The Vulnerary of Christ

LOUIS CHARBONNEAU-LASSAY

THE MYSTERIOUS EMBLEMS
OF THE WOUNDS IN THE BODY
AND HEART OF JESUS CHRIST

The Vulnerary of Christ

WITH THREE HUNDRED & FIFTY-NINE FIGURES
ENGRAVED ON WOOD BY THE AUTHOR

AND THIRTY-TWO PLATES

Translated by G. John Champoux

Angelico Press

First published in the USA
by Angelico Press 2020
Copyright © Angelico Press 2020

All rights reserved:
No part of this book may be reproduced or transmitted,
in any form or by any means, without permission

For information, address:
Angelico Press, Ltd.
169 Monitor St.
Brooklyn, NY 11222
www.angelicopress.com

978-1-62138-676-6 pb
978-1-62138-677-3 cloth

Book and cover design
by Michael Schrauzer

CONTENTS

EDITORIAL NOTE. ix

⊛ FIRST PART
*Representations of the Five Wounds of Christ
in Earliest Christian Art* 1

1 The "*Signaculum Domini*" 3
2 The "*Signaculum Domini*" in Medieval Heraldry 45
3 Observations on the Employ of
   the "*Signaculum Domini*" 61

⊛ SECOND PART
Depictions of the Wound in the Side of Christ 65

4 The Wound in the Side of Jesus 67
5 Lenticular Representations of the Wound
   in the Side of Jesus 87

⊛ THIRD PART
Representations of the Redemptive Shedding of Blood 93

6 Symbolic Thirst 95
7 The Heart, Fountain of Life and Holiness 99
8 The Springs of the Savior 107
9 The Mystical Wine-Presses 121
10 The Triple Precinct 131

⊛ FOURTH PART
Plants Emblematic of Christ's Five Wounds 139

11 The Trees of the Passion 141
12 Plants of the Divine Torture 155
13 The Garden of the Wounded Christ 161

⊛ FIFTH PART
Stones Emblematic of the Wounded Christ 175

14 Stones of the Passion 177
15 The Holy Grail 187

SIXTH PART
The Iconography of the Wounded Heart of Jesus 211

16 Beginnings of the Iconography of the Heart of Jesus . . 213
17 The Ancient Iconography of the Heart of Christ
    at the End of the Middle Ages 239
18 The Iconography of the Heart of Christ
    Posterior to the Renaissance 289
19 Ancient Testimonies of Piety in
    Small Provincial Towns 313
20 The Image of the Sacred Heart and the
    Coats of Arms of Sovereigns 341
21 The Astronomical Marble from the
    Charterhouse of Saint-Denis-d'Orques 353
22 Heart-Shaped Sundials 369
23 Reliquary Hearts 379
24 The Iconography of the Heart of Christ Abroad . . . 389
25 Varied Representations of the Heart of Jesus 405

SEVENTH PART
*The Iconography of the Heart of Jesus in the
Counter-Revolutionary Armies of the Vendée* 431

26 Rally-Badges, Also Called "Scapulars,"
    with the Image of the Sacred Heart 433
27 The Order of St. Michael of the Chouans 459
28 Old Vendean Jewelry 465
29 The "Cross of Father de Montfort" 479

EIGHTH PART
*Diverse Representations Relating to or Foreign to
the Cult of the Heart of Jesus* 489

30 Representations Relating to the Worship
    of the Sacred Heart 491
31 Blasphemous Representations of the Heart of Jesus . . 501
32 Hearts of Bewitchment 511
33 Epilogue and Refutation of Some Criticisms 517

INDICES 527

TABLE OF PLATES

PLATE 1.—*Ancient coins, first series* 18

PLATE 2.—*Ancient coins, second series* 23

PLATE 3.—*Ancient Christian jewelry* 35

PLATE 4.—*Cover to the Evangelary of Monza, gold and precious stones, 6th century* 39

PLATE 5.—*Ancient seals* 42

PLATE 6.—*Christ Jesus showing his five wounds and forming a Signaculum Domini. Reredos attributed to the Master of Liesborn, church of Lünen (Germany), 15th century. Photo Giraudon. Archives of the review* Regnabit, *1921–1929* 63

PLATE 7.—*Wound to the side dealt by the spear-thrust, detail of a retable attributed to the Master of Liesborn, church of Saint Mary on Höhe at Soest (Germany), 15th century. Photo Giraudon. Collection of the review* Regnabit, *1921–1929* 68

PLATE 8.—*Christ expired, surrounded by two thieves, is wounded on the side by the Holy Spear. Painting by Victor and Heinrich Dünwegge, 16th century. Photo Giraudon. Collection of the review* Regnabit, *1921–1929* 69

PLATE 9.—*Page from a notebook of the author dedicated to the Shroud of Turin. Charbonneau-Lassay archives* 73

PLATE 10.—*Miniature of an "Image of the World." Manuscript of the 14th century, Bibl. Nat. of Paris, French collection S. N., f° 136* . . 79

PLATE 11.—*Illuminated page from the Book of Hours for the use of Parcival of Dreux, 15th century (after 1472), belonging to M. Labarre of Marseille. Photo from Madam E. Rossollin, sent to the author. Charbonneau-Lassay archives* 82

PLATE 12.—*The living Christ wounded by the spear-thrust to the side of the heart, Konrad von Soest, reredos of the 15th century. Photo Giraudon. Archives of the review* Regnabit, *1921–1929* 86

PLATE 13.— *The Adoration of the Mystical Lamb by Hubert and Jan van Eyck, 1432. Detail of the central panel of a polyptych of Ghent cathedral (Belgium). Archives of the review* Regnabit, *1921–1929 (ed.).* 110

PLATE 14.— *The Christ of Bernardino Luini, one of the most prestigious masters of Milanese painting at the end of the 15th century. Notice that the cross crosslet held by the Savior is itself a symbol, at that time frequent and well understood, of the redemptive five wounds* 111

PLATE 15.—*Jesus crucified, source of the fountain of grace, Saint-Mesme chapel at Chinon* 112

PLATE 16.—*Jesus between the two boards of a winepress drawn and tightened by two strong screws. Stained glass window from the church of Sainte-Foy, Conches (Eure). Photo Nuhan Doduc (ed.)* 123

PLATE 17.—*Jesus laid on a winepress, stained glass window from the church of Saint-Étienne-du Mont, Paris, 1922. Photo Nuhan Doduc (ed.)* 124

PLATE 18.— *Triple Precinct, engraved stone, Church of St Pierre in Theillement (Eure), 12th century. Photo Gauthier Pierozak (ed.)* . . 134

PLATE 19.— *The Tree of Life and Pelican's Nest. Fresco attributed to Giotto, Santa Croce monastery, at Florence (Italy), 14th century. Photo Giraudon. Collection of the review* Regnabit, *1921–1929 (ed.)* . . 147

PLATE 20.—*Jesus and the Two Thieves by Giotto, at Palermo (Italy), 14th century. Pelican's nest in a cluster of foliage on top of the cross. Photo Giraudon. Collection of the review* Regnabit, *1921–1929 (ed.)* . . 148

PLATE 21.— *Crucifixion by Andrea di Nicolò (1502), Sienna. Pelican's nest on top of the cross. Photo Giraudon. Collection of the review* Regnabit, *1921–1929 (ed.)* 149

PLATE 22.— *Crucifixion by Matthias Grünewald. Polyptych for the altarpiece of Isenheim (Germany), 16th century. Bramble bush crown arranged in an inverted "magpie's nest." Photo Giraudon. Archives of the review* Regnabit, *1921–1929 (ed.)* 160

PLATE 23.— *The wound in the side of Jesus, marked by a ruby on the left side. Crucifix 12th–13th century, belonging to Canon Berjat, of Lyon. Photo from the collection of the review* Regnabit, *1921–1929* . . . 178

PLATE 24.— *Crucifixion scene, attributed to the Master of Marienlebens. A standard, held by Saint Hippolytus, bears the sign of the Rays of the Escarbuncle, or on a gules field on the original painting, a symbol of the radiant wound in the side of Jesus. Church of Saint Ursula, Cologne (Germany), ca. 1466. Photo Giraudon. Archives of the review* Regnabit, *1921–1929* 186

PLATE 25.— *Christ, seated on the side of a vat and surrounded by the instruments of his Passion, presses his hand to his right side, from which he causes his blood to spurt into the chalice. Hiéron du Val d'Or Museum, Paray-le-Monial, 15th century. Photo Giraudon. Archives of the review* Regnabit, *1921–1929*. 200

PLATE 26.— *Angels collecting the blood of Christ in chalices. Triptych by Niccolo da Foligno, 15th century. National Gallery, London. Photo Giraudon. Archives of the review* Regnabit, *1921–1929* 201

PLATE 27.— *Angels collecting the blood of Christ in chalices. Crucifixion by Giotto di Bondone, 14th century. Photo Giraudon. Archives of the review* Regnabit, *1921–1929* 202

PLATE 28.— *Angels collecting the blood of Christ in chalices. Crucifixion by Taddeo Gaddi, 14th century. Photo Giraudon. Archives of the review* Regnabit, *1921–1929* 203

PLATE 29.— *Angels collecting the blood of Christ in chalices. Calvary by the Master of Bruges, Cathedral of Saint-Sauveur (Belgium), 14th century. Photo Giraudon. Archives of the review* Regnabit, *1921–1929* 204

PLATE 30.— *Hosts fall from the Wound of Christ. Engraving from the Basel Museum, 15th century. Heitz Collection, Strasbourg; xi, No. 6.* Regnabit Journal *archives, 1921–1929 (ed.)*. 429

PLATE 31.— *The Sacred Heart of the Vendean General Athanasius Charette de la Contrie* 443

PLATE 32.— *The painting called "Sortilège d'Amour" by Jan Van Eyck, 15th century. Leipzig Museum (ed.)* 514

Editorial Note[1]

THE VULNERARY OF CHRIST, NOW FINALLY published for the first time more than seventy years after its author's death, contains exceptional findings by French Catholic archaeologist and symbologist Louis Charbonneau-Lassay regarding the five wounds of Christ, their symbolism, and their representations and meaning in Christian art.

LOUIS CHARBONNEAU-LASSAY: AN APPRECIATION

Born in Loudun (France) in 1871, the young Louis Charbonneau-Lassay developed an early interest in the Christian faith. In 1885 he joined the Catholic congregation of the Brothers of Saint Gabriel,[2] where he was given the name Brother René in 1891. It was there, over the course of many years, that he developed his vast Christian knowledge, while also teaching younger students for nearly a decade. During this period he also formed a close friendship with the local scholar Joseph Moreau de la Ronde (1831–1910), whom he supported and accompanied on many expeditions to explore old dungeons or excavate ancient graves to bring to light forgotten local history. Thus did Brother René develop his enduring passion for local archaeology. Several articles describing his findings were published in prestigious journals, and throughout his life he gathered together a significant collection of ancient artifacts (axes, swords, engraved stones, coins,

---

1 Although not cited in the text, much of the biographical material in this note is drawn from Pier Luigi Zoccatelli's foreword to this book's original French edition, *Le Vulnéraire du Christ* (Paris: Gutenberg-Reprints, 2018), and from Zoccatelli's book in collaboration with Stefano Salzani, *Hermétisme et emblématique du Christ* (Milan: Arché, 1996).
2 Founded by St. Louis Grignion de Montfort and originally called *Brothers of the Holy Spirit*.

etc.). These artifacts are on continuous display now at the Louis Charbonneau-Lassay museum in Loudun, which was founded after his death in 1946.

In 1903, triggered by a change in the French law regarding the separation of Church and State, the Saint Gabriel congregation was dissolved, and so, at one stroke, eighteen years after first joining the Catholic congregation and dedicating his studies to local archaeology and Christianianity, Brother René became again Louis Charbonneau-Lassay. As we shall see later, these events would in due course deeply influence Charbonneau's later work. From 1903 to 1925, he published over seventy articles on topics of prehistory, Celtic and Gallo-Roman archaeology, numismatics, heraldry, folklore, and local legends, culminating in a 500-page book on the subject of the "Castles of Loudun," which would earn him praise and recognition from the archaeological elite of his time.

During this period of his life, Charbonneau-Lassay also developed an unusual and remarkable artistic skill: rather than employ photographs or drawings to illustrate his articles, he would himself engrave wooden blocks by hand, sometimes utilizing for this purpose a simple pocket knife, and the resulting prints gave his publications a unique, timeless style. In so doing, he was in fact but following in the footsteps of many great Christian archaeologists who had published books in a similar manner at the end of the 19th century, among them Grimouard de Saint-Laurant, Dom Henri Leclercq, and Émile Mâle. During his lifetime Charbonneau-Lassay engraved literally thousands of coats of arms, sacred images, geometrical symbols, sacred objects of all sorts, ex-libris seals for friends, even portraits. Not only this, but he often also printed these engravings himself using an old 15th-century press he had acquired. Charbonneau-Lassay eventually acquired an old house in Loudun, an ancient Knights of Malta commandery, complete with Gothic windows, an enclosed garden, and a massive stone fireplace that still bore the Maltese Cross. To this venerable residence he added his own "mark" over the front entrance, with the following legend carved in marble by his own hand:

Editorial Note

The front entrance of Louis Charbonneau-Lassay's house in Loudun. Private collection.

BENEDICTIO DEI MANEAT SUPER INGREDIENTES
ET BONITAS EIUS PROTEGA EGREDIENTES[3]

Numbered among ancestors of this remarkable man are some of these very Knights of Malta. For Louis, however, chivalry did not remain some "dead letter" of ancestral prestige but became integral to the *aventure* of his life. As recalled by Pierre Delaroche, a close collaborator in his archaeological pursuits, Louis "was not one of those old scholars who amass documents in a sterile heap to preserve, with jealous care, for oneself alone," but someone who, "with superb politeness and amiable charm ... received those who might happen to knock at his door, thus tearing him away from his labors and causing him to waste precious time. No, rather did he open his home to them, spent hours showing them items from his collection, and answered their questions, all with perfect courtesy."[4]

3   "May God's blessing rest upon your going in and His goodness protect your going out." Cf. Deut. 28:6 and Psalm 121:8.
4   *M. Louis Charbonneau-Lassay (18 janvier 1871–26 décembre 1946). Éloge funèbre prononcé le 19 janvier 1947, à la Séance Publique de la "Société Historique du Pays de Loudunois,"* Loudun, 1947.

Besides his craftmanship and courtesy, another dimension of Charbonneau-Lassay's personal life must be considered: his ardent love for Christ, the unmistakable "background" to his last two books, *The Bestiary of Christ* and *The Vulnerary of Christ*. And this ardency of his inner life has no better witness than the prayer with which he concludes Chapter 21 of the present work: "O Heart! Who are the center of the Universe, the seat of the Infinite, and our Redeemer, have mercy on the dust of atoms that we are, be our Light and our Life now and at the moment we enter real life through Death's dark door."[5]

Here was a true man of tradition, at once craftsman, knight, and cleric, whose hand, head, and heart were boon companions in their praise of God.

THE GENESIS OF BESTIARY *AND* VULNERARY

Charbonneau-Lassay commenced focusing his research more closely on studies of Christian symbology after he was invited in 1922 to participate in *Regnabit*, a monthly French Catholic periodical. This publication, founded in 1921 and led by Father Félix Anizan (1874–1944), was dedicated to studies of Sacred Heart symbolism, but with a particular emphasis on a scientific approach: it published articles analyzing the dogmatic, moral, mystical, liturgical, artistic, and historical aspects of the Sacred Heart throughout the ages, with the purpose of showing its universal dimension. From 1922 to 1929, Charbonneau-Lassay published in *Regnabit* no fewer than 78 articles regarding the Sacred Heart and Christian symbology in general, always adducing archaeological evidence in support of his findings. All his articles were illustrated with numerous engravings of artefacts from his own or other collections.

The quality of Charbonneau-Lassay's articles and illustrations, which contrasted greatly with the rest of the work published in *Regnabit*, caught the attention of several readers, especially as our scholar kept introducing most unexpected findings. The devotion

5 Page 368.

Editorial Note

Louis Charbonneau-Lassay's office in the main room of his house in Loudun. Source: Charbonneau-Lassay Museum, Loudun. We thank museum director Mrs. Marie Haquet.

to the Sacred Heart was officially recognized by the Catholic Church in the 18th century in the wake of the mystical visions of Jesus unveiling his heart to a young nun, Margaret Mary Alacoque (1647–1690), in Paray-le-Monial, France. Charbonneau-Lassay had begun gathering more and more evidence that the devotion to the Sacred Heart had in fact existed centuries prior to the visions of Margaret Mary Alacoque, going back as far as the first centuries of Christianity. He was presenting undeniable archaeological evidence in his articles, and his readers were growing more and more fascinated with what he had to say. This very likely explains why Charbonneau-Lassay was contacted in 1925 by a mysterious and secret confraternity, the *Estoile Internelle* (*Inner Star*),[6] whose origins are said to date back to the Middle Ages. This strictly Catholic group was composed solely of twelve individuals, and did not entertain applications for admission to their number. When a member died the others would identify a qualified candidate who shared their values and invite him to join their confraternity. As it happens, one of Charbonneau-Lassay's close friends in the clergy, the elderly canon of the cathedral of Loudun, Théophile Barbot (1841–1927), was the Major at the head of the *Estoile Internelle*. Nearing his death, he determined to contribute what he could to Charbonneau-Lassay's work on the theme of Christian symbology, and, with the approval of the remaining members of the *Estoile Internelle*, offered him the opportunity to consult an old 15th-century notebook containing sketches and notes preserving (among many other symbols) a unique drawing of the cup of the Last Supper that contained the blood of Christ. This cup was in the form of congealed blood resembling a faceted stone. The notebook also contained other important Christian symbols regarding the Holy Spirit.

It is worth mentioning here as well that the *Estoile Internelle* kept the archives and rituals of another group called the *Knights of the Paraclete*, a Christian confraternity that had become inactive towards the end of the seventeenth century. The *Knights of the Paraclete* were a more open organization that welcomed into their ranks Catholic men and women who applied to join them, without any policy of limiting the number of members. However, for reasons that remain unclear, this organization came to be suspended, and was absorbed into the *Estoile Internelle* (possibly because some members were participants in both organizations). In the mid-1930s Charbonneau-Lassay would revive the *Knights of the Paraclete*, using the rituals and authority granted him by Théophile Barbot in 1925. But this is another story.[7]

In 1924, Louis Charbonneau-Lassay had become acquainted with French metaphysician René Guénon (1886–1951) after a

---

6 Perhaps a reference to 2 Peter 1:19–21.

7 See PierLuigi Zoccatelli, *Le Lièvre qui rumine. Autour de René Guénon, Louis Charbonneau-Lassay et la Fraternité du Paraclet. Avec des documents inédits* (Milan: Archè, 1999).

mutual friend, Olivier de Fremond, made the introductions. Guénon, having discovered Charbonneau-Lassay's articles about Christian symbolism in *Regnabit*, spoke very highly to his own circle of correspondents of the scholar and his work;[8] and he himself then collaborated with *Regnabit* from 1925 to 1927. He published a total of 18 articles, all doctrinal developments of various aspects of the the symbolism of the heart.[9] These articles were most often based on elements of Charbonneau-Lassay's work that had came to Guénon's attention. Even though Guénon's collaboration with *Regnabit* came to an end in 1927,[10] his friendship and respect for Charbonneau-Lassay endured unchanged until the scholar's death in December 1946. What is more, this friendship and respect was reciprocated, for we find Charbonneau-Lassay still addressing Guénon as a friend on November 11, 1945,[11] just a little over a year before his death.

Guénon commented in his articles on several of the symbols and archaeological findings treated by Louis Charbonneau-Lassay. For instance, the remarkable engraved heart of Saint-Denis d'Orques (chap. 21) is taken as an important reference by Guénon in his articles "The Secret Language of Dante and the 'Fedeli d'Amore,'"[12] "Radiating Heart and Flaming Heart,"[13] "The All-Seeing Eye,"[14] and "The Mustard Seed."[15] Furthermore, the sixteenth-century

---

8   Guénon wrote to his friend Guido de Giorgio, in a letter dated March 4, 1929, "There is nothing interesting in *Regnabit* except my articles and Charbonneau's."

9   See René Guénon, *Écrits pour "Regnabit."* A posthumous collection presented by PierLuigi Zoccatelli (Milan-Turin: Archè-Nino Aragno Editore, 1999). This collection of articles has yet to be translated into English.

10 Guénon resigned after a disagreement with the *Regnabit* censorship committee.

11 Letter from Louis Charbonneau-Lassay to René Guénon, dated November 11, 1945. Private archives.

12 *Insights into Christian Esoterism*, trans. H. D. Fohr (Hillsdale, NY: Sophia Perennis, 2001), p. 53.

13 *Symbols of Sacred Science*, trans. H. D. Fohr (Hillsdale, NY: Sophia Perennis, 2004), p. 399.

14 Ibid., p. 424.

15 Ibid., p. 426.

figure of Janus (chap. 18) is alluded to numerous times by Guénon, particularly in "Some Aspects of the Symbolism of Janus"[16] and "Heart and Brain."[17] He also dedicated a full article to the symbolism of the "Triple Precinct" (chap. 10), in which he referred repeatedly to Charbonneau-Lassay's findings.[18] It also appears that Guénon's attention was drawn to the mysterious "cup with a red stone" of the *Estoile Internelle* confraternity (chap. 15), as he discusses it in several articles: first in "The 'Cornerstone,'"[19] and then in "*Lapsit exillis.*"[20]

Finally, from 1930 to 1939, Guénon contributed highly favorable reviews of every new article published by Charbonneau-Lassay in the periodical *Le Rayonnement intellectuel,* a periodical directed by Charbonneau-Lassay. A number of these articles are now included in *The Vulnerary.*

Thus we see that, in his own work, Guénon frequently utilizes Charbonneau-Lassay as a reference. And in return we find numerous mentions of René Guénon in *The Bestiary of Christ* and *The Vulnerary*, wherein Charbonneau-Lassay draws in particular from Guénon's *The King of the World*[21] and *The Symbolism of the Cross.*[22] In *The Vulnerary*, Charbonneau-Lassay even speaks of Guénon's "incontestable authority" in matters of Christian hermeticism.[23] We have also found in the correspondence between the two men numerous proofs of the help Guénon provided in analyzing the symbolism of animals such as the lion, the sphinx, the amphisbaena, etc.

In 1925, as Charbonneau-Lassay was showing French cardinal Dubois the extensive collection of Christian emblems he had gathered over his lifetime, Dubois suggested that Charbonneau-Lassay compile these notes into a book on the theme of "Christian

---

16 Ibid., pp. 120–21.
17 Ibid., p. 410.
18 Ibid., in "The Triple Precinct of the Druids," p. 74.
19 Ibid., p. 274.
20 Ibid., p. 280.
21 Trans. H. D. Fohr (Hillsdale, NY: Sophia Perennis, 2001).
22 Trans. Angus Macnab (Ghent, NY: Sophia Perennis, 2001).
23 *Infra*, p. 524.

Editorial Note

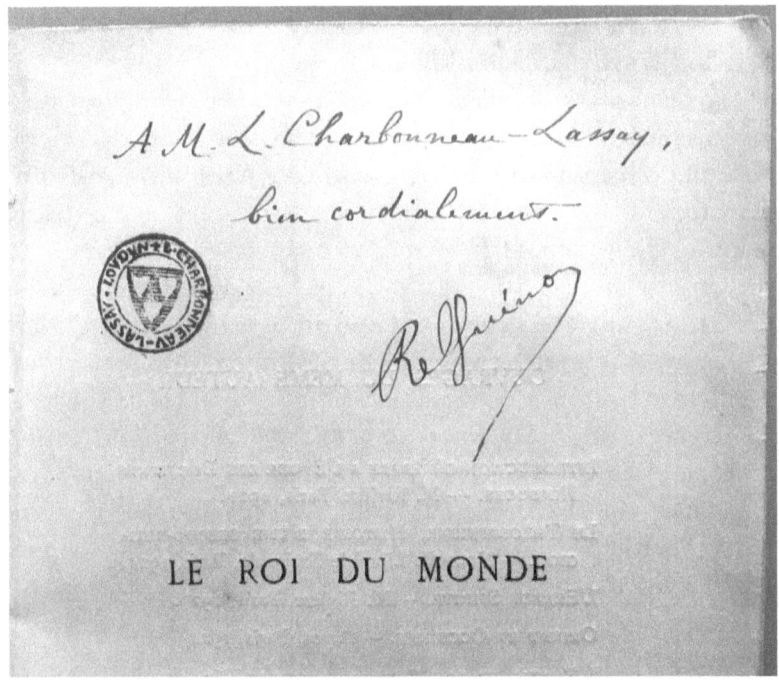

Autograph by Guénon of Charbonneau-Lassay's copy of "Le Roi du Monde." Private collection.

symbolism." In response to this suggestion, Charbonneau-Lassay commenced work on this project, which only came to an end with the completion of *The Bestiary of Christ* in 1936. However, owing to various setbacks, this book was only published in late 1940, during the Second World War. Nor did the setbacks end there, for, since the publisher (Desclée de Brouwer) was located at Bruges in Belgium, the Nazi-controlled French border posed an insurmountable challenge for any sizeable shipment of books to the publisher's subsidiary in Paris. Of the 500 copies from the book's first printing, about 250 copies were dispersed to the author and to paid-in-full subscribers. The remaining 250 were stored at the company's warehouse in Bruges, but in late 1942 Charbonneau-Lassay received the sad news that this remaining stock, along with his wood-cuts, had been reduced to ashes when fire consumed the publishing house — a fire caused, he was informed, by an electrical short-curcuit. A decades-long labor of love... A second printing of *The Bestiary* would finally appear in L. J. Toth's 1974 facsimile edition.

The Bestiary has since become a major reference work for Christian symbology. Imitating the format of ancient bestiaries, which were in use particularly during the Middle Ages, this book's primary focus was on the symbolism of hundreds of real and mythical animals (always supported by copious archaeological evidence) for the purpose of associating them with distinct doctrinal aspects of Christ. Reading the *Bestiary of Christ* in its entirety[24] gives one the impression that every living being upon the earth symbolizes a different facet of a universal Christ, a Christ not limited to a simple man, but a man whose dimensions encompass the entire universe. Defining God in Christian theology has always been a challenge owing to the impossibility of characterizing infinity without at the same time limiting it — this latter, of course, constituting the very nature of a "definition." Early theologians used apophatism[25] to circumvent this conundrum by defining instead what is *not* God. Charbonneau-Lassay's work, however, is rather different, indeed possibly unique in the sense that it takes another approach, for he shows that it is possible to intuitively grasp a sense of God's infinity in the context of symbolizing it by way of the indefinitude of things,[26] or the countless manifestations of everything that exists in the universe, whether in a life form or not. From this perspective, then — that is, through the use of symbolism applied to hundreds of animals in the *Bestiary of Christ* — Charbonneau-Lassay was able to show that any and every thing that exists can be taken to symbolize Christ, and thus

24 The English translation (New York: Parabola Books, 1991) was much-abridged.
25 Apophatic theology, also known as negative theology, attempts to approach the Divine by the way of negation, speaking of God only in terms of what God is not.
26 Mathematically indefinitude would be the limit of an equation that tends to mathematical infinity. Practically, indefinitude represents something that is unlimited from our human perspective, but that is not metaphysically infinite: indefinitude can be symbolized by the countless grains of sands on a beach, by the innumerable stars in the universe, etc.

offer to those open to this approach an understanding of divinity through indefinitude.[27] He had also planned to extend this exercise with several other books, such as the *Lapidary of Christ* (a compendium on precious or peculiar stones emblematic of Christ) and the *Florary of Christ* (a compendium on flowers and trees that also symbolize aspects of Christ). However, Charbonneau-Lassay suddenly halted development of these books in 1936 in order to focus his efforts instead entirely upon a new and rather mysterious project: *The Vulnerary of Christ*. This change of path seems to have taken place after he read the scientific work of Dr Pierre Barbet, a Catholic physician and surgeon. Dr Barbet had just published a book on the crucifixion of Jesus Christ based upon the anatomical features of simulated crucifixions he had performed on bodies donated to science. Through this exercise, Dr Barbet came up with two important findings:

a) Even though various artistic renditions of crucifixions throughout the centuries show nails piercing the palms of the hands of Jesus on the cross, Dr. Barbet showed that anatomically the nails alone could not realistically have held the body. Instead, Dr. Barbet determined that the nails would have had to pierce the victim's wrists, where a stronger bone structure allowed for fuller support.

b) The other intriguing matter was the water and blood escaping the side of Jesus when he was struck by the spear of Longinus.[28] Dr Barbet's theory was that the spear must have pierced the side of Jesus's body below the rib cage at a specific angle and penetrated deeply enough to strike and wound the heart's pericardium within the chest cavity. Typical of a violent death, then, the pericardial liquid, similar in color to water, would have escaped first, the blood following after.

---

27 This symbolizing of Infinity with indefinitude was mentioned by René Guénon in several of his own books, which shows the influence Guénon might have had on Charbonneau-Lassay's personal approach to Christianity. See René Guénon, *The Multiple States of the Being*, Chap. 1 "Infinity and Possibility" (Ghent, NY: Sophia Perennis, 2001), pp. 7–12.

28 "But one of the soldiers with a spear pierced his side, and forthwith came there out blood and water" (John 19:34).

As he was reproducing this phenomenon in his research facility, Dr Barbet noticed that the positions of the wounds he had produced on the crucified bodies fit exactly how the wounds appeared on the mysterious Shroud of Turin: the wound openings in the wrists and feet, as well as a wound at the expected location and angle below the rib cage could be clearly identified. From this evidence, Dr. Barbet concluded that the Shroud was genuine. Charbonneau-Lassay was persuaded also, and announced to René Guénon in a 1936 letter that he had refocused his work on Christian symbolism to a study of the five wounds of Christ.

Between 1936 and 1939, Charbonneau-Lassay published excerpts of his work in a periodical he founded called *Le Rayonnement intellectuel*, which had replaced the now defunct *Regnabit*. It is in one of these articles that he declared having discovered "things completely forgotten today, even by members of the clergy," by which he meant the significance of an ancient symbol still present in numerous liturgical objects and ancient art, called the *Signaculum Domini* (the Sign of God), a symbol also depicted in the already mentioned old notebook of the *Estoile Internelle*.

Charbonneau-Lassay completed the *Vulnerary of Christ* shortly before his death in December 1946, but it was never published, because the manuscript of this work was stolen by a man pretending to be a publisher, who "borrowed" it from Charbonneau-Lassay's beneficiaries, allegedly for consideration for publication. As of today, this original manuscript has still not been found, and in consequence a shroud of mystery has surrounded this enigmatic book ever since.

FINDING THE VULNERARY

Fast forward now to 2013. Gauthier Pierozak, an avid reader of René Guénon's work, built and made available to the public a web-based indexing tool for this metaphysian's collected works in French, including his articles published in *Regnabit*. For the purpose of adding them to the indexing tool, Pierozak also gathered copies of letters Guénon had sent to various correspondents, including a series of 26 letters to Louis Charbonneau-Lassay from

Louis Charbonneau-Lassay, sitting in the shadows of the Loudun castle's ruins. Source: Charbonneau-Lassay Museum, Loudun, from Mrs. Marie Haquet, director.

1924 to 1929. The content of these letters showed how much Guénon was involved in assisting the latter in his research on Christian symbolism. Then, having just completed the indexing tool, Pierozak was contacted by René Guénon's son, who, having heard of Pierozak's work transcribing numerous letters of Guénon's, asked if he could help organize his father's thousands of letters still stored in old shoe boxes, so they could be used as references for future publications. After agreeing to this plan, Pierozak worked daily, from 2013 to 2016, at transcribing thousands of pages from this correspondence.

As destiny would have it, one of the first sets of these letters he was given to transcribe was the correspondence of Louis Charbonneau-Lassay to René Guénon. These stretched from 1933 to 1945. It is in these letters, read for the first time in almost seventy years, that Gauthier Pierozak found, clearly explained for the first time, the story of the *Vulnerary of Christ*. Charbonneau-Lassay had been keeping Guénon informed about the progress of his new book, how the idea for it came to him, and what content he intended to include in the different parts and chapters. Holding these letters in his hand for the first time, reading them one after the other, one can imagine how Pierozak was overwhelmed in turn by feelings of awe, unworthiness, and gratitude, as some of the mystery surrounding the long-lost *Vulnerary of Christ* unfolded before his eyes.

As it had become clear from the letters that Charbonneau-Lassay was going to reuse most of the articles about the Sacred Heart he had published from 1921 to 1939 in various periodicals, Pierozak spent several months collecting the publications where these articles were printed, and using Charbonneau's letters to Guénon as a guide, was able to organize the contents of the *Vulnerary* according to Charbonneau-Lassay's descriptions in his letters. He then sent samples of his reconstruction of the book to some experts on Charbonneau-Lassay and let them know of his project to "resurrect" the original *Vulnerary of Christ*. It was after a very warm initial reception for this initial work that Gauthier Pierozak was unexpectedly informed that in fact at that very juncture the full archives of Charbonneau-Lassay had come into the possession of some individuals in Italy. The existence of these archives had first came to Pierozak's notice when reading a January 1947 letter to Guénon from a mutual acquaintance, Georges Thomas (aka Georges Tamos, or Argos) announcing the scholar's death. This letter reports that at his death Charbonneau-Lassay left behind "about 50,000 files, notes, drawings, engravings, pictures, etc., neatly organized in hundreds of folders." These were the materials he had gathered during the course of a lifetime of profound research. The *Bestiary of Christ* and the *Vulnerary of Christ* had been redacted from these archival notes. To this letter Guénon responded that the Charbonneau-Lassay archives should be preserved with the goal of one day completing the work he had initiated and taken so far on the subject of Christian symbolism. As it turned out, it was to Georges Thomas, who became the Grand Master of the revived Knights of the Paraclete after Charbonneau's death, that the archives were left according to the scholar's last will and testament, and subsequently the archives were passed on to other Paraclete members who, in turn, employed them in their own research. These archives were finally sold confidentially to a group of publishers in the early 2000s, after the last known member of the Knights of the Paraclete had passed away.

After Pierozak was informed in 2014 of the existence and current circumstances of the archives, a meeting was facilitated in Italy with the new owners of the archives, as a result of which he was granted access to them for the purpose of helping reconstitute *The Vulnerary of Christ*. It became clear, very quickly, that these archives represented an invaluable, unique depository of knowledge regarding long-neglected aspects of Christian symbolism, and furthermore that they contained material for a great deal more than two books only: there were as well thousands of notes and folders dealing with the Christian symbolism of stones and flowers, from which Charbonneau-Lassay had intended one day to complete a *Lapidary of Christ* and a *Florary of Christ*. However, neither of these projected texts had yet been commenced by Charbonneau-Lassay at the time of his death, but for some handwritten notes.

Having discovered that the owners of the archives were interested in selling them, and to avoid their being either lost, or divided and sold piecemeal to various collectors, Pierozak negotiated the purchase of the whole lot. In order to gather the large funds needed to acquire these archives, he set up a crowdfunding project in 2016 to which the response was overwhelming: in just a few weeks he had gathered the funds needed to purchase the Charbonneau-Lassay archives in full. He took possession of the archives in December 2016, exactly seventy years after the author's death. Gauthier Pierozak now had everything needed to reconstitute *The Vulnerary of Christ*, and the first French edition of the book was published in 2017, followed by a second edition in 2018.

TRANSLATING THE VULNERARY

As Gauthier Pierozak was reaching out to potential sponsors in the Fall of 2016 to help fund the purchase of the archives, the news of this project to reconstitute *The Vulnerary of Christ* reached the ears of G. John Champoux, the English-language translator of Jean Borella, a renowned French Catholic philosopher who has himself written extensively on Christian symbolism.[29] Occurring almost simultaneously in the early 1980s, Champoux's discovery of both Borella and Charbonneau-Lassay greatly impacted his life and launched his translating efforts, which have now extended over nearly forty years. When he learned of the project, Champoux immediately took up the task of translating *The Vulnerary* into English, once the reconstitution in the original French had been completed. After three years' labor, his translation of *The Vulnerary of Christ* is now finally available to the English-speaking public. Our wish now is that this work inspire others to undertake further study of the deep and inspiring meaning of Christian symbolism, and perpetuate the transmission of a knowledge that was very nearly lost...

---

29 *The Crisis of Religious Symbolism & Symbolism and Reality* (Kettering, OH: Angelico, 2016), for example.

Editorial Note

GAUTHIER PIEROZAK was born in France, where he obtained a degree in mechanical engineering with emphasis on mathematics. He came to the US in 1998 and currently lives in Oklahoma. He is the author of numerous articles on symbolism, with particular emphasis on the symbolism of the heart. He reconstituted and self-published the original French version of *The Vulnerary of Christ*, and he directs the websites www.index-rene-guenon.org and archives-charbonneau-lassay.org. His primary areas of study are currently the metaphysical aspects of the Infinite and the metaphysical dimension in *The Bestiary of Christ*.

G. JOHN CHAMPOUX, a retired registered nurse, has translated works by Jean Borella, Jean-Claude Larchet, and, as co-translator with Robert Proctor, Jean Hani. He is also author of *The Way to Our Heavenly Father* (Kettering, OH: Semantron, 2013), a book of commentaries and meditations on the Lord's Prayer.

FIRST PART

Representations of the Five Wounds of Christ

IN EARLIEST CHRISTIAN ART

CHAPTER ONE

The "Signaculum Domini"

I. FIRST OCCURRENCES

WE SEARCH IN VAIN FOR ANY CLEAR allusion in the earliest centuries of our era to the sufferings of the Redeemer during his Passion, whether in the decorations of the Roman catacombs or elsewhere. His divine personality only appears under the enigmatic and serene figures of a watchful shepherd in the midst of his flock, or of a fish.

For the Christians of those times the cross, which was the instrument of salvation, only comes before their eyes under the mysteriously emblematic figures of the letter X, or of a ship's anchor, a trident, or a ship's mast crossed horizontally by a yard. But nowhere do we encounter the cross under its gibbet-like form or under its stylized form with the four equal arms of a pre-Christian starry cross.

No more than their Master's torments are those of the martyrs recalled in these underground sanctuaries where his pursued disciples, some of whom had already shed their blood for him, came to adore him. These persecuted men and women lived there in a setting of contentment, grace, and serenity, where everything spoke of another life filled with infinite happiness in compensation for earthly sufferings and trials. Maternally, the Church compassed them about with peace, certainty, and hope so that, when the winds of hell blew more fiercely upon them, they might traverse the human path to the end without weakening.

The earliest dated representation we have of the cross in an X (also the initial of the Greek word XPHCTOC, *Christ*) was found at Palmyra in Asia. It was made in 147, as its accompanying inscription attests.[1]

---

[1] Dom H. Leclercq, *Dictionnaire d'Archéologie Chrétienne*, tome III, vol. II, col. 3048.

Part I: The Five Wounds of Christ in Earliest Christian Art

It first appeared, under its gibbet-like form and bearing its divine Victim upon its shaft, on engraved gems, the oldest of which is of gnostic origin; the others, orthodox in origin, are from the third and following centuries. But, on these records and on those of greater sculpted, carved, or painted size, Christ does not seem to suffer: the cross makes its appearance above all as the trophy of his victory. This is why, ordinarily, it is crowned, decked with laurels, bejeweled, adorned with many colors, ornamented.

Not until the fourth century is there manifested in Christian art a mysterious sign that will have an unprecedented vogue through all the intervening centuries until the end of the Middle Ages, a sign that nine-tenths of today's Christians no longer understand.

This sign is a cross, generally an equal-armed cross, which bears at its central point and on the ends of its branches — or even more commonly in the middle of it and between its arms — points, crescents, crosslets, nails, roses, heart-shaped leaves, etc. Sometimes the cross is not depicted, and the points, crescents, etc., are simply arranged in quincunx: 2, 1 and 2 as is said in heraldic language.

The early Middle Ages indicated this mysterious emblem under the words *Signum Dei, Signaculum Dei*, the sign or seal of God; and again, *Signaculum Domini, Signaculum Christi*. These last two terms are also more exact, for here only the Savior is involved, and the five chief sources for the shedding of his blood on the cross are indeed, in the Church's eyes, the final seal of the great act of the world's redemption and the mission on earth of the Christ of God.

The term *Signaculum Dei* was also given in the early Church to the sacrament of baptism because, although not an emblematic sign of the wounded body of Jesus, it is however the seal by which the Christian is marked as something belonging to God.[2]

Comparably, we find disks laden with a cross that ancient art often placed in the hand of the Savior, as well as other cross-bearing disks sculpted or painted onto the walls of churches, disks which the prelate consecrating the building anointed with chrism.[3]

---

2 Cf. A. Lerosey, *Hist. et Symbolisme de la Liturgie*, 311.
3 See Grimouard de Saint-Laurent, *Guide de l'Art Chrétien*, T. IV, 378, fig. 36.

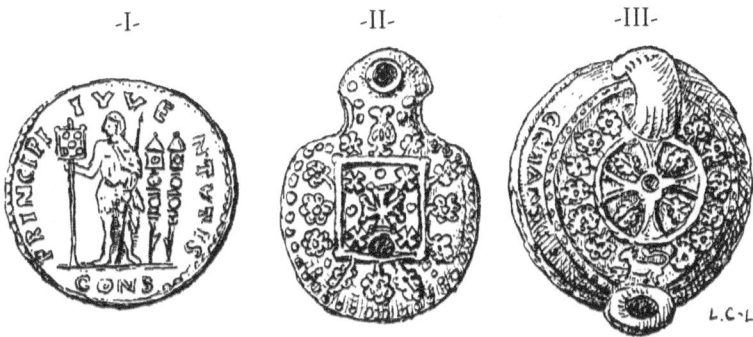

Fig. 1. —
Medallion of Constantin.

Fig. 2. & 3. —
Christian lamps from Egypt.

One of the very earliest reproductions known to us of this *Signaculum Christi* is found on a large coin or medallion of the emperor Constantine, struck between 314 and 337, where it occupies the middle of the *Labarum*, the imperial standard (Fig. 1).

Is this to say that there was no *Signaculum Christi* prior to these examples? Certainly not, although a by no means certain tradition claims that this mysterious emblem formed by a cantoned cross of four nails was brought from Antioch to Rome by St. Peter himself.[4]

Soon after Constantine, two Christian terracotta lamps, from Abydos in Egypt[5] and from Cairo, display a cross cantoned with four crosslets and four leaves. We also see it on a sculpture from the early monastery of Chaqqara, likewise in Egypt (Figs. 2, 3, and 4). The same symbol would be found also on a balance beam from Asia Minor.[6]

Fig. 4. — Sculpture from the Monastery of Chaqqara (Egypt), 6th century.

4 Cf. C. Sallas, *Sur les Quatre B,* in *Revue Archéolog.*, IIe Série, T. XXXIII (1877), 96.
5 Cf. Dom H. Leclercq, op. cit., T. III, vol. I, col. 541.
6 Ibid., T. V, Vol. II, col. 1689.

II. THE "SIGNACULUM CHRISTI" ON ANCIENT ALTARS

Among the most interesting manifestations of the *Signaculum Christi*, we must first mention its presence on altar stones consecrated by five anointings of Holy Oils. Christian archaeologists concur in acknowledging that, starting with the sixth century, such altars were consecrated in this way by special ceremonies, as they still are today.

Previously, the eucharistic sacrifice was celebrated indiscriminately on the sarcophagi of martyrs, on tables, or a stand of wood, stone, marble, silver, or gold. But starting with the above mentioned period at least, the Church decided that the middle of the sacrificial altars, destined to support the consecrated Bread and Wine, should be of stone. Since the eighth century, for greater convenience, consecrated stones cut into thin sheets reduced to small sizes and framed with metal or wood would enable the Mass to be said anywhere, on no matter what support, whether altar table or ordinary table, as is the case today.

The reason for this obligation to place the eucharistic Bread and Wine, the *Corpus Christi*, on a stone is moreover evocative. On the mount of Calvary, when the body of Jesus was unnailed from the cross, it was stretched out upon the earth, hands and feet pierced by the nails and the side opened by the spear — an oblation like none other, for which the very mountain was the altar. And it is this body pierced with five wounds that the five anointings and the five crosses on altar stones represent. The most scrupulous liturgist of the Middle Ages, William Durandus, bishop of Mende, states this expressly: "The [altar] stone designates," he says, "the humanity of Christ. The five crosses formed thereon signify that we should always hold present in our memory a remembrance of the Five Wounds of Christ, that He has suffered for us on the cross. For He received five wounds, namely to the hands, feet and side."[7]

---

[7] William Durandus, *Rationale divinorum officiorum* (1284), Book IV, chap. I, 49 and chap. LXXX, 9.

The "Signaculum Domini"

According to this same author, and in harmony with the altar stone's five crosses, the liturgy of the Mass divides up the sacrosanct part of the sacrifice into five parts: "[B]ecause on the cross alone took place the outpouring of blood in five spurts, the Canon of the Mass is divided into five parts, the first until the *Pridie*, the second until the *Memento*, the third until the *Praeceptis*, the fourth until the *embolis*[8] and the fifth until the end of the Canon."[9]

We should say at once that on the majority of altar stones, even since the sixth century, the central cross that represents the wound in the divine side is larger or more ornamented than the others. This is because, through this wound — even though inflicted after he was already dead and which therefore did not

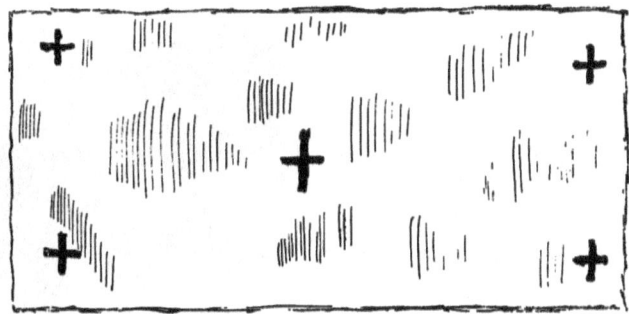

Fig. 5. — Middle of the altar-table from Vouneuil-sous-Biard.

cause the Savior any suffering — the spear struck his heart, thus going to seek out, right to their source, even the last, still warm reserves of the redemptive blood.

I am giving here the upper surface of two altars from the Merovingian period, the sixth and seventh centuries. One, originally from Vouneuil-sous-Biard (Vienne), is in white marble (Fig. 5); the cross in its middle, as simple as the others, is larger. This altar, which belongs to the Antiquaires de l'Ouest, at Poitiers, is today in the St. John Baptistry of this city.[10] The second one, originally from Ham (Manche), bears on the angles four small crosses, and its center is

---

8 That is, as far as *Sed libera nos a Malo*, which concludes the *Pater*.
9 William Durandus, op. cit., XL, 6.
10 See Dom H. Leclercq, op. cit., fasc. LXII, col. 1522.

marked with a beautiful ornamented cross (Fig. 6).

The Middle Ages continued (as we still do) to use the same type of altar stone: here is a stone composed of gray sandstone from a demolished altar, most likely of the twelfth century. I drew it for the pastor of Saint-Gilles of Île-Bouchard (Indre-et-Loire) in 1898 (Fig. 7). It is 0 m. 26 per side. Combined with this is the image of another, surely later than the first, which in 1924 was at Lussant (Charente-Inférieure), the rubbing of which was procured for me by Mr. Robert de la Tour d'Auvergne (Fig. 8). On the first of these stones the central cross stands out much more than on the other four; the five crosses are alike on the second one.

Fig. 6. — Altar table from Ham.

Fig. 7. — Altar stone from Île-Bouchard.

III. THE PASCHAL CANDLE'S FIVE GRAINS OF INCENSE

Like the altar to the right of which it stands in the Catholic and Roman liturgy, the Paschal candle is an emblem of Christ dead for the salvation of men and yet always living: the wax represents his body, the wick his soul, and the flame his

Fig. 8. — Altar stone from Lussant.

8

Divinity, his life, his love, and the saving brightness of his doctrine.

Cero caro Christi [the wax is the flesh of Christ], writes the eighth-century author of *The Key*, said to be by Saint Meliton.

Lit at the office of matins of the Easter vigil, during the time that symbolizes the sojourn of the body of Christ in the tomb, the Paschal candle shines for all the Offices until the *Assumptus est in cœlum* on Ascension Day, when the commemoration of the post-mortuary and earthly life of the risen Christ commences.

During all this time it keeps, embedded in the whiteness of its wax, the five grains of incense in the form of a cross fixed into it by the celebrant in the course of the aforesaid office.

The special ritual ceremony of the Paschal candle clearly seems to have arisen in northern Italy or among the Gauls before being adopted by Roman ceremonial practice. We do not know at exactly what period this striking symbol of Christ the redeemer and light of the world was introduced, but the composition of the *Exultet*, the wonderful *praeconium pascale*, which is sung between the ritual sprinkling of the grains of incense and their fixation in the candle, is attributed by some historians of the liturgy to St. Augustine, although by a greater number of historians — and more probably — to St. Ambrose of Milan, in the fourth century.

However this may be, we possess two formulas of the blessing of the Paschal candle composed in the middle of this same fourth century by Ennodius, bishop of Pavia; and Papebrock even has the origin of this ritual usage going back to the Council of Nicea in 325.[11] Its symbolism would be therefore as ancient as that of the *Signaculum Christi* and the five crosses of the consecration of altars.

What is of interest here is the liturgical and obligatory rule — probably as old as the use of the Paschal candle itself — to imbed in its wax the five grains of incense in a cruciform pattern; this wax being the mystical symbol of Jesus crucified, the five grains of incense imbedded as a cross in the candle necessarily represent (this is the opinion of all liturgists) the five principal wounds from which flowed the blood of Christ on the cross. They are not then, as some have written lately, an emblem of the five

---

11 Cf. Martigny, *Dict. des Antiquités chrétiennes*, 151.

great feasts of the Christian year, still less are they a symbol coming from Delphi into the West with the cult of Apollo.[12] Even though the early Church did not hesitate to borrow from the traditions of prior cults for her liturgies if they might serve her mystical thought, such is definitely not the case in the present instance.

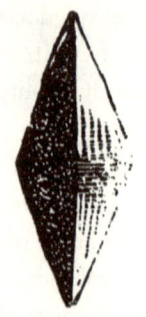

Fig. 9.—A Paschal candle's incense grain. Saint-Germain of Orly (Seine), 1935.

These grains of incense are imbeded in the wax in either an unfashioned or a worked and stylized state. Thus a foreshortened and abbreviated form of a spearhead or nail is often imposed on it. Even the one at the crucial center, which stands for the spear wound, is almost always similar to the others (Figs. 9 and 10).

Fig. 10.—A Paschal candle's incense grain. Saint-Pierre of Loudun. (Vienne), 1921.

This stylization is a very clear allusion to the tortures of crucifixion endured by Jesus and is in harmony with the form of *Signaculum Christi* given to the whole set of grains on the Paschal candle. It is a memento of the five redemptive wounds.

IV. THE "SIGNACULUM DOMINI" ON LITURGICAL OBJECTS

Incised as it was on the sacred stone of the altars and replicated on the Paschal candle, it is altogether logical that we should again find the "Seal of Christ" on objects with a liturgical use, above all on those connected with the sacrament of the Eucharist, that is, the mystical sacrifice where the Body and Blood of the Redeemer are offered: the body that was insulted by spear and nails, and the blood that flowed from the wellsprings opened by them.

The *Cabinet des Médailles* at the Bibliothèque Nationale of Paris possesses a wondrous salver or paten along with its chalice, both

---

12 Lanoé-Villène, *Le Livre des Symboles*, T. IV, 179.

in gold, which were found at Gourdon (Saône-et-Loire). These precious vessels were produced at the beginning of the sixth century.

The rectangular paten is decorated in the middle with a cross tiled with blood-red enamel, just as is a large decorated border of squared lozenges that forms the raised edging of the salver. The four angles of this edging are marked by cross-shaped cavities, and the angles of the inner rectangle are marked by four heart-shaped convolvulus leaves. The totality of the central cross and leaves or crosses replicates the theme of the five marks of the altar stones on which rest the chalice and paten during Mass (Fig. 11).

Fig. 11. — *Paten of Gourdon (S.-&-L.), 6th century.*

These are clearly leaves and not hearts borne by the Gourdon paten, for the rim of the chalice is decorated with an upright garland with the same leaves and the tendrils of a convolvulus. We will see that the blue color that fills the leaves of the salver was utilized elsewhere in figurations of the *Signaculum Domini*.[13]

This emblem also splendidly decorates the cup of the ministerial chalice of Ardagh, in Ireland, a most beautiful work of the eighth century that is today in the National Museum of Dublin. The cross evoking the divine wounds on this eucharistic vessel is

---

13 Cf. 1st Part, Chap. II, VII, p. 56.

inscribed within a very ornate circle and bears at its center and on the ends of its arms the five emblematic points.

I do not hesitate to number among these documents of the first Christian millennium the prototype of the metallic or ceramic host molds which are still in use in certain Near Eastern rites. In the liturgical art of the Ethiopian Copts, for example, the hosts produced by these molds bear an ornamental subject whose theme, like all sacramental things in these so traditional lands, must date back to the very time of the local liturgy's creation.

One example of these Coptic hosts, of a very ancient type, published in 1908 by Bernard Picard, has the form of a disk ornamented with a Greek cross adorned with small crosslets (Fig. 12). In the middle square, one cross symbolizes the wound to the heart and the four crosslets, made in an X to differentiate them from the other crosslets, represent the wounds to the hands and feet. Some have wished to see in the other crosslets positioned around the central motif an allusion to the multiple flagellation wounds. The host would be thus the memento of all the bodily wounds of the Redeemer. It bears this inscription in Greek lettering: ΑΓΙΟC ICXVPOC, *Agios ischyros*, "Holy and Mighty."

Fig. 12. — Host of the Ethiopian Coptic rite. According to Bernard Picard.

We know that even in the West, host irons were already in use in the sixth century, and that the motifs that decorated them were always symbolic.

The second millennium, above all during its first half, when a full-scale Christian symbolism animated all the arts and imparted a living intensity to souls, eucharistic vessels still often bore the "seal of the Lord."

On the magnificent ciborium of Alpais, which is in the Louvre and dates from the twelfth century, an angel displays a small disk that can only be the image of a host; this disk bears the cross and the five points of the *Signaculum* (Fig. 13).

I have noticed the same motif at Marseille on a reliquary of the fifteenth century. It would be easy, I think, to find many other examples.

Reliquaries, which play such a great role in the piety of the ancient Church — above all those containing relics of the True Cross or of martyrs, the sacrificed disciples of the Divine Sacrificed One — often bear the marks of the divine wounds. I give here only two examples:

Fig. 13. — One of the angels on the Alpais ciborium, 12th century. Louvre Museum.

For the first Christian millennium: the Merovingian reliquary of Saint-Bonnet-Avalouze is decorated on one of its sides with a *Signaculum Domini* formed with a cross, which bears empty mountings at its center and extremities; the one in the middle is marked with a small cross, which inclines us to think that the reliquary contained a fragment of the True Cross (Fig. 14).

The treasury of the Cathedral of Trier, in Germany, contains a very precious reliquary enclosing one of the nails that fixed the transpierced members of the Savior to the cross (Fig. 15).

Fig. 14. — Reliquary of Saint-Bonnet-Avalouze. Barbarian art, 6th–7th century.

Fig. 15. — Gold reliquary of the Holy Nail at the Cathedral of Trier, 10th century.

Fashioned in gold in the tenth century, this reliquary, a four-paneled stem with four bevelled edges at the corners, adopts the form of the sacred object it envelops. Its ornamentation of precious stones and emeralds is very rich. On its main section is inscribed a rather uncommon form of the *Signaculum Domini*: five enamel crosses are vertically aligned, the middle one white, the others blue.

On the reliquary of the Holy Nail it is not possible to see anything else, in the five crosses it bears, than an allusion to the five wounds of the crucified Savior.[14]

At the Cluny Museum in Paris, we find a beautiful reliquary of the thirteenth century composed of a quadrilobate piece set on the stem of a cup. As well, five large crystal cabochons are arranged like the points of the *Signaculum* on numerous coins of the same period; the rest of the decoration is made from red stones (Fig. 16).

Lastly, to conclude this brief review of the *Signaculum Domini* on liturgical and ancient objects, we cite a Byzantine processional cross at Emesa, which bears the five emblematic cabochons,[15] and also a censer from Lille on which "an angel holds in his hand a mysterious disk or seal, the Byzantine symbolism of which supposes that God always provides swift messengers that He entrusts with his orders for mortals."[16]

---

14 See Mgr. Barbier de Montault and Leon Palustre, *Le Trésor de Trèves*, p. 4 and Pl. II.

15 See Dom H. Leclercq, *Dict. d'Archéologie Chrétienne*, T. IV, vol. II, col. 2729.

16 Auber, *Hist. et théorie du Symbolisme religieux*, T. IV, 315.

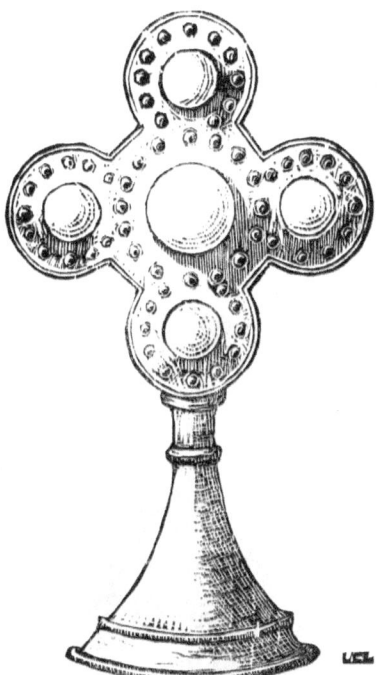

Fig. 16. — Reliquary in gold of the 12th century. Cluny Museum, Paris.

V. THE "SIGNACULUM DOMINI" ON LITURGICAL VESTMENTS

Although less frequently than on liturgical objects, we find the *Signaculum Domini* represented on the pontifical vestments which remain to us from from those remote times, or copied on monuments.

On the Imperial Dalmatic in the Vatican Treasury the holy emblem is formed by a Greek cross cantoned with the four nails of the crucifixion of Jesus, arranged, as we will see later, in the same manner as on numerous signet rings from barbarian times (6th–10th century).[17]

The *signaculum* is likewise placed on the front of a Benedictine abbot's vestment of the eleventh century brought to light by Dom Mabillon.[18] The vertical form already adopted by the goldsmith of

---

17 See Didron, *Annales archéologiques*, ann. 1844 (mai-déc.), 286.
18 Cf. Dom Mabillon, *Annales Ord. S. Bénédict*, T. I, Lib. V, 121.

Part I: The Five Wounds of Christ in Earliest Christian Art

the Trier reliquary of the Holy Nail is repeated here, an arrangement suitable for narrow and elongated spaces. We must not confuse the median orphrey of the above-mentioned cowl with the *pallium* of the higher clergy which, as Viollet-le-Duc tells us,[19] in agreement with Durandus of Mende, should regularly entail four purple crosses in front and four others behind[20] (Fig. 17).

The same symbol is again inscribed on the pectoral part of the chasuble, which Philip, bishop of Rennes from 1179 to 1182, bore on his seal; and we also notice it on the lower end of a maniple borne by a statue on a doorway of Chartres cathedral (12th–13th centuries)[21] (Figs. 18 and 19).

Fig. 17. — The five crosses borne by a Benedictine abbot of the 11th century. According to Mabillon, op. cit.

Fig. 18. — The Signaculum Domini formed by the band and four disks on the chasuble of Philip, bishop of Rennes, 11th century.

Fig. 19. — Lower part of the maniple of a statue on a doorway of Chartres, 11th–12th century.

19 Viollet-le-Duc, *Dict. du Mobilier* (s. v. Pallium).
20 William Durandus (13th c.), op. cit., ch. XVII, III.
21 Cf. Dumay, *Le Costume sacerdotal* in *Gaz. des Beaux-Arts*, 1877, num. 246, page 521.

VI. THE "SIGNACULUM DOMINI" ON ANCIENT COINS

Ancient coins are the mirror of the leading thoughts of the times in which they were struck. An incontestable reflection of the soul of each nation, the strength of its beliefs and the liveliness of its hopes, is preserved on them. And right from its beginnings, early Christian coinage marks its money with the sigil of the chief five wounds of the Savior: the *Signaculum Domini*.

We have seen that the first Christian emperor of Rome, Constantine the Great, placed the symbol of the five wounds on the very standard of the Empire, to which a large coin with his effigy bears witness. The money of ancient Gaul at the time of the kings of the first Frankish dynasty, the descendants of Merovech, frequently bore the same emblem.

As we know, these Merovingian kings did not reserve the striking of money exclusively to themselves in the territory subject to their sovereignty, but under certain guarantees authorized their vassals, the *leudes* [barons], to practice it in their own domains. This is why certain pieces of money in gold, silver, or bronze bear the name of what are today miniscule localities, but which were often, even at the very time this money was struck, no more than small hamlets or isolated dwellings in the countryside.

Among these coins whose composition was only under the control of the mint that issued them, a good number bear the *Signaculum Domini*. They were struck during the sixth and the two following centuries. I have reproduced a few examples of them here:

Plate 1, Num. 1. — A coin from Mans on which the cantoned cross with four points surmounts a step.[22]

Num. 2. — A coin from Niort that also bears a step, a Latin cross, and four symbolic crosslets. Within the compass of these two coins, as in several of those to follow, the cross represents

---

22 Cf. Adrien Blanchet, *Nouv. Manuel de Numismatique du Moyen-Âge et Moderne*, num.1.

Part I: The Five Wounds of Christ in Earliest Christian Art

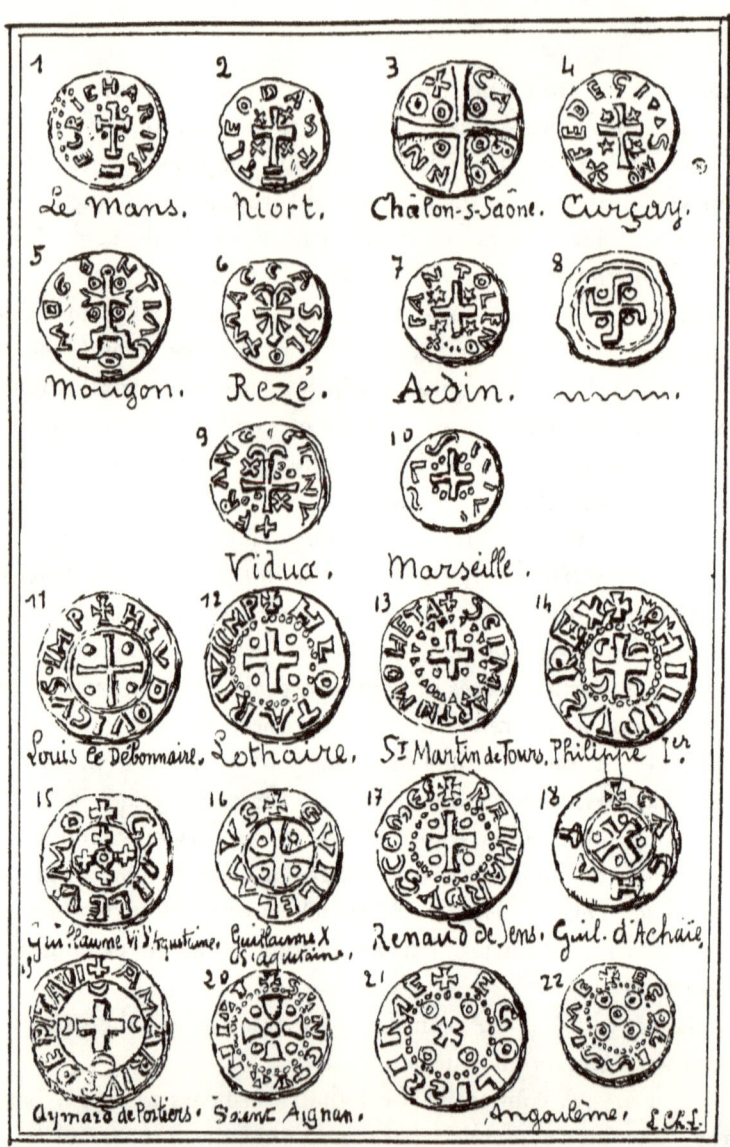

Plate 1. — *Ancient coins, first series.*

The "Signaculum Domini"

the wound in the side of Jesus, and the points and crosslets the wounds in his hands and feet.[23]

Num. 3. — A coin from Châlons-sur-Saône bearing four circles or ringlets around a Greek cross.

After these coins from the large towns, here are some that come from quite small localities:

Num. 4. — At Curçay, near Loudun (Vienne), the Leude Fedegius struck pieces where the central cross is accompanied by four stars.[24]

Num. 5. — Mougon of Touraine or Mougon of Poitou issued money where we see the cross between four small circles and standing on a pedestal or "calvary."[25]

Num. 6. — On pieces from Rezé, near Nantes, an anchored cross is cantoned with the four nails of the crucifixion. We will see later that this motif was frequently utilized for the sigillary and symbolic decorating of ring bezels.[26]

Num. 7. — The cross on the money of Ardin (Deux-Sèvres) is placed, as on the money of Curçay, between four stars.[27]

Num. 8. — Lastly, we mention that on another Frankish coin from the same period, but anepigraphic, the swastika (now improperly designated under the name of a "gammated cross") symbolizes, like the simple crosses on the preceding coins, the wound in the side of Jesus, and is accompanied by four points.[28] The unforewarned should not be alarmed: the swastika, a very ancient emblem for the very beginnings of life, was an emblem of Christ accepted by the early Church; and, in the Roman catacombs, an image of the Redeemer bears this swastika on his clothing.[29]

---

23 Cf. Charles Farcinet, *Les identifications géographiques des monnaies Mérovingiennes et le Catalogue de la Bibl. Nationale.*
24 Cf. Adrien Blanchet, op. cit., n° 74.
25 Cf. Adrien Blanchet, op. cit., n° 157.
26 Cf. Benj. Fillon, *Considération histor. et artistiq. sur les Monnaies de France.*
27 Cf. Charles Farcinet, *Essais numismatiques. Les monnaies mérovingiennes attribuées à la Vendée*, 13.
28 Cf. Dom H. Leclercq, *Dictionn. d'Archéol. chrét.*, T. III, v. II, col. 3096.
29 Ibid., T. III, vol. I, col. 610.

We understand that, in a coinage so dispersed and completely given up to the arbitariness of the countryside barons or of the minters who were often satisfied with more or less copying their neighbors or their predecessors without always clearly understanding the symbols they were reproducing, degenerations in emblematic standards were inevitable. Here are two examples of this among hundreds of others:

Num. 9. — Coin from Vidua: a cross with two crosslets and two groups of three points.[30]

Num. 10. — Coin from Marseille: a cross and four groups of two points.[31]

The sovereigns of the Carolingian dynasty only exceptionally granted to their chief subjects the right to strike money. On their own currency the *Signaculum Christi* frequently fills an entire side:

Num. 11. — Coin of Louis the Fair: the cross and four points.[32]

Num. 12. — The same subject on Lothaire's currency.[33]

Num. 13. — The same theme on coins from the royal abbey of St. Martin of Tours.[34]

Once more we see the emblem of the five wounds of Christ on the royal coinage of Philip I and of several leading vassals of the crown who, without being sovereign princes, had received or arrogated the right to mint money:

Num. 14. — Coin of King Philip I: the cross is accompanied by four crescents.[35]

Num. 15. — Coin of William VI, count of Poitiers and sovereign duke of Aquitaine: a cruciform combination of a circle and four crosslets.

Num. 16. — Coin of St. William X, count of Poitiers and duke of Aquitaine: a cantoned Greek cross with four points.[36]

---

[30] Cf. A. Blanchet, op. cit., num. 43.
[31] Ibid., num. 175.
[32] Ibid., num. 225.
[33] Ibid., num. 234.
[34] Cf. G. Cartier, *De la monnaie Tournois issue de celle de Saint-Martin*, Pl.
[35] Cf. A. Blanchet, op. cit., num. 238.
[36] Ibid., num. 314.

Num. 17.— Coin of Renaud, count of Sens: the same theme as the one on the previous piece.[37]

Num. 18.— Coin of William of Villehardouin, prince of Achaia: the cross in an X and four points.[38]

Num. 19.— Coin of Aymard VI, of Poitiers, count of Valencia and Die: a cross accompanied at the ends of its arms by four crescents.[39]

Num. 20.— Coin of the lords of Saint-Aignan: a central point of a cruciform cluster and four other smaller points form a *Signaculum Domini*.[40]

Nums. 21 & 22.— Two coins from the city of Angoulême: on the first, the *Signaculum Domini* is made with a crosslet and four circles or ringlets; on the second it is composed of five ringlets.[41]

Even more often than in prior ages, alterations and degenerations of the *Signaculum Domini* were produced in the hodge-podge of feudal coinage. This should not, however, invalidate the sense of the authentic model. We repeat, the significance of this model is the same as for the five crosses on altar stones and the five grains of incense on the Paschal candle. But, the field on the coin being enormously more reduced than the surface of the altar, the grouping of the five parts of the *Signaculum Domini* have undergone a restriction that has brought them together into the compact cluster we find throughout medieval heraldry.

On the very beautiful coinage of the last Capetians and Valois, the heraldic and royal Fleur de Lys is set between the arms of the cross. Might not there be some connections here with the redemptive wounds? It is not out of the question that someone at that time might have thought of this, for the chivalric pharmacopoeia preferred to treat the wounds of war with lily petals steeped for a long time in wine oil or spirits (*eau-de-vie* [that is, brandy or, literally, water-of-life]), these petals being applied by compresses to the wounds and held there by bandages. This way

---

[37] Ibid., num. 351.
[38] Ibid., num. 553.
[39] Ibid., num. 378.
[40] Ibid., num. 337.
[41] Ibid., num. 444.

of dealing with all bleeding wounds still exists in many rural areas in the west of France.

It is quite evident, we should add, that on money where, in the gaps between the arms of the cross, fleur-de-lys alternate with crowns, for example, or else where only leopards, lions, or towers are placed, the symbolism of these figures is simply heraldic: the cross that they surround is indeed connected with Christ's social sovereignty, but without any relationship to his redemptive wounds.

Outside of France, the emperors of Byzantium, more or less direct successors of Constantine, often represent the Lord Jesus Christ seated on the imperial throne, and on several of these representations he is surrounded by this very clear proclamation of his social sovereignty:

IHS·XIS·REX·REGNANTIUM
"Jesus Christ, king of those who reign"

Thus enthroned, Christ the Sovereign holds in his hand the book of his doctrine, the Gospel, on the cover of which is seen his "sign" and the seal of our redemption, the five symbolic points. The following coins are examples of this:

Plate 2, Num. 23. — Coin of Theodora: Christ standing holds in his hand the "Book" sigillated with five points (501 to 548).

Num. 24. — Coin of the emperor Michael: Christ in half-length likewise holds the Book (842 to 867).

Num. 25. — Coin of Romanus Argyrus: Christ is on a throne and carries the Book (1059 to 1067).

Num. 26. — Coin of Nikephoros Botaneiates: the same subject as on the previous coin, but the *Signaculum Domini* is also seen on the nimbus that glorifies the Savior's head (1078 to 1081).

Num. 27. — Coin of Alexios Comnenos: Christ holds the Book and blesses (1086 to 1118).[42]

---

42 According to *Monnaies Antiques, Grecques, Romaines, Byzantines et Gauloises*, Catalogue of collection A., Pl. XII, and *Recueil Numismatique*, passim.

Plate 2. — *Ancient coins, second series.*

The *Signaculum Domini* was also placed on coins in other countries:

Num. 28. — Coin of Canute the Great, king of England and Denmark (died 1036). The symbol of the five wounds is depicted here around the intersection of the first of the cross's two crossbars, which will become the "Cross of Anjou" later, and the so-called "Cross of Lorraine" today, and which since the time of Canute was especially placed on reliquaries for fragments of the True Cross.[43]

I will stop here with this very brief review of the representations of the *Signaculum Domini* on coins; the examples given will suffice to show how this emblem played an important role in the official symbolism of the old nations of Christian Europe.

---

43 Cf. A. Blanchet, op. cit., num. 534 and 535.

Part I: The Five Wounds of Christ in Earliest Christian Art

VII. THE "SIGNACULUM DOMINI" ON WEAPONS AND BATTLE-GEAR

The emblematic mark of the torment of Jesus Christ was too often represented on the currency of the Frankish leaders of all ranks for it not to be also engraved on any number of objects in their employ. And foremost among the objects held to be the noblest and most cherished by their national character were their weapons.

Except for those of the high aristocracy, the appearance of Frankish weapons was simple and rough, as was in general the art of that time, rather like the customs and lives of their possessors.

But the Christian faith, which only slowly tempered the habits of these semi-barbarians, nevertheless affected their spirit, for which Christ was an invisible living being, present in their midst, and the emblem of the wounds received on Calvary by this generous Redeemer was engraved on the weapons from which they were hardly ever parted, and on the metallic pieces of their sword-belts and other straps.

We will just mention, as regards offensive weapons, the presence of the *Signaculum Domini* on the following items:

I.—The Parenteau collection, which is at the Musée de Nantes, contains two long javelin heads found at Rezé (Loire-Inférieur). On the ailerons of one of them, two cantoned crosses, each with the four symbolic points, brings to mind the Savior's Passion. A bronze key found with the two javelins is also marked with a cross and the four emblematic points[44] (Fig. 20).

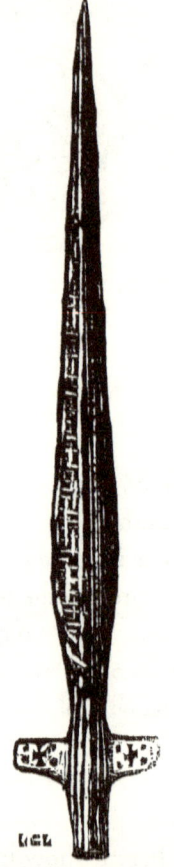

Fig. 20.—Javelin head 6th–7th century. Rezé (Loire-Inférieure). Parenteau collection, Musée de Nantes. Length 0 m. 60.

---

44 Cf. F. Parenteau, *Inventaire Archéologique*, Pl. 10, num. 4, p. 22 and p. 48, num. 3.

II. — A fine example of a Frankish battle axe, discovered between Villiers-Charlemagne and Meslay (Mayenne) about 1885, likewise bears a cross between four points square in form. Both of these weapons are from the sixth or seventh century (Fig. 21).

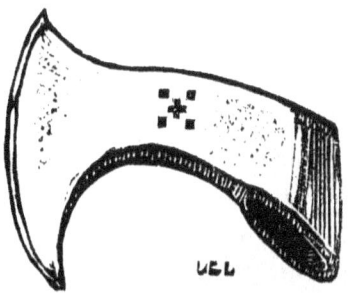

Fig. 21. — *Frankish battle axe, 6th–7th century, from around Meslay (Mayenne). According to a drawing by Fr. Sylvestre, 1898.*

III. — A large sword of an extraordinarily sharp metal, found near Cerizay (Deux-Sèvres) in the bed of the Sèvre-Nantaise river, carries, inlaid in the steel of its blade at the lower end, a drop of copper or gold marked in hollow relief with a cross accompanied by four small crosslets. This weapon, which was given to me by the archaeologist Gabriel de Fontaines, is from the ninth or tenth century (Fig. 22).

It was with such weapons that the Franks of those times wrote on the soil of Europe the first "Gesta Dei per Francos."

Fig. 22. — *Sword of the Carolingian period. From the author's study.*

The following centuries sometimes also marked their offensive arms with the "Seal of the Lord," and most likely it is this that is found on the mysterious sword, marked with five crosses on each of its flat surfaces, that Joan of Arc sought for in the soil of Sainte-Catherine-de-Fierbois and placed at her side.

We will surely never know at what period this weapon was forged.

Another sword, from the early years of the sixteenth century, shown at the Bacheleau home, 46 rue de Provence, Paris, in 1932, bears on the shoulder of its blade five minute crosslets arranged vertically, as we saw on the Holy Nail reliquary at Trier cathedral. By way of an appeal for divine protection, the presence of the *Signaculum Domini* on defensive arms and battle gear is perhaps easier to explain than on offensive arms, however more frequent this might be.

Our fathers of Western Christianity did not invent this practice, which in fact came to us with the barbarian art of the Ostrogoths, Visigoths, and Goths of the Ukraine, Crimea, and Dacia, through the valleys of Dniester and the Danube, through the roads of Illyria, Panonia, Norica, and Dalmatia — art sparkling and sumptuous despite its roughness. From the fifth to the ninth century it covered the West with heavy and complicated jewelry lined with brilliant stones, glass beadwork, glittering cabochons, and baffling interlaced designs that were displayed on every warrior's leatherwork.

*Fig. 23. — Buckle of a sword-belt from Soujouk-Sou (Crimea). According to J. de Baye (*Mém. des Antiq. de France, loc. cit.*).*

I. — The lovely buckle of a barbarian sword-belt that Baron J. de Baye brought to the attention of the antiquarians of France in 1907 dates back to the earliest Christian times of the Gothic race.[45] It was found at Soujouk-Sou in Crimea. The five mysterious crosses have the same arrangement there as on altar stones, with nail-framed cabochons placed over the small crosses at the corners (Fig. 23).

II. — A large clasp or fibula from Wittislingen, today in the Bavarian Museum at Munich, probably attached to war gear, bears a cross pattée set with cloisonné enamel and cantoned with four cabochons imbedded in the metal, which form the four emblematic points between the arms of the cross (Fig. 24).

III. — On the large buckles of sword straps from France the cabochons are most often only three in number. However, exceptions sometimes occur. This very simple hitch plate, for example,

---

45 J. de Baye, *Mém. Ant. de France*, ann. 1907, p. 97.

The "Signaculum Domini"

Fig. 24 — Large clasp from Wittislingen, at the Munich Museum (from a Hanfstaege photographic negative).

was found in a grave near the church of Saint-Maixent-de-Beugné (Deux-Sèvres) and collected by the marquis Charles de Cumont-Damas around 1890 (Fig. 26).

IV. — At the time of the Capetians and Valois, that is, for five hundred years, the *Signaculum* also sometimes appeared on knightly armor. It is seen on the visor for the helmet of Ulrick, Landgrave of Alsace, reproduced on his statue, which dates from 1334 and is found in St. William's Church, Strasbourg[46] (Fig. 25).

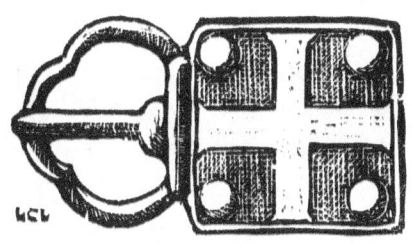

Fig. 25. — Visor for the helmet of Ulrick, Landgrave of Alsace, 14th century.

Fig. 26. — Buckle of a sword-belt from Saint-Maixent de Beugné, 6th–7th century.

46 Cf. Viollet-Le-Duc, *Dictionnaire du Mobilier* (s. v. Heaume).

V.—The same representation is found on the gorget of heraldic helmets on a stained glass window with the arms of the Landgrave of Hesse, Louis II, fifteenth century.

VI.—The German shields of the "targe" type, in the fourteenth century and during the following century, were rather frequently pierced with eye-holes arranged in various ways. One of these targe shields, at Bamberg cathedral, is decorated with a large cross and the eye-holes are arranged in such a way as to form the *Signaculum Domini* with it[47] (Fig. 27).

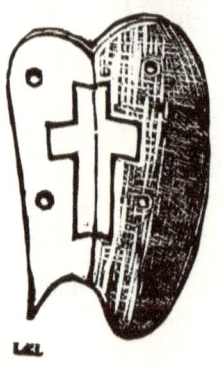

VII.—Again we find it, this time composed of five crosses, on a gauntlet with jointed iron strips from the fifteenth century (Fig. 28). It was passed by way of a trade from the hands of Count R. de Rochebrune to those of the Count of Chauveau, but does not appear today in the collections of this last connoisseur, collections generously given by his will, along with Keriolet castle, to the department of Finistere. This item was quite likely of French workmanship, and we find the emblem engraved in the middle of the metacarpus in the place occupied by metallic disks on the liturgical gloves of prelates during the same period.

Fig. 27. — 14th-century shield belonging to Bamberg Cathedral. This "targe" was copied by Demmin (loc. cit.) in more reduced dimensions.

On all these pieces of gear, the *Signaculum Domini* indeed appears to be, then, the sign of blessing by which a warrior virtually asks for the Lord's protection: *Per Crucem et Passionem tuam, libera nos, Domine,* "Through Thy Passion and Cross, deliver us, O Lord."[48]

Fig. 28. — 15th-century armored gauntlet from the collections of de Rochebrune et de Hauveau (from a drawing by Comte R. de Rochebrune).

---

47 See Auguste Demmin, *Guide des Amateurs d'Armes*, p. 311, num. 17.
48 *Roman Breviary* (*Off. of Rogations, Litany of the Saints*).

VIII. THE "SIGNACULUM DOMINI" ON ANCIENT CHRISTIAN CERAMIC PRODUCTS

We have already seen the symbol of the five wounds on two lamps from Egyptian Christian antiquity, one found at Cairo, the other one coming from the necropolis of Akmin. It is also to be met with in the far West on some ceramic products of the early Christian centuries.

It was thus that a Merovingian brick from Marans in Saintonge, part of the H. Jousseaume collection, was marked with a disk containing five crosslets in relief (Fig. 29). And the Musée des Grandes Écoles, at the Société des Antiquaires de l'Ouest at Poitiers, also owns a pot of the same date as the previous one, that carries a mark composed of a cantoned cross with four points in relief (Fig. 30).

Fig. 29. — Mark recovered by M. Gabriel de Fontaines on a brick from the 6th or 7th century, originating in Marans (Charente-Inférieure). Jousseaume Collection.

Fig. 30. — Mark sigillated five times on a fragment of Merovingian pottery. — Musée des Grandes Écoles, Poitiers.

Both of these marks were made by the pressing of a wooden or stone sigillary mold against the soft clay of the aforesaid objects before their firing in the potter's kiln.

An inspection of French museums would surely produce numerous similar examples: a decorative motif on a fifteenth century terracotta paving tile corroborates this assertion. It is comprised of a fleuroned cross cantoned with four cross-shaped flowers. This composition is closely related to certain documents from England connected with the same period. The drawing is thanks to the late Rev. Blanchet of Saint-Laurent-sur-Sèvre (Vendée). This paving is from the outbuildings of the Château des Rochers near Vitré

(Ille-et-Vilaine), which, in the seventeenth century, belonged to Madame de Sévigné (Fig. 31).

As is also the case for the Cross, the Anchor, the Tau, and the Constantian cipher for Christ, the X-over-P, we sometimes encounter the cross and points of the *Signaculum Domini* on ceramic or metallic objects much more ancient than Christianity; this is however an extremely rare occurrence, a perfect example being a terracotta disk of pre-Christian

Fig. 31. — *Decorative motif on a paving tile. Château des Rochers (I.-et-V.), 15th century.*

Fig. 32. — *Mark on pre-Christian pottery from Asia Minor (Louvre Museum).*

craftsmanship originating in Asia Minor and now at the Louvre (Fig. 32).

Should we see in the decorative motif of this object a purely ornamental subject in accord with the *Signaculum Domini* through sheer coincidence, or else a purposeful mark the symbolism of which, formerly precise, has become for us ungraspable? However this may be, the *Signaculum Domini* is not attached to this mark by any link and remains a specifically Christian and Christic emblem.

IX. THE "SIGNACULUM DOMINI" IN ANCIENT SCULPTURAL ART

The emblematic sign of the five principal wounds of Jesus Christ is often encountered in the sculpted ornamentation of early Christian art. We will cite only a few examples, taken from all over in the early Church:

On the ruins of a Christian chapel, at Baouit in Egypt, a freestone of great height bears in relief a cross and the four evocative

The "Signaculum Domini"

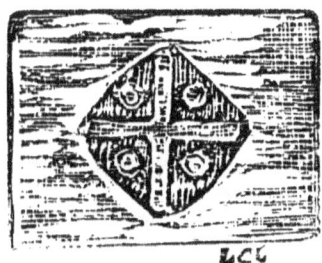

Fig. 33. — Chapel in Baouit, Egypt, 5th–6th century.

points of the divine wounds. This sculpture is from the fifth or sixth century[49] (Fig. 33).

At the same period, likewise in Egypt, at the monastery of Chaqqara, a gravestone was decorated with a *Signaculum* composed of a forked cross cantoned with the four nails of the Lord's Passion arranged as we have seen them on numerous Gallo-Frankish rings (Fig. 34). The first part of this chapter contains a reproduction of a beautiful *Signaculum* from the same monastery.[50]

At Mayence, a tombstone from the earliest Frankish period, probably from the sixth century, is ornamented with a cross and four cross-bearing circles[51] (Fig. 35).

In Ireland, the *Signaculum Domini* was more utilized, it seems, than anywhere else in monumental sculpture; this was, moreover, the favorite theme in the decoration of all religious works. I have already mentioned the ministerial chalice of Ardagh,[52] which is from the eighth century.

Fig. 34. — Sculpture from the monastery of Chaqqara, in Egypt 5th–6th century.

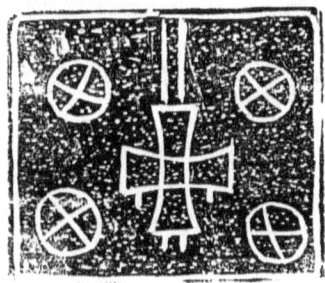

Fig. 35. — Upper part of a gravestone at Mayence, 6th c.

On sculptures of the same date, the symbol of divine torture similarly makes its appearance; one of the most beautiful is incontestably the funerary cross at Clonmacnois, in King's County, made for King Flann, who died about 915. The four points are found there on a central circle that encompasses Christ on the cross[53] (Fig. 37).

49 According to a photograph at the Louvre Museum.
50 Cf. 1st Part, Chap. 1.i, p. 5.
51 Cf. Maurice Prou, *La Gaule Mérovingienne*, p. 266.
52 Cf. 1st Part, Chap. 1.iv, p. 11.
53 Cf. Dom Leclercq, *Dict. d'Archéologie Chrétienne*, T. III, vol. II, col. 2, p. 18.

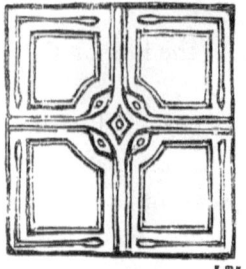

Fig. 36. — Central part of a grave-stone from Clonmacnois (Ireland).

And not far from this cross a slab reproduces the same emblem[54] (Fig. 36).

Among the numerous and important iconographic findings I possess thanks to the great kindness of Mrs. Edith E. Wilde of Winchester, is the drawing of the top of a cross from the cemetery of St. Breaca (Cornwall), which replicates the *Signaculum* (Fig. 38), as well as photos of the cross that decorates a small menhir now set in the gardens of Wharncliffe Hotel at Tintagel (Cornwall) (Fig. 39), and photos of two other sculptural pieces near the church and cemetery of St. Buryan (Land's End, Cornwall) (Fig. 40 and 41). These monuments are chronologically spread out across the entire Middle Ages, with this pattern unchanged in the course of centuries.

Concluding our survey with France, we will mention the beautiful medieval sculpture from Saint-Guilhem-le-Désert (Hérault), where the *Signaculum* is composed of five crosses with this

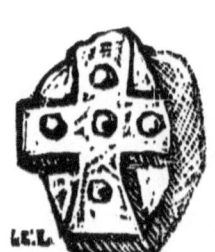

Fig. 38. — Top of a funerary cross, Saint Buryan cemetery (Cornwall).

Fig. 37. — Cross from the Clonmacnois cemetery (Ireland), 10th century.

Fig. 39. — Menhir from the Wharncliffe Hotel at Tintagel (Cornwall).

54 Ibid., col. 2023.

Fig. 40. — Stepped calvary at Saint Buryan (Land's End, Cornwall).

Fig. 41. — Cross at the top of another stepped calvary, Saint Buryan (Land's End, Cornwall).

inscription: HIC EST SIG(*naculum*) DEI (Fig. 42), and the central motif of a fifteenth-century sculpture, noticed formerly by Arthur Labbé in a house of the Saint-Jacques Quarter at Châtellerault (Vienne) (Fig. 43).

Chasing, in productions of the minor arts such as works on more or less precious metals, on ivory or wood, has often also represented the emblem of Christ's sacred wounds. We will just mention, for example, eburnean works: the cover for the Etschmardzin Evangelary, the leaves of the Murano Diptych, and an ivory from the Berlin Museum that is from the seventh or else the eighth century[55] (Fig. 44).

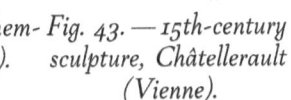

Fig. 42. — Saint-Guilhem-du-Désert (Hérault).

Fig. 43. — 15th-century sculpture, Châtellerault (Vienne).

Fig. 44. — On an ivory at the Berlin Museum.

---

55 Cf. Dom Leclercq, *Dict. Archéol. Chrét.*, T. I, vol. II, col. 2037 and T. II, vol. I, col. 784.

X. THE "SIGNACULUM DOMINI" ON EARLY CHRISTIAN JEWELRY

1. Signet rings.

Emblem of the bloody sacrifice that sealed the world's redemption, the *Signaculum Domini* possessed, on the signet rings where it was featured, a dual character: it was borne first by a Christian as a religious, benefic, and protective sign, and then, by a higher inspiration, as a sign of a hope of salvation based on the Lord's promises. On the other hand, it was also the instrument used by the sealer to authenticate his written promises, contracts, and commitments. And this instrument with which he sealed in his own name was the *Sigillum Christi*, the very seal of Christ himself. Accomplished in this way, the act by this very means took on, so to say, a religious value in its use, became an oath of truthfulness, loyalty, and fidelity.

Here we will be content to consider a few of these sigillary and religious rings which were not, in Frankish society, reserved for a particular category of citizen, but which anyone might bear and utilize socially. All these rings fall within a chronological span from the the sixth to the ninth centuries.

Plate 3, Num. 1. — Ring from the collection of Count R. de Rochebrune, collected from the bed of the Lay river at Mareuil (Vendée). This is a man's piece of jewelry.

Num. 2. — Ring originally from the Namur region.

Num. 3. — Ring with the name of Launoberger, originally from Allonnes (Sarthe).

Num. 4. — Ring originally from Nesle (Côte-d'Or), displaying the *Signaculum Domini* under a particular but still incontestable form.

With the rings to follow we come to a very expressive form of the *Signaculum Domini*, for, within the intervals between the arms of the cross are found the nails of the Crucifixion, symbolizing the four wounds in the divine limbs. Max Deloche was one of the first to point out this significance, and was the first to promote it with some reservations. Today we are convinced that it should be accepted with complete confidence.

The "Signaculum Domini"

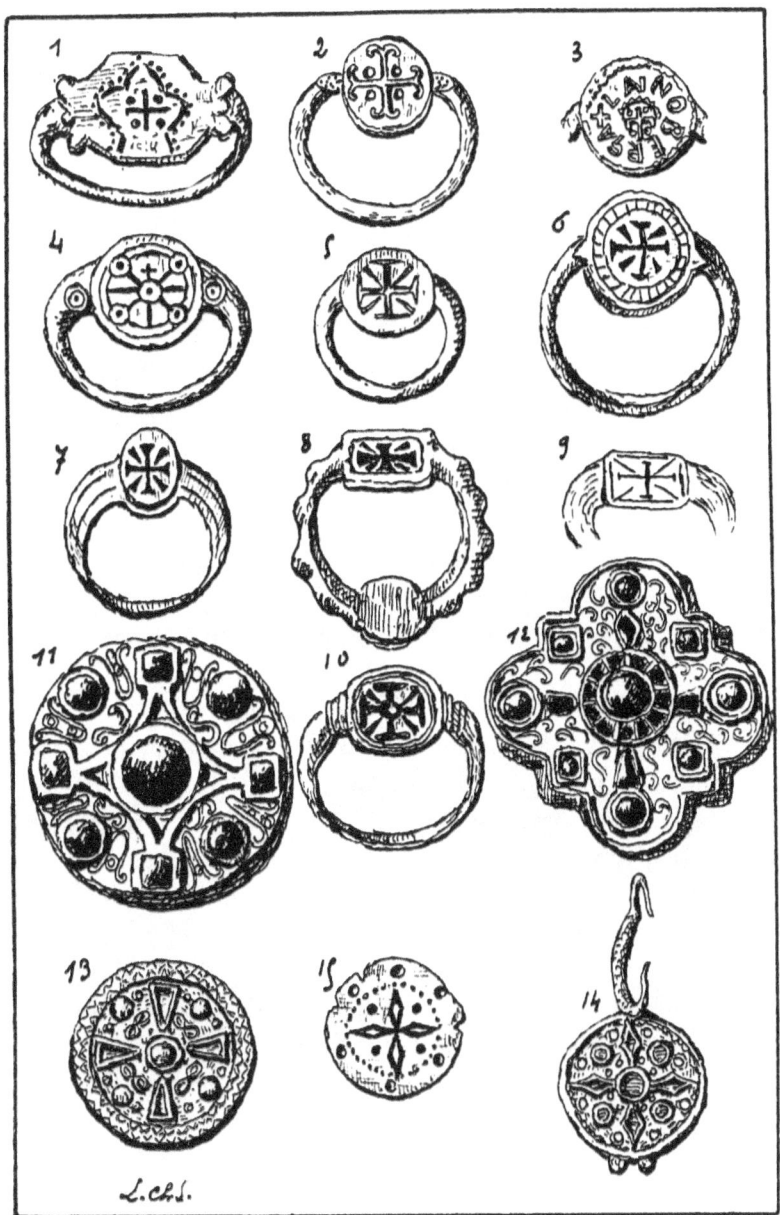

Plate 3. — Ancient Christian jewelry.

Num. 5. — Ring collected by the learned Fr. Moreau in a woman's grave at Aiguisy (Aisne).

Nums. 6 & 7. — Two rings from the Eck collection, originally from Marchélepot (Somme). The first, a very large one, is a piece of men's jewelry; the second comes from a woman's grave. A third ring, of the same provenance, has been reproduced by Deloche, and linked to them by him from the symbolic point of view; however, the form of the nails is less clear than for the other two.

Num. 8. — Ring from Resseigne, Namur province, found in a man's tomb in a Frankish necropolis. It has two chatons: on one, the emblem of the cross and nails; on the other, a Greek cross with crosslets.

Num. 9. — Ring originally from Lisieux. It is akin to the previous rings through the four simple features that most likely spring from the same thought.

Num. 10. — Ring originally from the Gallo-Frankish burials in the Old Cemetery at Loudun (Vienne); it is similar to those of Nums. 5, 6, 7, and 8, published by Deloche (collection of the author).

On the topic of these rings, we will just observe that until the thirteenth century Christ on the cross was always represented suspended by four nails. Some authors, Mgr. Barbier de Montault for one, have attributed to the Albigensians the use of crucifixions with three nails. It is likely that the bringing into Europe, at just about this time, of the Holy Shroud of Turin, which represents the two feet of Jesus placed one over the other and pierced with the same nail, was for many, more than just the Albigensians, the reason for the iconographic change produced at that time in the representations of the crucified Savior.

2. Jewels of all kinds.

The ring was always foremost among the jewelry of both men and women: the one piece that was the testimony of their conjugal union, sometimes the emblem of social rank when it bore noble or professional markings for example, and their instrument of witness when it was sigillary. This was and ordinarily still is the only secular jewelry that profits from a liturgical blessing at the celebration of the consecration of popes and kings, at the consecration of abbots, monks, and nuns, and at the marriage of the faithful. This was not, however, the only jewelry to bear, as a simple image of piety or as a protective sign, the *Signaculum Domini*. It often appeared on jewels that were simply luxury items.

Thus we find it not only in the decorative composition of the Byzantine cross of Bulla-Regia, which bears emblematic five disks at its center and on its arms,[56] but also on numerous clothing fibulae or clasps, such as the one from Elbeuf[57] (Plate 3, Num. 11), or the one published by Maurice Prou[58] (Num. 12), which was attached to the large cloak of the Franks called the *saga*. The sacred symbol is depicted on these jewels by an arrangement of pearls larger than the others.

Likewise on a great number of objects of Byzantine workmanship, earrings or buttons of large size[59] (Nums. 13 and 14).

On a small, ancient, formerly gilded bronze disk, originating in Orly (Seine), the central cross is made of four spearheads, just as it is on one of the earrings mentioned above, and the wounds to the four members are represented by simple points (Num. 15). This small plaque, pierced with holes on its rim, like the plaques on the pontifical gloves in the Middle Ages, was intended to be fastened by this means onto some material, leather or wood.[60]

XI. THE "SIGNACULUM CHRISTI" IN THE ART OF THE BOOK DURING THE FIRST CHRISTIAN MILLENNIUM

We have seen that on the coinage of the emperors of Constantinople, successors of Constantine the Great, Christ sits on the imperial throne and most frequently holds the book of the Gospels supported by his left knee.[61] Now, on the flat side of this book's

---

56 Cf. Dom Leclercq, *Dict. Arch. Chrét.*, T. V, vol. I, col. 1047.
57 Ibid., T. IV, vol. II, col. 2608.
58 M. Prou, *La Gaule Mérovingienne*, p. 274, num. 123.
59 See A. Parmentier, *Album Historique*, Livr. III, p. 46.
60 From the author's study.
61 Cf. 1st Part, Chap. 1.vi, pp. 22–23.

cover are, almost always, the five points that were the symbol of the five wounds of Christ on the cross.

Numerous liturgical books, above all during the first ten centuries, were marked externally in this way with the "Seal of the Lord," such as we see for example on the book cover held by Saint Cornelius in the Roman catacombs, reproduced by the renowned archaeologist, Commander J. B. de Rossi.[62] The five points on it are each made of two small concentric circles (Fig. 45).

Fig. 45. — The "sigillated" book held by Saint Cornelius, according to J.-B. de Rossi, op. cit.

The Evangelary of Saint Gauzelin (Fig. 46), from the Merovingian period, bears as a central motif of its cover's decoration a circle containing an X-cross made of four crosslets joined at the base to a central circle. This same motif is also found on several coins from the time of the first Frankish dynasty.[63]

Fig. 46. — The Signaculum Domini on the Evangelary of Saint Gauzelin.

Under its usual appearance as a cross and four points, the *Signaculum Domini* was introduced in the very text of liturgical books of this same period under the name of "diacritical points." At times we also find it joined with four Greek gammas, which symbolize the four Gospels and, by extension, their authors:

It thus appears, for example, on the splendid golden cover of the Monza Evangelary given by Theodelinda (Plate 4).

Mgr. Barbier de Montault explains that, in the Byzantine symbolic system, the four gammas are equivalent to a schematic drawing of books placed flat and seen from the side. He has also published the drawing of a Byzantine miniature of the eleventh

---

62 De Rossi, *Roma sotterranea*, T. I, pl. VI.
63 See *Gazette des Beaux-Arts*, ann. 1875, p. 276.

The "Signaculum Domini"

Plate 4. — *Cover to the Evangelary of Monza, gold and precious stones, 6th century.*

Part I: The Five Wounds of Christ in Earliest Christian Art

century that he accompanies with these words: "The Evangelists under the form of four gammas."[64]

On this document, the wounds of the divine members are symbolized by four hearts (Fig. 47).

The four evangelical gammas are found on a man's signet ring from Merovingian times, originating from the vicinity of Yverdon (Switzerland) (Fig. 48).[65] We have already encountered them on the Irish sculptures at Clonmacnois, for example.

On the Evangelary of Monza, the symbolic points are represented by

Fig. 47. — The Signaculum Domini *and the four gammas, Byzantine miniature, 11th century. Cf. Barbier de Montault, op. cit.*

four antique cameos which, here, just as on liturgical vessels, reliquaries, and other sacred objects where they have been so often inlaid, were only chosen as very precious ornaments, and solely to enhance the value of the object that bears them. This explains why these finely worked stones were employed without regard for the subjects with which they were decorated: the heads of pagan gods, emperors, and empresses, mythological allegories, or even somewhat indecent subjects.

Fig. 48. — Signet ring from the vicinity of Yverdon — according to M. Deloche, op. cit.

The *Signaculum Domini* also appears in the composition of a miniature from the ninth century contained in the sumptuous bible of St. Paul Outside-the-Walls at Rome, representing the Frankish king Charles II, the Bald, seated on his throne. The baldaquin that shelters the sovereign bears on the drapery that falls back behind the throne four figurations made of the cross and four points.[66]

64 Barbier de Montault, *Traité d'iconographie chrétienne* (Paris: Vivès, 1890), T. II, fig. 355, p. 281 and 282.
65 Cf. Max Deloche, *Les anneaux sigillaires et autres des premiers siècles du Moyen-Âge*, XXXV, p. 36.
66 See Max Petit and collab., *Hist. générale des Peuples*, T. I, p. 175.

XII. THE "SIGNACULUM DOMINI" IN SIGILLOGRAPHY

The metal molds for the ancient seals of the sacerdotal or mystical type, or of the armorial type, that bear variants of the *Signaculum Christi* are all connected with what we have said about the presence of this sign in the composition of armorial bearings; but personal signature marks, those designs that serve as flourishes, so common throughout the Middle Ages, have often placed their signers under the protection of the emblem of the Lord's five wounds. This revered *Signum* piously vouched for the faithfulness of the accompanying signature, as well as its authenticity, just as formerly it had done so beside the name of the sealer with the affixing of the signet ring's emblem-engraved bezel.

These personal signature marks, of necessity affixed to archival documents, are much less known than the seals in metal. To gain some idea of this more rarely visited realm, let us turn to the cartularies of early Spain, elder sister of that Portugal whose royal and national standards have always borne the sacred emblem.

From 954 the sovereign count of Barcelona, Borel, ended his name with a cross potent cantoned with four points (Plate 5, Num. 1); in 992, his successor Raymond Borel did the same (Num. 2). In 1018 it was Count Berenger (Num. 3); in 1076, Raymon Berenger II (Num. 4); in 1031, Raymon-Berenger IV (Num. 5) whose youngest son, the brother of Alfonso, named Raymond Berenger like his father, did not reign in Barcelona. This last Raymon Berenger ended his name with the flourish of a very particular *signum* in which the *Signaculum Domini* was joined to a star[67] (Num. 6).

A good number of the kings of Aragon, Castille, and Majorca have also taken as a motif for their signature the traditional emblem of the five wounds. Alfonso II's signature is composed of a recumbent rectangle with its angles reinforced by four emptied points, which makes it resemble on a linear plane certain fortified enclosures; a large cross is inscribed at its center (Num. 7).

---

67 Cf. E. de Fouchier, *Sphragistique roussillonnaise*, in *Mém. Soc. Agricole scientifique et littéraire des Pyrénées-Orientales*, p. 248.

Part I: The Five Wounds of Christ in Earliest Christian Art

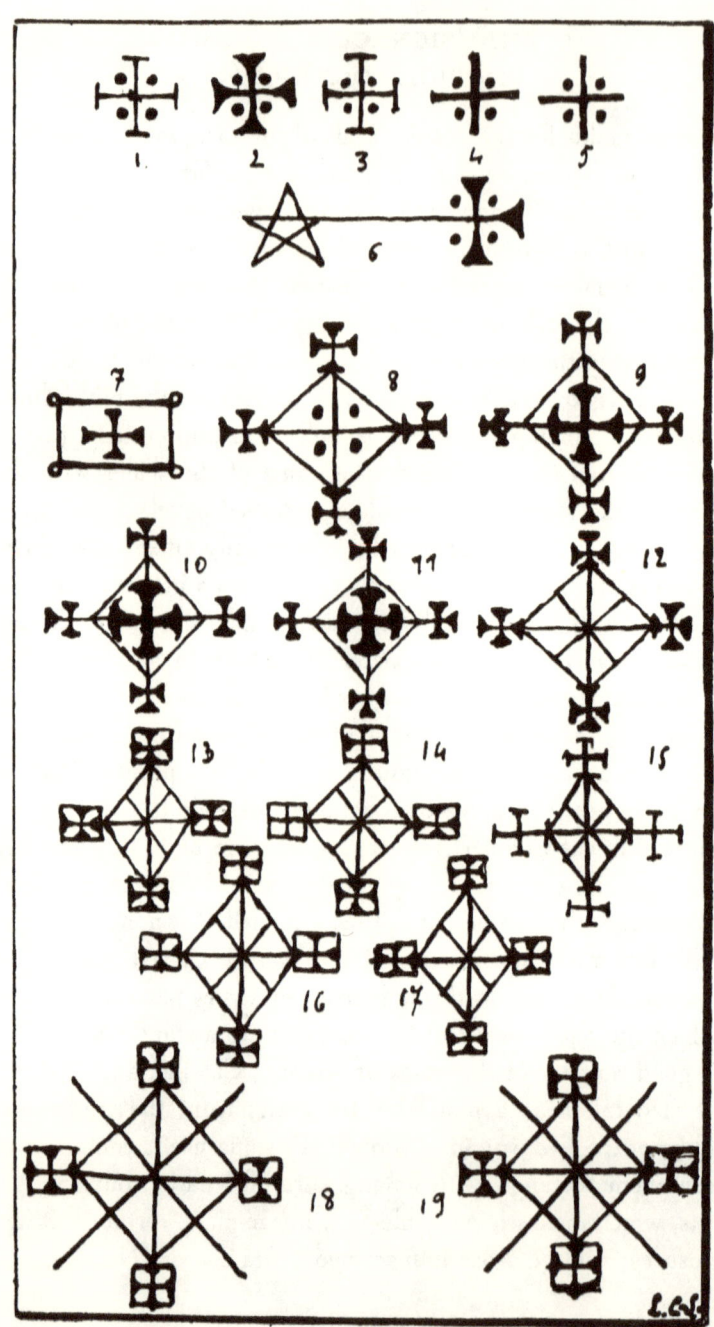

Plate 5. — Ancient seals.

The "Signaculum Domini"

The signature marks of other sovereigns of Majorca and Aragon are made with a square resting on one of its angles, or with a lozenge; these figures are transected by two diagonals in the shape of a cross, the ends of which give rise to four crosslets—which form a *Signaculum* made of five crosses.

The lozenge of Peter II (1196–1213) contains four additional points, a doubling of the traditional *Signaculum* (Plate 5, Num. 8); those of James I (1276–1311) (Num. 9), Sancho (1311–1324) (Num. 10), and James II (1234–1244) (Num. 11), kings of Majorca, enclosing a thick cross, those of James the Conqueror, of Majorca (1213–1311) (Num. 12) and the kings of Aragon and Castille, Peter IV (1395) (Num. 13), Martin (1376–1410) (Num. 14), John I (1458–1479) (Num. 15), John II (1468) (Num. 16), Ferdinand (1412–1416) (Num. 17), Alfonso (1416–1458) (Num. 18) and Ferdinand the Catholic (1474–1516) (Num. 19) are transected, in addition to the cross-shaped diagonals, by two other lines set in an X; moreover, the crosslets of their projecting angles are enclosed in small rectangular or squared frames.[68]

We also see these four framed crosslets at the angles of the lozenge-shaped coats of arms of queens Maria of Aragon (1396) and Maria of Castille (1445).[69]

And so, with all these signatures, the old emblem of the shedding of redemptive Blood is manifested again and again.

We will just add that, from 1388 to the eighteenth century, the Viguiers of Barcelona have used a wax seal on which, in a quadrilobate cartouche, "a square escutcheon tipped up, with pales of Aragon, bore another crest charged with a humetty cross charged with the four points of the *Signaculum Domini.*"[70]

---

68 Cf. E. de Fouchier, op. cit., pl. 7.
69 Ibid.
70 Ibid., p. 250.

Part I: The Five Wounds of Christ in Earliest Christian Art

Wood engraved with penknife by the author.

CHAPTER TWO

The "Signaculum Domini" in Medieval Heraldry

I. HERALDRY IN GENERAL

FOR OVER A HUNDRED YEARS THERE HAVE been those who repeatedly insisted that heraldry arose during the first two centuries of the second Christian millennium with the founding of chivalry and the remote expeditions of the crusaders.

This is a childish error. Heraldry is to be seen in all ancient civilizations: prehistoric tribes have had their totems and images which represented them; the Egyptians have had their sacred tokens that were "at first the personifications of their clans before being their tutelary deities";[1] both the pharaohs and the cities of Egypt have had their escutcheons, which were in fact coats of arms; Greek cities and Mediterranean countries have had their consecrated emblems, the images of which were preserved on their coins, and these emblems were in fact coats of arms; the Gaulish tribes have had their tokens and symbolic markings which were in fact coats of arms. But, at the time of chivalry and the Crusades, European heraldry was codified; use made armorial bearings a family or personal property of which the public power became the upholder. These bearings became, so to say, an integral part of a name, and, for each individual, were the representative symbol of one's blood, one's family stock.

Reviving the custom of the Gaulish warriors, the men-at-arms of early Capetian times had their personal or familial marks painted on their battle or ceremonial shields; from this arose the practice of representing them elsewhere, bearing them on small bucklers or shields called *escutcheons* or little shields.

Also clergy, lawyers, judges, and even simple merchants, imitating in this the men-at-arms, adopted escutcheons, while craftsmen

[1] Ph. Virey, *La Religion de l'ancienne Égypte. Le Totémisme*, p. 31.

ordinarily placed their professional marks, without escutcheons, within the circular framework of their seals or on their corporative banners. Later, craftsmen and guilds also adopted escutcheons: the marks of the first French printers (fifteenth and sixteenth centuries) are a witness to this.

The subjects covering these heraldic escutcheons were of all kinds, and their choice, for each blazon, stemmed from the most varied circumstances: religious, mystical, or hermetic emblems, military, feudal, monastic, ecclesiastic, or corporative life each contributed their ample share.

Religious emblems were among the most frequently adopted by each of these social categories. Among them the *Signaculum Domini*, which had enjoyed such great favor in all the sacred and secular arts during the previous centuries, could not help but still have a secure place in the heraldry of the second millennium.

It is in fact frequently encountered; but often, in the midst of numerous similar compositions, present-day heraldists do not always distinguish it from the others.

Since the codification of blazonry in the twelfth century, the round point, in the specialized language that it created and set apart, is termed "bezant" and was first termed "Bysans," from the name of the coins of Byzantium taken as the prototype of money in general. The ancient cross of the *Signaculum* cantoned by four points was therefore said to be cantoned by four bezants, without ceasing to be for all that a secular and yet real emblem of the five wounds of our Savior Jesus Christ.

And it was the same thing when the cross on the escutcheons was cantoned with crosslets, nails, crescents, flowers, squared points or lozenges, spearheads, or even stars. Have we not already met with all these details on Christian coins and jewelry from the first millennium of our era?[2] And the same is to be said when five bezants, five crosslets or five crescents are arranged 2, 1, and 2 on coats of arms or on the extremities of a cross on a coat of arms.

We should add that, although "bezants" are intermingled in medieval heraldry with the points of the old *Signaculum Domini*,

---

[2] Cf. 1st Part, Chap. 1. vi, pp. 17-23 and 1. x, pp. 34-36.

it should not be the same for the "tourteaux,"³ which are disks of too great a diameter to represent wounds; originally, they derived their name from the small circular breads that are still called "tourteaux" in the rural areas of western France.

According to the rules of blazonry, bezants are always gold or silver; the tourteaux are always of another color, but on images of the *Signaculum Domini* painted in manuscripts or represented on fabrics or other materials, the points of the emblem of the five wounds occur indiscriminately in gold, silver, or other colors.

Heraldic examples of all the foregoing details:

  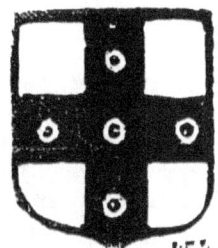

Fig. 1. — The Signaculum Domini on the Cicoteau coat of arms.

Fig. 2. — Coat of arms of Jehan de Blehen, 1374.

Fig. 3. — Escutcheon on the baptismal font of Saint Gulval (Cornwall), 15th century.

a. — The Cicoteau and Sicotteau families, in Poitou, bear on their coat of arms *Azure, a cross pattée argent, a bordure gules charged with six stars or, in orle*⁴ (Fig. 1).

b. — The seal of Jehan de Blehen, 1374, bears a shield charged with a cross cantoned by four crosslets⁵ (Fig. 2).

c. — The seal of Reynald of Argenteau, 1338, bears *a cross charged with five escallops and cantoned with four crosslets*.⁶ This shield probably has its point of origin in a pilgrimage to Jerusalem, Jerusalem's coat of arms being none other than the *Signaculum Domini*.

3 A "roundel" in English heraldry. — *Trans.*
4 See R. Petret, *Armorial poitevin*, p. 40.
5 Cf. Raadt, *Sceaux armoriés des Pays-Bas*, tome I, p. 343 and tome III, p. 1, pl. CXXI.
6 Ibid., tome II, p. 316 and plate XCII.

d. — On the baptismal fonts of Saint Gulval, near Peuzana (Cornwall), a coat of arms bears a cross charged with five points[7] (Fig. 3).

On the armorial bearings of the Bonvarlet, annulets and not points charge the cross[8] (Fig. 4). We have already seen the *Signaculum* formed by annulets on ancient coins. Some of them even belonged to the feudal period, and Bonvarlet is basically a medieval surname.

e. — There should be no doubt about any of these examples, and even less for this shield reproduced by La Colombière: *Sable, cross patonce and cantoned with the four nails of the Passion saltirewise, their points towards the heart of the shield*[9] (Fig. 5). We have seen the same subject on signet rings[10] from the sixth to the ninth century.

Fig. 4. — The Signaculum Domini on the Bonvarlet coat of arms.

Fig. 5. — The Signaculum Domini on the coat of arms reproduced by V. de la Colombière, loc. cit.

Fig. 6. — Cardinal Le Moine's coat of arms, according to the super-libris of Lemoine college, 17th century.

f. — The armorial bearings of Cardinal Le Moine (died 1313), founder of the renowned Lemoine College in Paris, is comprised of *three nails palewise in fess, on a chief gules charged with three bends, the shield surmounted by an episcopal cross with trefoiled ends, accompanied by four nails appointed to the heart of the cross.* This cross is a veritable *Signaculum Domini*.

Lemoine College has retained, as its very own, the coat of arms of its founder. We see them reproduced on book cover stamps and

7 Cf. J. T. Blight, *Churches of West Cornwall* (1885), p. 127.
8 Cf. *Dictionnaire du Blason* directed by Bénard (1772), Pl. III, n° 163.
9 V. de la Colombière, *La Science Héroïque*, 1669, p. 148, 149, fig. 51.
10 Cf. 1st Part, Chap. I.x, p. 34.

ex-libris of this institution during the seventeenth and eighteenth century (Fig. 6).[11]

g. — The Westerburg coat of arms bears *a cross cantoned by four times five crosslets 2, 1, and 2*, and the shield is stamped with a helmet, the crest of which is a disk reproducing the escutcheon itself (Fig. 7). This is the sacred emblem repeated five times.

II. THE CROSS CROSSLET

Among the numerous kinds of crosses, there are two typical forms adopted by medieval heraldry that, in themselves, recapitulate the *Signaculum Domini*. These are the Cross crosslet and the Cross of Jerusalem. We will speak at length about this last later.

Fig. 7. — The Westerburg coat of arms.   Fig. 8. — Bierley family coat of arms.   Fig. 9. — Blainville coat of arms.

The cross crosslet is a cross in which the extremities of the four branches are themselves crosslets, or, if you like, it is a cross made by the joining together of four small Latin crosses joined at their feet. The Bierley coat of arms is a perfect example of this: *Argent, cross crosslet gules*[12] (Fig. 8).

The armorial bearings of the house of Blainville bears *azure, cross argent cantoned with four cross crosslets*[13] (Fig. 9). In fact, this coat of arms entails a quintupled image of the *Signaculum Domini* condensed into a single heraldic whole. This is not a unique example. We have met with it already on the Westerberg coat of arms.

11 Cf. Joannis Guigard, *Armorial du Bibliophile*, T. I, p. 310.
12 Cf. P. Menestrier, *Nouv. méthode raisonnée du Blason*, 1770, p. 83 and pl. 9, n° 20.
13 Cf. V. Bouton, *Nouv. traité des Armoiries*, p. 234, n° 362.

The cross crosslet is therefore only a joining together in a single whole of an altar stone's five crosses and of the *Signaculum Domini*. The heraldry of Capetian times did not invent it, and we have encountered it at a much earlier date; but, for nobilary and other coats of arms, this era makes of it a dedicated figure, or, to speak in its own language, an "heraldic honorable ordinary."

Moreover, besides coats of arms, the cross crosslet was used as a mystical *Signaculum*, as it had already been on certain Frankish coins and on those of the Anglo-Danish king Sigefroi.[14] Also, with the same thought in mind, it was sculpted on one of the gables of the church of Saint Anthony at Padua (Fig. 10), and, lastly, the Cistercians of the Grande Trappe of Mortagne (Orne) appropriated it as a commercial mark for their abbey (Fig. 11).

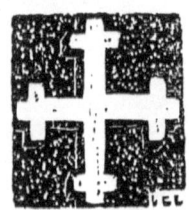  

Fig. 10. — Sculpture from the church of Saint Anthony, Padua.   *Fig. 11. — Commercial mark of the Grande Trappe of Mortagne (Orne).*   *Fig. 12. — Cross crosslet according to Abbé J. Corblet, loc. cit.*

Another kind of more rarely used cross crosslet involves a simple or cross pattee, or cross potent, or an entirely different heraldic type on the ends of which four small crosslets are traced[15] (Fig. 12).

At times, the Latin cross with a very long vertical, lower branch is seen as a kind of cross crosslet. In the ancient penitent and other confraternities of southern France, Spain, and Italy, processional crosses have assumed this form obtained by crossing the shaft of the cross at a distance from its crossing-point equal to the one that separates the small crossbars at its ends, or by

---

14 Cf. Adrien Blanchet, *Nouv. Manuel de numismatique du Moyen-Âge et moderne*, n° 536 and Pl. XI.
15 See Abbé J. Corblet, *Manuel d'Archéol. nationale* (1851), p. 368.

simply prolonging the lower crosslet by a shaft independent of the entire emblem: the cross Saint Claire holds in her hand as a scepter on a medieval painting in her church at Assisi is a perfect example of this[16] (Fig. 13).

The image of the heart of Jesus Christ is actually, for today's Catholics, an emblem of redemptive love more expressive than the image of the entire crucified body of Jesus; likewise, formerly, when its true and lofty significance was understood more generally, the processional cross in cross crosslet form, which evokes at once the five sacred wounds, was regarded as a more precise and more expressive emblem of the shedding of redemptive Blood than the natural image of the whole body of the crucified Savior.

Fig. 13. — *The cross of Saint Claire of Assisi, 13th–14th century.*

Small reliquary medallion of the 16th century, bronze and glass, red background, white cross. From the author's study.

III. THE ARMS OF THE KINGS OF THE CITY OF JERUSALEM

When the first crusaders had conquered the city of Jerusalem and Palestine from the Muslims in 1099, they organized a Latin realm at the head of which they placed Godefroy de Bouillon, duke of Lower Lorraine. Although he wanted to assume only the modest title of Baron of the Holy Sepulcher, he was truly the sovereign of a new dominion organized along the lines of Western feudal monarchies. The "Assizes of Jerusalem" established its laws and hierarchy.

---

16 See L. Gillet, *Saint François d'Assise*, p. 30.

Then, the following year, 1100, Pope Pascal II, approving everything that had been done in the Holy Places, conferred on the new Christian state of Jerusalem a coat of arms composed of the *Signaculum Domini*, the old and grand symbol of the Savior, formerly crucified on the very soil of the city. This coat of arms, made — contrary to the then quite recent rules of heraldry[17] — entirely in *or* and *argent*,[18] was thus fixed: *Jerusalem, city and kingdom, Argent with cross potent or, cantoned with four crosslets also or* (Fig. 14).

His brother and all the other kings, the successors of Godefroy de Bouillon, as also the princes of the houses that reigned in the Christian East or that inherited a possible right to the throne of the Holy City, bore this coat of arms. This is why we find it up to the end of the Middle Ages, and later, on the coinage of the kings of Cyprus, Armenia, Naples-Sicily, Anjou-Sicily, and Austria-Lorraine, as well as on the arms of the Lusignans, the Cornaros and a few other great lords.[19]

Fig. 14. — Coat of arms of the Christian kingdom of Jerusalem, 1100.

IV. MONOGRAM FOR THE CITY OF JERUSALEM

Not only was this an already centuries-old emblem of the five wounds that became, since the First Crusade, the coat of arms of Jerusalem and the new Christian kingdom of the East, but later it also became the heraldic monogram for the very name of Jerusalem, which the Latins of the time spelled HIervsalem.

---

17 According to heraldic rules, metal cannot be placed on metal. Only two metals, *or* and *argent*, are usually admitted. Cf. Woodcock and Robinson, *The Oxford Guide to Heraldry* (Oxford: Oxford University Press, 1988), p. 58. — *Trans.*

18 By affixing *or* on *argent*, the Pope might have wanted to represent Old and New Testament; the Mosaic law figured by *Argent* and Christian law by *Or*, both laws having been promulgated within the territory of this new crusader kingdom.

19 See Adrien Blanchet, *Nouveau Manuel de Numismatique du Moyen-Âge et Moderne*, nums. 592 to 595, and passim.

By combining the first two letters of this name, H and I, and by affixing the second letter over the crossbar of the first, while adding four crosslets, we obtain then a new and special form of the *Signaculum Domini*[20] (Fig. 15 and 16).

This heraldic monogram for the Holy City is not to be confused with its armorial bearings, but both are indisputable evocations of the crucified Savior's wounds.

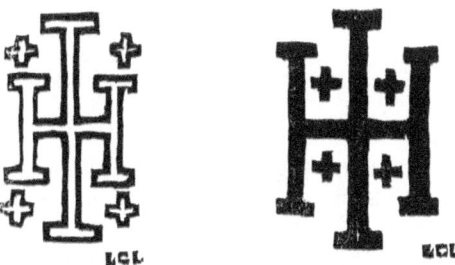

Fig. 15 & 16. — *The "Cipher" of the City of Jerusalem under its two most usual aspects. Cf. Brianville and Bouton, op. and loc. cit.*

V. THE COAT OF ARMS FOR THE KNIGHTS OF THE HOLY SEPULCHER AND SAINT CATHERINE OF MOUNT SINAI

At the time of the Crusades there was, in the church of the Holy Sepulcher at Jerusalem, a college of Canons Regular, later replaced by knights of the same name whose armorial bearings were again the *Signaculum* of the five wounds: *Argent with cross potent gules, cantoned with four crosslets of the same.*[21] This red of the five crosses was at once an emblem of the Savior's blood and the blood that the knights should be ready to shed in the service of the Christian faith.

This cross, which the Knights of the Holy Sepulcher still bear on their ample white cloak and from which is made the insignia of their Order (Fig. 17), was also combined with the Wheel on the insignia of the Order of Knights of Saint Catherine of Mount Sinai, established in the Middle Ages to protect pilgrims who made their

20 Cf. de Brianville, *Le Jeu du Blason*, p. 51. V. Bouton, *Nouveau Traité des Armoiries*, p. 38.
21 Cf. *Dictionnaire du Blason*, directed by Bénard, 1772, Pl. 24, n° 28.

Part I: The Five Wounds of Christ in Earliest Christian Art

Fig. 17. — *The cross of the Order of Knights of the Holy Sepulcher from the 18th century, according to a document furnished by M. de La Maroue.*

way to the tomb of the saint on the famous mountain.[22]

In addition, this same cross of Jerusalem has been likewise adopted for a century by almost all endeavors pertaining to the Holy Land. It even reigned triumphant just yesterday in the brilliant gems, on I know not what grounds, in the middle of the headband of the imperial crown assumed by the sovereign of the last German empire inaugurated at Versailles in 1871.[23]

VI. THE ROYAL AND NATIONAL COAT OF ARMS OF PORTUGAL

The coat of arms of Portugal is blazoned in this way: *Argent five shields azure, each charged with five bezants argent 2, 1 and 2, bordure gules charged with seven Castillian towers* (Fig. 18).

On these arms the five shields were at first arranged 2, 1 and 2, as are quite frequently the components of the *Signaculum Domini*. Thus we see them on a shield engraved, amidst numerous graffiti, by the first Portuguese colonizers of Angola, in the sixteenth century, on the rocks of some falls on the Congo river at Yeallala[24] (Fig. 19). Arranged in this way, and independent of the five white points it bears, these five escutcheons constitute the emblem of the five wounds of Christ. We will see, however, that they are related to an entirely different idea. Later, they were arranged in a cross, and it is in this way that they are depicted in the heraldic works of Hiérosema de Bara (sixteenth century) and heraldic works of the seventeenth century.[25]

22 Ibid., Pl. 25, n° 60.
23 See Bouton, op. cit., p. 566, fig. 855, n° 4.
24 Cf. *Angola*, edition of national printing house of Luanda, 1931, p. 9.
25 Cf. Hiérosme de Bara, *Le Blason des Armoiries*, Lyon, 1581, p. 206. – M. L., *Nouv. Méthode de Blason*, 1770, pl. 45, n° 8 and p. 394, etc.

The official coat of arms of the last king of Portugal, the unfortunate Carlos I, likewise bore the five escutcheons in a cross, and this is how the current Portuguese Republic displays them.

The very origin of these armorial bearings provides an explanation for their component parts:

As we know, around 1095 King Alfonso VI gave Portugal to his nephew, Henry of Burgundy, who assumed the title Count of Portugal. The latter's son, Alfonso Henriquez, defeated, at Ourique in 1139, the Saracen armies led by five emirs, and was proclaimed king by his warriors on the battlefield itself. On the

Fig. 18. — The coat of arms of the kingdom of Portugal, according to Hiérosme de Bara, Le Blason des Armoiries, 1581, p. 206.

Fig. 19. — Older appearance of the coat of arms of the kings of Portugal, depicted on the rocks of Yeallala (Angola), 16th century.

subject of this victory, the Portuguese chronicles relate that, on the morning of the battle, Henriquez saw a beam of light detach itself from the eastern sky at daybreak and form a circle around a cross, while an apparition of the Savior, displaying his bleeding wounds as a sign of victory, promised him triumph over the five emirs and the royal crown at the same time. In remembrance of this, Henriquez the Conquistador placed on his shield five shields representing the five conquered emirs, and charged each of these symbolic and commemorative shields with the Seal of Christ, made in the image of his five wounds.

A superb fresco in the church of the Portuguese at Rome represents the Savior appearing to Count Henriquez who, having become king on the evening of that day, continued, under the protection of the *Signaculum Domini* on his coat of arms borne by his standards, the conquest of the country, successively seizing from the Moors Leyria, Arranches, Santarem, Mafra, Cintra, and Lisbon, which he made his capital, which latter had previously been established at Guimarens.

The Portuguese kings who succeeded Henriquez granted to some lords the right to bear, like themselves, the shield with the five wounds on their coats of arms. This is why the blazon of the Mesia de la Serda is comprised of eight escutcheons argent charged with five bezants azure arrayed on the bordure of the shield.

VII. ON THE COLOR OF THE "SIGNACULUM DOMINI" IN HERALDRY

On Jerusalem's coat of arms the *Signaculum Domini* is *or* (gold), the color of triumph and sovereignty.

It is sometimes *argent,* which was formerly the color of immaterial and supernatural love, sometimes also *azure*, the color of the sky; and these two colors are often joined, as on the escutcheons of Portugal's armorial bearings, and on the reliquary of the Holy Nail at Trier, where the crosses that represent the wounds to the divine limbs are *blue* and the one corresponding to the wound to the heart *white.*

Most often the *Signaculum* is *red*, as on the insignias of the Order of the Holy Sepulcher and of Saint Catherine of Mount Sinai, where it evokes both the blood that the Savior has given for the salvation of the world and the blood that the knight should shed courageously for him.

More rarely the emblem of the five wounds is *green*, the color devoted to the virtue of Hope, for the sacrifice on Calvary which it recalls forms the basis for the hopes of a Christian. *O crux ave, spes unica* says the *Vexilla regis*, the immortal hymn of Saint Fortunatus of Poitiers.

Finally, we often find the *Signaculum Domini* colored *black*, the liturgical color of Good Friday, a color reminding us of the thick darkness that overspread Calvary while, from the gaping wounds of the Crucified, his redemptive blood poured out upon the world.

The round points of armorial bearing are not therefore ordinarily bezant-coins, above all when they are placed crosswise, or 1, 2, and 1, even when they are *or* or *argent*, but they are indeed so when one, two, three, four, six or more in number.

VIII. THE COAT OF ARMS OF THE REDEEMER

To the *Signaculum Domini*, a true coat of arms made of the five wounds of the Savior, which retained its favor everywhere until the end of the Middle Ages, the thirteenth century added another more expressly evocative symbol, at least for the majority of Christians. It is composed of a grouping of instruments from the Passion of Jesus brought together as trophies or arranged on the field of an escutcheon.

These hieratic compositions are called *The Coat of Arms of the Passion*, *The Arms or Blazon of Jesus Christ*, and sometimes *The Crest of the Five Wounds*. At first they included only five or six items: the Cross, Nails, Spear, Sponge, Crown of Thorns, and Whips. From the end of the thirteenth century, secondary items were added, waxing excessively complicated: they no longer evoke just the five main wounds of the Lord, but even anything recalling the various specifics of the evangelical accounts of the Passion: the seamless robe of the Savior and the dice used by the guards on Calvary to divide up his garments, the auger that perhaps served to make counter-sink holes in the wood of the cross for the nails, the hammer that drove them in, the basin in which Pilate washed his hands, the pillar of the scourging, the reed that was the scepter mocking the Lord, the lantern that alludes to his pursuit and arrest in Gethsemane, the cords that bound him, the repulsive thirty pieces of silver and Iscariot's purse, the sword and rooster of Saint Peter, the faces of Pilate, Caiaphas, and Herod... Sometimes, instead of being grouped, these objects are held separately by angels, or each one is placed on an escutcheon as we see on the keystones of Saint Matthias at Trier, on the stalls of Langeac, and elsewhere.

Here are a few examples of these *Coats of Arms of Jesus Christ* which enter, for quite good reasons, into the iconography of redemptive suffering:

Part I: The Five Wounds of Christ in Earliest Christian Art

1. — A painted coat of arms, of the fifteenth century, found in the ancient church of Cerizay (Deux-Sèvres), improves on a concise theme from the time of Saint Louis: the cross, nails, spear, sponge, and dolorous crown[26] (Fig. 20).

Fig. 20. — *Arms of Jesus Christ in the ancient church of Cerizay (Deux-Sèvres), 15th century.*

2. — In the castle keep of Chinon, where Jacques de Molay and the grand dignitaries of the Order of the Temple were incarcerated for long months, numerous designs engraved by knife-point on the wall are attributed, in all likelihood rightly, to these miserable captives. As we will speak again later about the most important of these engravings,[27] here we will just say that, among them, we find three representations, in trophy form, of the "Arms of Jesus Christ," the largest comprising a cross on two steps, four nails, a sponge, and a spear, the head of which is pointed towards the place occupied by the right side of the Crucified on the cross, a place indicated by an oblique mark (Fig. 21). Below all this is an inscription whose lettering is in accord with the date of the Templars' trial:

Fig. 21. — *Trophy with the "Arms of the Passion," 1308-1309, in the castle-keep of Chinon (Indre-et-Loire).*

ie requier a dieu pdon
(I beseech God's forgiveness).

26 According to the drawing of Dom Fourrier Bonnard of the Augustinians of Beauchêne.
27 Cf. 6th Part, Chap. 16.iv, pp. 233-37.

The "Signaculum Domini" in Medieval Heraldry

Another, smaller trophy again shows the spear leaning against the cross at the height of the wound to the heart. A third is composed of the cross, nails, vertical spear, and pillar; from each side of the titulus of the cross the glorifying *Sol et Luna* sigil testifies that, by the cross, was the glory of Christ raised on high: *regnavit a ligno Deus*, "God has reigned by the wood"[28] (Fig. 22).

3. — In the collection of the archivist François Eygun, of Poitiers, is found a mystical seal of the thirteenth century with a superb "Blazon of the Passion": semy with drops of blood, it is charged

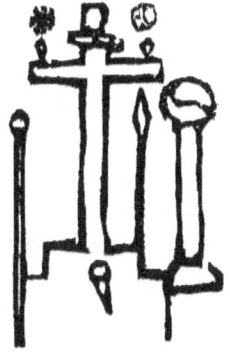

Fig. 22. — *Another trophy with the "Arms of the Passion," in the keep of Chinon, 1308–1309.*

Fig. 23. — *Coat of arms of the Passion on a seal from the collection of Fr. Eygun, from Poitiers, 13th century.*

with a cross flory and cantoned, in the first a crown of thorns, in the second a spear, in the third three nails, in the fourth a sponge. This is a perfect example of the emblematic motif that interests us here (Fig. 23).

4. — By way of other examples of instruments of the Passion represented separately on different escutcheons, I depict below the whip and rods that shield-bearing angels hold against their chests on the very beautiful stalls of the collegiate church of Langeac (Haute-Loire), sculpted "in anno Domini 1526" (Fig. 24 and 25).

---

28 Saint Fortunatus of Poitiers, the hymn *Vexilla regis prodeunt*.

Part I: The Five Wounds of Christ in Earliest Christian Art

Fig. 24. — One of the escutcheons of the Passion in the collegiate church of Langeac (Haute-Loire), 1526.

Fig. 25. — Another escutcheon from the collegiate church of Langeac, 1526.

Similar records of the same date are to be found in France by the hundreds; we will see several others subsequently upon which the transpierced heart of the Savior is represented overtly.

Doctor Paul Durand speaks of a *Book of Hours* printed in the sixteenth century in which an escutcheon bears the instruments of the Passion, and below them we find this description, which justifies the present chapter's title: *Redemptoris mundi arma*. And these instruments of his redemption are also a protective escutcheon, the efficacious shield of the Christian, of which a French manuscript of the fourteenth century tells, as cited by the same author — for the escutcheon that bears them is accompanied by these words: *C'est li vrais écuz aus Crestiens*, "This is the true shield of Christians."[29]

Wood engraved with penknife by the author.

29 Cf. Dr Paul Durand, *Étude sur l'Etimacia, symbole du Jugement dernier*, p. 35.

60

CHAPTER THREE

Observations on the Employ of the "Signaculum Domini"

IN THE PREVIOUS CHAPTERS WE HAVE ascertained successively:

1st — That, during the fourth century, a sign made its appearance in Christian iconography that symbolically alluded to the five wounds received by Christ on the cross;

2nd — That, nearly as soon, the Christian liturgy employed this emblem to mark the sacred stones of its altars and the Paschal candle, both of which represent the body of the God-Man in Catholic symbolism;

3rd — That this emblem, the *Signaculum Domini*, was utilized in the Church at the same time as the most venerable symbols of Jesus Christ, the cross, the anchor, the fish, the dolphin, the dove, the chrismon under all its forms, the alpha and omega, the grand eucharistic emblems, etc., and that its favor continued during the Middle Ages more intensively than that of the majority of other emblems;

4th — That we find the emblem of the five wounds, not only on the altars and the Paschal candle, but also on liturgical objects and vestments, on coinage, on offensive and defensive weapons, on products of the ceramic industry, on products on sculptural art and the art of the book, on jewels and ivory, in all the branches of heraldry and sigillography. And, if we wanted to press our research further, we would have certainly come upon this emblem upon household objects, on the old tools of craftsmen, on ancient furniture, and on a great variety of instruments;

5th — That this extraordinary frequency of employ has consecrated the *Signaculum Domini* forever, and that today we are obliged to admit that this emblem of the wounds of Jesus was one of the strongest expressions of the Christian people's love and confidence towards their Redeemer;

6th — That this emblem is still represented on altars, on the Paschal candle, on the coat of arms of Jerusalem and Portugal, on the insignia of the Knights of the Holy Sepulcher, on numerous objects of piety produced in Jerusalem and Palestine;

7th — That, despite this limited yet current employ, nine-tenths or more of Christians no longer know about it, and that many among those who, by personal position, still employ it, do not know or understand its exact significance;

8th — Finally that, on the greatest number of ancient reproductions of the *Signaculum Domini*, the piece that corresponds to the wound to the heart of the Crucified, whether cross, point, crescent, heart, flower, lozenge, annulet, etc., is of more important dimensions than those of the other pieces, or more ornamented. This intention to differentiate it from the others corresponds to a greater, more loving veneration for this wound than for those in the hands and feet. We will see later that this particular cult of the wound in the side has quite naturally led to the exteriorizing of the cult of the heart of Jesus under its anatomical form, which it contained in potency and towards which it inevitably oriented thought; but here, as in all such cases, the symbol has necessarily preceded the thinking responsible for interpreting it.

Plate 6. — Christ Jesus showing his five wounds and forming a Signaculum Domini. *Reredos attributed to the Master of Liesborn, church of Lünen (Germany), 15th century. Photo Giraudon. Archives of the review* Regnabit, *1921–1929.*

SECOND PART

Depictions of the Wound in the Side of Jesus

CHAPTER FOUR

The Wound in the Side of Jesus

1. WHAT IT WAS IN REALITY

IT WAS ON THE HAPPY DAY WHEN JESUS saved us. Nailed to the wood of his cross, the tortured divine Victim had sensed death achieving its conquest within him, and, with one last effort towards the world, he had cried out that his redeeming work was consummated.

Next, in the unexpected night that had suddenly fallen over it, as the earth trembled with emotion and rocks split apart, Jesus bowed his head and rendered up his soul to his Father.

Then, as the hour of the sabbath approached, his own had to quickly take him down from the cross to be able to bury him. But, before allowing them to do as they wished, soldiers approached to break the legs of Jesus and of the two others crucified with him, so as to finish them off. But, seeing that the Savior was already dead, they did not break his legs. "But one of the soldiers with a spear opened his side: and immediately there came out blood and water."[1]

The wounds to his hands and feet, as well as the bruises over his entire body, had stopped the life of the Victim and satisfied justice. The wound from the spear-thrust, a wound of supererogation, brought forth from the very body of this corpse the blossoming of a divinely fecund life, and satisfied infinite munificence and love (Plates 7 & 8).

And since that time, and for evermore, the Christian world has lived and will live from this life springing forth, through his side, from the opened heart of Christ Jesus!

---

1 John 19:34.

Part II: Depictions of the Wound in the Side of Jesus

Plate 7. — *Wound to the side dealt by the spear-thrust, detail of a retable attributed to the Master of Liesborn, church of Saint Mary on Höhe at Soest (Germany), 15th century. Photo Giraudon. Collection of the review* Regnabit, *1921–1929.*

Plate 8. — Christ expired, surrounded by two thieves, is wounded on the side by the Holy Spear. Painting by Victor and Heinrich Dünwegge, 16th century. Photo Giraudon. Collection of the review Regnabit, *1921-1929.*

Part II: Depictions of the Wound in the Side of Jesus

But, in its physical reality, what was this activity of the soldier's weapon on and in the very body of Jesus? At what precise place did it enter into his flesh?

Artists in all genres of the first thirteen centuries generally represent the Savior as wounded on the right flank, above all because of inspired texts that, however, have nothing of the humanly historical about them. Others clearly felt that the heart could not have remained beyond all injury in the complete torture of the divine body, thus siding with the common mistake that would have the human heart to the left, in the chest's inner cavity, because this is where its beating is perceived, and so situate the wound on this side. Some represent the wound at the very top of the chest, others at the level of the lower sides. For some this was only the prick of an arrow, whereas others make of it an opening that cleaves through half the chest.

Now we do have, as to what exactly this lateral wound was, a detailed testimony the true value of which only came to light quite recently.

Before bringing forward this testimony let us first listen to the Gospels:

In Saint Matthew, Chap. 27, verses 59–60: "Joseph of Arimathea having obtained from Pilate the body of Jesus wrapped it in a clean linen shroud and laid it in a new tomb that he had hewed out of a rock."

In Saint Mark, Chap. 15, verses 45–46: "The centurion... gave the body to Joseph. Then Joseph, buying a linen shroud and taking him down, wrapped him up in the linen shroud and laid him in a sepulcher which was hewed out of a rock. And he rolled a stone against the door of the tomb."

In Saint John, Chap. 19, verses 38–42: "Joseph of Arimathea... came and took away the body of Jesus. Nicodemus also... came bringing a mixture of myrrh and aloes, about a hundred pounds' weight. They took the body of Jesus, and wrapped it in linen cloths with the spices, as is the burial custom of the Jews. Now in the place where he was crucified there was a garden, and in the garden a new tomb where no one had ever been laid. So... they laid Jesus there."

The Wound in the Side of Jesus

Hear now the wonder: without any miracle, solely by action at a distance — a very short distance, where there was no real contact — solely by the action, I say, of ammoniacal fumes from an *unwashed* tortured body on the surface of a white shroud imbued with aloes — and because the juxtaposition of linen thus exposed and a body lasted for more than twenty-four hours but less than thirty-six in the darkness of the tomb — a *spontaneous photograph* of the body became fixed, as a *negative*, on the linen!

Certainly this sacred shroud, which was kept successively at Constantinople, Lirey, Chimay, Chambery, and which is now, since 1535, at Turin, was always the object of ardent veneration because of the miraculous image that was thought to be seen there. But it was only in 1898, when Signor Pia photographed it — which had not been done before — that his prints revealed: 1) the representation of the body of Jesus on the Shroud of Turin is not a painting made by hand; 2) it is a "negative" of natural and spontaneous photography of physico-chemical origin; 3) this print reveals details about the redemptive sufferings that surpass to an extraordinarily degree the bounds of human knowledge prior to the scientific inventions and studies of more recent times.

At nearly the same time, Paul Vignon, a doctor of natural science, assisted by Commandant Colson, a professor at the Ecole Polytechnique, Yves Delaage, of the Academy of Sciences, and Dr. Hérouard, professor at the Sorbonne — and then, after them, Vandervelde, a doctor at the Gand Laboratory, and de Bourgade-La-Dorie, director of the review *La Rayons X* — have undertaken scientific studies that have come to a satisfying explanation of the natural phenomena to which we owe the Turin image.

Since then their scholarly labors have been summarized and popularized by several authors: E. Faure, Father de Malijay, and the Right Reverend d'Armailhac, S.J., the latter in the *Semaine Religieuse de Paris*; and further, parallel to these writers, by a Parisian lecturer of great merit, Paul Le Cour, who has had this advantage over many others: at Turin in 1898 he was able to study the Holy Shroud with his own eyes when Signor Pia photographed it.

Now, just what do we see on this peerless document with respect to the wound in Jesus's side?

First of all, we see that the spear-thrust was dealt to the right side of the body, in conformity with the practices of the Roman infantry, by a soldier trained in striking at that side because, in battle, the adversary was covered on the left by a shield.

Next, we see that the weapon has penetrated the thorax a little above the level of the elbow's inner fold. Its penetration into the flesh produced a back and forth opening, the wide axis of which is parallel to the two sides between which passed the point that parted but did not break the ribs.

Speaking very briefly in his work on the blow from the spear, Vignon only specifies this: "...There exists on the image of the Shroud, in the region that corresponds to the right side of the body, a lens-shaped stain; its length, related to natural proportions, is about 4.5 centimeters. Connected to this stain, toward the bottom, are other stains that have the look of a bloody flux. This blood would have flowed while the man was upright. The sum total of these stains immediately remind us of the wound made by the spear-thrust to the chest of Christ.... If the blow had been dealt in the least obliquely from right to left, the weapon would surely have pierced the heart...."[2]

Now this obliquity, already natural to the movements of a lancer striking a man placed in front of him, would become, it seems to me, even more normal for an aim situated a little higher than himself.

Then Vignon, as a qualified anatomist, adds that, had the weapon not reached the heart itself, which is hard to accept, it would have at the very least severed the major vessels that issue from it, for, still keeping with the testimony of the Shroud, the quantity of blood and colorless liquid — also coagulated — that came from this wound, made in a dead but still interiorly somewhat warm body, indicates that everything that might still run from it had been poured out and immediately congealed in the air. And

---

2 P. Vignon, *Le Linceul du Christ — Étude scientifique* (Paris: Masson, 1902), p. 96.

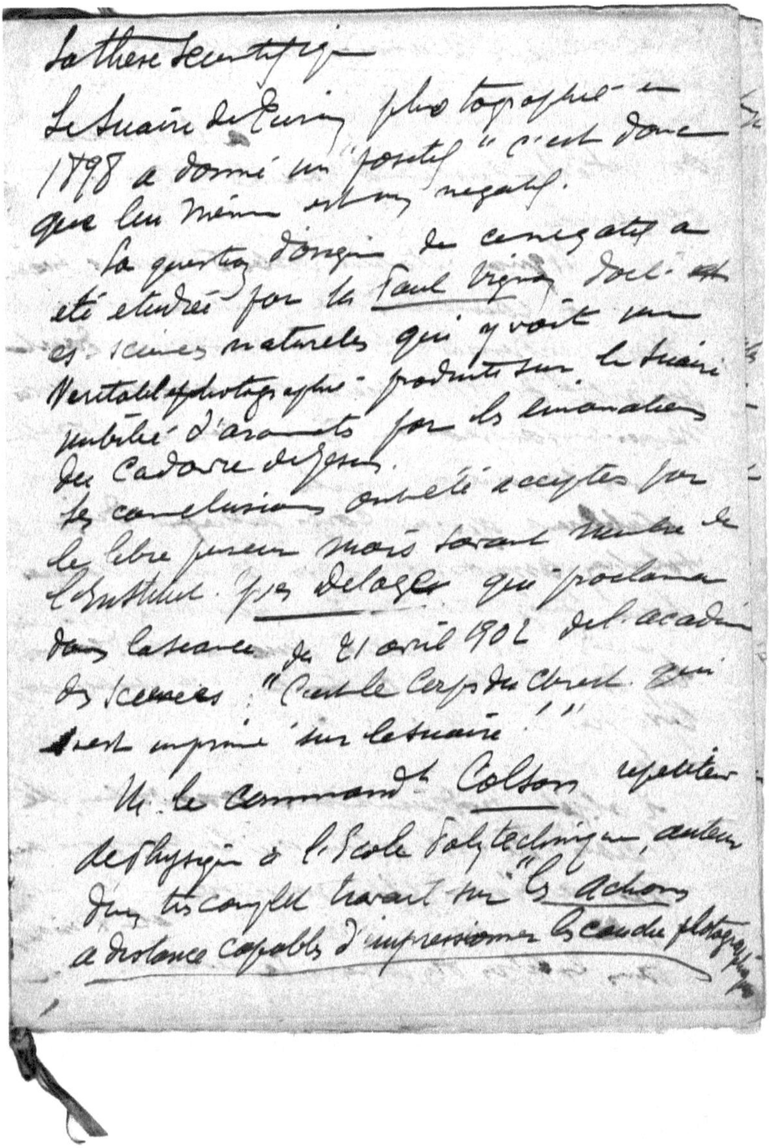
La thèse scientifique
Le Suaire de Turin photographié en
1898 a donné un "positif" c'est donc
que lui même est un négatif.
La question d'origine de ces négatifs a
été étudiée par M. Paul Vignon Doct. ès
sciences naturelles qui y voit une
véritable photographie produite sur le suaire
imbibé d'aromates par les émanations
du cadavre de Jésus.
Les conclusions ont été acceptées par
le libre penseur mais savant membre de
l'Institut Yves Delage qui proclama
dans la séance du 21 avril 1902 de l'académie
des sciences: "C'est le Corps du Christ qui
s'est imprimé sur le suaire!"
M. le Commandant Colson répétiteur
de physique à l'École Polytechnique, auteur
d'un très complet travail sur "les actions
à distance capables d'impressionner les plaques photographiques

Plate 9.—Page from a notebook of the author dedicated to the Shroud of Turin. Charbonneau-Lassay archives.

this is one more reason for not doubting that the heart, source and last preserve of vivifying liquids, has been truly struck and opened.

Here then is what was on and in the Savior's breast, this wound that parted before the world the curtain of flesh drawn over the Jewel of love where the blood of our redemption was wrought and whence it sprang forth.

2. THE HOLY SPEAR

Since early Christian times, first at Jerusalem, then at Antioch, Byzantium, and after that at Rome, people have venerated the lethal weapon, the mysterious key that opened to us, on the cross, the Holy of Holies: St. Gregory of Tours, Bede, and Arculf speak of it, and its history is quite well-known.

I wished to learn whether its shape and size were in complete agreement with the data from the Shroud of Turin.

Kept sheltered from all approach for good reason, accessible only to the titular cardinal of Saint Peter's, who shows it twice a year to the people, it cannot be photographed, but, thanks to the kind auspices of the Right Reverend Leon de Lyon, curator of the Franciscan Museum of Rome, I was nevertheless able to obtain the sufficiently exact tracing of it reproduced here. Moreover, this tracing is in perfect accord with the FORMA FERRI LANCEA D. N. JESUS XPI, executed about 1640 in the crypt of St. Peter's at Rome, and also with the drawing made from life, in 1599, by G. Grimaldi, a cleric of the Vatican Basilica, a drawing today at Milan's Ambrosian Library.

This is a stout weapon whose socket is reinforced with two rings; its offensive part, endowed with a median ridge, could deal a terrible blow; its double edge, corroded by oxidation, has lost a little of its width towards its middle, but at its base this width remains intact.

Baudouin, emperor of Constantinople, broke off its point when he gave it to our St. Louis of France along with the other great relics of the Passion, and later the sultan Bajazet offered the spear itself to Pope Innocent VIII. In the seventeenth century, Benedict XIV had a cast made in Paris of the point preserved at that time at Sainte Chapelle and found that it fit perfectly on the spear-head in Rome. In 1793 this point was brought from Sainte Chapelle to the Bibliothèque Nationale where it still was three years later; since then, though, no one seems to know what has become of it.

The Holy Spear was 25 centimeters high altogether but, lacking its upper end, it is no more than 0.21 meters. In its entirety, the offensive tip must have been, within one or two millimeters, 13.5 centimeters in length. At its greatest breadth it measures 4.5 centimeters.

Now, referring back to the passage from Vignon's study on the Holy Shroud cited above, we read that the lateral wound of Jesus, as inscribed on the Shroud, is likewise shown to be 4.5 centimeters.

Evidently the soldier, for his part wishing to bring about and assure the death of the Crucified, had to vigorously thrust his weapon into the middle of his chest; so that, by making it enter beyond the point where it reached four and a half centimeters in width, even in the thorax of a very strong man, the heart would have had to be seriously wounded.

Fig. 1.—*The Holy Spear preserved at Saint Peter's in Rome.*

From the viewpoint of a specialist in military archaeology, first with reference to the tracing on the opposite page and, in other respects, to the specialized works of Rich, Demmin, Maindron, etc., as well as to items in our museums, the Holy Spear does not correspond to those shafted weapons utilized above all by Roman cavalry and designated by the names *contus* and *lancea*, nor to the *pilum* of the legionnaires of the regular infantry. To me it seems more related to certain so-called "barbarian" Germanic or Gaulish arms, or even to certain spearheads of eastern antiquity, which would suggest that the soldier who pierced Jesus's side belonged to one of those groups of allied auxiliaries enlisted by the Romans to reinforce their national legions, and who could undoubtedly retain their personal arms to the extent that they fulfilled the conditions required by Roman hoplomachy.

III. REPRESENTATIONS OF THE WOUND TO JESUS'S SIDE IN ANCIENT FRENCH ICONOGRAPHY

So now we have a sufficient basis for thinking we know rather exactly what the spear spoken of by St. John was and what the injury it inflicted on the side of Jesus. I will not reiterate here, from apostolic times onward, the adorations of our first fathers in the Faith that were spontaneously drawn towards the sacred wounds and, above all, to the supreme wound in his chest.

However, a feeling of respectful constraint kept early Christian artists from graphically depicting the body of Jesus on the cross insofar as crucifixion was still in use as an especially shameful punishment, and remained so even for some time after its abolition. We have to go to the end of the fourth century or the beginning of the fifth to ascertain, on a precious ivory in the British Museum, a sure depiction of the Savior's death on the cross. This shows us the Crucified girded with a narrow waist-band, the "titulus" above his head. To the right a soldier brandishes his spear, to the left Mary and John stand erect. Throughout the Middle Ages these four personages will form the basic ingredients for every small-scale crucifixion.

During the period of the Merovingian dynasty representations of the crucifix spread, but quite slowly, while, to the contrary, an extraordinary profusion of emblems of the five wounds multiplied everywhere.

Symbolized by the grouping of crosslets, small circles, and points already forming what will be later called the *Signaculum*

Dei, we see this emblem of the five wounds on coins, on both offensive and defensive weapons, on pottery, on all kinds of jewels, on vessels or liturgical objects, etc. In all these compositions the sign marking the wound to the side is always distinguished from the others, either by a greater size, a choice place at the center, or a different color, so that we find ourselves compelled to make this seemingly illogical observation: the only wound inflicted on the Savior after his death and from which he did not suffer is more honored, more glorified than those that had truly made him a "Man of Sorrows," the Redeemer who ransomed us by the shedding of his living blood. This homage by our first artists can only be explained by the certainty that overwhelmed their thoughts: the wound to the side was the selfsame wound to the physical heart of Jesus; that is, to the central point of this life that he had sacrificed for our ransom and the source of the blood that he had shed.

If the crucifixes of romanesque times, especially those of the Limousin enamellers who represent Jesus fixed to the cross by nails, do not generally bear the mark of the wound to his side, this is because, ordinarily, they show us a Jesus still alive on the cross, where he often appears rather in triumph than as a victim. However, from this period onwards we know of Christs where the side wound is quite particularly glorified. Two among them — we will speak of them again — which seem attributable to the 12th to 13th century time period, bear at the site of the spear-thrust a ruby imbedded in the metal that forms the wound (Plate 23, page 178), as well as a minuscule cross, as though its author wanted to make clear that the wound to the heart was preeminently the redemptive wound, since he marked it by a kind of repetition of the sign of Redemption already offered to our eyes by the cross that bears the entire body of Jesus. Is it not as if he had written: your salvation has come from this very point, let your gaze and your adoration dwell on this above all?

However evocative these tributes offered to the wound in his side might be, it must be acknowledged that they are however less so than the representations of this same wound separated from the body of the Savior, representations by which sight and thinking go more directly to this wound alone, and stop there.

If we come down now to the times of our last direct Valois, irrefutable documents show us the divine wound, not only as the source of the redemptive blood, but also as the dwelling place, as the opened jewel-case of the heart of Jesus, itself wounded by the spear.

Here are some examples:

— *The Image of the World*, a very beautiful manuscript in the Bibliotheque National from the first part of the fourteenth century and which later belonged to the duke Jean de Berry, shows us the wound in the side of Jesus Christ, isolated and depicted as having the width of the Holy Spear[3] (Plate 10).

— I possess several wax impressions of a small, unpublished seal or signet, engraved with the name of Jehan Coste and discovered in the Paris-Versailles region; it comes from the papers of Father Davin, who was one of the most erudite contributors to the review *L'Art Chrétien*.[4]

With a first glance at this small seal (Fig. 2), we easily surmise that Jehan Coste has quite simply wanted to compose "canting arms," that is, an emblem interpreting his own surname, Coste, and to do this he has represented under the form of a crescent the wound to the *costé*, "side," of Jesus Christ. And to distinguish it, to make the subject matter entirely explicit — recalling the Holy Grail, that wondrous cup in which all the poems of his time would have Joseph of Arimathea collecting, on Calvary, the blood that flowed from the spear-thrust to the *costé* of Jesus — he placed the image of the Holy Grail below the bleeding wound.

Fig. 2. — Seal of Jehan Coste

To what time period can we attribute this composition? The name IOHAN COSTE is written around the signet with those small lower case Gothic letters used exclusively on seals from 1350 to the end of the fifteenth century.

In the opinion of several sigillographers, this lettering seems attributable to the first part of the fifteenth century. This is said

---

3 *Bibliothèque Nationale, fonds français* 574, f° 136.
4 I have received them from his nephew, the abbé Davin, curé of Sigournais (Vendée).

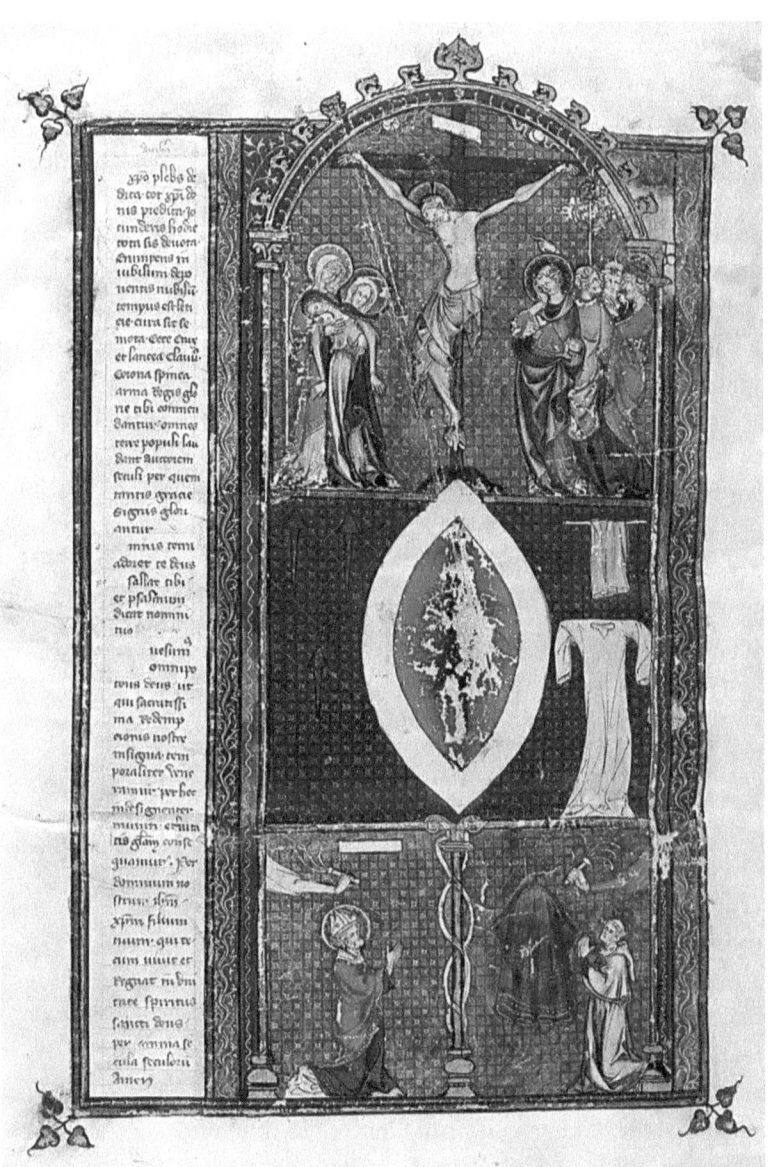

*Plate 10. — Miniature of an "Image of the World."
Manuscript of the 14th century, Bibl. Nat. of
Paris, French collection S. N., f° 136.*

Part II: Depictions of the Wound in the Side of Jesus

with reservations, however, because the seal is so small, so that only slight pressure need be applied to make the imprint. In short, this lettering could be from the last years of the fourteenth just as well as from the second quarter of the fifteenth.

By merest chance, could we be in the presence here of the seal of that Jehan Coste who was, along with master Girard d'Orléans, one of the two painters commissioned by John the Good and to whom Prost attributes the famous portrait of this prince in the collection of Roger de Gaignières? John the Good died in 1364, but his painters might have been younger than himself, and above all in the case of Jean Coste, who is shown by documents to be under Girard's direction.

For the seal in question to have been his, it would have had to be engraved in the last quarter of the fourteenth century. As we have seen already, this is possible but not certain.

In the Caillaut and Martineau *Hours*, printed at the end of the fifteenth century, a wood-engraving also represents the side wound as a large bleeding slit, placed in a finely wrought cup that also evokes the memory of the wondrous Holy Grail.

I have copied it here (Fig. 3), extracted from all that surrounds it on the fifteenth century engraving: crucifix, angels, spear, sponge, pillar, rods, whips, etc.

Fig. 3. — The wound to the side of Jesus on a cup. Detail of a 15th century engraving. ("Hours" of Caillaud and Martineau)

But some will say that these imaginative depictions show only the exterior wound, the physical fountain of the divine blood and mystical birthplace of the Church, nothing more, and that the idea of the wounded heart of Jesus is not obvious here.

Actually, it is not always expressed outwardly, but it is also not as absent as might be supposed. The mystical birthplace of the Church is a theological concept which the artists of the Middle Ages knew very well how to embody when they worked for theologians, but, for

80

The Wound in the Side of Jesus

the mass of the faithful, the wound in the side was almost always just a conduit for the redeeming blood and, by it, their thought went back to the heart that is the fleshly source of this blood.

This is what a talented master illuminator shows us amazingly well by parting somewhat the margins of the supreme wound in order for us to see there, at its center, the spear plunged into the transverberated heart.

This is seen on a very fine Psalter manuscript from the fifteenth century belonging to Pierre Labarre of Marseille.

The page that bears this evocative composition (Plate 11), and of which I reproduce only the lower part here (Fig. 4), is entirely surrounded with a gold-enhanced grisaille; the depths of the wound are golden and the blood that weeps, dark red. In the midst of a *semy* of blood droplets, all the instruments of the Passion are arranged around the page, but all that appears of the redemptive Victim's body is this gaping wound in the depths of which the spear traverses a golden heart pierced by the spearhead, which means that, in the pious illuminator's thought, the blow that transpierced the chest attained also the heart that dwelt there: "The body is only the dwelling-place of the heart," as one of the heroes of the Round Table had already said three hundred years earlier.[5]

There we have it: the external wound is, strictly speaking, just the open jewel-case wherein lies Christ's wounded heart; this is the

Fig. 4. — *The wound to the side and heart of Jesus. Detail from an illuminated page of a 15th century Psalter, from the Labarre collection, Marseille.*

5 Cf. J. Boulanger, *Les Romans de la Table Ronde,* Les amours de Lancelot du Lac, XX.

Part II: Depictions of the Wound in the Side of Jesus

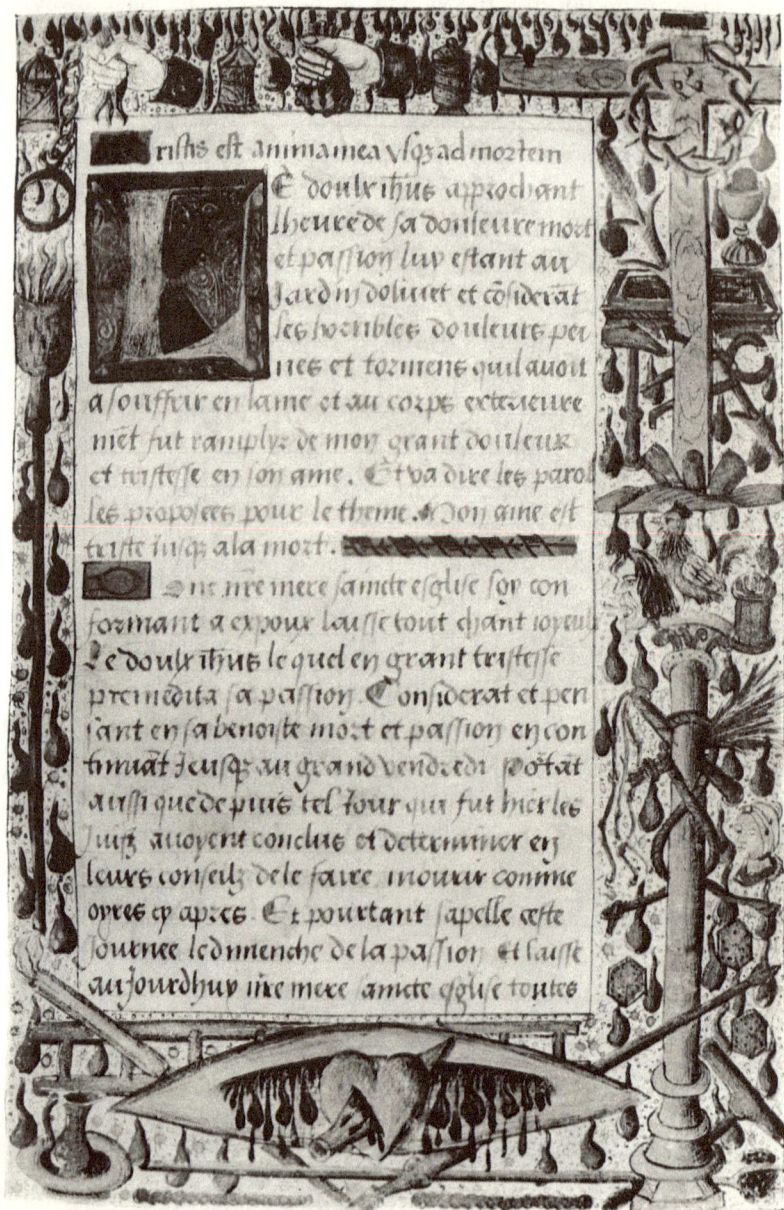

Plate 11. — Illuminated page from the Book of Hours for the use of Parcival of Dreux, 15th century (after 1472), belonging to M. Labarre of Marseille. Photo from Madam E. Rossollin, sent to the author. Charbonneau-Lassay archives.

bloody path followed by the blade and which, now, remains open to us. Could an image convey this idea more explicitly? Then there is another, only conjectured scene: the old image-maker, a contemporary of Queen Anne, straightens himself above the just-painted vellum and murmurs the *Venite adoremus* before wiping dry his brushes!

And now, would you like to know what the preachers of former times said to the people about the sacred wound whose images we have just studied?

I have before me a true gem for the bibliophile, *The Passion of Our Lord Jesus Christ preached to the Parisians by Reverend Father Olivier Maillard*, printed in the year 1513, in Gothic lettering similar to the more ancient lettering in the Psalter manuscript of Marseille. This small booklet bears the typographic mark of Jehan Petit, one of the best among the early masters from the beginnings of French printing. Its text is as follows:

> ... And the body of Jesus remained affixed to the cross. The Jews came before Pilate saying: There are two thieves here. The day of Passover is at hand. They must be taken down from the cross and, if they are not dead, put to death. And about the fourth hour of the afternoon there came a troop of armed men. In the words of Landulf, when Mary perceived them she started to weep. They laid the thieves on the ground and broke apart their legs. The Virgin Mary thought they were going to do the same to her Son. But, when they saw that Jesus was already dead, they did not break his legs. Then, with his spear, one of the soldiers opened his side and there immediately came out blood and water. And Mary said to them: I beg you, give me the body of my Son that I may place it in a sepulcher. One of the soldiers with a proud bearing (*superbus*) answered her, and it is commonly said that this was Longinus, who took his spear and thrust it right to the heart of Christ and opened his side just before the torrent of blood and water.
>
> Christ says to the devoted soul: Arise, my beloved, my dove, my beautiful one, come into the clefts of the

rock, into the hollow places of the wall. Thus the dove builds its nest among the rocks, and when a bird of prey would seize it, it flies away to its refuge. For Christ, it was not a complete enough satisfaction to redeem us: He wanted to open his heart! *Non satis Christo redimere nos: sed voluit aperire cor!*

And, miraculously, blood and water came out, as symbols of the two sacraments of Baptism and the Eucharist, which could not happen naturally. Water figures the sacrament of Baptism, blood that of the Eucharist. All that was done for you who suffer temptation. You should have recourse to Christ, saying to him: You have willed that your side be opened, I beseech you, enable me to dwell in the midst of your heart! *Vos voluisti latus vestrum aperire: precor ut in medio cordis vestri valeam habitare.*

No, when teachers of present-day piety recommend to souls the wound in the side and heart of Jesus as a comforting refuge in life's worst trials, they are teaching nothing new, no more than did Olivier Maillard claim in 1513 to preach a new theory to the Parisians, or to point them towards a hitherto unknown shelter. At the place of the wounded heart of Jesus, as with everything that is the object of adoration, today's Christian rediscovers, in bending the knee to the ground, the incontestable trace of the knees of all his ancestors.

IV. DEPICTION OF THE WOUND TO THE SIDE OF A LIVING JESUS

In the previous chapter I was led to state that artists of the fifteenth century have at times represented Jesus still living and yet wounded from the spear-thrust to the side of the heart, and I should add — which seems incontestable to me — that this unusual feature could not be an instance of a mistake. To be persuaded of this, just read Émile Mâle's luminous work, *Religious Art in France: The Late Middle Ages*, about how the artists and craftsmen of this

The Wound in the Side of Jesus

era were in full possession of both a pure spirit of orthodoxy and of the sacred texts that then governed Christian iconography.

And I think I have come upon what motivated their thinking in the present case by assuming that they wanted to show in this way that the heart of Jesus — the wounded heart so often depicted in this fifteenth century — had had an actual and physical share, by repercussion, in the expiatory sufferings of Jesus before his last breath.

It seems to me that this depiction of the wound on the living Jesus must have been explained to everyone, because, when no longer understood after the Renaissance, only a century and a half later, it was interpreted by some according to its material aspect alone, which contradicts the express text of Saint John: "But...when they saw that he was already dead...one of the soldiers with a spear opened his side" (19:33-34).

Rome intervened then with just cause, and by the decree of January 18, 1638, Urban VIII prohibited "images of the not yet expired Crucified where the wound to the side is seen, because the opinion that maintains that Longinus pierced the living Redeemer with his spear is heretical."

These depictions are therefore condemned since that time, and one must abstain from creating such works anew, but it remains perfectly permissible to reproduce those of the fourteenth century, at the very least as an accepted document for studies in sacred iconography (Plate 12).

Central part of the Franciscan family coat of arms. Wood engraved with penknife by the author, after a copper by Ignatio Luchesini, 17th century.

Part II: Depictions of the Wound in the Side of Jesus

Plate 12. — The living Christ wounded by the spear-thrust to the side of the heart, Konrad von Soest, reredos of the 15th century. Photo Giraudon. Archives of the review Regnabit, *1921–1929.*

CHAPTER FIVE

Lenticular Representations of the Wound in the Side of Jesus

1. IN FRANCE

SINCE THE BEGINNING OF THIS WORK WE have been engaged in showing how, since early Christian times, our fathers applied themselves to creating—in order to continually remember the shedding of Jesus's blood—more or less mysterious emblems, hardly appreciated today. And yet both their existence and role in memorializing the bloody drama that unfolded from the praetorium of Pilate to the summit of Golgotha are incontestable.

This hidden symbolism, at least since the fifth century, under the appearance of grains of incense on the Paschal candle and the five crosses of altar stones, under the more veiled form of dots, crosslets, and the various marks of the *Signaculum Domini* inscribed on the coins of Christian nations, on books, seals, ceramic products, on weapons and liturgical objects, in the heraldry of the nobility, ecclesiastics, and corporate bodies, as well as elsewhere, are to be constantly rediscovered today under the eyes of whoever studies the history of the religious or secular arts of times past.

For nearly all of these evocations of the five chief wounds of the Savior, the cross, the dot, the mark, or whatever the sign that represents the wounded side of his divine body is more important, more ornate, more honored than those that evoke the wounds to his four limbs. We repeat, this is because the creators of this symbolism did indeed want to indicate by this that the four streams of blood issuing from the hands and feet are derived from this unique source, the heart of the Crucified, the wound in which was one and the same with the gaping wound left in the flank of Jesus when the legionnaire withdrew the point of his spear, and from which escaped the torrent of blood and water.

What is more, we will also see in the following chapters how this intense cult of the redeeming blood is hidden, "to sing its hymn of the precious blood," under the sparklings of the escarbuncle and stones of a reddish color, under the wonderful petals or supple leaves of a great number of plants, and how, in the incision made by the arboricultural industry in the trunk of resinous trees, Christian thought again sees the everywhere sought-for image of the open wound in the Savior's side.

A day finally comes when, without however growing weary of depicting the divine wounds with purely conventional images, iconography is emboldened to go so far as to give, especially to the wound in the side, a form more akin to the one the passage of the nails and the spearhead must have left on the pierced body. The blow dealt by this weapon was therefore sometimes represented by a crescent and, most often, by a kind of reddish quite elongated ellipse, comparable to the geometrical curve of a lens or, even better, to the transverse curve of a spearhead. To better distinguish this figure, drops of usually blood issue from it and fall to earth. Here are some examples:

— On a beautiful manuscript book of the fourteenth century, *The Image of the World*,[1] which in the following century belonged to the duke Jehan de Berry, the Savior's lateral wound, lenticular in form and of a dark red color, is seen in the middle of a miniature, where it is surrounded by nails, evocative of the other wounds, and the seamless robe. Above is the scene of the crucifixion of Jesus (Plate 10).

— In the cathedral of Limoges, on a column of the first span of the ambulatory, on the epistle side, a defaced angel holds a shield, also defaced, on which the side wound is at the center of the four emblematic signs of the wounds to the limbs; from its lower edge fall drops of blood. This is a fifteenth century *Signaculum Domini* (Fig. 1).

— A small bronze cross of the fifteenth century found in the vicinity of Orléans; its four globular extremities are marked with

1 Bibliothèque Nationale of Paris, *fonds français* S. N., folio 136.

a point; in the middle, a small shield bears a lenticular figure of the wound to the side: this is a normal variant of the *Signaculum Domini* (Fig. 2).

2. IN SPAIN

Painted and fixed on wood, a small tooled leather piece from Vic in Catalonia also represents the wound in a lenticular form from which issue drops of blood. The accompanying three nails complete the evocation of the redemptive tragedy, and the whole is placed at the center of a crown of thorns covered on its upper part by a dove with its wings extended. The head of the symbolic bird is encircled with a nimbus of glory — sixteenth century (Fig. 3).

I have at hand hundreds of iconographic documents related to the Passion of Jesus Christ that come from all the arts and all Christian peoples: the one presented here is the sole one of these placed in symbolic contact with the dove and a direct evocation of the redemptive agony. What was the creative thinking behind this relationship?

The dove seems to be there only with its significance as an emblem of love, the Savior's divine love, which made Him accept death for the salvation of men: "Father, not my will, but thine be done";[2] for the love that brings a being to sacrifice itself for those it loves: "The good

Fig. 1. — Sculpture from the Cathedral of Limoges, 15th century.

Fig. 2. — Small bronze cross, 15th century. Orléans region.

Fig. 3. — Motif in relief and painted on leather, 16th century. Vic (Spain).

---

2 The Gospels: St. Matthew (26:39), St. Mark (14:36) and St. Luke (22:42).

Shepherd gives his life for his sheep."[3] And this corresponds to one of the thoughts dear to St. Thomas Aquinas, namely that "the chief sentiments at play in the soul of Jesus during the Passion, validating his acceptance, are obedience and love."[4]

3. IN ENGLAND

England, which was at the end of the Middle Ages — as were moreover all Christian lands of the West — so fervent with regard to the wounds, blood, and heart of Jesus Christ, still retained, from the time when it was Catholic, a very rich iconography.

We find there impressive images of the Savior's chief wound under the lenticular form: one of them, noticed near Coventry, is seen in the midst of an assemblage quite similar to the motif of the Vic leather. Here we have a stone shield painted a purplish-red color. The ellipse of the wound is dark red and the nails that encompass it are black. Nails and wound are bordered with gold as a sign of glorification. Above are the cross, the crown of thorns, the spear, and sponge[5] (Fig. 4).

At Cambridge, in the chapel of the renowned Royal College, a brass sheet covers the tomb of Robert Hacumblen, provost of the aforesaid college from 1509 to 1528; it bears the image of the prelate in full regalia and, near his head, is an escutcheon charged with the five wounds of Christ represented by the bleeding lenticular cuts (Fig. 5). A banderole that seems to issue from the mouth of the deceased has him say these words:

"Thy wounds, O Christ, are my sweet remedy." *Vulnera Christe tua michi dulci sint medicina.*[6]

From the same period, or at the end of the fifteenth century, a stained-glass window found in the sacristy of a church at Sidmouth (Devonshire) bears an escutcheon where we see the five wounds of Jesus depicted by small ellipses magnificently crowned;

3 John 10:11.
4 Rev. Félix Anizan.
5 Document received from Mr. J. Thom, of London, 1923.
6 Document received from Mr. Littlechild, former warden of the chapel of the Royal College of Cambridge.

Lenticular Representations of the Wound in the Side of Jesus

from each of them fall veritable downpours of blood, and, on the banderoles, five inscriptions tell Christians that they are the efficacious and rich treasures of divine help: the wounds of the hands are thus acclaimed as being fountains of *Wisdom* and *Mercy*, those of the feet as fountains of *Grace* and *Holy Comfort*, and the wound to the heart as fountain of *Everlasting Life*[7] (Fig. 6).

These indications of the mystical order recall a painting from the same period, probably Flemish, where phylacteries around Jesus crucified proclaim the wounds of his hands as being the wells

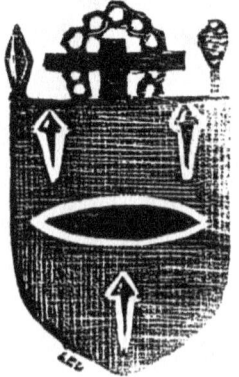

Fig. 4. — *Escutcheon of painted stone. End of 15th century. Coventry (England).*

Fig. 5. — *Escutcheon from the tomb of Robert Hacumblen. Royal College of Cambridge, 1528.*

of *Justice* and *Knowledge*, those of his feet the wells of *Strength* and *Prudence*, and the one of his open side the well of *Mercy*. And these two compositions, which bring a Christian to his knees before the inexhaustible store of spiritual consolation offered him by his Redeemer, echo the creative thinking behind the "fountains of life" which show the blood of the divine Crucified One collected in a large basin where men go to seek and find their spiritual regeneration. We will speak of this later.

Among many other examples, we will conclude with the escutcheon of an engraving stemming from the canton of Saint Gall, in Switzerland, on which the lateral wound in lenticular form is encircled with a radiant halo and set on the Roman legionnaire's

7 Documents and information received from Mrs. Edith Wilde of Winchester, and from Rev. Woolcombe, Vicar of Sidmouth, 1923.

Part II: Depictions of the Wound in the Side of Jesus

Fig. 6. — Escutcheon on stained-glass at Sidmouth (England), 15th century.

spear. Around it, four nails evoke the wounds to the feet and hands — sixteenth century[8] (Fig. 7). Later, we will see how the beautiful documents from the very same time, in France and England especially, feature, not the lenticular wound, but the heart of Jesus set on the spear or transpierced by it.

Fig. 7.—Escutcheon of an engraving stemming from Saint Gall (Switzerland), 16th century.

8   Document received from Rev. Leon de Lyon, curator of the Franciscan Museum at Rome, 1925.

THIRD PART

Representations of the Redemptive Shedding of Blood

CHAPTER SIX

Symbolic Thirst

THIRST IS EVEN MORE PAINFUL THAN hunger: pushed to extremes, it becomes an atrocious torment; those who die by torture have no hunger—they thirst. In the symbolism of desire, thirst holds first place because, like thirst, unquenched desire can be a painful torment for mind and heart, and for the soul that animates both. Every desire arises from an unsatisfied love; this is surely why the Ancients tied Eros, the child Love, to the symbolism of desire, just as they tied thirst to the same symbolism.

Two thirsts are expressed by Christian symbolism in its writings and emblematic iconography, the two great loves that govern the world: the love of God, of Christ, for the human soul, and the love of a human soul for its God, its Savior.

This thirst of the human soul, of the saintly soul, for the One from whom every good thing descends, was symbolized in several ways by the iconography of the early Christian centuries: doves, peacocks, and other birds drink from a cup filled with the divine blood or pick at the eucharistic grape; a stag and its doe lean over clear fountains or over the four springs that issue from a mystical knoll; later there are griffins and various other animals that rear up to slake their thirst from an overflowing basin.

And all these symbolic images are modeled on the text from a psalm of David: "As the hart panteth after the fountains of water; so my soul panteth after thee, O God. My soul hath thirsted after the strong living God."[1]

Christ responds to this expression of vehement desire in many Gospel passages, notably in St. John: in the temple of Jerusalem "Jesus stood and cried, saying: If any man thirst, let him come to me and drink" (7:37).

---

[1] Psalm 42 (Vulgate 41):2–3.

On a low pillar or pedestal having served as a credence table, near an altar, and relegated in the last century to farming uses of an old rural priory in the vicinity of Carentan (Manche), an inscription of the sixteenth century or beginning of the seventeenth bore these words: SI Q SIT VENIAT AD ME ET BIB, which should be read in this way: Si quis sitit veniat ad me, et bibat, "If anyone thirsts let him come to me and drink." At the lower end of

Fig. 1. — Inscription on stone, vicinity of Carentan (Manche), 16th century.

the Gospel text the wounded heart of the Redeemer pours forth its living torrent into a eucharistic cup[2] (Fig. 1).

Here the inscription and the motif of the Breton pedestal have the same mystical significance as the ewers or aquamaniles of the same era which pour their purifying or refreshing stream of water through the wound in a heart which can only be the Savior's.

Turning over a few more pages of John's Gospel, we read that, on Calvary, nailed to the gallows cross, Jesus, "knowing that all things

[2] Document received from Canon Lerosey, former director of the major seminary of Saint Suplice in Paris.

were now accomplished, that the scripture might be fulfilled, said: I thirst" (19:28). Then those who came to crucify him brought to his lips, at the end of a reed, a sponge drenched in vinegar.

And so Christian spirituality has taken, among other texts, this word "I thirst" [*sitio*] — the penultimate word uttered by the Redeemer before dying — in order to make of it the literary symbol experienced by him in the place of souls ransomed at the price of his sacrifice. This is what the vase, the reed, and the sponge are saying when represented near the cross in Christian iconography.

Wood-engraving by the author.

CHAPTER SEVEN

The Heart, Fountain of Life and Holiness

THE SOCIÉTÉ DES ANTIQUAIRES DE l'Ouest possesses in one of its museums at Poitiers, that of the Augustinians, a seventeenth-century vase whose decoration is integral to this work. It is a large hydria or flagon, a water fountain about 35 centimeters in height, potbellied like a Provençal jar and equipped with two handles in the manner of ancient amphorae.

Made of terracotta, it is covered with a greyish-green glaze; its broad neck was formerly closed by a lid of the same nature whose prominent center would have ended in a more or less ornamented knob.

For its overall decoration, this vase bears, at its neck, the radiant face of the sun and, at its base, the heart of Jesus, the lower end of which is prolonged in a spigot for drawing out the liquid inside. This heart is surmounted by a cross placed between two rigid flames, sharply bent into crooks; it is therefore an incontestable image of the heart of Jesus Christ (Fig. 1).

Fig. 1. — Water-fountain from the museum of the Augustinians, at Poitiers.

At first glance, the transformation of the Sacred Heart into a common sink faucet seems a daring if not utterly disrespectful boldness; yet, as unenthusiastic as I am about the symbolism of the seventeenth century (an often anemic heir to that of the Middle Ages), this time it seems to have attained an unaccustomed rightness and fullness of meaning, having been, it seems, directly inspired by the sacred books and not by the insipid sentimentalism that almost always serves it poorly.

Part III: Representations of the Redemptive Shedding of Blood

But it is the casing of an older well that will have, I do believe, something to say about the enigma of the heart of the Poitiers drinking fountain: In the courtyard of the Bois-Rogues castle, near Loudun, where Francis I had once brought Maximilian Sforza, Duke of Milan, for a quite relative and most lordly captivity, there was still in the nineteenth century a well from the Renaissance period where the following inscription was inscribed under the monogram of the name of Jesus charged with a cross whose shaft bore the Sacred Heart: *Haurietis aquas in gaudio de fontibus salvatoris.* "You will draw in joy the waters of the fountains of salvation."

This well no longer exists, and the inscription I reproduce here (Fig. 2) is preserved only by the copy made on July 23, 1863 by the Loudun scholar and archaeologist Joseph Moreau de la Ronde, by way of comparison with the inscription engraved on the well of his own patrimonial residence at La Ronde, near Loudun, which also bore, but in seventeenth century lettering: *Haurietis aquas in gaudio fontibus salvatoris. Isayæ II.*

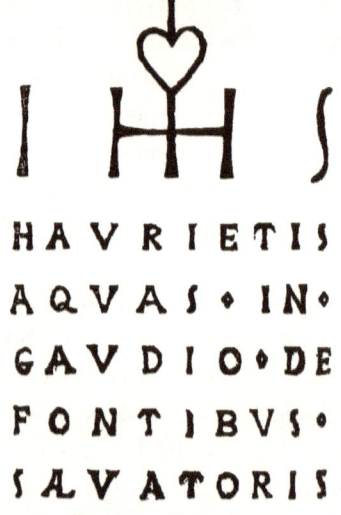

Fig. 2. — *Inscription on a 16th-century well. Château du Bois-Rogues, near Loudun (Vienne).*

The well of La Ronde, like that of Bois-Rogues, has been razed and filled; but upon the demolition of its coping the stone carrying the inscription was embedded above the door of a garden pavilion, where it still stands (Fig. 3). The reference it gives to biblical words is not completely accurate: they are not from the prophet Isaiah's second chapter, but from the twelfth, verses three and four, where they begin with this magnificent passage: "You will draw water with joy from the fountains of salvation, And you will say in that day, Give thanks unto the Lord of Israel, call upon his name, and declare before the people his wonders, and proclaim that he is a safe haven."

> # HAVRIETIS AQVAS
> # IN GAVDIO DE FONTI
> # BVS SALVATORIS ISAYAE II

Fig. 3. — *Inscription on the well of the De la Ronde château, near Loudun (Vienne).*

And so, as for the thought that presided, during the first half of the sixteenth century, on the epigraphy of the Bois-Rogues well, there was no doubt, no hesitation: the "source of salvation," the "fountain of the Savior," or, according to the translation of Saint Bernard, the "font salvatrice," our Poitou forebears would have said at the time that this is the very heart of Jesus the Savior, the heart that on the stone of the well is only one with the redemptive cross, with the name of Jesus, I. H. S. And it is in view of this, in immediate relation with this, that the *Haurietis aquas* of Isaiah is laid out.

And, for those who would go further than the apparent and superficial materiality of words, the limpid water of the well, life-giving and purifying, is nothing more than the material image, the emblematic figure, of the invisible divine gift sprung from the heart and streaming forth to give back to souls salutary joy, purification, and the life of justice.

Outside of this interpretation it seems impossible to give any plausible and solid meaning to the compenetration, to the juxtaposition, of heart, cross, monogram, and biblical text.

And this same thought, this proclamation that the heart of the Savior is indeed the source of our redemption through the blotting out or — why not use the common word — "washing" away of human guilt, this thought seems less overtly but just as clearly expressed on the Poitiers drinking fountain. There is no inscription to tell us of the secret consolation, but is it not an eloquent language to have the beneficent liquid flow from the Divine Heart itself? Does not the hand of the potter, that has thus stabilized the pot in its charitable office, seem to have wanted to make it cry out to all: O you who are defiled, come to me who am the source and means of all purification and you will you find again the living splendor of your souls?

And the words of the current *Litany of the Sacred Heart* come to mind of themselves:

> *Cor Jesu, fons vitae and sanctitatis.*
> Heart of Jesus, fountain of life and holiness.

And further, when the same liturgical text greets his heart with the title "fountain of all consolation," does not our thought reflect back on the "in gaudio" of Isaiah's book?

Surely, by applying to the heart of Jesus the *Haurietis aquas* of the prophet, the inspirer of the Bois-Rogues sculpture was not an inventor, but rather one who has come after so many others.

In his magnificent study, *Sermon of Saint Bernard on Our Lord's Nativity*, Dom P. Séjourné reproduced the passages by which the great abbot showed his twelfth-century monks the "the sources of the Savior": the "source of mercy" that purifies; the "source of wisdom" that satisfies the soul; "the source of grace" that sprinkles it and makes it grow; the "source of zeal" from which the heart of the Christian draws its ardor. And the great mystic adds: Behold, here are the fountains about which Isaiah spoke beforehand: "You will draw with joy the waters from the springs of the Savior." Then, having contemplated these four springs that he relates to the wounds in the four limbs of the crucified Jesus, the saint recollects himself, and turning his gaze to the gaping wound of the heart, designates it as the supreme source, the very source of life, of the true life which begins for us with the utterance of the last sigh from our chest.

This is why I am sure that, if the great abbot of Cîteaux had seen the Poitevin potter model in clay the heart-fountain that decorates the Antiquaires of the Ouest's hydria, he would have inclined his head before this evocative image, murmuring the *Haurietis aquas* of Isaiah.

I will dare go even further along this same track in the realm of iconographic interpretation on the subject of another water vase, respecting which the incomparable artist who conceived it seems to have obeyed a mystical inspiration quite close to the one guiding the ceramist of the Poitiers drinking-fountain.

Three leagues from Loudun and the castle of Bois-Rogues where the heart of Jesus surmounted the inscription on a well, at the very time when the biblical word was engraved there, the Gouffier d'Oiron, dukes of Roannais, resided at Oiron, their princely abode, where they created a center where the arts — all the arts — were held in high honor.

At that time Hélène de Hangest, Duchess of Roannais, had crafted those marvelous earthenware pieces called Oiron in the nearby workshops of Saint-Porchaire, pieces that are the purest, the most splendid jewels of French ceramics and whose least remnants are prized today, literally, far more than their weight in gold.[1]

Fig. 4 — Le Pelican on an Oiron earthenware, 16th century.

The former Dutuit collection had three Oiron pieces; one of them, a water-pitcher, bears on the curvature of its belly, on a milky-white background decorated with wild, bewitching intertwinings and arabesques of various colors, a monochrome cartouche on which an emblematic pelican opens its breast so as to give, by the washing of its blood, life to its brood (Fig. 4).

Is this empurpled source opened at the heart of the bird which, by this means, restores existence to dead beings, very different from the idea of a fifth source opened in the divine side spoken of by St. Bernard? For, let us not forget, in medieval Christian

---

1. We know of only six or seven entire pieces of Oiron earthenware, which have been listed in the Rothschild collection and in the former Sauvageo and Dutuit collections at the Louvre. The only extant earthenware chandelier, embellished with the monogram of Henry II, was purchased by Dutuit at the end of the nineteenth century for 91,000 francs less expenses. This speaks to the magnificence of these pieces and their present-day astronomical value (Cf. *Les Arts*, year 1902, num. 18, p. 3).

iconography, from the tenth century to the Renaissance, the pelican striking itself "to the heart" is an emblem of revivifying redemption, and not of the Eucharist.

Let us listen to William of Normandy, one of the most trustworthy masters of symbolism in the twelfth century, who in his *Divine Bestiary* tells us: "The pelican's young, having grown larger, strike their father with their beaks, and the latter, in his just anger, kills them; but three days later he returns to them, pierces his side, and, shedding his blood on them, recalls them to life." Then William applies this touching fiction to Jesus the Savior. All this unfolds in ninety-five verses, too long to reproduce here.[2]

Albert the Great, Vincent of Beauvais, and Hugh of Saint-Victor all explain the symbol of the pelican by the same fabulous story; for all of them the young birds, rebellious and chastised to death, are purified, washed, pardoned, and restored to life merely by the ablution of paternal blood, and not by its incorporation as food. The dead cannot be fed. And even though Saint Augustine, commenting on Psalm 101, had a presentiment that the pelican would become a eucharistic emblem, his idea found no echo in medieval iconography.

That is why, when St. Thomas Aquinas, in the *Adoro te* hymn of his *Office of the Blessed Sacrament*, in turn applies the figure of the pelican to the Savior, he will also express the idea of the human soul's redemption by the purifying washing in the divine blood, and not by the act of eucharistic nutrition:

> *Pie Pellicane, Jesu Domine*
> *Me immundum munda tuo sanguine,*
> *Cujus una stilla salvum facere*
> *Totum mundum quit ab omni scelere.*

> Good Pelican, Lord Jesus,
> Wash my defilements in your blood,
> One drop of which is enough to save
> The entire world from all its sins.

---

2. Cf. C. Hippeau, *Le Bestiaire Divin de Guillaume, Clerc de Normandie*, VI (Caen: Hardel, 1852), pp. 93 and 207.

At the very time when the great ceramist of the Duchess of Roannais was bending the soft curves of the handles and decorating the contours of his ewer, du Bartras,[3] in his Ronsard school style, gave the symbolic pelican the same mystical meaning as the authors of previous centuries. Only after all these, by adulteration, by ignorance of the thinking of the great centuries of Christian intellectualism, did the pelican become one of the late symbols of the Eucharist. This is why the artists, sculptors, painters, and carvers of the Middle Ages placed it almost always at the top of the cross or in the branches of the "Tree of Life."

On an old ewer, I see the pelican in direct conceptual relationship with the fiction that shows it purifying, resuscitating, and reviving from the source of its heart, and by all the vital fluid of its heart, blood and water, its guilty and mortally chastised children. Do we not actually have here, in the most fervid symbol of its bestowal, that water seen by St. John on the island of Patmos "issuing from the right side of the Temple," and "which saves all who are touched by it,"[4] this purifying source upon which all the mystic soul of the Middle Ages looked with the joy of "the hart [that] panteth after the fountains of water," as Psalm 41 says, and magnified in so many ways?[5]

Am I too daring when I bestow on the Oiron ewer's pelican an anagogical value almost equal to that of the Poitiers heart-fountain, and with nearly the same meaning? For the two inspirers of these

---

3. Cf. Hippeau, op. cit., p. 96.
4. Ezekiel 47:1–12 is actually where the reference to the "right side" occurs, a passage with echoes in Apocalypse 22:1–2. — *Trans.*
5. This is the same idea of purification by washing, by the bath, that has presided over the composition of the "fountains of life" by which the fifteenth century glorified the redemptive activity of the Precious Blood, and which has inspired some pages by the eminent teacher Émile Mâle that shine with the lovely, pure light of sacred archaeology (*Religious Art in France: The Late Middle Ages*, trans. M. Mathews [Princeton, NJ: Princeton University Press, 1986], pp. 104ff.).

   The common theme of these "fountains of life" is implemented in this way: the cross where Jesus expired is raised from a basin into which the blood of these five wounds and above all that of the heart, as from five wellsprings, runs in such abundance that the basin is completely filled.

vases, as well as for the thinking that decorated the Bois-Rogues well, the water that flowed from all these brought physical and material revivification and purification for bodies, while from the Savior's open heart—whether represented under its own form or by the wounded pelican—poured out for souls "the source of life and all holiness."

And so that no one is fooled to the point of believing that this symbolism was once intended exclusively for the intellectual elite of the faithful—for from its highest point the piety of this symbolism can uplift even the simple, descending from level to level down to, ultimately, the lowest ebb of the arts—I will conclude by engraving the image of a holy-water stoup quite popular in my neighborhood; one of those poor bedside holy-water stoups at which our forefathers, whether they wore a homespun jacket or a linen blouse, and our grandmothers, whether in dresses of drugget or fustian, blessed themselves.

Fig. 5.—*Holy-water stoup Loudunais countryside, 17th or 18th century.*

This stoup is made of the coarsest seventeenth- or eighteenth-century earthenware, like the old plates of country hearths, and its polychrome ornamentation is of the most childish naïvete. Now, its bowl, the bowl where the sacramental and holy water settles, is made of the very heart of Jesus (Fig. 5). It was therefore from Christ himself that the Christian's finger would draw the salutary, exorcising, and protective water. Here too we could have written: *Haurietis aquas in gaudio fontibus Salvatoris.*

CHAPTER EIGHT

The Springs of the Savior

MORE THAN ANYTHING ELSE IN THE spectacle of the physical world, two things seemed striking to the eyes and minds of early man: the sun and springs, springs above all. That their thinking dwells so continually on the sun is only because it is itself the splendid source of two of the elements essentially necessary for earth's living creatures: heat and light.

In all lands, the primitive peoples who in those exceedingly remote ages witnessed the youth of the world sought out, when establishing the first human dwellings, the fortunate neighborhood of springs from which quite pure water issued. In their gratitude for the benefits that came to them from it, their childlike, fertile imaginations peopled these springs with mysterious sprites, and often gratuitously attributed to them the most wondrous qualities, as if it were impossible for all these springs not to have such qualities! And, in naïve homage, their hands cast various precious objects into these fountains with their pure, upwelling waters.

The semicivilized from among our Gallic and Gallo-Roman tribes carried on the practice of thank-offerings to springs and their imaginary divinities. But once Christianity organized in the West, almost everywhere the new cult consecrated the most renowned springs to select, often local saints.

Also, what is more natural than seeing—since the era of the Roman catacombs—early Christian artists symbolize the helping gift of the varied graces God bestows on man under the figure of generous springs?

See how the painters have covered the inner surfaces of these subterranean chambers where the glorious remains of the Martyrs have been laid in the peace of Christ. Everywhere the artist has reprised images of eternal rest, serenity, and happiness: in the shade of palm trees a shepherd watches over his flock in a flowering vale; fish swim in peaceful waters; winged children gather

Part III: Representations of the Redemptive Shedding of Blood

lilies; orantes pray, their eyes and arms upraised; doves, peacocks, phoenixes, frail butterflies soar or perch in the midst of foliage and blossoms, while, very much in a place of honor, upright on a rock or grassy knoll, stands the Lamb with glorious head. At its feet, from the knoll that bears it, four springs well up and form four rivers over which deer bend to drink deeply.

The Lamb is Christ, the savior of the world; the rivers that rise at his feet are the grace of eternal life he pours forth through the four Gospels on the four parts, the only ones known at that time, of the ransomed world; and the deer are the faithful souls who have realized what David has said of himself: "As the hart panteth after the fountains of water; so my soul panteth after thee, O God."[1]

Elsewhere, about a hillock from which rivers flow, there are saints who stretch out their supplicating hands towards the Lamb, as in the crypt of Saints Marcellinus and Peter.

In the sixth century, this is represented as well on the large mosaic in the basilica of Saints Cosmas and Damian. It seems the entire Church stands beneath the symbol of the twelve lambs that advance towards the four springs issuing from a rock where the divine Lamb stands erect.

Also among the Gauls, and at the same time, the symbol of the mystical springs was favored. I will give only one example: a very beautiful engraved semi-precious stone from the rich collection of Count Raoul de Rochebrune, a lapis lazuli on the bright blue of which the artist has depicted not the Lamb, but the Monogram of Christ — the superimposed X and P — set on a hillock like a triumphal flag (Fig. 1). In the basin out of which the regenerative waters issue, two deer eagerly quench their thirst. Then the theme comes to a conclusion: because it is to the divine springs, and not to the pernicious springs, that the deer direct

Fig. 1. — Intaglio on lapis-lazuli, 5th century. Collection of Count R. de Rochebrune.

---

1 Psalm 41:2.

The Springs of the Savior

themselves, a glorious crown is prepared for them in heaven, and doves hold it above their heads.

This superb intaglio, which was in the Parenteau collection before its entry into the Rochebrune, was in all likelihood found on the southern border of Deux-Sèvres and the Vendée. It appears to be attributable to the fifth century.

Sometimes, about the same era, it is the stag and his doe that imbibe this divine gift together beneath the gaze of the Savior-Lamb; perhaps never has iconography conceived for conjugal, Christian life a more discreet, a more worthy, a more gracious emblem, or a more perfect design as well.[2]

Later, two other mystical springs make their appearance in the field of the iconographic art: from the Lamb itself, struck to the heart, a large stream of blood gushes into the cup of the chalice placed at its feet; this is the emblematic source of the Eucharist (Fig. 2, Plate 13). And, perched on the edge of its nest, above its brood, which it purifies and thus resuscitates, the pelican also pours out blood from its breast; here it is no longer the source of the eucharistic gift, but the source of purifying and redemptive grace.

Fig. 2. — Badge on a liturgical glove, 13th century. Jean Martin Collection, Lyon, 1902.

With the same sense of purification achieved by the virtue of Jesus's lateral wound, the symbol of the earthen vase presents itself to us as a less striking and more hidden image. In the beautiful pages dedicated to *St. Bonaventure's Sermon on the Benefits of the Heart of Jesus*, Dom Séjourné has already told us of this emblem of the square terracotta flask with an opening on the side, of the gloss which tells us that this flask is the image of the body of the Lord, made of human clay, and which, through the opening of its side, has poured out life.

---

2   Silver reliquary casket from the church of Aïn-Zirara; cf. Poinssot, in *Mémoire des Antiquaires de France*, 1903, p. 33.

Part III: Representations of the Redemptive Shedding of Blood

Plate 13. — The Adoration of the Mystical Lamb by Hubert and Jan van Eyck, 1432. Detail of the central panel of a polyptych of Ghent cathedral (Belgium). Archives of the review Regnabit, *1921–1929 (ed.).*

The Springs of the Savior

Plate 14. — The Christ of Bernardino Luini, one of the most prestigious masters of Milanese painting at the end of the 15th century. Notice that the cross crosslet held by the Savior is itself a symbol, at that time frequent and well understood, of the redemptive five wounds.

Part III: Representations of the Redemptive Shedding of Blood

Plate 15. — *Jesus crucified, source of the fountain of grace, Saint-Mesme chapel at Chinon.*

The Springs of the Savior

It seems quite likely that earthen vases were actually once molded, in accordance with the text of the gloss, in the many medieval abbeys where the monks were potters and, even more, ceramic artists. Very few, no doubt, are those that have come down to us, and I have not had as yet the pleasure of encountering any.

Jesus's lateral wound, with its meaning in this instance as eucharistic source, appears more clearly in the second half of the Middle Ages, though sometimes figured in isolation from the Lord's body.

Thus we find in a miniature from the *Hours* of Caillaut and Martineau painted in the fifteenth century,[3] beside the Crucified surrounded by the instruments of his Passion, the wound in his side is figured separately within the very opening of a large chalice. And its very property as a eucharistic emblem (together with the quality of a canting and personal coat of arms) should be recognized as well in the heraldic image of the same sacred wound in the "costé" of Jesus, represented in crescent form, on the previously mentioned seal of Jehan Coste (fifteenth century), above the chalice into which falls the blood that spurts from the wound.[4]

Do not these two compositions seem inspired by the incomparable poem of the Holy Grail, which by itself alone cast upon the Christian world at the end of the exclusive reign of Christian beauty in art a thousand times more poetry than the whole horde of old pagan fictions with which, to harmful effect, the Renaissance imbued the religious art of France?

Sources of regeneration as well, the divine wounds also nurtured, for medieval piety, the "divine winepresses" and the impressive "fountains of life" where soiled men rid themselves of the deadly stains of sin.

Never more than in the last three centuries of the Middle Ages did the Christian world fall prostrate with more vehement piety and confident hope before the blood from the side and four limbs of Jesus. What five wonderful sources, inexhaustible generators of the most precious graces and the most desirable virtues we have here! And the mystics of those days asked from each of them one of these salutary gifts.

3 Cf. op. cit., p. 103, fig. 57.
4 Cf. 1st Part, chap. 4, III, p. 194, Fig. 2. — Seal of Jehan Coste.

Part III: Representations of the Redemptive Shedding of Blood

We have already mentioned in the preceding chapter how, as early as the eleventh century, St. Bernard, in his *Sermon on the Lord's Nativity*, showed in the wounds of the divine members the sources of *Mercy* and *Wisdom*, *Grace* and *Zeal*, and in the wound on the sacred side the very source of *Life*. On the other hand, theologians and mystics from the eleventh century up to our own time have understood and defined the gift of life that flows for souls from the heart and gaping side of Jesus pierced. Let us see how this spring of the Sacred Heart and the other four wounds that are, so to speak, only derivatives of it, since the redeeming blood they pour out comes therefrom—how, I say, these springs were figured in the creations of our old image-makers. In the fifteenth century art is inspired more strongly than ever by the theme of the mystical springs; it no longer shows this by lines and colors only, but the theme is made to cry aloud through words that bring this thinking to a fullness of expression and precision.

For example: on a 15th-century stained-glass window in the sacristy of the old Catholic church of Sidmouth (Devonshire), which has been a reformed temple since the 16th century, a splendid coat of arms bears the five wounds of Jesus, designated as the source of spiritual good (Fig. 3).

Surmounted by golden crowns, they appear there as five oblong purple wounds from which blood escapes in abundance. Above the wound corresponding to the right hand of the Crucified One, an inscription in Gothic cursive tells us: 𝔚𝔢𝔩 𝔬𝔣 𝔚𝔦𝔰𝔡𝔬𝔪; for the wound to his left hand: 𝔚𝔢𝔩 𝔬𝔣 𝔐𝔢𝔯𝔠𝔶; for the wound to his right foot: 𝔚𝔢𝔩 𝔬𝔣 𝔊𝔯𝔞𝔠𝔢; for the wound to his left foot: 𝔚𝔢𝔩 𝔬𝔣 𝔊𝔬𝔡𝔩𝔶 𝔠𝔬𝔪𝔣𝔬𝔯𝔱; and for the wound to his side, which directly pours the blood of the heart: 𝔚𝔢𝔩 𝔬𝔣 𝔈𝔳𝔢𝔯𝔩𝔞𝔰𝔱𝔦𝔫𝔤 𝔏𝔦𝔣𝔢, "source of the eternal life."

Whatever the choice of word—*wel* (well), spring, source, or fountain—the idea remains the same.

On a miniature, probably of Burgundian or Flemish origin also from the fifteenth century, the phylacteries[5] around Jesus

---

5 Long unfurled ribbons, as on the Sidmouth coat of arms, on which are placed explanatory inscriptions.

crucified, the inscriptions on which I have already mentioned, recognize similar gifts in the sacred wounds: for the right hand: Source of Justice; for the left hand: Source of Wisdom; for both

Fig. 3. — The "Springs of the Savior" on a coat of arms with the five wounds at Sidmouth Church (Devonshire), England, 15th century.

feet, nailed to one another: Sources of Strength and Prudence; and, for the bleeding side: Source of Life and Mercy.

Does not this inspiration to ask for mercy at the same time as life from the wound to the heart — which, if it is the center of life, it is so for goodness as well — seem most reasonable, most logical? Is not the mercy of God for our souls the necessary, indispensable complement to the gift of spiritual life, for want of which this life would not know how to resist the deadly attacks of our all too frequent guilt?

These old mystical artists knew the soul like our anatomists know bodies!

If the divine wounds are, for our soul, sources from which flow the life and also the virtues which are, etymologically, its "strengths," they are also the sources of effective remedies for its debilities, for its most dangerous diseases.

This is what an image of Robert Hacumblen, engraved on a brass sheet covering his remains in the King's College chapel at Cambridge, of which he was provost from 1509 to 1528, proclaims like a voice from beyond the grave (Fig. 4). With his hands joined on a canonical cope with swan feathers, a long phylactery unfurls towards the emblematic image of the five wounds, engraved on a bronze coat of arms; and on the supple streamer, which a breath seems to flutter, we read these words in Gothic lettering:

Fig. 4. — *The five wounds, "sources of spiritual remedies" on the brass of Robert Hacumblen's tomb in King's College chapel at Cambridge (England), 15th century.*

> Vulnera Christe tua michi dulci sint medicina.[6]
> Thy wounds, O Christ, are my sweet remedy.

---

[6] Knowledge of these two interesting English documents I owe to the most kind Mrs. Edith E. Wilde, member of the Archaeological Societies of Hampshire and Essex; I have engraved them on wood, the first after a photograph obligingly communicated by the Rev. C. K. Woolcombe, Vicar of Sidmouth Church, the second after a very beautiful rubbing graciously sent by Mr. W. P. Littlechild, a former cleric of the chapel at King's College, Cambridge. — Most respectful thanks.

But as if in his eyes the five wounds were not, strictly speaking, five distinct sources but five streams fed by the same common and deeper source, here is another English artist who, at the beginning of the sixteenth century, sculpting a pulpit at the church of Combourg (Cornwall), clearly states that the five wounds are the fountains of *Piety, Comfort, Grace,* and *Mercy,* and, for the lateral wound, *Eternal Life.* But, even though he has indeed depicted all five on the coat of arms that bears them, only one sheds its torrent, and thus gathers together the gifts of all.

This is not a simple opening made in the flesh by a spear, it is the very image of the wounded heart, which, in the midst of the pierced hands and feet, bleeds into the open cup of the chalice, like the Lamb "stricken to the heart" on the older emblem; a splendid image of the eucharistic gift in which the soul finds all together the most precious spiritual gifts and the most munificent giver that can be.

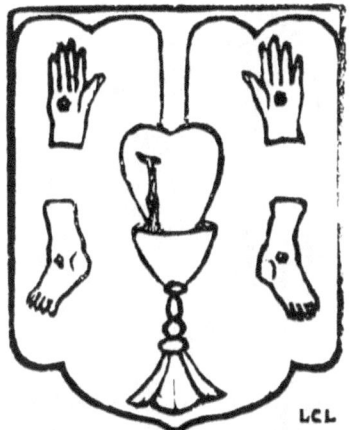

Fig. 5. — *The Five Wounds, sculpture from Camborne's old church (Cornwall).*

A little later, in 1549, still in England, when the regions of Devon, Norfolk, and York rebelled in favor of the Catholic faith — as later on in France the Vendeans would rise against the Convention — the insurgents took as a rallying sign a coat of arms similar to that of Combourg: between the pierced hands and feet, the Sacred Heart bleeding into a chalice (Fig. 5).[7]

To return to the spiritual sources, to the sources of the Savior, let us note how since Saint Bernard in the eleventh century, until the sixteenth century, the theme of sacred wounds as generous fountains of divine graces has not changed. Especially with respect to the wound of the heart it remained invariably the same: for artists as well as for theologians

---

7 From a sketch kindly communicated by Mrs. E. E. Wilde.

and mystics it is the source of eternal Life, "Wel of everlasting life." As long as the artists maintained the symbolic representations of the holy wounds, as mystical sources or fountains, whether in the artistic domain of the crucifixions or in that of coats of arms, this theme received, from the first of these domains, a stamp of sanctity and from the second, a character of nobility that kept a dignified bearing well-suited to the lofty thought that it interpreted. But when, after the Renaissance — during which the sobriety, the sometimes quite naïve simplicity, and the extraordinary energy of expression of the religious symbolism of the Middle Ages foundered — painters, sculptors, or engravers wanted to translate the old theme of the mystical springs, they found themselves in an odd situation, and finally, instead of wounds glorified by a truly royal heraldry as on the coat of arms of Sidmouth, or more simply, like the one at Cambridge, or like those — the most natural of all — on the just mentioned crucifix, these artists felt compelled to construct architectural forms, monumental and complicated fountains, in imitation of the marmorean basins of Italian gardens, with projections upon which they had the poor taste of hanging the severed limbs of the Savior in an overall arrangement that brings to mind vulgar comparisons.

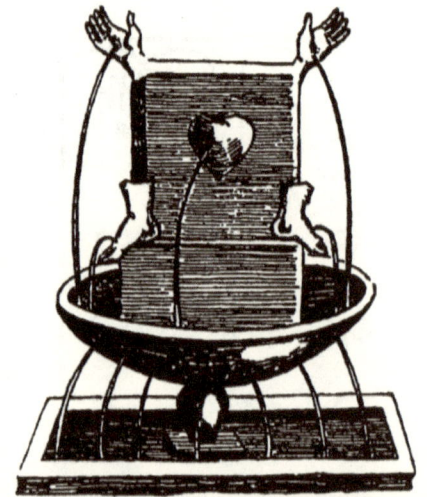

Fig. 6. — *The fountain of grace, after an engraving by Frédéric Boutrais, 17th century.*

The fountain of grace by the engraver Frédéric Boutrais shown here belongs to this late and pitiful school (Fig. 6).

Admittedly, in its decline the Middle Ages has also, as we have seen, in France, England, Germany, and elsewhere, represented the holy wounds by the figures of the heart, hands, and feet of Jesus separated from his image in its entirety; but at least it placed them on the wood of the cross, or, which was much more common and better still, on escutcheons. There, by this fact alone, the heart, hands, and feet of Jesus became "motifs," "furniture" of sacred heraldry, and their presentation in an isolated state was accepted and consecrated by the precise rules of the highest, the most choice art that the human mind has invented, glorifying through it all that it wants to place above the ordinary, all that it wants to treat "nobly."

What we have just said is surely only a brief glimpse into the way in which the old Christian image-makers have illustrated on glass, stone, bronze, or vellum this evocative theme of the "springs of the Savior" created by the loftiest souls, set forth by the holiest writers of the time; it is enough, however, to show a little how the artists also helped to direct souls to these divinely precious springs, these still life-giving and healing Siloes, springs that everlastingly retain their generous efficacy.

Wood engraved with penknife by the author.
Detail of a commissioner's seal from New Spain.
After an engraving published by Gonzaga,
De origine Seraphieae religionis, *1587.*

CHAPTER NINE

The Mystical Wine-Presses

IN THE PREVIOUS CHAPTER I HAVE already stated that the fifteenth century had driven the worship of the redeeming blood to the outer limits of human sensibility. Many saints have known what they have called "the folly of the cross," but the end of the Middle Ages alone has known what might be called a love mania for the divine blood of the Crucified, and it might be said that the symbolic winepress was indeed the most excessive iconographic invention of this feeling in a religious world where human vocabulary sometimes no longer had strong enough terms at its disposal.

Emerging from the splendid serenity that the thirteenth century had imposed on the manifestations of Christian art, the following two centuries caused these manifestations to lapse, through an excessive search for pathos, into a sometimes disconcerting realism that the artists of the time, those of the end of the 15th century especially, have often conveyed in all its crudity. "To better express the horror of the Passion," says Émile Mâle, "and convey that Jesus has shed his blood to the last drop, he was placed under the screw of a winepress; his blood flowed like the juice of the grape and ran into the vat. This is the theme known as the Mystic Wine Press."[1] It is also called "the winepress of love."

The prophecy of Isaiah contains these impressive verses, which were the starting point for the symbolic winepresses:

> Who is this that comes from Edom,
> with dyed garments from Bosra,
> this beautiful one in his robe,
> walking in the greatness of his strength?

---

[1] Op. cit., p. 110.

Part III: Representations of the Redemptive Shedding of Blood

"I, that speak justice, and am a defender to save."
Why then is thy apparel red, and thy garments
like theirs that tread in the winepress?
"I have trodden the winepress alone..."
— Isaiah 63:1–3 Douay

And St. John the Evangelist, echoing the distant prophet of Israel, says of the Christ of God:

"He was dressed in blood-stained garments" (Apoc. 19:13).

Already the mystics of the first half of the Middle Ages had represented Jesus under the figure of the vintager who, having harvested his grapes, tramples them underfoot on the floor of the press. This is what we see in the *Hortus deliciarum* of the abbess Herrarde, thirteenth century: beneath the trampling, wine flows from the drain spout of the press, and the Church, represented by a pope, prelates, and nuns, brings to the press an abundance of grapes.

In this scene Christ is the sole presser. But by the end of the Middle Ages art dared to do much more: the Redeemer himself becomes the fruit of the vine and takes his place under the boards of the press, according to what Augustine had said,[2] seeing in him the divine Grape, represented by the grape that was for the Hebrews the sign and token of the Promised Land.[3]

And this theme of the mystic winepress was particularly dear to the prestigious stained glass window painters at the time of Kings Louis XII and Francis I. In magnificent pages known worldwide today, and to which I can here only refer, Émile Mâle has spoken beautifully of these dazzling works of art. Their general theme? It is this: A stained glass window from Conches (Eure) shows Jesus standing between the two horizontal boards of a press of this time, which are brought together and tightened by two strong screws (Plate 16); blood flows from the divine wounds and, through the drain spout of the press, falls into the vat of life. On another stained

2 *Expositions on the Book of Psalms*, vol. III (Oxford: John Henry Parker, 1849), Psalm 56, pp. 58–59.
3 Numbers 13:23.

The Mystical Wine-Presses

Plate 16. — Jesus between the two boards of a winepress drawn and tightened by two strong screws. Stained glass window from the church of Sainte-Foy, Conches (Eure). Photo Nuhan Doduc (ed.).

Part III: Representations of the Redemptive Shedding of Blood

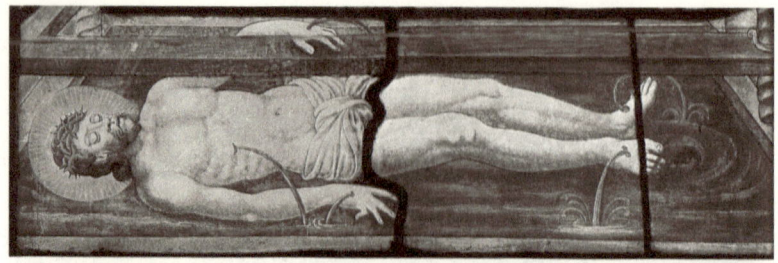

Plate 17. — Jesus laid on a winepress, stained glass window from the church of Saint-Étienne-du-Mont, Paris, 1922. Photo Nuhan Doduc (ed.).

glass window, at Saint-Étienne-du-Mont, Paris, Jesus is lying on the winepress (Plate 17); the pope, cardinals, bishops, saints, and the faithful pour his blood, which is wine, into casks. It is the reserve of redeeming treasure for ransoming men until the end of time.

An engraving from the first half of the sixteenth century, owned by the Cabinet des Estampes in Paris, seems to sum up all these representations of the Mystic Wine Press in the great French art of that time. Mâle analyzes it as follows:

> The subject was conceived as a strange epic in which triviality mingled with grandeur: it is both the poem of the vine and the poem of the blood. First we see the patriarchs and men of the Old Law planting the vines, watched over by the eye of God. After long centuries of waiting, the harvest time finally comes; the apostles pick the grapes and place them in the vat. But it is not the grapes that we see under the press, it is Christ himself; it is not the juice of the grapes that flows from the vat, but the blood of a God. Henceforth, this blood is to be the potion of mankind. A great barrel drawn by a Dantesque team—the lion of St. Mark, the ox of St. Luke, and the eagle of St. John—and driven by the angel of St. Matthew—carries the divine liquor over the world. The Church is born and will henceforth be the guardian of the blood. The four Fathers of the Church set it aside in barrels; farther along, a pope and a cardinal let the barrels down into a cellar with the help of strong ropes; an emperor and a king, transformed into workmen, aid them. The blood preserved in the cellars of the Church will be dispensed to the faithful; and in fact, in the middle ground we see confessing sinners, who will take communion once they are absolved of their sins.[4]

Great art was not alone, however, in appropriating the theme of the Mystic Wine Press: we find it reduced symbolically on

4   É. Mâle, op. cit., pp. 120–22.

poorly known small objects. They were however in vogue at the very time specified above.

It is no longer the sacrificed body of the Redeemer shown in the press, but only his heart, and the symbolic reduction could not be more satisfactory from the viewpoint of the idea as much as with regard to the material realization of these small objects: the grape is the natural crucible where wine is wrought under the heat of the summer sun; the heart is the crucible and reserve where the blood and the love of Christ for us have been wrought. In addition, the abstract form of the grape is identical to the abstract form of the heart: both fall within the general pattern of an inverted triangle.[5] And medieval symbolism, even in the final hours of its decline, was not indifferent to morphological similarities of this kind. The heart taking the place of the grape was therefore in full accord with the spirit of traditional symbolism.

The reduction theme of small objects that will occupy us is presented on larger scale by a magnificent embroidery from the same period (Fig. 1).

There is, in the Naples Museum, a large "altar canon card" embroidered with small point on white muslin from the beginning of the 16th century in the royal abbey of Fontevrault, then of the diocese of Poitiers, for Charles of Lorraine, Archbishop of Reims. I reproduce here the winepress that is on it, but cleared of the surrounding leaves and thistle flowers that are only a heraldic allusion to the name of the prelate, the recipient of this altar canon card: these are the "thistles of Lorraine." We see there the divine heart between two horizontal

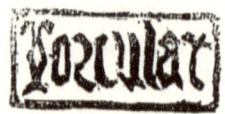
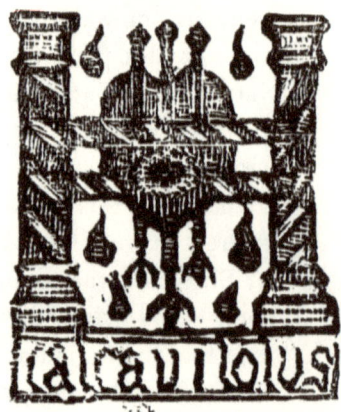

Fig. 1. — *The mystical winepress embroidered on an altar canon card, 16th century.*

---

5 What the Hindu texts constantly call "the triangle of the heart."

The Mystical Wine-Presses

pressure bars operated by two stout vertical screws. Above and below are these words taken from Isaiah's text:

Torcular calcavi solus
"I have trodden the winepress alone."

Fortunately, I am able to compare this iconographic document with a thin copper plaque found in the Angevin region around Fontevrault, sent to me by the Rev. Ballu, a parish priest of Parnay (Fig. 2).

Fig. 2. — The mystical winepress on a copper plaque, 15th or 16th century.

This object dates from the end of the fifteenth or beginning of the sixteenth century; the lines that make up its design are embossed, and small holes all around indicate that this plate was to be fixed on either a wooden board or a cloth, such as pontifical gloves. It is six centimeters in diameter.

We see the heart lying between the two presses: above, the divine hand blesses from a cloud; below is a basin, the profile of which reminds us of the Sagro Catino of Genoa, for receiving the blood that will flow.

This same iconographic theme is found in small jewelry of the pendant or, as they were called at the time of their manufacture, "pentacol" type, which represent in the same way the heart under the grip of the press. They are from the same time as all the items just mentioned.

One of them is in the Apollo Gallery at the Louvre Museum, Paris (Num. 437). It is in gold, and I depict it below (Fig. 3). Three small globules that look

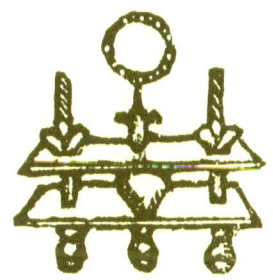

Fig. 3. — Small mystical winepress in gold. Louvre Museum, Apollo Gallery, num. 437, 16th century.

127

like bells hang below the press, such as we see beneath many religious or secular pendants from the same period (for example, with small gold pendants and gems representing Christ on the cross, an armed centaur, the pelican and its brood, from the Dutuit collection owned today by the City of Paris).

Another press of the same kind, but without globules, in silver, was found in 1898 in excavations Madame the Marquise de Cintré was having made in her castle of Boulaye, at Treize-Vents (Deux-Sèvres). It was a mistake not to do a drawing of it while I held it in my hands at that time. I truly did not know then exactly what it meant.

At the Château of Granges-Cathus, in Saint-Hilaire-de-Talmont (Vendée), the underside of the grand stone staircase is adorned with a very large number of carved medallions with heraldic motifs and various emblems. On several of these medallions the winepress of love is represented exactly like those on the small jewelry with which we have just dealt, although with this difference: two streams of blood, which look like ribbons, flow from the press (Fig. 4).

Fig. 4.—The symbolic Wine Press on a stone medallion at the Château of Granges-Cathus, Saint-Hilaire-de-Talmont (Vendée), 16th century.

On the topic of this item and small winepress jewelry, one might well ask if they are at times emblems of secular love, because the hearts seen on these do not bear, like that of the Fontevrault altar canon card, the spear wound, but neither does the embossed copper plate from the same region, and yet the divine hand blesses and consecrates its sacrifice.

Some may therefore wonder if this small winepress jewelry might not be secular objects, because the poor human being, who has only the same words to express the love that God bears us and his own love for himself, his fellow human beings, and God,

The Mystical Wine-Presses

often employs the same emblems as well to externalize these same feelings. However, it is very likely that these small items of women's jewelry can be rightly viewed as objects of devotion, for clearly we do not see how this idea of the winepress, derived from a biblical text mystically applied to the heart of Jesus Christ, can be suitably transposed with the human heart smitten by earthly love.

It is the same — despite its secular environment — for the winepress on the stairs of Granges-Cathus, from which two streams of blood flow, for the shedding of blood, commonly used in the iconography of the heart of Jesus, is used only exceptionally, if ever, in the iconography of the human heart — except for the heart of the Virgin Mary pierced with seven symbolic swords. But this involves, in this circumstance, the translation of a sacred text into an image.[6] The thousands of human hearts of all dates that we see everywhere pierced by the arrow of love are never bloody, although sometimes the stricken are most cruelly wounded.

If we were to see only two ornamental ribbons below the Granges winepress, we would have to agree that they could only be the ends of a chain enabling the jewelry to be worn around the neck, just like the one at the Louvre. The overall similarity of the Granges-Cathus winepress to the motifs shown on the Fontevrault embroidery and the copperplate from the same region enables us to see in this the mystical press just as reasonably as the press of worldly love, if indeed this symbol was used in our ancestors' sumptuary art.

*Sketch by the author of the mystic press
from the mosaic of Kabr-Hiram, 6th century.
Charbonneau-Lassay Archives (ed.)*

6   Luke 2:35. — *Trans.*

CHAPTER TEN

The Triple Precinct

IN THE CENTURIES FOLLOWING THE PEACE granted by Constantine to the Church of Christ in 313, the question arose among Christian theologians about knowing what is the actual import, in the cosmos as a whole, of the shedding of the divine blood poured out for the world on the summit of Calvary; and the opinion almost unanimously acknowledged by them was that, if God has created intelligent, reasonable, and therefore responsible living beings on planets other than ours, the Passion of Christ must have merited for them an influx of divine graces, distributed to them according to whatever mode—unknown to us—it pleased God to adopt.

We have a reflection of this theory in a famous hymn of the bishop-poet of Poitiers, St. Fortunatus (6th century), the *Pange lingua gloriosi lauream certaminis*, which the Latin Church has included in its liturgical office for Good Friday:

> *Felle potus, ecce languet;*
> *Spina, clavi, lancea*
> *Mite corpus perforarunt;*
> *Unda manat et cruor:*
> *Terra, pontus, astra, mundus*
> *Quo lavantur flumine!*

> Given gall to drink, behold, he languished;
> The thorns, the nails, the spear
> His tender body pierced;
> Water poured out with the blood:
> The earth, the sea, the stars, the world
> Are bathed in this sacred flood.

Singular circumstances have enabled me to avail myself of a source of information, which does not belong to the ordinary field of bibliography and is at least equally trustworthy, concerning several hermetic-mystical groups of the Middle Ages, their doctrines, and symbolic practices.

Now, this ancient emblem of the Three Precincts is presented as the ideogram for the scope of the Redemption on a universal plane (Fig. 1).

Fig. 1. — *The Triple Precinct, graffiti of the Templars, at the castlekeep of Chinon, 1308.*

The emblem of the Triple Precinct is very old and has been found on the menhirs of Suèvres (Orléans region) and Kermaria (Brittany), as well as on other megaliths. The ancient meaning of this symbol will no doubt always elude us, but, as for the Druidic and Gallo-Roman eras, with their prolongations over the following centuries, what René Guénon has said for his part,[1] namely, that these precincts with their avenues of access represented the three successive main degrees of initiation, seems perfectly acceptable.

It would not even seem surprising to me to detect traces of this symbolism, on the fringes of the specifically Christian meaning, in this or that milieu of Catholic society throughout the Middle Ages. During this period, did not the life of the whole social organism rest on successive initiations, often marked at each level by ritual ceremonies? Thus, the priesthood, monasticism, knighthood, the universities, coteries of alchemists, groups of Christian hermeticists more or less orthodox, craft, industrial or agricultural corporations, shipping, even criminal associations, were ritualized.

All these diverse groups living in the heyday of idealism had their figurative emblems, their heraldry, whose origins were almost always of a religious order. Christianity created many of these emblems, as it had done since its birth, to mysteriously express its dogmas and doctrine, but, for either use, it first accepted and then adapted to its own beliefs and customs all the symbols of

---

[1] "The Triple Precinct of the Druids," in *Symbols of Sacred Science*, trans. H. D. Fohr (Hillsdale NY: Sophia Perennis, 2001), p. 76.

the cults that preceded it and that would permit this adaptation, either by their already acquired meanings or by new meanings lent expression by their forms.

Why would the symbol of the Triple Precinct, found on the megaliths of Gaul and the Parthenon, or on common Roman objects, have been tossed aside by Christian emblematics? In fact, we know that it was not, since the Triple Precinct is present on both secular (Plate 18) and monastic churches, and on religious objects. Let us just say that it falls into the category of symbols that current "ignorance" no longer understands, or else totally ignores.

Everyone knows that, for Western hermeticism generally and for the Christian symbolism of geometrical figures, the square represents the world, that it is literally the *Mappa Mundi*, the "map of the world," our *mappemonde* [Fr.], the terrestrial and celestial planisphere. That being so, three squares inscribed one within the other, with a single center, that is to say forming one and the same set, represent the three worlds of the encyclopedias of the Middle Ages: the terrestrial world where we live, the firmamental world where the stars bear their radiant globes on immutable routes of glory, and finally the celestial and divine world where God resides and, with him, the pure spirits.

The Triple Precinct lent itself admirably to the symbolism of the redemptive reach: the cross, which traverses two-thirds of it, shows the direct efficacy of the sacrifice of Calvary on the terrestrial and astronomical worlds, but stops at the threshold of the angelic and divine world, which does not need redemption. When the three concentric precincts are orbicular, the symbolism remains the same; only, instead of being set in the angular form of a *Mappa Mundi*, it is based on the sphericity of the terrestrial globe and on the circular spread of the horizon line, which delimits, for us, the world of the stars; the divine world itself can be adapted to all regularly drawn forms.

On a funerary disk, in bone, of the Merovingian period, collected by the Rev. Courteaud, parish priest of Adilly, the cross, by contrast, extends over the small circle in the middle and over the second, but not over the third, larger than the other two (Fig. 2). This symbolism thus seems more logical, the earth being

Part III: Representations of the Redemptive Shedding of Blood

Plate 18. — Triple Precinct, engraved stone, Church of St Pierre in Theillement (Eure), 12th century. Photo Gauthier Pierozak (ed.).

The Triple Precinct

Fig. 2. — *Funerary disk in bone, originating from a Merovingian grave, Amailloux (Deux-Sèvres).*

small, the firmament much larger than it, and both — the one containing the other — being only like bits of dust in the hand of the Almighty, whose habitation is endless immensity.[2] More logical, in fact, this form, which proceeds in a direction the reverse of the first, is also rarer, however, in iconography, because in the eyes of our fathers a grave defect disqualified it, so to speak: it is not, in its linear entirety, the traditional and many-centuries-old emblem of the Triple Precinct. It is only one of its diverse variants or degenerations, more understandable than some others, such as for example the one at the castle of Chinon, whose curvilinear features I do not understand (Fig. 3). Several years ago, farmers living in the ruins of the Abbey of Seuilly, in Touraine — where Rabelais lived — brought to light the lower courses of a 14th-century chapel behind the actually inhabited buildings. On one of the stones of this edifice I have noted a quite clear graffiti of the Three Precincts, based on an octagonal plan very reminiscent of that of several ancient baptisteries;[3] and, remarkably, the "avenues" of the old pre-Christian symbol are, this time, clearly replaced by the cross (Fig. 4). Indeed, this is the affixing of a Christian theme onto an ancient motif. The point that occupies

Fig. 3 — *Variant of the Triple Precinct, graffiti of the Templars, at the castlekeep of Chinon, 1308.*

2   Consistent with the abbreviated shape of the universal circles in the "scheme of the world" from the Kalendrier des Bergiers, 1480 (Paris: Payot, 1926), p. E. XXXV.

3   See, in particular, the plans of the baptisteries of the Lateran, Rome, and Albenga, Italy (see Dom H. Leclercq, *Dict. Arch. Chrét.*, tome II, vol 2, cols 419 and 422). And also the baptismal font of Timgad (see Alb. Ballu, *Les Ruines de Timgad*, pp. 42-43).

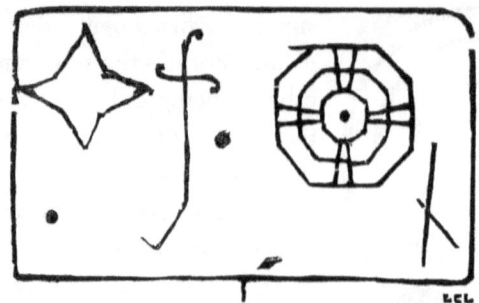

Fig. 4. — The Triple Precinct, graffiti of the Abbey of Seuilly (Indre-et-Loire) 14th, 15th century.

its center, and that is sometimes replaced by a small square or a tiny cross — hieroglyphs of the altar — is the ideogram for the Seat of Divine Presence and Peace. Here the traditions of the West are in accord with those of the East. Christianity has annexed to this symbolism a more particular idea of love and mercy. Does not the Latin Catholic liturgy officially make this word of the Bible its own: *Suscepimus, Deus, misericordiam tuam in medio templi tui,* "We have received thy mercy, O God, in the midst of thy temple"?[4]

And this theory, which is also that of the *Shekhina*, of the "Real Presence of God," in Hebrew mysticism, is singularly akin to what some hermetic-mystical brotherhoods of the Middle Ages have called the *"Great Refuge"* — enveloped by imperturbable Divine Peace — and the *"Kingdom of Blessing,"* at the center of which is enthroned the God of Life, the One whom, two centuries before our era, the Book of Enoch named "the Eternally Blessed."[5] It is also possible that the same idea of the "Ineffable Presence" is mysteriously enclosed at the center of the three squares that adorn a stone from the old Merovingian or Carolingian church of Ardin (Deux-Sèvres), now demolished (Fig. 5).

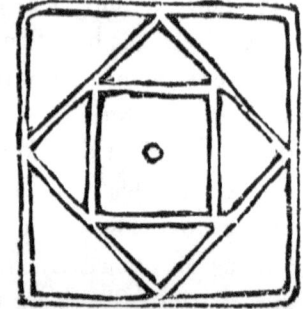

Fig. 5. — Decoration on one of the stones from the ancient church of Ardin (Deux-Sèvres), Gabriel de Fontaines collection, at St-André-sur-Sèvres.

4   *Missale Romanum* — Office for the feast of the Purification of the Virgin (introit of the Mass).
5   See *The Book of Enoch*, 77:2, trans. E. Isaac.

This, then, is at least one of the meanings Christian thought has given to the ancient emblem of the Three Precincts. Making thus manifest the effective scope of the Redemption for the terrestrial and firmamental worlds — but not for the divine world — the Middle Ages applied this emblem to the *Macrocosm*, or "universal world" of the ancients.

Perhaps, and this seems quite likely, Christian thought also applied it, according to its customary method of analogy, to the human microcosm, to the individual "little world," which its hermeticists and philosophers called "the world abridged"?[6]

This is only an hypothesis, or, if you will, a deduction, which may explain another medieval variant of the Triple Precinct, which is perhaps more than a simple degeneration of the ancient type, and in which the cross traverses the three squares of the emblem. It is drawn, for example, in a set of graffiti on one of the stones removed from the inner casing at the base of an old round castle-keep in Loudun (Fig. 6), built in 1206 by Philip Augustus and demolished by Richelieu. These graffiti are from the fourteenth century.

Fig. 6. — The Triple Precinct, on a stone from the ancient round-tower keep of Loudun (Vienne). Lapidary collection of Moreau de la Ronde.

Contemplatives of the Middle Ages have discerned three distinct parts in the human *microcosm*:

1st. The *carnal element*, governed by one of four temperaments: the choleric, the sanguine, the phlegmatic, and the melancholic. This element procures *bodily strength*.

2nd. The *intellectual element*, governed by the intelligence, itself directed by faith. This element procures *knowledge*.

3rd. The *moral element* for things of the soul, governed by conscience, served by the will, and which, well- or ill-directed, determines one's eternally happy or accursed state. Understanding it in this way, it seems to me that Christian thinkers of the past

---

6   See *Les Œuvres de M. Jean Belot, curé de Mil-Monts, Professeur aux Choses Divines et Célestes*, 1654 edition, p. 299.

were able, according to their usual method, to make the individual microcosm comparable to the universal macrocosm, and to symbolize it, like the latter, by three squares or three circles, each representing one of the human elements. The dominion of the figurative cross of Christ over the three of them is thus quite clearly warranted.

In the field of Christian thought, I see little other possible explanation for this variant of the Triple Precinct; but, I repeat, this is only a hypothetical — although, I think, quite likely — inference from what was said above regarding the traditional type of the Triple Precinct emblem accepted by mysticism as an ideogram of the redemptive scope of the death of Christ.

FOURTH PART

*Plants Emblematic
of Christ's
Five Wounds*

CHAPTER ELEVEN

The Trees of the Passion

IN FOLLOWING BOTH THE THREAD OF THE evangelical narratives of the Passion of Jesus and the inspirations of their own heart, the people of the past dedicated several trees and plants to the symbolism of the divine torture, either because they were found specifically named in these stories or because they were thought suitable to remind themselves expressly of their Savior's sufferings. In this part I will speak only of the plants dedicated by the Christian symbolism of the learned and ancestral traditions, the naïve beliefs of the good Christian people, to a representation or precise evocation of the main wounds received by the Savior during his Passion.

I. THE OLIVE TREE

Because Jesus suffered his painful agony in Gethsemane's Garden of Olives near Jerusalem, olive trees clustered in groups in the fields where they are cultivated, or thus represented in works of art, have always evoked, especially in southern countries, the dreadful sweat of blood that Jesus shed during his agony, which, as the Evangelist tells us, trickled to the ground.[1]

On the other hand, among other symbolic aspects attributed to it, the olive tree, because of the oil produced by its fruits, was one of the symbols of Christ illuminating the world. So then, like the Pascal candle, like the escarbuncle and many other emblems, this tree is linked to the particular symbolisms, quite often brought together, of blood shed for the redemption of the world and the spiritual light offered to souls by the Savior's grace and by the bright splendor of his doctrine.

---

1 Luke 22:44.

Part IV: Plants Emblematic of Christ's Five Wounds

II. THE TREE-CROSS

The tree-cross is any species of tree which, either as it is naturally, that is to say, as a living plant, or as an image, represents the cross in any of its forms: an ordinary cross, a cross in a tau, a T, or a forked cross in a Y.

Fig. 1.   *Fig. 2.*

Paintings from the catacomb on the Ardeatine Way, at Rome. Christ under the symbol of the sacrificial Bull, near the tree-cross.

At the time of the Roman persecutions, it was one of the most hidden emblems of the divine gibbet. "In the first Christian centuries," says Dom Guéranger, "often the cross is simply a tree whose sight recalls the one that was the instrument of salvation."[2]

In Rome, the catacombs of the Ardeatine Way have, in number, the most expressive representations of this symbol, little-known today. A forked tree, which represents the gallows cross in a Y, holds the chief place in a peaceful landscape; near this tree an ox and ram symbolize the divine Victim in their quality as sacrificial animals, or a dove, figure of the Christian soul, arrives after a long flight before the tree of salvation, or two doves stand on either side of a cruciform trunk from the foot of which part two long and supple branches (Figs. 1, 2, 3, and 4).

Dom Guéranger has established the symbolism of these allegorical images quite well,[3] perfectly summarized moreover by this ancient text from the preface of the Masses for the Passion and the Cross: "It was necessary that life be restored to us

---

2 Dom Guéranger, *Sainte Cécile de la Société romaine aux deux premiers siècles*, chap. XIII, p. 286. Similar expressions are found in Dom Leclercq, *Dict. d'Arch. chrét.*-passim and L. Delattre, *Carthage*, p. 83, etc.

3 Op. cit., pp. 286–88.

there where death had come to us and that the one[4] who, from the top of a tree, had subjugated us, was in his turn overthrown by a victor raised on another tree."[5] We have here a double allusion both to the Edenic tree of Good and Evil and to the tree that bore the God-made-man at the hour of his torment.

Fig. 3.   Fig. 4.

Soul and tree-cross. Paintings from the Ardeatine Way, at Rome.

The frescoes of Ardeatine do not preserve, far from it, the only examples of the tree-cross in primitive Christian art. In Marseille, to mention only one item, a small column discovered underground in this city also shows us the symbolic tree with two rising branches, with this peculiarity: it carries between them the sacred monogram of the "XPist," which here evokes the body of Jesus on the wood of the cross[6] (Fig. 5).

This monogram derived from the Constantinian chrismon was especially in common use from the beginning of the fifth to the seventh century.

This was the time when the bishop-poet of Poitiers, Saint Fortunatus, sang of the

Fig. 5. — The Christ Tree on a Christian sculpture from Marseille. After Ed. Le Blant, op. cit.

---

4 The infernal serpent.
5 Quote from the *Vitis mystica*, 12th–13th century, XLVI, 3.
6 Cf. Ed. Le Blant, *Nouveau Recueil d'Inscriptions chrétiennes de la Gaule* (Paris: n. p., 1892), p. 209.

Tree of the Cross in immortal stanzas that the Latin Church repeats every year on the most tragic days of her liturgy:[7]

Arbor decora et fulgida,	O lovely and refulgent Tree,
Ornata Regis purpura	Adorned with purpled majesty;
Electa digno stipite	Culled from a worthy stock, to bear
Tam sancta membra tangere.	Those limbs which sanctified were.
Beata cujus brachiis	Blest Tree, whose happy branches bore
Pretium pependit saeculi	The wealth that did the world restore;
Statera facta corporis	The beam that did the Body weigh
Tulitque praedam tartari.	Which raised up Hell's expected prey.
Crux fidelis, inter omnes	Faithful Cross! above all other,
Arbor una nobilis!	One and only noble Tree!
Nulla silva talem profert,	None in foliage, none in blossom,
Fronde, flora, germine.	None in fruit thy peers may be.
Flecte ramos, arbor alta	Bend thy boughs, O Tree of glory!
Tensa laxa viscera,	Thy relaxing sinews bend;
Et rigor lentescat ille,	For awhile the ancient rigor,
Quem dedit nativitas	That thy birth bestowed, suspend;
Et superni membra Regis	And the King of heavenly beauty
Tende miti stipite.	On thy bosom gently tend!

In the sigillography of the Middle Ages, the tree is often set on the ogival seals of prelates, monks, and clerics; and quite frequently, then, its stylized foliage, ordinarily beneath which peacocks or doves are shaded and feeding, is presented in a cruciform arrangement. In other compositions the intention is clearer still, and this is how it appears on the coat of arms of the city of Guernica, in Basque country. Does its name perhaps come from *quercus*, oak, or *quercetum*, oak grove? Hence, on Guernica's coat

---

7 Venantius Fortunatus, hymns *Vexilla Regis* and *Pange lingua gloriosi*, in *Brevarium Romanum* (Office of the Passion). Eng. trans. from *The Hymns of the Breviary and Missal*, ed. Matthew Britt, O. S. B. (London: Burns Oates & Washbourne, 1922), pp. 123, 127.

of arms, the tree is accompanied by two wolves holding a lamb in their jaws; and we see, emerging from its foliage, the bare ends of a cross (Fig. 6).[8]

On the Kingdom of Aragon's ancient coat of arms, a denuded cross completely emerges from the top of the tree. It is shown in just this way on a document from the beginning of the sixteenth century reproduced here (Fig. 7).

This composition recalls that the cross has been identified with the "Tree in the Midst," the "World Axis" Tree, the biblical Tree of Life, which is one of the mysterious figures of Christ—the ideal tree that is supposed to spring up, says René Guénon, "at the center of the world, or rather of a world, that is, of a domain in which a state of existence, such as the human state, is developed."[9]

A medievalist of merit, Émile Lambin, professor of archaeology at the Trocadero, wanted to see the tree-cross, recapitulated mysteriously, even in the cruciform aspect given to oak leaves represented in isolation on an interior capital from Notre-Dame de Chartres.[10]

Fig. 6. — *The coat of arms of the town of Guernica, in Basque country. See P. Le Cour, op. cit.*

Fig. 7. — *The kingdom of Aragon's ancient coat of arms. After V. Bouton,* Nouveau Traité des Armoiries, *p. 571, fig. 861.*

---

8 Cf. Paul Le Cour, *L'Arbre sacré de Guernica,* in *Atlantis,* tome III (1929), num. 23, p. 44.
9 René Guénon, *The Symbolism of the Cross,* trans. Angus Macnab (Ghent, NY: Sophia Perennis, 2001), p. 54.
10 See E. Lambin, *La Flore des grandes cathédrales de France,* p. 44. Cf. fig. p. 48.

Part IV: Plants Emblematic of Christ's Five Wounds

At the monastery of Santa Croce in Florence[11] there is an admirable fresco attributed by Vasari to Giotto, 14th century (Plate 19): it shows the Savior nailed to a large cross from the trunk of which springs long stylized branches in arabesque foliage whose ends bloom in busts of prophets, next to which texts drawn from their writings are displayed.[12] One miniature from a manuscript in the British Museum offers a fine analogy with the Santa Croce painting; also, quite a number of medieval crosses terminate at the top with a tuft of foliage where the pelican often nests (Plate 19 to Plate 21). Without taking leave of the walls of Florence, we have several examples of these, such as the cross in Nicolas di Pieto Gerini's crucifixion in the church of Santa Croce, as well as Don Lorenzo di Giovanni's in the Uffizi Gallery, both from the 15th century.

Fig. 8. — *Hibernal phase of the cruciform abalone of La Pochetière. From a large sketch of Abbé Libeau, in Fief-Sauvin; about 1892.*

From the Middle Ages, and ever since, in religious houses, castles, private lodgings, and at country crossroads, trees have been trained and cut in a cruciform pattern. I saw several of these on rural roads, at entrances to estates in the Vendée, Anjou, and the Nantais: the one of which I made a sketch (Fig. 8) was from the beginning of this century, near the hamlet of La Pochetière in the Fief-Sauvin (Maine-et-Loire). It was an abalone whose shoots were cut every two or three years. Elsewhere these are oaks, maples, boxwoods, yews, hawthorns, etc.

And this symbolism of the tree-cross, whether as a living plant or figuratively, is always inevitably — like all Christian crosses with

---

11 Cf. Lady Eastlake, *History of our Lord*, vol. II, p. 195.
12 See Grimouard de Saint-Laurent, *Guide de l'Art Chrétien*, tome II, plate XIX, p. 353.

Plate 19. — *The Tree of Life and Pelican's Nest. Fresco attributed to Giotto, Santa Croce monastery, at Florence (Italy), 14th century. Photo Giraudon. Collection of the review* Regnabit, *1921–1929 (ed.).*

Part IV: Plants Emblematic of Christ's Five Wounds

Plate 20. — Jesus and the Two Thieves by Giotto, at Palermo (Italy), 14th century. Pelican's nest in a cluster of foliage on top of the cross. Photo Giraudon. Collection of the review Regnabit, *1921-1929 (ed.).*

The Trees of the Passion

Plate 21. — Crucifixion by Andrea di Nicolò (1502), Sienna. Pelican's nest on top of the cross. Photo Giraudon. Collection of the review Regnabit, *1921–1929 (ed.).*

four arms, or those with two branches bifurcated in a Y—the evocation of crucifixion suffered by Jesus, and therefore of all the wounds received by him on the cross.

I add that, even apart from the thought of the cross, the Savior was often represented in iconic compositions by a tree. In *The Garden of Virtues*, painted in the *Somme le Roy*, in 1295,[13] seven trees are depicted around a larger tree, which reads: "C'est le iardin des Vertus, li VII arbres senefient les VII vert(us) dont cest livres parle, l'arbre du milieu senefie Ihucrist sous qui croisent les Vert(us)" [This is the garden of virtues, the seven trees signify the seven virtues about which this book speaks; the tree in the midst signifies Jesus Christ beneath whom the virtues grow].

III. TREES WITH ILLUMINATING AND MEDICINAL CONCRETIONS

A large number of trees, over the whole surface of the ancient world, produced by exudation to the surface of their trunk or branches, either of themselves or as a result of wounds to their bark, concretized and oxidized saps that are in various ways precious for mankind.

Depending on whether these saps are soluble in pure water or only in distilled spirits, European trade has classified them into two categories: the *gums*, such as the solidified sap of cherry, peach, the acacia-gum tree of Egypt or Arabia, the dragon palm; and the *resins* produced by coniferous trees and some others: pine, fir, larch, terebinth, lentisk, incense tree, etc. Needless to say, in our Far-Western countries, the most ancient resins used are those from local conifers, especially pine and fir.

The symbolism that dealt with these concretized saps never distinguished the gums from the resins, but was only interested in their respective properties.

From these local trees of the West, ancient Europe extracted pitch-resin, yellow pitch, from which was made, formerly and up until the last century, large torches and especially candles that

---

13 *Bibliothèque Mazarine*, num. 870, folio 61.

were, along with some fatty substances, the commonest way of lighting for people of modest means.

Man has always caused a more abundant exudation of coniferous saps by making incisions in the sides of the trees that produce it. He did the same to obtain a larger production of usable gums.

The Greeks, and after them Westerners, flavored the wines of certain soils with selected resins, and all the ancient pharmacopoeia made of them a frequent use which increased when, in the course of the centuries, Christian pilgrims, the crusaders, and the first great travelers, had made better known in Europe the solidified saps of palm trees of all kinds, the rare gums of Egypt, Ethiopia, Arabia, and all the Near East: red sandalwood, dragon's blood, myrrh, etc.

In the monastic or learned circles of the Middle Ages, these substances were used as remedies, recalling passages from the sacred books that mention them, such as these fiery lines in the book of Jeremiah: "Is there no balm [i.e. gum or resin] in Galaad? or is there no physician there [to prescribe them]? Why then is the wound of the daughter of my people not closed?"[14] And further: "Go up into Galaad, and take balm, O virgin daughter of Egypt: in vain dost thou multiply medicines, there shall be no cure for thee."[15]

Is it perhaps the resin of the Aleppo pine, which for lighting, as for all other uses, is the most esteemed of those harvested in Palestine and Syria?

These substances, so precious in those distant times, looked to for light and healing, thrust themselves on the minds of the ancient symbolists, for, more remarkable to them than the real extent of their efficacy, these resins, these gums, are obtained by an injury made to the trunk of the tree that yields them.[16]

---

14 Jer. 8:22.
15 Ibid. 46:11.
16 According to Matthiolus, the Ancients purified themselves before tapping liqueur-producing trees and especially incense trees, and lived in continence during the time of tapping. They had great respect for these trees and this was shown in many ways. Cf. Matthiolus, *Commentaires sur Dioscoride*, 1655 ed., chap. LXXIII, p. 49.

Part IV: Plants Emblematic of Christ's Five Wounds

And the ancient symbolism took man in the needy misery of his flesh and prostrated him before what trees wounded in their side and the sap that flowed from the wound represented, namely, the open side of Christ, and basically the heart pierced by the legionnaire's spear, from which the redeeming blood and water flowed out upon the world (Fig. 9).

Fig. 9. — Easterners wounding the side of a wine tree to collect its sap. After a 14th-century miniature reproduced by the "Magasin Pittoresque."

In any case, are not these gums, these resins, the sap, the very blood of the tree, coagulated at the wound's margin, and purified by the frigid hoar-frost of snowy lands, or singed by the burning suns of Eastern skies?

Most often translucent and having crystalline fissures, resins and gums quite deceptively give the appearance of being precious stones that our people of Landes and, along with them today's commerce, call "vegetal gems." And their colors, which range from the very pale yellow tints of human lymph to the dark red of blood, once more connect them by these similarities to the symbolism of the divine blood issuing from the wounded side of Jesus.

The Trees of the Passion

Fig. 10. — Seal of Barthlémy Lubin, cleric, 13th century.

This is undoubtedly what the mystical seal of Barthlémy Lubin, a thirteenth-century cleric, indirectly refers to, its emblematic tree epitomized by a cruciform branch, with two cone-shaped fruits that tell us it is a resinous tree bearing within itself a source of light and healing (Fig. 10).

And here again we have the dual symbolism of spiritual light and divine blood.

And was not some symbolist thinking about the real or fictitious medicinal properties of resins and gums when, in the fifteenth century, on the tomb of Robert Hacumblen, Canon Provost of the Royal College of Cambridge, and beneath his coat of arms that bear the five bleeding wounds of Jesus, he wrote these words:

Vulnera Christe tua michi dulci sint medicina
"Your wounds, O Christ, are my sweet remedy."

A rubbed impression of the monogram of the Celestines, by the author. Archives Charbonneau-Lassay (ed.).

CHAPTER TWELVE

Plants of the Divine Torture

I. ST. JOHN'S WORT AND THE RODS

IN ST. MATTHEW'S ACCOUNT OF THE SAVIOR'S last hours (Matt. 26–27), Pilate ordered that Jesus be beaten before being delivered to the Jews to be crucified; and the other evangelists confirm that he was scourged.

This cruel treatment, shown by the Shroud of Turin to have been literally atrocious, has always struck the minds of Christians of all lands; but in the fourteenth century, and especially the fifteenth, "an insatiable imagination," says the master, Émile Mâle, "set to work on all the circumstances of the Passion."[1] This was the time when the author of the *Orologe de la Passion*, John Quantin, described the scourging with such excess that one could say with Tauler that both "blood and flesh flowed"[2] on the divine body; the time when Olivier Maillard dared to specify the number of wounds that Jesus then received and which would have been, he said, five thousand four hundred seventy-five(!);[3] the time also when the illuminators and engravers on wood represented Christ at the pillar, literally riddled with wounds all over his body, "from the soles of his feet to the top of his head," as a sacred text says.

Broussolle reproduced one of these fourteenth-century miniatures from the Bibliothèque Nationale of Paris,[4] and Mâle a fifteenth-century woodcut from the same repository.[5]

To evoke the torture of this dreadful scourging, artists allegorically depicted bundles of rods that we surmise were hard and

---

1. Émile Mâle, op. cit., p. 85.
2. Tauler, *Exercitatio super Vita et Passione Salvatoris nostri*, CXXIV.
3. Olivier Maillard, *Hist. de la Passion* (1493) and see also, *Passio domini nostri Jesu Xri a reverendo p. Oliverii Maillard Parisius declamata*, Jehan Petit s. d. (1513).
4. Abbé Broussolle, *Le Christ de la Légende dorée*, p. 254.
5. *Cabinet des Estampes*, Bibliothèque Nationale — Mâle, op. cit., p. 104.

flexible, and impressive whips that angels hold on the vaults or friezes of so many churches of that time, as at Langeac in Treves, and in a hundred other places. They are also found in all the trophies of the Passion figured everywhere (Fig. 2). On the other hand, the people of the country, no doubt the first to evoke the poor Savior torn by wounds in all his flesh, chose a humble and precious plant, St. John's wort, which, about 1900, and since that time, I have heard called "Flagellation grass" in the Vendée.

Fig. 1. — *Full-grown leaves of the Millepertuis Forest of Fontainebleau, 1932.*

Two reasons have determined this choice: the first is that, among the plants native to our country, the *millepertuis* [St. John's wort][6] — and it is from this that its name is derived — bears leaves that are riddled with many small holes, (once called *pertuis*[7]) (Fig. 1), and the second is that St. John's wort is one of the best herbs for treatment of bleeding wounds, and all the old medical books praise the balm made from its leaves and flowers macerated in oil, as well as the wound-treatment obtained by their infusion in good wine.[8]

II. THE THORNS OF THE CROWN AND THE REED

We know, in particular, from the studies of Rohault de Fleury,[9] that the crown Jesus wore was not a band of two or three intertwined branches surrounding his head from forehead to occiput, but in reality a kind of cap or tiara made of extremely prickly marine rushes, *Zisiphus vulgaris*. In the thirteenth century, Bishop William Durandus of Mende was not mistaken: "The crown of thorns was braided," he says, "with marine rushes, as we have

6. The *Hypericum perforatum* of the botanists.
7. The literal translation of *millepertuis* would be then "a thousand small holes" — *Trans.*
8. See especially: Dr Vergnes, *Le Millepertuis*, in *Voile d'Isis*, tome XXXIV, (num. 115) pp. 482-85.
9. *Mémoire sur les Instruments de la Passion* (Paris: Lessort, 1870), *passim*.

Plants of the Divine Torture

seen in the treasure of the king of France, rushes whose tips are no less hard or sharp than thorns."[10]

The artists who, shortly after Durandus and since then, *represented* the crowned Savior were not so well-established as the good bishop, and figured a twist of two or three spiny strands of Western shrubs; it sometimes has the appearance of a simple braid, as on the forehead of Gerini's Christ, at the Santa Croce in Florence; the German artists, on the contrary, like Grünewald, make the crown a veritable bramble bush arranged in an inverted "magpie's nest" (Plate 22).

And it is in accord with these works of art, if not even before the arts, which hardly represented Christ with thorns on his head prior to the thirteenth century, that Christians of all ranks found a quite natural evocation of the painful diadem in the hostile stalks of the *hawthorn* and *bramble*, the *eglantine* and *rose-bush* that they saw daily. I have seen in a humble dwelling near Château-Neuf-sur-Sarthe (Maine-et-Loire) a crown made of two strands of braided hawthorn, fixed to the head of the bed and serving as a frame for a crucifix.

In the parody of royal coronation to which Pilate's lackeys subjected the Savior, a reed replaced the sovereign scepter and was put in his right hand, says St. Matthew.[11] We find this reed on many documents of the art from every age, either in the form of any rod whatsoever, or reeds from our rivers and marshes.

III. HYSSOP AND SPONGE

Now the Victim hangs on his gallows, nailed by His four limbs. His blood, which has already flowed from the wounds of his scourging, is gushing, now, out of the four holes made in his hands and feet by the nails; his life is exhausted as his veins are emptied, his body is shaken with spasms of agony, and a complaint escapes his fevered lips: "I thirst." And the soldiers who guarded him take a *sponge* and fix it to the end of a *hyssop* stalk, dip it in a vessel full

---

10. *Rationale divinorum officiorum*, Book VI, chap. LXXVII, 17.
11. Matthew 27:27–31.

of vinegar, and bring it to his mouth. "And when Jesus had taken the vinegar, he said: All is consummated, and gave up his spirit."[12]

Historically, this is how two humble plants entered, at the most tragic moment, into the emblematic future of the divine sacrifice:

A humble plant issuing from the bottom of the marine waters that purify all things, the sponge, used daily in bathings of everyday life; and the hyssop that the Mosaic Law used in rites of

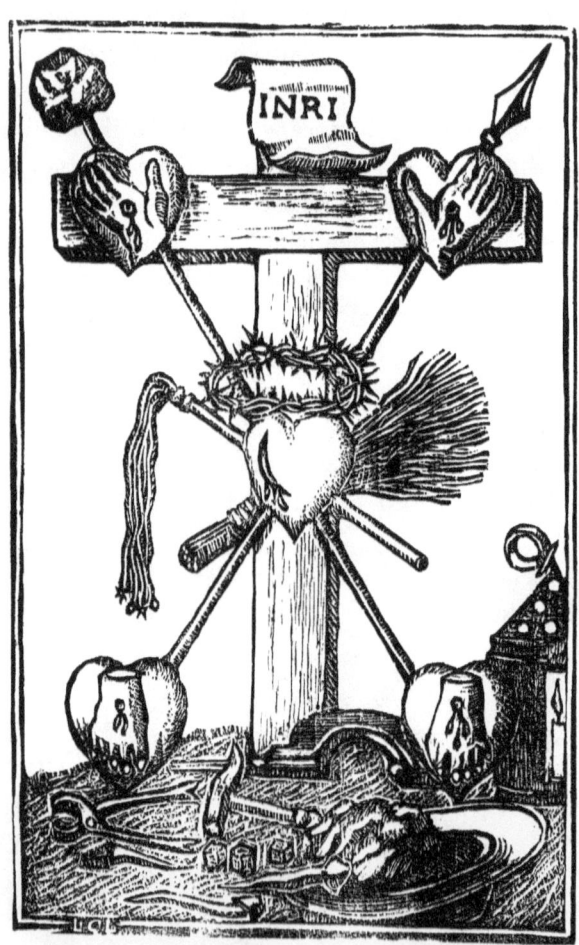

Fig. 2 — Engraving from the end of the 16th or 17th century. After an engraved copper plate from the monastery of the Capuchins of Aalst (Belgium). There we see, most notably, the sponge and the stem that bears it, the rods and the crown of thorns.

12. John 19:28–30.

Plants of the Divine Torture

purification, especially those concerned with the leprosy of men[13] and houses,[14] with those who tend the dead,[15] and the sacrifice of the red cow,[16] the hyssop, whose name is on the lips of the Christian liturgy when it sings after David: *Asperges me hyssopo et mundabor*, "Sprinkle me with the hyssop and I shall be cleansed."[17] Both sponge and hyssop were the last two objects that touched, while he was still alive, the supreme purifier, about whom John the Baptist had spoken: "Behold the Lamb of God. Behold, him who taketh away the sin of the world."[18]

And this is why the sponge and the stem of hyssop figure in all the trophies and "*Arma Christi*" (Fig. 2), in the figures of the symbolic *Etimacia*, in the mystical representations of the Last Judgment.

Sketch of the keystone of the lateral aisle of Glasgow Cathedral, sent to the author by an English correspondent, in 1923. Charbonneau-Lassay archives. An engraving on wood was created by the author from this sketch and printed in The Bestiary of Christ[19] *(ed.).*

13. Leviticus 14:2–8.
14. Ibid., 14:49–53.
15. Numbers 19:18.
16. Ibid., 19:6.
17. Psalm 51 (50 Vulgate).
18. John 1:29.
19. French ed. (op. cit.), p. 101, fig. IX. The 1991 English translation of *The Bestiary of Christ* does not reproduce this figure. — *Trans.*

Plate 22. — Crucifixion by Matthias Grünewald, polyptych for the altarpiece of Isenheim (Germany), 16th century. Bramble bush crown arranged in an inverted "magpie's nest." Photo Giraudon. Archives of the review Regnabit, 1921–1929 (ed.).

CHAPTER THIRTEEN

The Garden of the Wounded Christ

I. THE STRAWBERRY AND STRAWBERRY PLANT

THE MEDICINAL PROPERTIES OF THE strawberry plant and its fruit, although always held in less favor, are similar to those of St. John's wort. They can however explain its entry into the flora of the wounded Christ.

Matthiolus tells us in fact that "the leaves and root of this plant are very well adapted to cure wounds and ulcers, and curtail all bloody stools."[1]

Those illuminators who so skillfully decorated the fine manuscripts of the Middle Ages seem to have left us — in the frequent use they have made of representations of the fruiting strawberry plants — a reflection of the symbolism attached to this plant. They have brought it, a little everywhere and most graciously, into their decorative works; but more especially, it seems, into those pages devoted to the festivals of the Savior's and the martyrs' sufferings.

A *Book of Hours* manuscript from the fifteenth century, in the Clermont-Ferrand library, contains a "descent from the cross" accompanied by a band decorated with the image of various plants among which is the strawberry.

I have before me the reproduction of two miniatures of German origin published by Father Karl Richstaetter. Their ornamentation is made of strawberries and strawberry leaves in the midst of stylized palms: on the first, an angel holds, by its strap, a shield charged with the wounded heart and the four other wounds of Jesus (Fig. 1); on the second, two angels spread a veil bearing the same motif (fifteenth century)[2] (Fig. 2).

---

[1] *Les commentaires sur Dioscoride*, ed. 1655, Liv. IV, Chap. XXXVIII, p. 385.
[2] Karl Richstaetter, S.J., *Die Herz-Jesu-Verehrung des deutschen Mittelalters* (Paderborn: Bonifacius, 1919), p. 406.

Part IV: Plants Emblematic of Christ's Five Wounds

Fig. 1. — *From a breviary, 1470–1480. According to K. Richstaetter, op. cit.*

Fig. 2. — *Einlegebildchen, 15th century. According to K. Richstaetter, op. cit.*

In a work by Alphonse Labitte[3] we find the reproduction of a late fifteenth-century decoration made entirely of flowering branches and strawberry fruit, and the whole surrounds a liturgical salutation to the divine Victim, to the "salutary Victim," the *O salutaris hostia*.

In the very rich collection of the scholarly bibliophile from Marseille, Pierre Labarre, a fifteenth-century Book of Hours written, it is believed, at the abbey of Saint-Victor of Marseille, bears, on the page where the "Office of the Holy Cross" begins, a frame of strawberry branches.

The same collection contains another medieval manuscript that includes, also at the "Office of the Holy Cross," a strawberry branch with its leaves, flowers, and fruit. Finally, side by side with the previous item, a superb book, executed in 1518 for the marriage of Marguerite de Lévis-Mirepoix to Miraud de Vériville,

3 Alphonse Labitte, *Les manuscrits et l'art de les armes* (Paris: Menais, 1893), fol. 322.

bears on the page with the wording *Missa de Quinque plagis Christi*, a most lovely border of strawberry leaves, flowers, and fruit.

Concerning this last item, Labarre has affirmed: "I believe, like you, that this decoration of strawberries adorning the Mass of the Five Wounds of Christ is a symbolic decoration. This can also be proven with other examples."[4]

We can thus conclude that, even if the strawberry was not exclusively reserved by the arts at the end of the Middle Ages to emblematically decorate the pages devoted to the divine torture, this plant was at least, for this use, the object of a marked preference on their part. And this preference is consistent with the medicinal properties then recognized by the ordinary pharmacopeia.

Does not the reddish hue of unequal intensity, formerly known as the "color of crushed strawberry," remind us, together with the appearance of a bloody flesh, of those old brocades and moiré silks from which the red altar vestments are often made and used for the solemnities of the dolorous Christ and the martyrs?

II. THE POPPY

After the first sermons which presented to the people — in the light of the Gospel accounts — the Savior abused on all sides by his tormentors, Christians, contemplating in spirit, continuing to follow these accounts, their Savior hung upon the wood of his torment, could not but represent him completely bathed in the blood issuing from the punctures of his crown, the lacerations from his scourging reopened by the wrenching off of his robe, the jagged holes of the nails and the spear cleaving his heart deep in his chest. And the red body of the sacrificed One, upraised between earth and sky by the shaft of the cross, appeared to them like a purple flower outstretched by the Earth towards Heaven in a supreme gesture of repentance, love, and hope.

And when, going out after their prayers, the faithful went along country paths, the red flowers, bright red and blooming in the verdure, appeared to them like distant images of the redemptive flower, blooming in the scarlet and the purple of its sacrifice. So too was

4 Letter to the author, July 31, 1924.

Christ a flower for the learned themselves: did not St. Jerome write, towards the end of the fourth century, "Our flower is the destruction of death; and died that death itself might die in his dying."[5]

And on the lips of those who knew, having come from leafing through the biblical verses which, by the same love for their Savior, they also associated with the coral, the blood of the murex, the hematite, carnelian, ruby and the precious carbuncle: in Genesis the Messiah "washes his vesture in the blood of grapes";[6] in Isaiah he "treads the winepress" of Bosra and emerges blood-red;[7] in the Apocalypse he appears as a horseman covered with a coat dyed with blood, and riding a white horse,[8] etc.

Prior to the introduction of the rose to our Western countries, surely the poppy of the fields, the red poppy, was the first to seem a perfect evocation of him whom the holy books show dressed in red, which is probably why we often find it in the sculptural art of France.[9] Is not the shape of this flower a little like a dress, and its color of the most beautiful red? So it seems that Honorius of Autun identifies it with the "flower of the fields" of Solomon's *Song*, which was always regarded as an emblematic figure of Christ.

The mantle, the red garment was already in early antiquity an attribute of sovereign princes, which is why, in the praetorium of Pilate, his persecutors threw a scarlet cloth over the shoulders of the humiliated Savior: *Et induunt eum purpura... et ceperunt salutare eum: Ave, Rex Judaeorum.*[10] In the Middle Ages the supreme judges were also dressed in red because they had the power to punish by death, and so also the executioners who shed blood by the authority of the former. This is probably why Saint Bruno d'Asti attributes the red color to justice.

5 Letter 75, *To Theodora*, trans. W. H. Fremantle, in *A Select Library of Nicene and Post-Nicene Fathers of the Christian Church*, Second Series, Vol. VI, *St. Jerome: Letters and Select Works* (Oxford: James Parker & New York: The Christian Literature Co., 1893), p. 155.
6 Genesis 49:11.
7 Isaiah 63ff.
8 Apocalypse 19:13.
9 See E. Lambin, *La Flore des grandes Cathédrales de France* (Paris: Aux bureaux de la Semaine des constructeurs, 1897), p. 64.
10 Mark 16:17, 18.

The Garden of the Wounded Christ

The Knights of St. John of Jerusalem, today known as Malta, once wore a red habit to go to battle, both because their Order was born where the Lord's blood flowed and because they should remember to be always ready to shed their own in his service.

Less well-known, the Johannite monks were also attired in red: "There is," says the Protestant Alexander Ross, "an order of Johannites [who] wear a red garment to represent Christ's blood, and on the breast thereof is woven a chalice, to show that in his blood our sins are washed."[11]

No flower of our region was more suitable than the humble poppy to symbolize these clothes, themselves memorials of the redeeming blood, and whose emblematic sense Christians of former days understood just as Christians of today understand the emblematic sense of black, red, white, or purple liturgical vestments in the offices of the Church.

III. LYCHNIS

In the general body of flower lore, this plant is related to the symbolism of Christ illuminating souls, as we shall see later on with the carbuncle, sometimes called *Lychnites* by the ancient Greeks,[12] that is connected to the symbolism of his blood. We allude to it here only insofar as it is tied to the remembrance of the Lord's Passion, whence the name, the *Lychnis-Cross of Jerusalem*,[13] commonly given to it everywhere.

IV. THE RED ROSE

The Rose was charged by the human spirit with a great number of superimposed symbolic meanings, but we have to speak here only of the red rose, which the entire Middle Ages has called "the Rose of the Passion."

11 *Pansebeia: or, a View of All the Religions in the World*, 6th ed. (London: Gillyflower & Freeman, 1696), p. 241.
12 Lucian calls it *The Lamp*, Lychnis in *The Syrian Goddess* (trans. H. A. Strong [London: Constable, 1913], p. 72).
13 See *Catalogues Villemorin-Andrieux*, Paris; and all others.

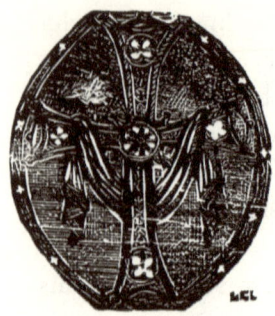

Fig. 3. — *Central motif of a fresco at Deir-el-Abiad, 5th–6th century. See G. Lefebvre,* Dict. arch. Chrét., *loc. cit.*

Fig. 4. — *German document published by K. Richstaetter, op. cit.*

Fig. 5. — *German document published by K. Richstaetter, op. cit.*

Already in the twelfth century the *Mystical Vine*, attributed by some (making it a little older than it really was) to the pen of St. Bernard,[14] dedicated seven chapters to *"the Rose of the Passion"* as an emblem of the divine blood that flowed — from the circumcision of Jesus to the spear thrust on Calvary — by seven effusions, says the author. Thus we read in the twenty-third chapter: "Behold how the crimsoned Jesus blossomed forth in this rose. See his whole body; is there a single spot where the rose is not found?... Examine the wound of his side, for the rose is still there, although of a paler red because of the admixture of water."[15] We find this scarlet rose, blooming in the opening of the divine side and in the blood spurting from each of the other four great wounds of the Crucified, celebrated by the arts until the decline of pure and great Christian symbolism during the sixteenth century.

Among the Christians of Egypt, before Islamism, the wounds of the Lord were symbolically represented by roses or eglantines. Thus it was that, on a fresco of Deir-el-Abiad, rose-like flowers mark the place of divine wounds on the wood of the Cross[16] (Fig. 3).

Barbier de Montault also noticed this Rose of the Passion on a host-iron of the thirteenth century, and another one of the thirteenth from Saint-Médard, Thouars

14 Now attributed to St. Bonaventure. — Translator.
15 *The Works of Bonaventure*, vol. 1: *Mystical Opuscula*, trans. José de Vinck (Quincy, IL: St. Anthony's Guild Press, 1960), p. 200.
16 See G. Lefebvre, *Deir-el-Abiad*, in *Dictionnaire d'Archéologie Chrétienne et de Liturgie*, tome IV, vol. I, col. grav. 3663.

(Deux-Sevres).¹⁷ At the same time, many knights of France and neighboring countries placed on their shields a cross cantoned by four roses as a *Signaculum Domini*: an *Arma Christi* escutcheon from the fourteenth century, painted on a manuscript from Paris' Arsenal Library, presents us with a set of the Instruments of the Passion in which the Rose marks the location of the five wounds of Jesus.¹⁸

Other examples. Two German documents of the fifteenth century, published by Father Richstaetter: the first one represents the Divine Heart pierced by the spear, surrounded by a kind of "rosary of the five wounds" where each wound is represented in the calyx of a rose (Fig. 4); the second consists of an angel holding a vertically raised rose in which rests the heart of Jesus, the source of redeeming blood¹⁹ (Fig. 5).

Fig. 6. — Germanic document sent by Rev. Leon de Lyon.

I owe to Father Leon de Lyon, curator of the Franciscan Museum in Rome, another Germanic document a little older than the preceding ones. On this we also see, in the center of a rose, the heart pierced vertically by the spear (Fig 6).

On some fifteenth century works of art we even see an entire rose bush in bloom with five evocative roses, such as the one a Rodez sculptor stylized on the divine crest placed at the foot of the statue of Christ in this city's cathedral (Fig. 7).

Fig. 7. — The Five Roses on an eschuteon sculpted under the feet of a statue of Christ standing in the cathedral of Rodez, 15th century. According to an anonymous sketch.

The sixteenth century continued, at least in its first half, the same tradition, and one of the most expressive

---

17 *Traité d'iconographie chrétienne*, tome 2 (Paris: Société de librairie ecclésiastique et religieuse, 1898), pp. 155–56.
18 Arsenal Library, num. 288.
19 K. Richstaetter, *Deutsche Herz Jesu Gebete, 14 und 15 Jahrhunderts* (Regensburg: Kösel & Pustet, 1921), pp. 38 and 51.

Part IV: Plants Emblematic of Christ's Five Wounds

figurations is that of the Holy Spear, on an altar canon card in the royal abbey of Fontevrault embroidered for Charles of Lorraine, Archbishop of Rheims: the sacred weapon stands upright and, along its shaft, the blood falls in large drops which, at its foot, turn into a large rose (Fig. 8).

Some examples are still to be found in the next two centuries in popular works still somewhat traditional, such as this curious processional cross of Levens, in Provence, which carries as trophies most of the objects mentioned in the evangelical accounts of the Passion, and, at its center, the heart of Jesus on a stylized rose[20] (Fig. 9).

Since that time, the impassioned symbolism of the rose has disappeared in Western Europe; perhaps it has been slightly better preserved in the Danubian countries: the most recent document I was able to collect comes from Walachia. It is a drawing of a tomb from the nineteenth century, signed Lancelot and dated 1860. A large rose fills the central junction of a cross, and four others mark the place of nails (Fig. 10). This is the traditional type.[21]

Fig. 8. — *Detail of the ornamentation of an altar canon of Cardinal Charles of Lorraine, 16th century.*

The red rose is undeniably then one of the iconographic emblems of the blood of Jesus Christ and his wounds, the main one in particular, "the ever-living wound in the side of the Crucified One."[22]

V. AMARANTH

The varieties of this plant form a family endowed with a very extensive habitat area, since *Amarantes* flourish from India to the Far West. The most beautiful are those called Early Splendor (*Amaranthus tricolor*), which is fiery red; Cockscomb (*Celosia*

20 Communication from Father J. Catteau of Nice, 1924.
21 Library of the Count of Monti de Rezé, Castle of Fief-Milon, Le Boupère (Vendée).
22 Marcel Prévost, *La retraite ardente* (Paris: Flammarion, 1927), p. 74.

Fig. 9. — Processional cross from Levens (Maritime-Alps), 17th–18th century.   *Fig. 10. — Tomb from a cemetery in Walachia, 19th century.*

cristata), of various red hues; the *Soleil Levant* amaranth whose flowers and leaves are carmine red; Love-Lies-Bleeding (*Amaranthus caudatus*), a beautiful blood-red, which was more especially *the* red hue for the popular symbolism in the West. Its flowers bloom in a paniculated spike and their terminal plume falls like a sheaf of stalactites of coagulated blood.

The amaranth possesses this property, which from early times held the attention of men: cut and dried out, its flowers keep their color and, when soaked in water, recover their freshness and their stem its greenness: "*Armarantum purpureum*," says Matthiolus, "is a kind of red cluster... the more it is cut back, the more beautiful it becomes... Once it is dried, after no more flowers are found, and soaked in the water, it will grow green again and serve to make garlands and bouquets in winter..."[23] That is why this flower was named *Amarantos* by the ancient Greeks, "the unwithering one," which explains why it was made one of the emblems for "perpetual duration," "immortality."

The amaranth, later dedicated by the Christian people to the evocation of the divine blood because of its color, combined with this emblematic role, because of its ancient symbolism, the role of symbolizing the perpetual duration of the redemptive efficacy as well, just as the previously seen symbolic drawing of the "Three Precincts" represents the infinite immensity of its reach.[24]

VI. THE ADONIDE

All mythologists have related the misfortune of Adonis, that admirable ephebe whom Venus loved, and who a boar ferociously tore from her formidable defenses.[25] While falling on the grass, the fable tells us further, the drops of Adonis's blood were changed into so many unknown flowers which have preserved since then, for the admiration of men enveloped by their delicate fragrance, the beauty of the blood of Adonis. This flower of such marvelous origin would be, the ancients tell us, our *red anemone*, to which the botanists have given the name of *Adonis Æstivalis*, the *Adonis*, still called the "Drop of Blood" by country folk in Italy.[26]

More Christian, the dialects of our southern regions of France call the adonide the "Sangue de Diou," the "blood of God."[27] There is no need to belabor the point: the purple adonis has in this way entered into the flower lore of Christ Jesus. Was it first expressed by a Montpellier humanist, a gardener in the Aude valley, or a country squire from Gascogny? What matter, since the inspiration was happy and our French folklore gained, for its part, one more flower in the Redeemer's sheaf.

23 Op. cit., Liv. IV, Chap. LII, p. 390.
24 Cf. Part 3, Chap. 10.
25 See in particular: Mario Meunier, *La légende dorée des dieux et des héros* (Paris: Librairie de France, 1925), p. 133.
26 See Angelo de Gubernatis, *Mythologie des Plantes*, tome I (Paris: Reinwald, 1878), p. 285.
27 Anon., *Remedies and Recipes*, p. 32. [No further information provided. — Trans.]

VII. GENTIAN

A short mention should also be made of the gentian. Known for its remarkable medicinal properties, discovered by Gentius, King of Illyria, in the second century before our era, the gentian exhibits in its root a particularity that has not escaped ancient Christian herbalists, and brought it, through them and by the paths of folklore, into the emblematic realm of the dolorous Christ, under the name of *Gentiane Croisette* or *Gentiane croisetée* [crosslet gentian].

Old Matthiolus explains it as follows: "It produces red flowers on top surrounding the peak of the stem. Its root is white and long and very bitter to the taste, and is interrupted here and there in several places, in the manner of a cross, from which it derives its name: the *Cruciata*."[28]

VIII. PASSIONFLOWER

Lastly we have the most singular and exceedingly gracious of flowers dedicated to the memory of the Savior's sufferings. Its entry into the flora of Christ is not very old, since it is generally accepted that this plant was introduced into Europe by the first Spanish monks returning from America; and it is a fact that they acclimated the passionflower of the New World to Spain. It was first known in France under the name of *grenadille*, because of the Kingdom of Granada, the first European land to see it bloom.

Other documents seem to indicate that the West knew of the passionflower a little earlier, either through the Crusades or through the first travelers returning from South and Central Asia, a part of the world where it grows.

What is no less certain, this strange flower began to enjoy, in the sixteenth century among Catholics of the West, a vogue that started first — to borrow an expression of Edmond Joly — by "crucifying the slender fingers of Spanish virgins."[29] This is because, leaning over it to pluck its petals, the people, by their loving regard, saw in its component parts the venerated forms of almost

---

28 Op. cit., Liv. III, Chap. III.
29 Edmond Joly, *Theotokos. — Marie dans l'Art* (Paris: Spes, 1932), p. 78.

all the objects involved in the torture of the Son of God: the thorny crown, the hammers and nails, the cross, the vessel of bitter drink, and finally the very heart of the Savior upheld on the tip of a spear. The passionflower, says Huysmans, is that "unique blossom of a purplish blue, its seed-vessel simulating the cross, its styles and stigmas the nails; its stamens mimicking the hammer; its thread-like fringe the crown of thorns — in short, it represents all the instruments of the Passion"[30] (Fig. 11).

IX. THE PAULOWNIA FLOWER

The paulownia, originally from Japan, was introduced to Europe only in recent times, and received its current name from Anna Paulownia, daughter of Tzar Paul I of Russia, who reigned from 1796 to 1801. The entrance of this flower into the florary of Christ is not therefore old; the testimony of Father Leon de Lyon convinced me, however, that in certain monastic settings, at least in Danubian countries, the Japanese flower now bears a genuine allegorical trait: it conveys the mourning of the mother of Jesus at the burial of her Son.

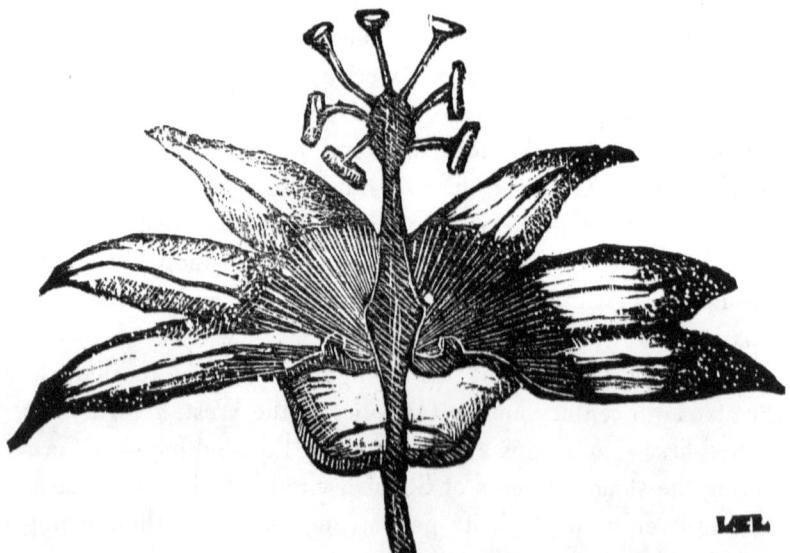

Fig. 11. — Cross-section of a Passionflower.

30 *The Cathedral*, trans. C. Bell (London: Kegan Paul, Trench, Trubner, 1922), p. 201.

Even though, in these same regions, the shape of the leaves and fruit of the paulownia have connected it with the iconic heart of Jesus Christ, we will speak here only of its flower (Fig. 12).

The Evangelists tell us that Joseph of Arimathea asked Pilate for the body of the Lord, and this was granted. Joseph therefore had the Savior taken down from his cross to bury him. The same sacred authors also specify that Mary Magdalene and Mary mother of Joseph were present at this funereal scene, but do not speak of Mary, the mother of Jesus. Nevertheless, St. John, having written that before the Victim's last breath, his mother stood with himself at the foot of the cross, Christian art, from the first millennium, always placed Mary among the witnesses of the descent from the cross, and towards the end of the Middle Ages, it depicted her sitting on the ground with the corpse of her son on her lap. Great was and great remains the fondness for this theme in Catholic statuary and piety: henceforth these "pietàs" will be for all time.

And it is to this dolorous Virgin that deeply moved souls have dedicated the paulownia flower. Its mauve color, of a very soft bluish tint, is suitable for the superhuman resignation of her who had the strength to climb Calvary on the bloody trail of her Son, and stay there until the end. Now the paulownia flowers, nestled one within the other, held together by a thread and joined in a circle, are placed each year, in May, on the neck and brow of the statues of the mother who weeps over the torn, pierced and stiff corpse of her Son.

Let the curtain fall now on the sight of these flowers gathered to recall the redemptive tragedy: it is a poem written, painted, and carved by our fathers, with all their faith and their most ardent love.

Fig. 12. — The flower of the Paulownia.

Part IV: Plants Emblematic of Christ's Five Wounds

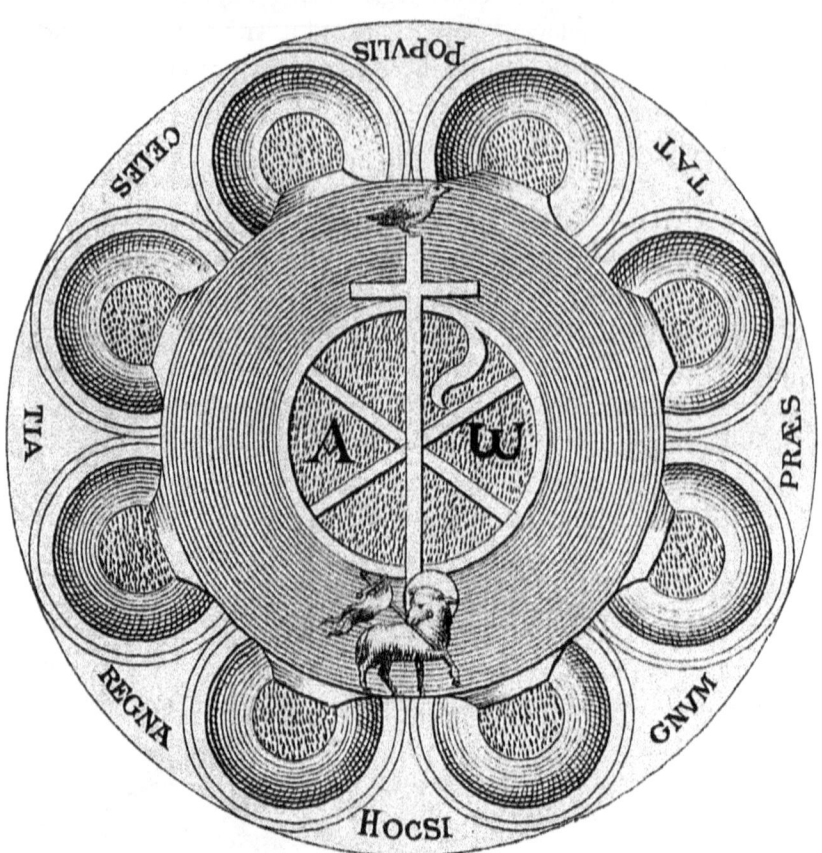

Plate 22. — The Rose of Saint John, the altar stone of Besançon cathedral, 10th century. This was the emblematic rose used for the cover of the original edition of the Bestiary of Christ *(ed.).*

FIFTH PART

*Stones Emblematic
of the
Wounded Christ*

CHAPTER FOURTEEN

Stones of the Passion

I. THE CRIMSON JEWEL CASE
OF THE REDEEMER

AT AN EARLY PERIOD CHRISTIAN SYMbolism devoted gemstones of a red color to the cult of the blood that the God-Man shed for the salvation of the world and of the wounds through which the divine blood left his heart where it had been wrought.

Thus we see arrayed, in the jewel case of the Son of God, the carbuncle, which is a dark red ruby, the balas ruby, which is the royal ruby (from the Greek *balen*, king, *baleinaios*, royal) and represents the light red color of the human blood's *serum*, the garnet, hyacinth, hematite, carnelian and red coral, which represent, along with the carbuncle, the dark tint of the blood's *coagulum*. Not only were these gems the preferred choice for the decoration of reliquaries related to mementos of the Passion and to depict the sacred wounds in the *Signaculum Domini*, but sometimes even for marking their anatomical position on the very body of the Crucified. When, along with these red stones, the diamond and the rock crystal, its poor relation, or even the golden topaz are used, this is only to recall the divine nature of the sacrificed Victim and his kingship.

Here are some examples:

—A Christ of the twelfth or thirteenth century, property of Canon Berjat, vice-rector of Fourvières, at Lyon (1923), bears at the location of the wound in the side a light red and transparent precious stone; probably a balas ruby. This beautiful work of medieval art is 35 centimeters high overall, while the Savior's body, from the feet to the top of the crown, measures 14 centimeters (Plate 23).

—An inventory of the treasure of the cathedral church of Paris, drawn up on July 23, 1416, contains the following mention: "The cross of gold has VIII large emeralds and XXI balays, the one in the middle larger than the others. On the diadem of the crucifix

Part V: Stones Emblematic of the Wounded Christ

Plate 23. — *The wound in the side of Jesus, marked by a ruby on the left side. Crucifix 12th–13th century belonging to Canon Berjat of Lyon. Photo from the collection of the review* Regnabit, *1921–1929.*

are IIII large diamonds and the nails of the two arms and feet have III large diamonds; in the crown on the head are VIII small diamonds, with an empty place for a balay in the breast; there are XXII pairs of large pearls under the diadem, and in the diadem are III bezels, and in each one three pearls..."[1]

If the notary who made the inventory of the metropolitan treasure of Paris specified without hesitating that the empty place in the breast of the Crucified was missing a balas ruby, this is because he knew by testimony that there was previously a stone of this nature to be found there, or else that other examples known to him assured him of this.

— In his book *The Rhine*, Victor Hugo, describing Freiburg cathedral, wrote the following: "What I admired most in one chapel museum was a Byzantine figure of Christ, about five feet high, brought from Palestine by a bishop of Freiburg. Both Christ and the cross are of gilded copper, enriched with brilliant stones. Christ, fashioned in a barbarian style, is clad in a finely crafted tunic; a large uncut ruby represents the wound in the side. A stone statue of the bishop, with its back to a nearby wall, contemplates it adoringly."[2]

— On evidence, which should be incontestable, from Count Claude of Monti de Rezé, I can reference here with complete assurance another medieval Christ unearthed near Plougasnou (Finistère), which he had in hand and that bore, inlaid in the middle of the chest, an oblong, non-translucent, red stone, most likely a hematite or carnelian. This Christ was of bronze.

II. THE "RAYS OF THE ESCARBUNCLE"

Among precious stones, the escarbuncle foremost and the balas ruby have captured the attention of the early symbolists of the wound in the side of Jesus: what marvelous things are told about these precious gems! The old fictions of the naturalists of Antiquity tell us that escarbuncles were formed in the head of the most terrifying, dreadful asps, and that only powerful spells would let them

---

[1] Cf. *Revue archéologique*, 2nd series, tome XXVII (1874), p. 399.
[2] Victor Hugo, *Le Rhin*, Edit. Nelson, tome II, p. 147.

be taken away: "You should know that the asp carries in its head the very shiny and precious stone called a carbuncle, and when the magician who wants to remove the stone speaks his words, as soon as the fierce creature realizes it, it puts one of its ears into the ground and covers up the other with its tail, and in this manner it becomes deaf and does not hear the words of the conjuration."[3]

And then there is the assurance that, "by the will of our Lord Jesus Christ," the escarbuncle stone shines in the darkness; also Guillaume de Machaut (c. 1300–1377), writing to Agnes of Navarre, tells her: "All those with sight compare you to the escarbuncle that lights up the darkest night."[4]

And, if we can believe Estienne Binet, who wrote in 1600, the balas ruby also emits luminous rays: "once set in place the ruby shoots forth a cloud-encircled fire; suspended in the air, it blazes and, because of this, is called the balas ruby. In Italy, *baleno* means lightning."[5]

Also our "chansons de gestes" and the legends of our provinces are themselves full of these marvelous fables. Knights of the epics carry off at spear- or sword-point the crimson escarbuncle. Elsewhere, all night long heavenly carbuncles enclosed at the heart of crystal ciboriums illuminate sanctuaries of dream and castles of faerie where invincible and formidable warriors prostrate themselves with face in the dust before the angels who carry the Grail.

We will see later that in the fifteenth century the mystics of the "Estoile Internelle," most likely thinking of this divine Grail, represent the wound in the side of Jesus by a mass which, set in a ciborium, overtops its rim. This could be the figure of an escarbuncle or of any red stone whatever, as well as clotted blood.

From the color of blood, to which the color of the escarbuncle and ruby is actually related, as also from their completely fictitious nocturnal luminosity and radiance, springs everything that the symbolists have imagined in order to glorify, by these precious

---

3 Brunetto Latini, *The Book of the Treasure* (*Li Livres dou Tresor*), I, 139, trans. Paul Barrette and Spurgeon Baldwin (New York and London: Garland, 1993), p. 109.
4 Guillaume de Machaut, *Le livre dou voir dit*.
5 Estienne Binet, *Merveilles de la nature*.

stones, the "most precious and divine blood of Jesus Christ": is it not from the spear-thrust and from his heart still filled with blood that the light promised "to every man coming into this world"[6] has

Fig. 1. — *Painting from the end of the 15th century. Netherlandish school. Rays and blood issue together from the divine side.*

sprung forth, the light promised to the ancient nations who, to speak as the Church does, "sat then in darkness and the shadow of death"? Surely it is to evoke this heart, bleeding fount and luminous source, that at the end of the fifteenth century a painter from the Netherlandish School, whose work is at Brussels, made both rays and blood spurt from the wound in the side of Jesus (Fig. 1).

6 John 1:9.

Part V: Stones Emblematic of the Wounded Christ

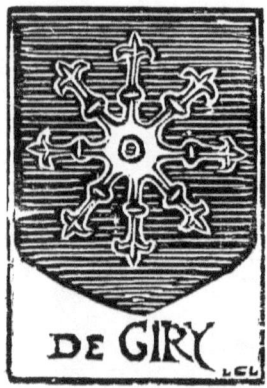

Fig. 2. — *The Rays of the Escarbuncle on the blazon of the de Giry family.*

And also, to symbolize this blood and light, since the twelfth century heraldists have represented the escarbuncle on the escutcheons of the nobility by a central ring from which proceed eight very stylized rays decorated with fleurons, the sum total of which is akin to the patibular monogram for the word Xhrist — as it was written then — the letter X placed on the ✠. And this figure was called the "Rays of the Escarbuncle"[7] (Fig. 2). In the twelfth century, the sovereign counts of Anjou, the Plantagenets, adopted it for their personal arms, and this is why we see it on the shield of Geoffroy Plantagenet on a large enamel from Mans. On the royal doorway of Chartres cathedral the large shield held by the Twins bears the same "Rays of the Escarbuncle," with a precious gem cut in five facets at its center (Fig. 3).

The "Rays of the Escarbuncle" also decorate the shield that Thibaut of Champagne bears on his large equestrian seal.[8] And the Abbey of Saint Victor in Paris likewise bore the "Rays of the Escarbuncle" in its arms; from there it has recently passed to the coat of arms of Fontenay-sous-Bois, near Paris, a former territorial dependency of the famous abbey.[9]

This favor bestowed by medieval and Christic symbolism on the escarbuncle ruby and the balas ruby

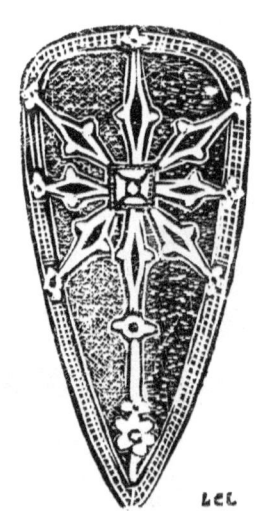

Fig. 3. — *The Escarbuncle and its "rays" on the large shield of the Gemini on Chartres cathedral, 13th century.*

---

7 That is, the radiance of the escarbuncle.
8 Archives nationales, Paris.
9 Cf. P. Le Cour, *L'Arbre sacré*, in *Atlantis*, tome VI (1932), p. 44.

182

explains why Saint Peter Alcantara, speaking of the wound to the side and heart of Jesus, calls it "this ruby of priceless worth."[10]

At times an emerald, topaz, or sapphire was transposed into the "Rays of the Escarbuncle," but even in this case the name *Rays of the Escarbuncle* was retained in heraldic language, even though it was expressing the diurnal shining of the aforesaid stones and even though its center was of their color. It was said then to be "allumé" with *sinople* for the emerald, *or* for the topaz, and *azure* for the sapphire.

Thus the arms for the dukes of Cleves, for example, were emblazoned "gules, with rays of the escarbuncle or allumé sinople," and the Schomberg "gules, with rays of the escarbuncle allumé azure." And that proves to the heraldist of today that this transposition of precious stones other than the Christic escarbuncle and ruby into the rays is a concession subsequent to an original rule.

Besides, this concession is justified by the fact that the medieval symbolic system devoted all precious stones to God-made-man: in the spirit of this symbolism the diamond, the pearl and the white rock crystal represent Christ's divinity, the purity of his earthly life, and also wine, which is his eucharistic blood; the topaz, his universal sovereignty and his triumphal resurrection; all the red stones represent his blood and, by this very fact, allude to his dolorous Passion and death; the sapphire, turquoise, emerald, olivine, and aquamarine were emblems of his royalty and his power over heaven and earth; jade and the dark stones symbolized his descent into hell, etc.

III. GEMS OF THE TORTURED CHRIST

Stones of secondary value, hematite (the name is derived from the Greek word *haima*, blood), jacinth, carnelian, and coral — more often utilized than the more precious and costly ruby and garnet — represent just the blood of the Redeemer. To hematite and carnelian the popular beliefs of the Middle Ages attributed various

---

10 *Treatise on Prayer and Meditation,* trans. D. Devas O. F. M. (Charlotte NC: TAN Books, 2008), p. 75.

properties, the chief one of which was the staunching of the flow of blood from wounds; the bishop of Rennes, Marbode, who died in 1123, has assured us of this.[11]

The mystical symbolism of these stones was revealed in sacred texts applied by the Church to Jesus Christ: "He was clothed in a robe dipped in blood."[12] "Your lips are as a scarlet thread."[13] "Who is this that cometh from Edom, with dyed garments from Bosra... Why then is thy apparel red?"[14] etc.

And, when the coral was mottled with white patches, the Song of Solomon was called upon: "My beloved is white and red."[15]

In the art of ancient jewelry, beads of carnelian, hematite, jasper and coral, fashioned into the form of droplets and inserted

Fig. 4. — *Italian jewel with silver filigree and three "droplets" of red coral. Toulouse, 1925.*

Fig. 5. — *"Droplet" of red coral in a silver setting, 17th century. Owned by Mme Gandon of Temple Loudun (Vienne), 1926.*

into gold, silver or bronze settings, were worn as a pendant or, as it was called at the time, a "pentacol," and piety connected these objects to the symbolism of the blood of Jesus (Fig. 5). Would jewelry of this kind made in more recent centuries, not with a single drop, but with three, have any relationship to the cult of the three drops of the blood of Jesus Christ contained in a costly reliquary

11   Cf. Marbode, *Le Lapidaire*, XX, de Corneolo.
12   Apocalypse 19:13.
13   Solomon, Song of Songs 4:3.
14   Isaiah 63:1-2.
15   Song of Songs 5:10.

discovered at Mantua in April 1605 and in honor of which Vincent IV of Gonzaga, duke of Mantua, established the Military Order of Knights of the Precious Blood (Fig. 4)?

With the exception of the escarbuncle, heraldry ordinarily represents all other precious stones as small lozenges, or rectangles crossed by at least four lines, or by hemispheric beads. On the *Signaculum Domini* of the *Estoile Internelle* this is how the five wounds are represented (Fig. 6). And these words, which indicate that our Savior was wounded for our iniquities, accompany the emblem: *Ipse autem vulneratus est propter iniquitates nostras.*

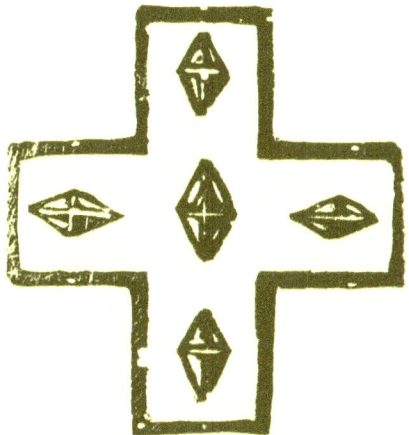

Fig. 6. — The jeweled Signaculum Domini *of the* Estoile Internelle, *end of 15th century.*

Plate 24. — Crucifixion scene, attributed to the Master of Marienlebens. A standard, held by Saint Hippolytus, bears the sign of the Rays of the Escarbuncle, or on a gules field on the original painting, a symbol of the radiant wound in the side of Jesus. Church of Saint Ursula, Cologne (Germany), ca. 1466. Photo Giraudon. Archives of the review Regnabit, *1921-1929.*

CHAPTER FIFTEEN

The Holy Grail

I. THE EMBLEMATIC OF THE HOLY GRAIL

AS WE HAVE PREVIOUSLY SEEN,[1] IN THE religious art at the end of the Middle Ages a schematic representation of the wound in the side of Jesus quite often appears under the form of an elongated ellipse from which fall, at times, drops of blood.

Moreover, the artists of that time have set this reference to the injury from the spear-thrust horizontally in the open bowl of a ciborium, and this theme recurs so often in their works that we clearly need to explain its frequency. This is because it is an allusion to a poetic theme that, in Western Christianity and during the entire Middle Ages, enjoyed the greatest favor in all social circles: the *Tale* or *Legend of the Holy Grail* or *Graal*.

At the time, this word *graal* had a very clear meaning for everyone: a *graal*[2] was a vessel. Even today the country folk of the basins of the upper Garonne and its tributaries say a *grazal*, while those of Provence say a *gral*, *gralon*, or *grallon*. What is actually involved, then, is a sacred vessel whose "story," wondrous beyond all others since it begins at the very foot of the throne of the Eternal, is everywhere told.

When therefore Lucifer, having revolted against God, was vanquished by Michael in the heights of heaven, the Almighty, before hurling him into the abyss, made the incomparable emerald, appearing on and protecting his brow as a dazzling diadem, fall at his feet. Then, when God created the first human couple in Eden, He placed there, among other marvels, a matchless cup shaped from Lucifer's emerald by the jewelers of heaven. But Adam and Eve sinned against

---

1 Cf. 2nd Part, Chap. 5.
2 According to the province and its dialects, such variants as *Gréal*, *Grasal*, *Gradal*, *Grail*, and even *Grolle* were also in use. Cf. L. de Laborde, *Glossaire français du Moyen-Âge*, pp. 333–34, 336.

thrice-holy God, and the implacable angel who brandished the flaming sword drove them out of Eden without the couple having had time to take the archangelic cup, the *Grail*, with them. Finally, their earthly days complete and their children having relinquished them to the ground, Seth, the son of Adam who was acceptable to the Lord, obtained from him re-entry into forsaken Eden to take from there the Grail which, from his hands, passed into those of his son Enos. During the Flood the sacred vessel was lost and no one knew what had become of it until the day when Jesus, on the eve of his death, assembled his disciples in the Upper Room to celebrate with them his last Passover. And that is when the Grail was set before him, filled with wine. And Jesus, having distributed to all the bread he had said was his very body, he leaned over the wine-filled vessel and spoke again: "This is my blood."

On the very next day Jesus was put on the cross and died for the ransom of men. Then a soldier, making sure he was dead, pierced his side with the blade of his spear and from the wound flowed blood and water.

Then, says the Grail legend, Joseph of Arimathea drew near to the Crucified, held out the sacred Grail to the gaping opening in his side, and collected the blood and water in his cup. And this blood and this water, more precious than the treasures of all the worlds, remained in the Grail and coagulated, forever incorruptible. And Joseph took the Grail home.

Such is the first part of the poem which, as we see, embroiders on Bible and Gospel contexts as it sees fit.

And the narrative continues in this way: when Jesus had ascended back to heaven and his Church was established under the authority of Peter, his first disciples were scattered to the four corners of the world to preach the good news of Christ dead on the cross and forever resurrected to assure eternal life for souls of good will. Then Joseph, the knight of Arimathea, and his son Joseph, whom Peter had made bishop, took the Grail, the "Holy Vessel," with them and crossed mountains, valleys, and seas with it, and happened to settle at the end of the world, in the isles of Great Britain. But soon afterwards, Joseph, his son, and his nephew Alain were put in prison by the king of the country, Crudel, without however being dispossessed of their treasure. Fortunately for them King Mordrain, having conquered Crudel, freed the captives, who then went and settled in an isolated spot where they could live in peace.

This is a good time to digress at length and recall that there existed, in the parts of Great Britain inhabited by tribes of Celtic origin (precisely those among whom we find the earliest evidence of the Grail legend), old traditions predating by far the Christian era, traditions that revolved around a magic spear and a sacred basin or cauldron.

The great local divinity of the Celts of these countries was the goddess *Don* or *Dona*, and one of her children is the god *Lug*, the cult of whom was dear to the insular Celts as well as to the Amoricans of French Brittany, the Picts of England, and the Pictones of Poitou.[3] Dona possessed a large bronze magic vase or basin that contained all the seeds of life for humans, animals, and plants, and as well the "seeds," so to speak, of all good things and every happiness, so that all the other gods wanted to possess it for themselves (Fig. 1). On the other hand, Lug, the son of Dona, had in his possession a divine and talismanic spear which, by itself, assured the defense and preservation of anyone who bore it.

Fig. 1. — The sacred basin of the Celts on a Gallic coin. From Hucher, Le Saint Graal, *p. 4, and* L'Art Gaulois, *Vol. II, p. 6, N° 2.*

When the origin and nature of such a myth is studied, it is hard not to relate it in a certain sense to that universal cult of a divinity creating and preserving life expressed by the ancient world's mysteries of Cybele, Attis, Osiris, and Tammuz in the Near East, not to neglect also the symbolic and pre-Christian significance of the cup and spear to the cult, in China, of the curved and the straight swords set in a perpendicular junction with each other.

---

3 In the days of Gaul's independence, the small town where I write these lines, *Loudon*, was dedicated to him: *Lugdunum*, the *dun* of *Lug*, the hill of *Lug*.

Then came the preaching of the Gospel beyond the Channel and the fruitful apostolates of Saint Patrick, his companions, and their disciples; then were the old menhirs and the stones of the cromlechs covered with crosses and other Christian symbols, while, at the same, the imagination of the faithful related the basin of Dona and the spear of Lug to the vessel and spear of the Gospel accounts of the Last Supper and the Passion of the Savior. What is more, we are told that the old druids had brought together the sacred basin of Dona, under the name of the vase *Azewladour*, and the spear of Lug, and that, by heavenly inspiration, had sent them to Jerusalem. It is these that were used, the one by the Savior at the Last Supper and the other by the centurion on Calvary.

Later, after the Saxon invasion of Great Britain at the beginning of the sixth century of our era, a rather poorly defined prototype of another legend is born, the legend of Artus or Arthur, a kind of demigod king, his wife, Queen Guenivere, and the heroes of his court: Perceval, Gawain, Lancelot, Bors, Kay, Galeriet, Yvain, Tristan, Hector, and many others, and above all Galahad, the knight with a totally pure soul, who certain versions end up identifying with Christ himself.

This mingling of Celtic mythology and heroic and fabulous traditions with a naïve and splendid Christian poetry passed over the Channel, and those writers who wrought the first links in the poetic chain of French national literature were inspired to once more embellish in its details the earliest theme. Under their pen Arthur reigns in a court similar to those of Charlemagne or the first Capetians; his knights combine in themselves the warrior heroism, the noble and total generosity, the impetuous and sincere faith, as well as the human weaknesses, of the great French barons. And when they gather round Arthur in his palace at Camelot, whether about his throne or table, the Round Table, the spear and the sacred vessel of Calvary and the Last Supper appear to them at times, filling them with happiness and procuring for them the goods and the most delicious foods they might desire.

Now, one day, the Holy Spear, the lance from whose point blood constantly seeped out, and the "holy vessel," the Grail, disappeared from Arthur's palace to go into another castle unknown

The Holy Grail

to all of them. Then the companions of Arthur, the "Knights of the Round Table," parted into all of Great Britain in search of the divine treasure; and, along the path of each one, there reared up against them the most hazardous adventures, the most bitter dangers and battles, the most diabolical enchantments, which have in view superhuman tests of their strength of character, of their martial valor, and of their moral worthiness. Finally, only three from among them — Galahad, Perceval, and Bohors — arrive at the Grail castle, the home of Pelles the Fisher King, and they were witnesses and beneficiaries of the most amazing wonders, the first of which was the healing of the Fisher King, for Pelles had been maimed long since and could not stir from his bed. Now when, by a divine inspiration, Galahad took the bleeding spear and touched him with it, his healing was sudden and complete.

This heroic and marvelous theme, having come into France at the time of the first Capetian kings, long remained in oral form; it was repeated, more or less complete, from castle to castle and from town to town by troubadours and trouvères, told and retold in every literate circle, and it was only at the end of the twelfth century that it seems to have been written down. This was the work of Chrétien de Troyes, who published, about 1180, *The Story of the Holy Grail*; then came Wolfram von Eschenbach, a German Templar who drew, in France, his inspiration and documentation from Guyot de Provins and wrote, about 1210, his *Parzival*, followed later by *Titurel*. The pseudo-Walter Map, who was a member of the Order, or Third Order, of Cîteaux, published, around 1220, *The Quest of the Holy Grail* and, about the same date, Robert de Boron composed his *Roman de l'Estoire dou Graal*.

Seen as a whole, the above mentioned works indicate that there were three major centers where the cult of the Grail was — we will venture to say — especially intense: the center of Ireland and England (Somerset and Glamorgan); the center of western France (Anjou, Poitou, and Brittany), and the Franco-Spanish center north and south of the eastern Pyrenees.

Each of the previously cited authors have more or less dwelt on the various evangelic facts which, under their authorship, have given to the Grail a more or less eucharistic, a more or less passionist character: Chrétien de Troyes mentions the two offices of the Grail, at the Last Supper and on Calvary, and above all sings with enthusiasm of "the bright lance with sparkling blade" from which

> a drop of crimson blood would drip
> and run along the white shaft and
> drip down upon the squire's hand
> and then another drop would flow.[4]

For Wolfram von Eschenbach, the Grail bore a host, and we will come back later to his particular idea of the Grail; Walter Map, to whom is attributed *The Quest of the Holy Grail*, dwells above all on the eucharistic aspect and mentions the Round Table of King Arthur next to the table of the Lord's Last Supper. Ultimately, he defines the sacred Grail in this way: *Ce est l'escuele ou Ihesucriz menja l'aignel le ior de Pasques o ses déciples*, "It is the platter in which Jesus Christ partook of the paschal lamb with his disciples."[5] But he does not forget that the legend calls for the Grail to be on Calvary too: speaking of the lance that a squire at arms held *tote droite sus le Saint Vessel*, "upright over the holy vessel," he tells us that the blood issued from its point and *contreval la hanste couloit, chavit dedenz*, "running down the shaft was caught therein."[6] Robert de Boron, for his part, specifies that the Grail was a *veissel moult gent ou Chriz fesoit son sacrement*, "a very noble vessel with which Christ performed his sacrament";[7] then later he adds that the Grail was *ce veissel précieux et grant ou estoit le sanctissime Sang*, that "noble and precious vessel, containing that holiest of blood,"[8] which Joseph of Arimathea collected from the side of Jesus when he took him down from the cross.

4 *Perceval or the Story of the Grail*, trans. R. H. Cline (Athens, GA: University of Georgia Press, 1985), p. 88.
5 *The Quest of the Holy Grail*, trans. P. M. Matarasso (Baltimore, MD: Penguin Books, 1969), p. 276.
6 Ibid., p. 275.
7 *Joseph of Arimathea, a Romance of the Grail*, trans. J. Rogers (London: Rudolf Steiner Press, 1990), p. 7.
8 Ibid., p. 15.

The Holy Grail

We repeat: the popularity of these various versions of the Grail legend was immense in the Middle Ages,[9] those times during which "the Passion was in fact the sole study."[10] Just one example: in the province of Poitou alone the names of the heroes of the Grail romance appeared as given names in many genealogies of the fourteenth and fifteenth centuries — those of the Rouhault, the Colloigne, lords of Pugny, and in the illustrious house of the Chabot, where we see that Guesdin Chabot named his children at baptism Lancelot, Perceval, and Tristan. Fifty further examples could be cited.[11] And this reminds me that Philip the Bold, for his Louvre castle, wanted the tapestry makers of Arra to create a series of tapestries representing the story of Perceval;[12] and this subject was repeated by artists of the same craft through all the rest of the Middle Ages.[13]

Since the twelfth century, the arts have shown us lambs wounded to the heart that bleed into ciboriums (Plate 13); and

Fig. 2. — Vase of the Holy Blood, fountain of salvation. 17th-century print adapted from a theme created by image-makers of the Middle Ages.

9 The Grail "was amazingly famous in the Middle Ages." L. de Laborde, loc. cit.
10 Émile Mâle, *Religious Art in France, the Thirteenth Century*, trans. M. Mathews (Princeton NJ: Princeton University Press, 1984), p. 225.
11 See P. Beauchet-Filleau, *Dictionnaire des Familles du Poitou*, passim.
12 Cf. Eug. Muntz, *La Tapisserie*, p. 120.
13 Ibid., p. 122.

later, the blood from Christ on the cross falls into a chalice set on the ground (Fig. 2) or on an altar-stone (Plate 25). Elsewhere it is angels that collect the redemptive blood in precious cups (Plates 26 to 29). All these works of an art that only wants to pray are so many allusions to the moving poem that was repeated everywhere at the time. Finally there came this more direct evocation of the image of the holy wound set within the cup, which in this way seemed to be the divine fountain of purification, regeneration, and life. *Haurietis aquas in gaudio de fontibus Salvatoris,* "you shall draw waters with joy out of the Savior's fountains" (Isaiah 12:3) (Fig. 2).

Here is a reproduction of the imprint of the small seal of Jehan Coste, who lived at the very end of the fourteenth or the earliest years of the fifteenth century; Coste, playing upon his name, took for an emblem the wound in the "costé," the side of Jesus, and we see it in the field of his seal under the form of a crescent that bleeds into a large cup (Fig. 3).

Fig. 3. — Seal of Jean Coste, 14th century. The original belongs to Canon Davin, of Versailles, collaborator of the Revue de l'Art Chrétien.

During the rest of this same fifteenth century, and above all in the last third, not only does the divine wound surmount the cup but quite often it is even situated within its bowl, as it is for example on this marvelous engraving where the cross stands with lance and sponge upright on either side, bearing at its focal point the Sacred Heart encompassed by the crown of thorns — the Heart that summarizes here the entire Person of the sacrificial victim. This heart bleeds and two angels raise toward it an elaborately wrought cup that contains an oblong image of the opening through which the lance passed to reach it (Fig. 4).

On the *Book of Hours* of Caillaut and Martineau, who are of the same era, Christ is represented on the cross, and behind him are all the instruments of the Passion; behind him is also a large cup, held by two kneeling angels, which contains the bleeding ellipse of the divine wound (Fig. 5).

Finally, in a series that would draw us too far afield, we will cite just this one page from the 1512 "Besançon Hours" at the

Fig. 4. — The sacred wound inside the cup. Print from the second half of the 15th century. Collection of review Regnabit, *1921–1929.*

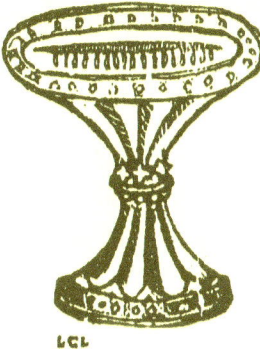

Fig. 5. — The sacred wound in a cup, detail from the Caillaut & Martineau Book of Hours, 15th century. See É. Mâle, Religious Art in France: The Late Middle Ages, *p. 103.*

Fig. 6. — The divine blood in a cup. The Estoile Internelle *collection, 15th–16th century.*

Cluny Museum in Paris. It also includes a richly jeweled cup held up by two angels under a ceremonial pavilion opened wide by two other angels; in this open ciborium we again see the same symbolic ellipse (Fig. 7).

Fig. 7. — The sacred wound in a cup. From the Besançon Hours, 1512. Cluny Museum. *Engraving modelled on an overly faint photograph.*

Are not these cups, these ciboriums, containing the exterior source of the blood, not in the direct line of that other cup, that Graal spoken of by Robert de Boron, that "noble and precious vessel, containing that holiest of blood" that Joseph of Arimathea collected from the side of Jesus in taking him down from the cross?

There is also another cup about which I have already spoken in the previous chapter while studying the Christic symbolism of precious stones, the cup of the members of the *Estoile Internelle*, which is at least as old as the just cited fifteenth-century documents. In the writings related to this group that were conveyed to me, the Holy Grail is not directly involved, and yet the chief insignia of this institution is not a star, but a ciborium in which a red stone should be placed (Fig. 6). We have previously seen that the ruby escarbuncle, hematite, carnelian, bloodstone, coral, and all stones of a reddish color were placed by our fathers of the Middle Ages among the number of emblems of the divine blood. One drawing from the collection of the Estoile Internelle represents this cup and its stone quite explicitly, for below it we read this Gospel text: ... *Unus militum lancea, latus ejus aperuit et continuo exivit sanguis et aqua*, "a soldier opened his side with a lance, and there came out blood and water."[14]

It is with respect to this red stone of the Estoile Internelle that I come back to what Wolfram von Eschenbach said about the Grail in *Parzival*, because for him the Grail is a stone[15] that he calls *lapsit exillis*, a rightly untranslatable expression that some interpret as *lapis e coelis*, "the stone fallen from heaven," which alludes to the emerald fallen from Lucifer's forehead; others derive *lapsit exillis* from *exilium* and translate it as "exiled stone" — exiled from heaven — which amounts to the same thing. Onto this stone, von Eschenbach tells us, a dove came soaring down from heaven every Good Friday and lay there a small, white host; and it is this host that endowed the stone with the virtue, which all other versions of the Grail legend attribute to the "Holy Vessel," of being the never-failing source of everything good, of all things delicious and comforting, and of also being the leaven for all purity, all chastity.

But the *exillis* stone is nevertheless clearly the Grail for, in *Titurel*, this same von Eschenbach has erected for it on Montsalvat a temple inspired by that of Solomon, where it must be guarded by chosen knights, the "Templists."[16] Surely, Eschenbach's writing hints at the idea of linking the Order of the Temple, to which he belonged, with the kind of spiritual center the Grail was at that time, and about which a number of more or less hermetic groups

---

14 John 19:34.
15 Surely a stone shaped into the form of a cup.
16 See the study by M. Oswald van den Berghe, *Le Temple du Graal*, in *Annales Archéologique*, tome XVII, July 1857, pp. 216–26.

gravitated: the Chevalerie du Graal, the Massenie du Saint Graal, and other much less known groups. Miss Weston claims some of these groups still exist in England. It is possible in fact that at least one of those found today dates back rather far in the past. Almost all the others, in England as well as in France, are only quite recent institutions, highly fanciful enterprises that stem only from reveries and from their founders' zeal for a self-generated culture. This does not mean that, in France, there was no equivalent to the English group.

What remains and will remain, in France as in England, is the attention that scholars of the greatest merit have given, for half a century now and above all in these last years, to the poems of the Middle Ages, and especially those concerned with the Holy Grail; foremost among them in France we will mention: Van den Berghe, Hucher, Tonnelat, Pauphilet, Nitze, J. Boulanger, and Loth.

In more or less specialized circles, on the other hand, the historical, literary, philosophical, mystical, or ascetic aspects of the Grail legend are studied, a legend that some people regard as a kind of prophecy, a theme *à clef* related to a body of oral, highly traditional, and today secret teachings that reappear sporadically in the religious world, kept, it is said, by custodians for a providentially favored elite with a view to this mission. And this seems to be based on what the Arthurian legend says: even though every knight seated at the Round Table benefits from seeing the Grail and shares in its blessings, after its disappearance only three — Perceval, Bohors, and Galahad — gained by their virtues and their valor the privilege of being the guardians of the "Holy Vessel," and of knowing its mysteries.

The oral teaching involved here would have flourished since the earliest Christian centuries and fallen almost into forgetfulness after the peace of Constantine in 311 and until the brief Carolingian renaissance, after which it would have suffered a new eclipse during the tenth century. But during the eleventh and twelfth centuries — sometimes called the "cycle of the pure idea" — its influence on lofty minds would have been considerable until, under the reign of Saint Louis, it would disappear anew. A historic enigma, if you like, about which one should only speak with reserve.

To return to the medieval iconography of the divine blood, we will conclude by citing this great and splendid illuminated page from a manuscript book in the Bibliothèque Nationale at Paris,[17] which shows us the legendary Round Table presided over by King Arthur and around which a score of knights are seated with him as kings, crowns on their heads, cloaks hooded and lined with ermine, while two angels fly over the center of the table bearing up the dazzling Holy Grail (Fig. 8). Both these angels and this cup are absolutely similar to those works of art of the same period pointed out above.

Fig. 8. — The Holy Grail from a miniature in a manuscript from the Bibliothèque Nationale, Paris, 15th century.

The "Legend of the Holy Grail" was therefore an efficacious leaven of inspiration for our people. And it remains, after the *Imitation of Christ*, the most prestigious, the most fruitful, literary masterpiece left to us by medieval society. Rest assured, its glory and its active role are not dead.

II. THE HOLY GRAIL AND THE VESSELS OF JERUSALEM, GENOA, AND VALENCIA

It is quite evident that the Grail of the poems of the Middle Ages was not a material cup that celestial personages bring to the court of King Arthur or to any other place, but a purely ideal allusion to the cup used by Jesus at the Last Supper. Anyone who hopes to see it come forth, dazzling and miraculous, from excavations undertaken in the ruined ramparts of Montsegur, in the grottoes of Sabarthes, or elsewhere, will be disappointed in their expectations: no one on Earth today knows what has become of the vessel over which Jesus inclined to let fall the unprecedented words of love and infinite power: This is my body, and this is my blood.

However, in the course of the passing centuries three vessels, among all others the most venerated, were deemed as having served, in the hands of Jesus, at the first eucharistic transubstantiation:

17 French collections, 112.

Part V: Stones Emblematic of the Wounded Christ

Plate 25. — Christ, seated on the side of a vat and surrounded by the instruments of his Passion, presses his hand to his right side, from which he causes his blood to spurt into the chalice. Hiéron du Val d'Or Museum, Paray-le-Monial, 15th century. Photo Giraudon. Archives of the review Regnabit, *1921–1929.*

The Holy Grail

Plate 26. — Angels collecting the blood of Christ in chalices. Triptych by Niccolo da Foligno, 15th century. National Gallery, London. Photo Giraudon. Archives of the review Regnabit, *1921–1929.*

Part V: Stones Emblematic of the Wounded Christ

*Plate 27. — Angels collecting the blood of Christ in chalices.
Crucifixion by Giotto di Bondone, 14th century.
Photo Giraudon. Archives of the review* Regnabit, *1921–1929.*

Plate 28. — Angels collecting the blood of Christ in chalices. Crucifixion by Taddeo Gaddi, 14th century. Photo Giraudon. Archives of the review Regnabit, *1921–1929.*

Part V: Stones Emblematic of the Wounded Christ

Plate 29. — Angels collecting the blood of Christ in chalices. Calvary by the Master of Bruges, Cathedral of Saint-Sauveur (Belgium), 14th century. Photo Giraudon. Archives of the review Regnabit, *1921–1929.*

these were the chalice of Jerusalem, the cup of Genoa, and the chalice of Valencia in Spain.

The first two, discovered in the Holy Places in the course of the Crusades, were brought back to Europe on the eve of the spread of the French poems about the Holy Grail; it is possible that, in writing them, the authors had their thoughts turned towards one or the other of these vessels. Also, from a variety of old documents, we know thoughts of the Grail had come unbidden to the minds of those who revered these vessels at Genoa or Valencia at a time when the aforesaid poems were fresh in everyone's memory and everywhere recounted.

The Chalice of Jerusalem

But, before the cups at Genoa and Valencia had become objects of veneration for the people of the West, the Christian East had known another chalice that was regarded, perhaps more rightly so, as being the Lord's. In the year 640, the Gallo-Frankish bishop, Arculf, saw and touched this cup in the course of a voyage to Palestine, about which the monk Adamnanus has left an account. There we read: "Between the Basilica of Golgotha and the Martyrium there is a recess [Lat. *exedra* = "a small chamber, or chapel, attached to the side of a church"] in which is the cup of the Lord, which he blessed and gave with his own hand to the apostles [at] the supper on the day before he suffered, and as he and they sat at meat with one another; the cup is of silver, holding the measure of a French quart [a *setier*], and has two little handles placed on it, one on each side."[18]

The Gaulish *setier* is equivalent to seven liters, forty-four centiliters.

Let us note in passing that the capacity of this chalice and its form of a vase with two lateral handles should connect it to many of the large "ministerial chalices" used during the early Christian centuries to distribute the Eucharist to the crowds.

The Venerable Bede, who lived from 675 to 735, speaking of the Jerusalem chalice, adds some details to Adamnanus's text:

18 *The Pilgrimage of Arculfus in the Holy Land*, trans. J. R. Macpherson (London: Palestine Pilgrims' Text Society, 1895), p. 11.

"In the street which unites the Martyrium and Golgotha," he states, "is a [chapel] in which is the cup of our Lord concealed in a casket. It is touched and kissed through a hole in the covering. It is made of silver, has two handles, one on each side, and holds a French quart."[19]

This vessel was no longer found in Jerusalem when the crusaders took this city, and no one knows what became of it. It is therefore impossible to reach any verdict on its authenticity. All that is certain is that it should not be confused, as we will soon see, with the Genoa and Valencia vessels, which are not in silver.

The Sagro Catino of Genoa

In 1101, the Genoese found this vase in the mosque of Caesarea, William of Tyr tells us, when it was captured by assault and, abandoning the gold and all kinds of riches to the other crusaders, kept for themselves the cup that was indicated as being the cup of the Lord's Last Supper.

By reason of its form, the Genoese designated this vessel by the name of *Sagro Catino*, "the sacred bowl." This is a basin of green and translucent material that they believed to be emerald; it is hexagonal, without a stem, and furnished with two small handles of the same material; its diameter is 32 and a half centimeters, with a capacity of about three liters (Fig. 9).

The Sagro Catino was soon transported to Genoa and deposited in a niche of an inner wall of the cathedral church of Saint Lawrence. A group of Genoese knights, the *Clavigeri*, had the keys to the powerful locks that shut up this niche, and once each year the archbishop of Genoa showed it from afar to the people.

With the twelfth century, Geoffrey of Monmouth informed his contemporaries about the legend that claimed that the Sagro Catino had been a present from the Queen of Sheba to King Solomon, which later, from king to king, had become the property of Herod, and which, after a misunderstanding, was found

---

19 *On the Holy Places* in *The Miscellaneous Works of Venerable Bede*, vol. IV, trans. J. A. Giles (London: Whittaker and Co., 1843), p. 407. Cf. J. Hoppenot, *La Messe dans l'Histoire et dans l'Art* (Paris: Desclée de Brouwer, 1906).

The Holy Grail

in the Upper Room where Jesus, finding it to his liking, had made use of it.[20]

A short time afterwards, the renowned Genoese Dominican, Jacobus de Voragine, archbishop of Genoa (d. 1298), is quick to assure us that the Sagro Catino was indeed the vessel used by the Savior at the Last Supper with his disciples, "then by Nicodemus" when he gathered up the final drops of the blood of Jesus after taking him down from the cross.[21]

Later, John of Autun, the author of the chronicles of Louis XII's reign, formally identified the Sagro Catina as the Holy Grail of Arthurian legend: in 1502 he states: "Le Roy fut ouir

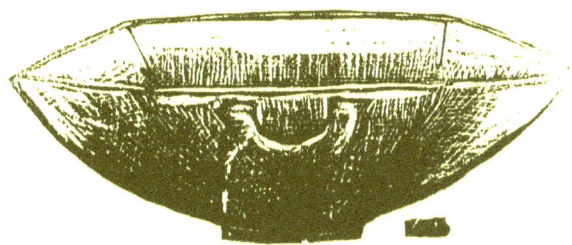

Fig. 9. — The "Sagro Catino" of Genoa.

messe... en l'églize de Sainct Laurenc qui est le grant domme et cathédralle de Gennes où fut par les chonoynes de là, après messe, monstré le riche vaisseau smaragdin, c'est assavoir le précieux plat au quel Notre Seigneur Ihésucrist mangea avecques ses appostres le iour de sa Ceine, et est celuy plat qu'on appelle le Sainct Graal." ("The King heard Mass... in the church of San Lorenzo, which is the great duomo and cathedral of Genoa where, after Mass, he was shown by the canons of the place the rich emerald vessel, which is to wit the precious dish with which Our Lord Jesus Christ did eat with his apostles the day of his Last Supper, and this is the dish called the Holy Grail.")

The fact that this vessel was thought to be cut from an enormous emerald would be all too well in accord with the legend that had the Grail made from the heavenly emerald decorating, as we are told, the brow of Lucifer before his fall.

20 See Rohault de Fleury, op. cit., p. 275 and *Rev. archéologique*, ann. 1845.
21 Jacobus de Voragine, *Chronicon Januense*, Chap. XVIII.

Then, too, the low and large form of the Sagro Catino also connects it to the use Walter Map assigns to the Holy Grail when he designates it in this way: "It is the platter in which Jesus Christ partook of the paschal lamb with his disciples."[22]

It was believed, in fact, that it had been successively used for the eating of the ritual paschal lamb, for the consecration of the bread, and then for the consecration of the wine.

We can understand, then, the intense veneration surrounding the Genoa vessel at a time when historical criticism was something almost unknown. Nonetheless, what remains is that the first vessel preserved at Golgotha as being the vessel of the Last Supper was in silver, whereas the one from Caesarea and then Genoa is of a vitreous material of an emerald-green color.

In 1805, after Napoleon had assumed the title of king of Italy, he ordered the Sagro Catino transported to Paris, where a commission of members from the Institute of Paris was formed to study it in all its aspects. The results of these studies were registered in a report from Millin de Grandmaison, and two certainties emerged: first, that the Sagro Catino is indeed, and indisputably so, a vessel of a very high antiquity; next, it is made of a vitreous paste and not of emerald.[23]

Returned to the city of Genoa in 1816, the Sagro Catino was accidentally broken in the course of the trip; restored since then, it has resumed its place in the niche of the church of San Lorenzo.

The Valencia Chalice

One of the expeditions by Western knights to the Holy Land in the course of the Middle Ages brought back to Valencia a vessel said to be the one Jesus took into his hands to transubstantiate within it the wine into his blood in the course of the Last Supper.

It is composed of a most beautiful agate-onyx hemispheric cup, with a more bell-shaped bowl of the same material forming its base, with a straight stem decorated with a large node midway. The agate base is encompassed by a large metallic circle that

---

22 Walter Map, op. cit., p. 276.
23 Cf. Millin de Grandmaison in *Magasin Encyclopédique*, ann. 1807, v. 137–50.

bears four ascending branches — all of this edged with pearls and precious stones. The two highly curved handles also connect the cup and agate foot, and all these metallic parts are decorated with interlacings Hispano-Moorish in style (Fig. 10).

Like the Sagro Catino of Genoa, the Valencia chalice is not the vessel designated by Palestinian tradition in the early centuries as being the Savior's, which Bishop Arculf venerated in the chapel of Golgotha and which was made of silver.

Fig. 10. — The Chalice of Valencia, in Spain.

But for eight centuries all of Christian Europe will center its fervor on the wondrous vessels that were believed to harbor the unheard-of mystery of a love that only a God, author and master of matter and the laws that govern it, could actualize. This is why, even though the piety of our forebears may have gone astray about them, these cups have been imbued with, have been sacralized to such a degree of intensity, by a sum of adoration and fervor unequalled on earth, that they remain even today, in spite of everything, incontestably most holy objects worthy of all respect.

Moreover, because of the role they have played, these vessels are for us records that no one engaged in studying the history of the Holy Grail, or the history of the worship of the Eucharist and the the divine blood shed on the cross, can ignore.

In concluding, we should add that in the fifteenth century there existed in France another chalice that has not had the glorious reputation of the previous ones, but which was neverethless claimed to fulfill the same role and divine function. It was jealously guarded in the treasure of Jean de France, Duke of Berry, and the 1416 inventory of this prince's furnishings and precious

Part V: Stones Emblematic of the Wounded Christ

objects mentions it in this way: "The chalice from which Our Lord drank at the Last Supper, lined with gold, inscripted about with black letters. Gold valued at XXXIII livres tournois."

It seems extremely probable that this chalice was only a reproduction of either the Genoa Sagro Catino or the Valencia chalice.

The heart above a Chalice. Detail from a German engraving of the 15th century (see La Dévotion au Sacré-Cœur de Jésus au moyen-âge allemand, *by Richstaetter S. J., Ratisbon). Reproduction on wood with penknife, by the author.*

SIXTH PART

*The Iconography
of the
Wounded
Heart of Jesus*

CHAPTER SIXTEEN

Beginnings of the Iconography of the Heart of Jesus

TO THE REPRESENTATION OF THE LATeral wound of Jesus placed in the bowl of a cup succeeded, by the end of the fifteenth century, many representations of chalices and ciboria into which a heart, pierced and placed immediately above these sacred vessels, bled directly. It is the same idea, but with this difference: instead of connecting the cup with the main and ultimate wound to the body of Jesus through which his blood flowed, it is put, in the second instance, in immediate relationship with the crucible of love where the Redeemer's blood was wrought before being shed with his life through all his wounds. England and France have preserved numerous examples prior to the second third of the sixteenth century.

With the creation of these last iconographic themes, one can say that the symbolism of the Sacred Heart was complete; everything drawn, painted, engraved, or carved afterwards is only a variant of the main emblems created up to that point.

But from when do the first representations of the heart of Jesus Christ, of the "Sacred Heart," date? For all too many Catholics, piety towards the divine heart is a late idea, originating in the seventeenth century out of the sentimental spirituality spread by Jesuits and other preachers. For some others — among those who are obliged to recognize that the faith of the Middle Ages, above all, honored and adored as we do the redeeming heart — this is only an idea sprung from the overly pious spirit of this medieval society imbued with a most tender poetry as well as a surprising realism. And might it not be said that, for a few, the cult of the heart, the center of all saving love, would derive at once from the "courts of love" and exalted meditations of nuns?

In any case, it is admitted by them, almost as sure knowledge, that the Christian soul of the first millennium did not, and could not, have even the shadow of a thought for the fleshly heart of Jesus, seat of his emotional feelings, and that this conception is situated quite outside the domain accessible to it.

For all the more reason it will seem absolutely astonishing to them that the entire priesthood of a pagan people of one of the very earliest human civilizations had for the heart of the One God — placed by it, as much as it could conceive, above its gods — a thought, a quite particular regard, since it ascribed to this heart all that the divinity itself possesses of perfections: creative power, science, infinite beauty, goodness and justice, and, from this idea, this priesthood shaped the whole nation with its proud sovereigns, its artists, its scientists, and its amazing architects.

Yet this is what discoveries made by advanced studies in Egyptology, especially in the first half of the twentieth century, make it possible to affirm with positive material records: writings, lapidary inscriptions, sculptures, art objects, etc., all things whose admirable testimony cannot be disputed.

I. THE HUMAN HEART AND THE CONCEPT OF THE HEART OF GOD IN ANCIENT EGYPT

Since the time of its first historical dynasties, around 3300 to 2600 BC, Egypt's monuments reveal it to have been a highly civilized nation; the statues and sculptures we have from this time are of an art whose perfection confounds us, and, when the Pharaohs of the fourth dynasty — Cheops, Chephren, and Mycerinus — raised or allowed the priests to raise, between 2840 and 2680 BC, the mysterious sanctuaries that are the Great Pyramids of Giza, the science of the Egyptians in astronomy, cosmogony, geometry, and geodesy was such that it took our sophisticated instruments of today to catch up with them; and their mathematical methods allowed them to solve, in the just-mentioned fields of science, calculations our scholars still find stunning.[1]

[1] See Rev. Théophile Moreux, *La Science Mystérieuse des Pharaons* (Paris: Doin, 1923).

Now, before, and again at that time, while the pontiffs of Memphis and Thebes were the guardians of science as well as religion in Egypt, they still preserved the worship of the true God — altered it is true, but clearly designated by the hieroglyphs on the monuments of the third and fourth dynasties, for example, as being the One God, the unique God. A spiritual entity, He appears as quite different from the *gods*, who were only totems or deified ancestors, beginning with Atum (the Ancestor[2]), one of whose sons, Osiris, became one of the ministers of the sole Godhead, entrusted with presiding over the weighing of souls on the threshold of the "kingdom of transformations."

As for the One God, often personified by the Sun, he was called according to locale, time, and sacerdotal school, Amon or Ra or Aton; and some of his perfections were personalized under other names. The rather late cult of certain animals was only a distortion of a totemism that seems to have been, at origin, purely heraldic.

It is of this unique God that the pagan of Egypt speaks who, at that time, wrote the papyrus in the British Museum where we read this phrase: "Great God, Lord of Heaven and Earth, who made all things that are. O my God, O my Master, who made me and formed me, give me an eye to see, an ear to hear your glories!" Where do we find, in the classics of ancient Greece and Rome, prayers similar to this one?[3]

What stands out from one's first contact with books specializing in the latest religious discoveries in Egyptology[4] is that the Egyptian people long retained the notion of first truths, and that,

---

2 Quite comparable to the Adam of the Bible.
3 Cf. Philippe Virey, *La Religion de l'ancienne Égypte* (Paris: Beauchesne, 1910), p. 13.
4 The following pages are based above all on four recent books: *La Religion de l'Ancienne Égypte* by Philippe Virey, former attaché to the French archaeological Mission at Cairo; *La Science Mystérieuse des Pharaons* by Father Théophile Moreux, director of the Bourges observatory; *Rois et Dieux d'Égypte* (Paris: Armand Colin, 1923) by Alexandre Moret, professor at the Collège de France, and *Mystères Égyptiens* (Paris: Armand Colin, 1923) by Alexandre Moret. Also various works by the renowned scholar Gaston Maspero.

on the other hand, even though it was not "the nation in whom all nations were blessed" (Gen. 22:18), there must have been in this people, and especially in their priesthood and in their intellectual elite, very lofty and spiritually very pure souls that God favored with marvelous illuminations and intuitions. Let us not be surprised: Melchizedek, spoken about in Genesis, and the three Magi of the Gospels were not Hebrews, and yet the first prefigured the Eucharist and the second discovered the newly born Christ: "The Spirit of God blows where it wills."

That is why, when faced with passages from the sacred texts of Egypt, some of today's greatest scientists, such as Alexandre Moret, a professor at the Collège de France and Director of the École Pratique des Hautes Études, do not hesitate to regard certain chapters of Ancient Egypt's theological writings as a kind of pre-Christianity; also Moret, in his magnificent work *Mystères Égyptiens*, boldly titles one of its finest chapters: "The Mystery of the Creating Word."

It is the remains of these very ancient beliefs from the height of Egyptian splendor that, collected in the Hermetic Books, surprised our first Christian teachers to such an extent that one of them, Lactantius († 325), said: "Hermes has discovered, I do not know how, almost all truth."

Now, from some of the oldest records, let us see what an amazing place is given to the *human heart* in this conception of religious psychology that had not yet, or only very little, penetrated the polytheism and zoolatry of the last centuries of Egyptian decadence.

In hieroglyphics, the sacred writing where often the image of the thing represents the very word it designates, the heart was however only represented by an emblem: the *vase* (Fig. 1). Is not the heart of man indeed the vase where his life is contin-

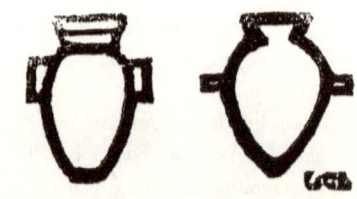

Fig. 1. — *The vase, the hieroglyphic emblem of the word "heart."*

ually elaborated along with his blood, the vase where the good or bad passions, which govern his will and sometimes dominate him to the point of tyrannizing his intelligence, are born and grow and where they die?

At the very birth of the human race, which the pyramid of the Pharaoh Pepi II relates in its own way, Atum, the first man, draws his children from his own breast by dividing his heart in nine portions, and each one became a complete human being; thus were born the ancestor gods and goddesses Atum, Shu, Tefnut, Geb, Nut, Osiris, Isis, Set, and Nephthys. And this suggests that man transmits life by his heart, as we will see later the Word of God create life with his Heart.

From the heart comes all that man knows and can do, and it is from the heart that human activity seeks its inspiration; this is what is confided to us by the stele of that prestigious Pharaoh of the fifteen century before our era, Tut-Ankh-Amon, who has just been restored to us in the midst of the incredible splendor of his funerary treasures. The text that speaks of him on the stele textually vouches that "he meditated deeply on the happiness of his people by *communing with his own heart.*"

And when Ramses II reproaches his officers for ill-supporting him during a battle, he tells them: "No longer will I bear you in my heart"; then, turning to his father who is in heaven, Amon-God, he dares to speak in this manner: "What are you doing, O my father Amon? Is it for a father to not sufficiently watch over his son ... and what are these Asians for thy heart?"[5]

This indeed then has to do with the heart of God, of Amon-God, but only — and the evidence for this is quite clear — of the metaphorical Heart of God as the seat of divine affection. But do not some of our Catholic liturgical texts sometimes implore in similar tones?

Oh! the human heart, how idealistic Egypt loved it! Just read the poetic fable of Bata, who sacrificed himself but whose heart would not die and which was reborn and transformed each time a new blow, of itself mortal, happened to strike it; until finally Anubis revived Bata by finding his wandering heart and putting it in water. And, with the return of his heart, Bata came back to life.

---

5 Cf. Virey, op. cit., p. 117.

But it is especially in the judgment of souls, at the end of earthly life, that the heart appears as the complete summary of a man. This weighing of the punishable acts of each human existence is expressed on the monuments of ancient Egypt by sculptural scenes quite comparable in sum to those that show us, on our Romanesque and Gothic churches, the particular judgment of the acts of our lives, with St. Michael who weighs small souls in the presence of the angel committed to our protection and Satan, our accuser.

What does Egyptian sculpture show us? Before the throne of Osiris, in charge of the judgment of the dead, with his assessors all about him, and near Maat, the divine personification of Truth, a scale is raised; beside or above the scale, a hybrid monster, "the devourer," the Godhead's dispenser of justice, is about to seize the soul if the just weighing proves unfavorable (Fig. 2).

Fig. 2. — *The Truth and the Heart in the scales of judgment. Details from paintings on the casket of a priestess of Amon. Cf. Ph. Virey.* Religion de l'Ancienne Égypte, *p. 157.*

In one of the pans rests the deceased's heart by itself under the guise of a hieroglyphic vase in which are the bad works of life that are to be judged. Then Maat-Truth advances, detaches from her headdress the white ostrich feather that is its chief feature (sometimes even she herself is seated on the pan,[6] but, since she is a spiritual substance, only the white feather bears down ever so lightly...) and a perfect balance must immediately be achieved between the heart-vase and the immaculate feather; otherwise, it is the justice-dispensing monster who triumphs, and the soul will not be received into the realm of happy transformations.

---

6   Maat holds in her hand "the sign of life," a small *cross* in the form of a Tau furnished with a loop at its summit (see engraving).

Beginnings of the Iconography of the Heart of Jesus

Behold: on the stone of his tomb is Ramses VI, whom the beautiful goddess-ancestor, Isis, daughter of Atum, leads by hand before the terrible tribunal of her brother Osiris. And before Osiris and his assessors, before incorruptible Maat-Truth, the Pharaoh makes his "mea non culpa," since here only the evil committed matters.

And Ramses begins: "Honor to Thee, great God who has certainty! I come to Thee, O my Lord, I present myself to contemplate thy glory. I know thee, I know thy name, and I know the names of the forty-two deities who are with thee in the hall of Truth.

I did not put iniquity in the place of righteousness.

I did not do what the gods detest.

I did not kill or cause to be killed treacherously.

I did not betray anyone.

I did not shed the tears of the poor," etc. Forty-three counts are thus rejected by the Pharaoh, who concludes by crying out: "I am pure, I am pure, I am pure!"

And while the Truth is watching him and getting ready to drop her terribly light feather onto the scale, the gemstone scarab, which occupies the middle of the heart in the royal mummy, repeatedly invokes the magical word that was said over it when it was consecrated by the hierodules: "O heart, who was my heart on earth, you who come from my mother and are needed for my transformations, do not testify against me, do not overwhelm your father, O my heart!"

But Maat-Truth has just dropped the feather of her diadem, the two pans of the scale oscillate, and stop at the precise point of perfect equilibrium. Ramses is justified.

— On his funerary stele preserved in the Turin Museum, and translated by Chabas, Beka, before unfolding his "mea non culpa" like Ramses VI, sums it up in advance with these winning words: "I myself was just and true, without malice, *having put God in his heart.*"[7] God, Beka indeed says *God* in hieroglyphs: "*Neter*"[8] and not one of the *gods*. Beka well understood that a heart

---

7 *Records of the Past*, vol. X, Egyptian Texts (London: Samuel Bagster and Sons, n. d.), p. 7.

8 Ibid.

within which God dwelt and which lived for him could not be condemned since he possessed him at the very center of his life!

After him, and with almost the same meaning, the book of the *Song of Songs* (8:6) will say to the soul: "*Pone me ut Signaculum super cor tuum.*" "O God, put me as a seal upon thy heart!" And well over a thousand years later another word, more expressive still, that of Saint Paul, will echo him: "And I live, now not I: but Christ liveth in me" (Gal. 2:20).

So, for religious Egypt the heart was everything in man: the seat of his intellectual faculties, as well as the passions that, along with them, govern his will; the vase of life where the soul leaves behind in quitting the body the deposit of actions accomplished with it, and lastly the tabernacle where the just carry the divinity when, through their virtues, as Beka boasted, they have put God himself within themselves.

Egyptian thought had the highest regard for the human heart and, outside of its physical role, made it of such importance that it rose, of itself, towards the heart of that unique divinity that the priesthood of this country recognized as possessing omnipotence and all perfections to the ultimate degree of totality and infinity.

It is the Pharaoh Amenhotep IV, also known as Akhenaten, whose beautiful and graceful bust is in the Louvre, and the Queen Nefer-Neferu-Aten, his wife, who together composed the splendid canticles that many monuments still standing have preserved for us. In one of these hymns, addressed to God, to God-Aten, that is to say, considered under the radiant emblem of the solar disk, we read at random from a very long text words such as these: "Thou hast created the earth in thy heart, when thou wast alone...thou hast made the seasons of the year give birth and growth to all that thou hast created...thou hast made the distant sky that thou mightest rise up into it and see from there all that thou hast created, thou alone... Thou appearest in the form of the living Aten, thou risest up radiant, thou departest and returnest; thou art in my heart."[9]

9 Cf. Moret, *Rois et Dieux d'Égypte*, p. 64.

It is therefore, according to the hymn of Amenhotep-Akhenaten, from the very heart of God that the divine exploit of the great creative act emanated: "You created the earth in your heart...."

This same conviction is repeated on the funerary inscription of a priest of Memphis, the text and meaning of which have been clarified by Breasted, Maspero, and Erman. It turns out that the theologians of the School of Memphis distinguished in the work of the Creator God the role of creative thought, which they call the share of the *heart*, from the role of the instrument of creation, which they call the share of the *tongue*. Therefore, in God, every word is a concept of the heart, and, for this to be realized, speech is needed; so every divine act is formed as a thought of the heart, as an utterance on the tongue.[10]

The heart of God is therefore looked upon by the sages of Egypt, not only as the initial source of creative power, but also as the seat of divine thought, and by this means God possesses the infinite knowledge of all things. On the Leyden papyrus we read in connection with God designated under the name of Ammon: his heart knows everything, his lips taste everything.

Another theological school made known by monuments from the Ramessid era (nineteenth dynasty; circa 1250 BC) exhibits another theological theory according to which God—the only God whose nature (literally: name) is a total mystery—is presented as consisting of three divine entities that are a true trinity-unity: *Ptah*, *Horus*, and *Thoth*. Ptah is the supreme person and represents divine *intelligence*; Horus, according to a tradition already ancient at that time, is the *heart*; Thoth is the *word*, the instrument of divine works. Ptah is so designated as Supreme Being because the whole triad proceeds in some manner from him; he is, according to the very text of the aforementioned document: "the One who becomes Heart, the One who becomes Tongue."[11]

The second person of this trinity, Horus, the Divine Heart, was represented under the emblematic sacred figure of a hawk or

---

10 Cf. Moret, *Mystères Égyptiens*, p. 122. See also Louis Charbonneau-Lassay, *Le Bestiaire du Christ*, Chap. 11.
11 Cf. Moret, ibid., p. 126.

Fig. 3. — *The name of Horus on the royal banner of Chephren, according to Maspéro.*

falcon. From the time of the fourth dynasty, that is to say nearly three thousand years before our era, it bore, on the sovereign banner of Pharaoh Chephren, the double crown of North and South Egypt, and a heart-vase appears in the hieroglyphic formula of Horus' name (Fig. 3).

The falcon-king, the falcon-god, was the totem, that is, the genius and family symbol, of the Pharaohs considered as sons, as earthly emanations of, the divinity, as was also the emblem of Horus, the Heart of God. On the beautiful statue of the same Chephren, the sacred hawk presses its heart against the nape of the Pharaoh, whom it protects, and clasps his head with its outspread wings (Fig. 4).

Does not this pose, however, indicate much more than simple protection? It is of course expressive, since the divine bird covers with its heart the very cerebellum of the sovereign at its most sensitive point, at the level of the "bridge of Varolius," and since its body shelters that bundle of cervical nerves some anatomists call "the tree of life." But is there not still more?

Many of Egypt's sacred sculptures show us priests, orants, or other participants using magnetic passes on a subject; all the bystanders sometimes favor an elite person in this way, a newly born Pharaoh for instance; and, concerning the reigning Pharaoh Hatshepsut, one text tells us plainly that "the gods continually cast their life fluids after her every day."[12]

Fig. 4. — *Statue of Chephren, Cairo Museum.*

With the interplay of all this suggestive evidence, might not this be

---

12 Moret, *Rois et Dieux d'Égypte*, p. 26.

a transmission of this nature: a kind of intimate communion by emanation and absorption of the ardent divine fluids between the heart of the bird-god and the brain of the Pharaoh Chephrem?

A thousand years after him, when on his throne — the first of his thrones — the sumptuous Tut-Ankh-Amon sat in all the splendor of his magnificence, his two arms also rested, naked, between the extended wings of the large lapis lazuli hawk... and among the Egyptians, as among the Hebrews, the idea of power and authority was connected to the arms.

I do not want to exaggerate or create a context and say that the sometimes quite bizarre theology of the old Egypt has contained in it, so to speak, a kind of prehistory of our Catholic worship of the Divine Heart, no; but all the same I thought it well to show here how much of its thinking was about, and what a place and role was recognized for, the Heart of the almighty, omniscient and all good God; a religion that was coarse and material in some ways, almost devoid of asceticism, yet so lofty in some of its dogmas and so eloquently expressive in its formulas of adoration and prayers.

And I will hazard to say that, if our holy doctors of the medieval centuries had been informed about what the discoveries of recent times have revealed concerning the ideas and other matters of ancient Egypt, we would surely be finding reflections of the Sacred Heart in patristics and perhaps even the liturgy: the Roman ritual accepts, in the *Office of the Dead*, the testimony of the Sibylline oracles, which concurs with those of the prophet-king: "*teste David cum Sibylla.*"

Surely the physical heart of Jesus, which was first adored as the foremost redemptive wound and bodily source of the Savior's blood, is not to be compared with the purely metaphorical heart, which the Egyptians could only regard as the source of beauty and other divine perfections; but this fact remains: for the heart of God as for the human heart, they represented this metaphorical or corporal heart as distinct from the rest of the human form by a common hallowed emblem with such an expressive symbolism: the hieroglyphic vase. What remains is that, more than any other ancient people, it was through their heart that they gazed upon the Godhead, whom they addressed and beseeched to take pity on them, just as they beseeched their own hearts not to testify against them at the final hour.

And so we cannot fail to glimpse how this regard of the Egyptian soul for the hearts of God and man was in no way a response to a particularly sentimental state of mind. The religious elite of Egypt, as misguided as it may have been in its general theology, seems too scientific, too speculative, to have let itself be led, in this matter, by emotions rather than by serious and reasoned reflections.

II. FIRST OCCURRENCES

The physical organ that is the very center of our vital organism has always been considered by man as the noblest part of himself; however, the most ancient depictions of this organ are more rare than those of several other parts of the human body, the eye and the hand, for example.

The oldest representation of a heart as the center of a living organism goes back many thousands of years before our era; it is found in the prehistoric and Aurignacian cave of Pindal, near Oviedo (Spain). It is a heart figured in red color, in its anatomical place on the body of an elephant, and this drawing pertains to the hunting magic of primitive man.

Much less certain are the hearts reported as existing on prehistoric monuments of neolithic times, for example in Brittany and Bas-Poitou, especially when it comes to heart-shaped reliefs on granite, granulite, and mica schist rocks where erosion or crumbling have left protuberances on the rock surface that hint at such shapes.

In the classical art of Greece and Rome at the time of Christianity's birth, the heart appears quite often, easily confused moreover with the stylized ivy, linden, and convolvulus leaves used in epigraphy, on the border, or in various decorative motifs. Also, some drawings are of a very uncertain interpretation, such as the sign engraved in early Christian times on a marble of Antium, which is perhaps the image of an ivy leaf,[13] perhaps that of a heart, because the branches, such as those from its summit, were at that time one of the emblems of renewal, resurrection. And below this drawing are engraved these words: *Spes in Deo* (Fig. 5).

Fig. 5. — *Inscription on a marble, at Antium. First Christian centuries.*

In other respects, the heart is indisputably present on various jewels, trinkets, and toiletry articles, like this Gallo-Roman and most probably Christian object of bone or ivory from the collection R. de Rochebrune (Fig. 6); also like those metal beads about which we are told by Arthur Martin: "The pagans made their children wear beads that sometimes had obscene forms to ward off evil spells, according to Varro, or the form of a heart to instill, according to Macrobius, manly courage."[14]

Fig. 6. — *Object in bone, Gallo-Roman period. Count R. de Rochebrune Collection.*

Thus, in the words of Macrobius (5th century), in his time there was bestowed on a simple image of the heart a power to sway induced simply by wearing and habitually viewing it. And this idea probably included even more than the simple power of a psychic "support," of a spiritual symbol acting through the constant evocation of a thought pointedly called to mind. This concept related by Macrobius is in any case singularly suggestive.

Among the Roman art objects decorated with heart-shaped ornaments is a series of dishes and lamps in terracotta, of Christian

---

13 Cf. Dom Leclercq, *Dictionnaire d'Archéologie Chrétienne.*, tome I, vol. II, col. 2489, fig. 820.

14 Arthur Martin, *Divers monuments d'orfèvrerie*, in *Mélanges archéologiques*, tome I, p. 113.

origin, which merits our attention. They were almost all collected in the ancient Kingdom of Carthage, Tunisia, Eastern Algeria, Tripolitania. These artifacts, many of which are due to his personal research, have naturally caught the attention of Father Louis Delattre, the founding scientist of the *Lavigerie Museum* at St. Louis de Carthage, and he has published the most remarkable results in some valuable studies.[15]

Let us first look at some of these heart-shaped patterns: the most common type is a heart on which a cross is drawn with shallow lines. This cross is extended at the top, splitting into two lines that bend to the right and to the left and curl to form the contours of a leaf (Fig. 7). Father Delattre and Dom Leclercq rightly recognize in these leaves stylized grape vine leaves. A lamp decorated with similar motifs came out of the excavations at Timgad.[16]

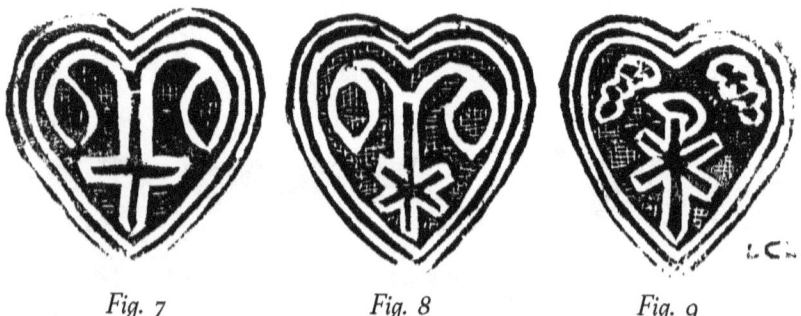

Fig. 7   *Fig. 8*   *Fig. 9*

Hearts represented on pottery of the Roman period collected in the region of Carthage (Tunisia).

A second type carries, inside the heart, not a cross but a primitive monogram of the Savior: I placed on X, the initials of "Iesus-Xrist" (Fig. 8).

Finally, a third variant is adorned with the Constantinian monogram of Christ, the combined Greek *chi* and *ro*, the first letters of the sacred name XPICTOC, *Xristos*. Two stylized grapes are placed above it (Fig. 9).

15 Louis Delattre, *La représentation du Cœur de Jésus dans l'Art chrétien*, Tunis, 1927, brochure. — *Symboles Eucharistiques — Carthage* (Tunis: Aloccio, 1930).
16 Albert Ballu, *Les ruines de Timgad* (Paris: Neurdein Frères, 1911), p. 165.

Beginnings of the Iconography of the Heart of Jesus

With all this ornamentation, three things are beyond all dispute. First, hearts are involved here and not just any scutiform motif. Dom Leclercq says: "It is possible to ask if these hearts are not mere decorative motifs, leaves for example. We will say, along with Father Delattre, we do not think so."[17] Second, these hearts enclose in their contours the cross or certain monograms of the Savior. Finally, vine branches and grapes are undeniable eucharistic symbols.

The chief question remains: do these hearts represent the very heart of Jesus or are they images of the Christian heart filled with the love of Christ and marked with his seal, the heart of the Christian in which the Christ abides by his grace, in which he is present through his Eucharist; that is: are they the expression of what is called the "spiritual habitation," the mystical dwelling of Christ in the Christian heart?[18]

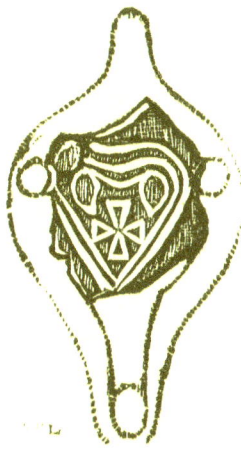

Fig. 10. — *Fragment of a Christian lamp from Carthage, 5th century, that bears a heart at its center. Lavigerie Museum of Carthage.*

Father Delattre was very concerned about this issue for quite a while, until the day when he was finally able to discover, at Carthage itself, a terracotta fragment that had been the center of a Christian lamp (Fig. 10). Now, this shard carries a heart in the field of which is inscribed a cross surmounted by the two symbolic vines. And this artifact illuminates the question happily, for Father Delattre himself, after examining thousands of Christian lamps from that time, formulated a kind of law that seems perfectly well founded, that is, that the subjects decorating the center of Carthaginian lamps are, almost always, directly related to the Savior of the world.

The most authoritative and severe critic of early Christian symbolism, Dom Henri Leclercq, has made much of the artifacts

---

17 Dom Leclercq, op. cit., fasc. 84, col. 1091.
18 Symbols of this "habitation" have been numerous on art documents in every era, as we will see in chapter 18 of this work.

supplied by Father Delattre, and, of these, he compares two bronze lamps of the same date, found in Catania, whose handles are cordiform; and one of these handles is decorated with an openwork cross cut into its perimeter (Fig. 11). This comparison is all the more judicious because other bronze lamps reproduced by the learned Benedictine bear, with their handles carved in the same manner, either the cross or the Constantinian monogram of Christ.[19]

The illustrious founder of the Lavigerie Museum has returned to God without seeing one of his greatest desires realized: to find an entire lamp bearing at its center the heart stamped with the cross and symbolic grape leaves. "The lamp of which we have only a fragment must not be the only one issued from the mold that served to shape it. We must not, therefore, despair of ever tracking down a good copy. Perhaps it exists in some museum or private collection."[20] Christian archaeology has not yet had, as far as I know, the satisfaction of seeing the fulfillment of Father Delattre's wish; it can, however, safely make its own these lines from Dom Leclercq: "Might we venture to ask if we do not have here the oldest monumental witnesses to the devotion to the Sacred Heart of Jesus? Up to the present day we have not been able to find any attestation of this devotion in the Fathers of the Church. A sentence of St. Paulinus of Nola is very imprecise. We have to wait for the writings of St. Gertrude and St. Mechtilde, of the Cîteaux order, to collect the oldest incontestable testimonies to this devotion. Now, it seems, the earthenware dishes and lamps of Carthage compensate for this silence."[21]

Fig. 11. — *Bronze lamps from Catania. Cf. Dom H. Leclercq, op. cit.*

---

19 Dom Leclercq, op. cit., fasc. 84, col. 1209, 1210, figs. 1 and 8, 6 and 7.
20 Delattre, *Symboles eucharistiques*, p. 81.
21 Dom H. Leclercq, op. cit., fasc. 84, col. 1091.

We might also venture to bring together with these hearts, and especially the central heart of the fragment of the Carthaginian lamp, the testimonies of the honor accorded especially to the mark of the wound in the side of Jesus in the first representations of the great symbol of the five wounds, the *Signaculum Domini*, at the very time when the Carthaginians were molding their lamps (fourth or fifth century).

Dom Leclercq is quite right: texts are much, but texts are not everything. And our best wishes are extended to the researchers of Carthage, hoping that tomorrow the privileged soil they examine will yield further precious revelations.

III. MEDIEVAL EMBLEMATIC

We have just seen that the hearts on the Carthage lamps, which are from the fourth or fifth century, can be accepted, because of the signs they bear, as the oldest representations known so far of the heart of Jesus Christ; and this attribution is thus regarded as based on solid evidence by expert archaeologists such as L. Delattre and Dom H. Leclercq.

During the centuries that followed the date of these objects, the representation of the human heart is sometimes present in Gallo-Frankish art, but becomes rarer in Romanesque and early Gothic art, at least until the end of the thirteenth century. Would the heart of the Savior not have been figured during these seven or eight centuries during which, however, the fervor was extraordinarily ardent for the place of the wound in his side, especially from the eleventh to the end of the thirteenth century, a period during which wonderful mystics, the best of the best — St. Bernard, William of St. Thierry, Guerric of Igny, the author of the *Vitis mystica*, Saints Lutgarde, Mechtilde, Gertrude, and the first Franciscan saints — echoed the praises of the heart wounded on the cross? So far we do not know of a single artifact from these centuries unmistakeably clear enough for us to be absolutely sure.

In the *Novissimum organon*, a review written by the Hiéron school,[22] an author who identifies himself only as "a doctor of

---

22 Num. for July–September 1898.

theology and canon law," has spoken at length about a marble from Castel Sant'Elia, near Nepi (Italy), which, according to him, dates from the sixth or seventh century and bears three hearts covered with grapes. Finally, after reading this — the author provides no image of the document — we do not know if these are actually hearts, even though the author says so, or grape clusters, or leaves. The document is retained only for the sake of inventory.

This absence of the Sacred Heart in art was quite striking to Baron Alexis de Sarachaga, the founder of Paray's Hiéron Museum, who drew attention to this lacuna and enlisted the help of several of his collaborators, without any actual results.

Personally, however, Baron de Sarachaga saw a mysteriously veiled representation of the heart of Jesus in the heart placed by medieval art in the hand of statues and images of St. Augustine, the heart of the "City of God." The work of the Bishop of Hippo bearing this title was indeed one of the favorites in the Church at that time, and it was the bedside book, so to speak, of our King St. Louis. Sarachaga, who several times paid me the honor of speaking with me about this question, said: In the *Apocalypse*, St. John explains that the heavenly Jerusalem has no need of sun or moon to enlighten it, because the divine Lamb is the lamp (Rev. 22:24), just as the heart of the City of God that Saint Augustine raises in his hand can only be the heart of the Lord (Fig. 12).[23]

Admittedly, on certain questions of archaeology, the founder of the Hiéron sometimes deceived himself to a baffling degree, but I know that some medievalists have regarded his hypothesis on the Augustinian heart as worthy of acceptance. He assured me that my late friend, Bishop Barbier de Montault, whose reputation for great archaeological expertise was known throughout Europe, was of this number, and I am not surprised at this, although he was previously of another opinion.[24] On the other hand, I do

---

23 The statue depicted here is only from a late period and after the Middle Ages; but the very characteristic attitude of the saint is basically the same for all his medieval statues.

24 He initially saw in the heart, whether with flames or not, the emblem of the ardent piety of the saint (Barbier de Montault, op. cit., tome II, p. 300).

not know what historical basis Sarachaga relied on to write that "the Templars of France, England, and Portugal bear the Sacred Heart since their initiation by St. Bernard."[25]

Fig. 12. — *Saint Augustine raising towards Heaven the heart of the City of God.*

In fact, we must come to the tragic days of the dissolution of this famous Order to have an incontestable image of the glorified heart of Jesus, which in truth was traced by one of its chiefs in circumstances that suggest it was not the first.

Before addressing this in the next section, let us examine some of the many images the Middle Ages devoted to the wound in the Savior's side, images that make the almost total dearth of any direct representations of the Divine Heart itself most surprising to later centuries that saw these images carved, embroidered, engraved, or painted everywhere.

On one of them, a miniature from a manuscript book of the eleventh or twelfth century (Fig. 13), the centurion has just withdrawn his spear from the flank of the Victim, and blood and water gush forth together. And, according to the sacred text, bystanders exclaim: "This is truly the son of God."[26]

The cope of St. Louis of Anjou, Bishop of Toulouse and nephew of our king St. Louis, bears an embroidery that shows us Nicodemus, embalming the sacred wound with a perfume of myrrh and

---

25 Letter to the author, from Marseille, July 13, 1917.
26 Matthew 27:54, Mark 15:39, Luke 23:47.

Part VI: The Iconography of the Wounded Heart of Jesus

Fig. 13. — Soldiers acclaiming the Savior on Calvary. Miniature, 11th or 12th century. From Revue de l'Art Chrétien, *1870, p. 300.*

aloe, before depositing the body of Jesus in his tomb[27] (Fig. 14). Nicodemus, who holds the spherical vase containing the perfume, wears on his head a cap, for he was a "doctor in Israel" (John 3:10); this detail makes it likely that the inspirer of this scene was familiar with the universities or great episcopal schools of his time.

Fig. 14. — The embalming of the wound in the side of Jesus on the cope of St. Louis of Anjou. From l'Art Chrétien, *1879, p. 308.*

27 John 19:39.

Beginnings of the Iconography of the Heart of Jesus

Finally, in the last image (Fig. 15), carved on an ivory in the Cluny museum, the date of which is close to that of the cope of St. Louis of Anjou, the spear bearer (in Greek *longinos*) — whom we call St. Longinus — after having struck the divine body with the spearhead, adores the wound he has just opened right to the heart of the divine sacrificial Victim.

Fig. 15. — *The adoration of the spear bearer before the injury he has just made to the side of Jesus. From the* Revue de l'Art Chrétien, *1879, p. 305.*

In all these works, do we not feel that the thought of their time was wholly centered on this bloody cavity in the side of Jesus, in the depths of which rested, inert now and yet alive, an invisible heart which was, however, clearly seen by everyone, which the mystics of that time invoked by name, and before the mysterious irradiation of which everyone fell down in adoration?

IV. THE HEART ENGRAVED BY THE CHIEFS OF THE ORDER OF THE TEMPLE

Let us cast ourselves in thought back to the year 1308. The Grand Master of the Knights Templar, Jacques de Molay, and the seventy-two principal leaders of this powerful Order had been arrested, by order of Philip IV of France, on the 13th of October, 1307, and afterwards interned in the towers of the castle of Chinon, in Touraine. There they will remain until the spring of 1309.

While at Chinon, the Grand Master Jacques de Molay and the principal dignitaries of the Order occupied the castle's dungeon. And this is where Cardinals Fredol, Suzy, and Brancaccio came to interrogate them on behalf of Pope Clement V who, that year, resided at Poitiers. They were therefore examined in relation to the extremely serious charges against their Order, which involved faith and morals, the abandonment of the monastic spirit and its obligations, and practices forbidden to religious orders such as financial speculation and banking, etc. These accusations were certainly exaggerated, and many, like that of idolatry, completely unjust. The cardinals were not misled: they welcomed the Templars' protestations of repentance for anything of which they were actually guilty, and declared them worthy of forgiveness. However, and this is undeniable, the Order of the Temple had departed from the spirit of its foundation, no longer fulfilled its purpose, and had strayed far from its obligatory path. The Church, which had approved the Order of the Temple on condition that this spirit would be kept and its initial goal pursued, was therefore justified in dissolving it as a monastic and military order and returning its members to secular life or allowing them to enter into other orders.

Less lenient, the Estates General of the Kingdom, then meeting in Tours and sitting in sovereign and civil court, formally condemned all Knights Templar, and their leaders were led back to Paris where, finally, Molay and his chief officers were condemned by the jurists to be burnt at the stake, and everyone else to perpetual prison.

Long before they left Chinon, the leaders of the Temple, even if they did not know the tragic destiny that awaited them, knew themselves to be in the hands of their enemies and had to wonder with anguish what would be their fate. And, on the wall of their prison, one of them deeply engraved an irrefutable testimony of their common repentance, of their anguish, and also of their faith, of their hope in eternal salvation (Fig. 16).

Beginnings of the Iconography of the Heart of Jesus

This document consists of a set of "graffiti," figures engraved with a knife in stone over a length of about 0 m 85, and 0 m 70 in height. They are cut primarily into four major dressed stones:

The first has at its center a cross placed on a mound, which evokes Calvary. On one side of this cross a figure haloed like a saint, who bears an oval shield on his arm, is kneeling in front of another cross against which a spear is leaning to the height at which would be found the wounded side of Jesus. Above, another

Fig. 16. — The large Templar graffiti from the castle keep of Chinon.

cross, which surmounts a small circle, supports a larger one. For reasons I have explained elsewhere,[28] it is possible to see in this haloed figure the very founder of the Temple, Hugues de Payns[29] (who was never officially canonized, but who could be venerated in his order as a "venerable," or perhaps a "blessed," as was the case with Gerard Tunc of Martigues for the Knights Hospitallers of Saint John of Malta). On the other side of this central cross, a mystical Calvary consists of a large cross against which the spear is again pointed at the place where its spearhead struck the divine flank, and on the cross itself the five wounds of Jesus

---

28 Louis Charbonneau-Lassay, *Le Cœur rayonnant du donjon de Chinon*, (Milano: Archè, 1975).

29 Generally *de Payens*.

Part VI: The Iconography of the Wounded Heart of Jesus

are evoked by the nails and a mark that relates to the lateral wound of the divine body. Beneath this assemblage recalling the redeeming torture a steady hand engraved this cry of anguished repentance: IE REQUIER A DIEU PDON, "I beseech God's forgiveness" (Fig. 17).

ie requier a dieu pdon

Fig. 17. — *The repentant inscription in the castle keep of Chinon.*

And the lettering of these words is of the purest epigraphy in use at the time of the dissolution of the Order of the Temple.

On the *second stone* we see an isolated lance near two hooded persons who wear the same mantle as the figure engraved on the first stone; and between them an extended hand similar to the so-called "Hand of Fatima" Arabic talisman.

The *third stone* shows a heraldic square quartered, on each section of which is the same figure as on the shield of the personage on the first stone. Below, an isolated square bears the same subject. This figure is also found in several former commanderies of the Temple without anyone now knowing exactly what it means[30] (Fig. 18).

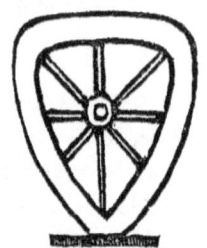

Fig. 18. — *Large eschuteon on the tombstone of a Templar of the commanderie of Roche-en-Cloué (Vienne).*

The *fourth stone* is more interesting: we see in fact someone of monastic appearance whose face, already quite naively rendered by the poorly equipped engraver, has been regrettably mutilated. This monk, this saint crowned with a

---

30 I have encountered it in two Poitou commanderies. Cf. Louis Charbonneau-Lassay, *Le Cœur rayonnant du donjon de Chinon*, p. 16.

nimbus much more pronounced than the one on the first stone, wears his hood thrown back. Within the nimbus that enhaloes it, a deep recess leaves the head in flat relief and emphasizes the particular holiness of this person as one of the Elect. In all likelihood this is St. Bernard, who was in his lifetime the law giver for the Order of the Temple, who had it approved by the Pope at the Council of Troyes in 1128, and made it a subsidiary branch of his Order of Cîteaux.

This saint, set in profile, contemplates a heart in heraldic style very carefully carved into the stone, a heart that sends forth a whole burst of lengthy rays. Beneath the heart and in the glory of its light an escutcheon bears the royal fleur-de-lys of France.

Is not this heart — the center of a source of light and glory — the very one adored and invoked by the Church as the hearth of all light and glory, as the "fiery furnace of love"?

Now, here we have an absolutely precise historical date: between the spring of 1308 and that of 1309.

The ancient royal château of Chinon, 12th, 13th, 15th centuries. Within the enclosure, the castle-keep of Coudray, built by Philip Augustus. Wood engraved by the author (ed.).

The castle-keep of Coudray, Chinon.
Wood engraved by the author (ed.).

CHAPTER SEVENTEEN

The Ancient Iconography of the Heart of Christ at the End of the Middle Ages

I. HEART-SHAPED DEPICTIONS OF THE FIVE WOUNDS

FROM FATHER FÉLIX ANIZAN I HAVE received an unsigned seventeenth-century engraving from a Capuchin monk of the monastery of Aalst (Belgium), which may well be of Franciscan inspiration. It was obtained by the imprint of an etched copper plate and I traced an exact copy of it with a woodcut.

This quite evocative composition represents a large cross planted on a hillock; half-way up this cross the wounded heart of the Savior is brought forward under a crown of thorns while, behind it, the whip and the bundle of rods are set as trophy with sponge and spear crossing each other in saltire. At the place where the spear and the sponge join the horizontal branch of the cross, and at the foot of these two objects, the two pierced hands and two pierced feet of Jesus appear on the convex surface of four hearts of similar appearance to that of the central heart. The nails of the crucifixion and other objects mentioned by the Gospel accounts of the tragedy on Calvary are strewn about haphazardly on the hillock (Fig. 1).

Faced with this somewhat strange composition, two questions arise of themselves for the iconographer. First: exactly what idea inspired it? Then, second: has this idea already been conveyed by the figurative arts before the time of the engraving of Aalst, or are we then in the presence of a new theme?

When we carefully examine the ancient iconography of the lateral wound and the heart of Jesus Christ, it often seems that the mystical artists of the late Middle Ages were haunted by a clear desire to make it well understood that the Savior's heart, struck by the legionnaire's spear only after the acknowledgment

Part VI: The Iconography of the Wounded Heart of Jesus

Fig. 1. — Engraving on copper originating in the convent of Aalst (Belgium), 17th century.

of his death, nevertheless had its actual share of suffering in the redeeming torment. As I have already said in previous chapters, it did not escape them that, without being directly struck first of all, the heart, center and end point of our physical sensations, had necessarily felt the mortally painful repercussions of all the offenses inflicted on all the limbs, all the muscles, all the nerves, and all the organs of the person of Jesus.

Is it not under the influence of this idea that the greatest artists of the past, who were neither naïve nor misinformed, have committed this anachronism of representing the spear wound, open and bleeding on the body of the living Christ? In the fifteenth century Mantegna did this on his *Ecce Homo*, which is in the Louvre (Fig. 2), and so was it done before him, at the end of the fourteenth century, by that anonymous master whose picture appeared at the Exhibition of the French Primitives, and which shows us Jesus Christ crucified, still alive and speaking, and yet wounded by the spear-thrust to his side. Now, neither the Christ of pity of Mantegna, nor especially the living Crucified One of the Primitives, are images of the risen Jesus adorned with all his wounds become glorious; no, both of them, and the artists who did likewise, indeed show us Jesus in the last hours, the last minutes of

Fig. 2. — Ecce Homo, Mantegna (Louvre), 15th century.

his human life, yet stricken with the wound to his side. Were they just distracted? Who would believe it? I prefer to think that they wanted to have us understand that the heart, wounded only after death, had however actually shared in all the pains of the Passion, and that the spear only opened, only "lanced," dare I say, an organ already heavy with suffering and overwhelmed with gore-blood.

In any case, is not this the idea that presided over the composition of the Aalst engraving? The whips, the rods, and the dolorous crown are put in immediate contact with the heart, and the pierced hands and feet are one with four images of the heart placed on the spear and the sponge as if to indicate the direct relationship between the sufferings of the pierced limbs and the heart itself, which took in their after-effects and hoarded them all up.

There remains the question of whether the theme I believe to be that of the Aalst etching was conveyed in the arts during the Christian ages preceding the time when this etching was made.

I do not really know of any other composition that is absolutely the same, but many of the artifacts I have in hand seem related to the same inspiration.

— At the beginning of the seventeenth century that saw the Aalst's piece engraved, and in the same region, Hubert Germijs, "abbot and lord of Saint-Trond," used an ogival seal with a crest bearing a cross composed of four hearts appointé, and charged in its center with another heart.

It is probable that, on the original seal, this central heart would have borne the spear wound; Th. De Raadt, who brought this seal to our attention,[1] does not mention it, but he says that he himself knew of it only through two "quite damaged" imprints, borne by authentic documents from 1620 and 1630. Note that this involves an ecclesiastical seal stamped with a cross and abbatial mitre (Fig. 3).

Fig. 3. — Ogival seal of Hubert Germijs, 17th century.

[1] Th. de Raadt, *Les sceaux armoriés des Pays-Bas*, tome I, p. 487 and Append. ix, p. 7, num. 168, Bruxelles, 1898.

For anyone who has studied the iconography of the five wounds, this composition is nothing but a cross evocative of the five wounds to the limbs and heart of Jesus Christ, but surely the same motif, treated by a heraldist before the Renaissance, would have been more expressive.

— We have an example in this watercolor drawing inside the back of a 1528 English book which belongs to Mrs. Rodolph, of La Haye: On the branches and in the center of a cross in an X, termed in blazonry *saltire ecoté* (a charge quite common in English heraldry), are five hearts; the middle one is opened by the wound of the spear and the others are attached to the wood of the cross by nails (Fig. 4). Is this not the same subject as on the engraving of Aalst?

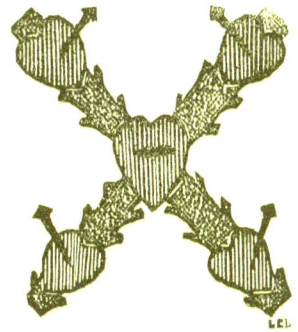

Fig. 4. — Saltire ecoté inside the back of an English book, 1528.

This ecoté cross, that is, a cross that still bears the "stubs" [*écots* in French] of poorly pruned side branches, is wine colored, the hearts are red, and the nails are black.

Did someone want to recall, by the choice of a cross in an X, the initial letter of the word Xhrist? This is quite likely; there were still at that time gold coins bearing the victorious inscription: *XPC vincit, XPC regnat, XPC imperat*, "Christ is victorious, Christ reigns, Christ commands."

Father Richard was therefore quite right when he wrote in *Regnabit*[2] about the heart-shaped representations of divine wounds, that artists of past centuries had sometimes represented the cross with five wounded hearts instead of the five wounds.

Here is an example of this heart-shaped representation of wounds even older than the previous ones: dealing with the ancient iconography of the Evangelists, Mgr. Barbier de Montault reproduced, in his *Traité de l'iconographie chrétienne*,[3] a Byzantine

2 "La blessure du côté et la blessure du Cœur de Jésus du XIe au XIIe siècle," in *Regnabit*, Oct. 1922, p. 389.
3 New ed. (Paris: Société de librairie ecclésiastique et religieuse, 1898), tome 2, p. 281 and plate XXXV, num. 357.

miniature of the eleventh century (Fig. 5), whose meaning remains obscure to anyone not somewhat initiated into the figurative language of those distant times, and for which he gives, moreover, an altogether insufficient explanation since he keeps solely with the symbolism of the Evangelists.

Before discussing it, you will recall that I had occasion to mention, in the first part of this work, about an arrangement of the cross and four roses, the age-old acronym for the five wounds that consists of a cross with symmetrical arms accompanied, between the arms, by four crosslets, four rings, sometimes four crescents, or four roses. This symbolizes the side wound of Jesus, represented by the cross, while the wounds to his limbs are represented by the other signs. From the fifth to the sixteenth century, this motif, the *Signaculum Domini*, is found everywhere.

Fig. 5. — Byzantine miniature of the 11th century, according to Mgr Barbier de Montault.

Reproduced at the center of the Byzantine miniature is this acronym for the five wounds, but here each wound to the limbs is figured by a heart, hence the four hearts about the cross.

Now here is a probably much less well known interpretation: in the figurative and mysterious language of ancient Christian iconography, the four Evangelists were sometimes represented in the Byzantine Empire by the Greek letter *G*, the *gamma* (which looks like our letter *L* inverted), repeated four times; here, the frame itself of the miniature is made of four gamma, gamma-brackets, so to speak, separated by dots.

This composition taken as a whole is, then, a mysterious acronym for the Divine Master showing his wounds and placed in the center of the emblem, at least as mysterious, of his four inspired historians. This is a motif that the entire medieval period was justly fond of, and so often represented by both the Christian East and West in the form of Christ sitting, teaching or blessing the earth, in the midst of the four evangelical animals, the Man, the Lion, the Eagle, and the Ox.

We should not be surprised to see the Evangelists figured by signs as obscure as the gamma. In the paintings of the Roman catacombs they are well hidden from us under the emblem of four manuscripts rolled up and set upright in a scrinium, that is to say with a seal or in a cylinder intended for rolled parchments.

The already mentioned motif of the cross between four hearts is also seen, as early as the sixth century, on the famous golden salver of Gourdon, a motif that can almost certainly be interpreted as yet another evocation of the five wounds of the Lord.

In truth, the cult of the wounded heart of Jesus Christ does not have its origin in the deep meditations and exaltations of theologians or teachers of the past, or in the conceptions of our old artists; it does not have its source in the revelations, the visions, the inspirations of the saintly men and women of any time or in the zeal of a particular religious order; it comes wholly and directly from the sole worship of the divine blood and the five chief wounds from which it poured, according to the word of the Nicene Creed, "for us men, and for our salvation." By this well-marked route, the cult of the wounded heart goes back to the very birth of the Church.

Of course, theologians, artists, doctors, saintly men and women, and religious orders, have added to, each has quickened, according to the providential views and according to their time, the cult of the five wounds, the worship of the open heart of Christ Jesus. But no, none of them has invented anything new. And when I look at Calvary, in spite of the darkness that enshrouds it with mourning, I see, already, worshipers of the pierced heart: Mary, "the dolorous Mother who stands upright," John, Magdalene, and, surely from that moment, the legionnaire whose spear tip has just initialed with a flourish the "Consummatum est" of the Crucified One, who withdraws it from the open chest while his captain proclaims that this One, truly, is indeed the Son of God, whose heart, even now, pours forth blood and water through his wound!

Part VI: The Iconography of the Wounded Heart of Jesus

This is why, after John among the frightening crags of Patmos saw him standing and yet immolated, the first artists of our Faith represented the Lamb on the mountain, alive and triumphant, yet with a stream of blood gushing in an arc from his chest; while their successors later conceived a sacred acronym where the five main wounds were symbolized and brought together, so that they would soon be united and focused for us in the single image of the heart forever open and radiant. "En alterum Signum," Pope Leo XIII will say, "This is the last sign."

II. HEART-SHAPED MOLDS

Some documents just pass by like shooting stars in the sky; by happenstance they emerge from the earth for a moment, or from the shadows into which the indifference of the ignorant had deemed them buried; then, quite quickly sometimes, other fortuitous causes plunge them once more under a new shroud of oblivion, whenever not entirely destroyed forever.

Hence the great utility of fixing their images so that their memory, so that, above all, whatever still throbbed in them for the souls of former times, may at least survive their own destruction a while longer.

The great and magnificent religious poets who were once the simple people of France have often shaped with so much faith, so much resignation, and so much hope these lowly testimonies of their piety, just like those of all their loves. Both such witnesses vibrate like lyres for those who know how to question and understand them.

Jewelry Mold from Saint-Laurent-sur-Sèvre (Vendée), 14th century

In 1903, one of the heads employed at the laundry of Saint-Laurent collected, in excavations made on the grounds of this location near an unfinished church, a small stone mold made to cast two pendants at once, but broken by a pickaxe.

The shape of one of these objects was crushed, the other produced a kind of openwork medal, composed of an irregular pentagonal band and furnished with a heart in the middle also made of a flat band whose branches are wound inside in the shape of a cross.

In 1904, in an article in the *Revue du Bas-Poitou*,[4] I only indicated this discovery, but ten years later I sought in vain to know what had become of this object.

All I have is the drawing made from a wax imprint communicated to me by Father Blanchet (Fig. 6).

When compared to a number of jewels from western France, from the Raoul de Rochebrune and Parenteau collections, which bear inscriptions and are thus dated by their paleography, the Saint-Laurent mold is classified as dating from the fourteenth century.

This is surely a devotional jewelry mold, since the heart is marked with the Cross.

But what is this heart?

The heart of a Christian full of devotion for the mystery of the Cross? This is possible, but not certain.

Is it the heart of Our Lord Jesus Christ?

To unreservedly assert this today would be too rash; more reckless still would be anyone maintaining the exact opposite.

I will venture to say this: The heart of the Saint-Laurent mold is, with regard to the iconography of the heart of Jesus, a possible but problematic artifact. The solution called for can only be given by comparing similar artifacts that are easier to distinguish. Why should we not expect them?

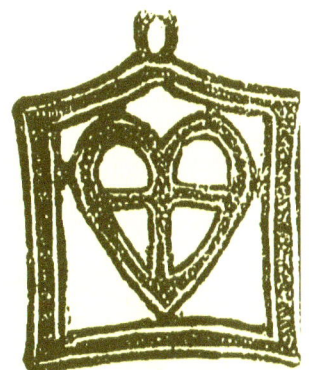

Fig. 6. — Saint-Laurent-sur-Sèvre (Vendée), 14th century.

A Host-Mold from Vic, in Catalonia, 14th century

Another artifact of great importance in the history of devotion to the heart of Jesus is an iron mold for the manufacture of eucharistic hosts from the fourteenth century. This mold was found a few years ago in the rich display cases of the Episcopal Museum of Vic. It contains two large host-molds for the celebrating priest and a single host-mold for the simple communicant. What has

---

4 1904, fasc. II.

become of it during the infernal storm[5] that, in Catalonia, has obliterated so many treasures of art, especially religious art?

This precious artefact was pointed out to me in 1922 at a residence in Madrid by Father Antonio Capuano, O. M. I., to whom Canon Llado, of Vic, had disclosed its existence. Through them I was able to obtain, from Don Gudiol, the learned curator of the Episcopal Museum of Vic and professor of sacred archaeology, a notice written by him in 1902, in the *Veu del Montserrat*. From this I have excerpted in full what follows:

"The most interesting of the two hosts," he states, "is the one on the right. In two concentric circles that frame the subject as a whole,

Fig. 7. — Iron host-mold from Vic, 14th century.

a quatrefoil bears, between its re-entrant angles, tips containing barely visible annulets. Within this quatrefoil is seen a cross raised upon a heart, and two similar crosses on each side of the heart; a horizontal line (forming a terrace) is placed under the whole and beneath which we see the letters XPS (Fig. 7).

"In this heart and these three crosses we see an express allusion to the sacrifice on Calvary, and also see quite clearly indicated the object to which the XPS sigil refers, which is the very name of Christ.

"This being so, we should recognize, in the heart that is the main object of the composition, an explicit representation of his heart

---

5 Spanish Civil War (1936-1939). — *Trans.*

opened on Golgotha and shedding the last drops of his blood. That is surely a manifestation, a representation of the Sacred Heart of Jesus.

"The other large host directs our thoughts solely to sacrifice on Calvary. Within a quatrefoil similar to the other host is engraved a crucifix and the letters IHES, signifying the name of Jesus...

"Certain details of great importance," Don Gudiol adds, "enable one to say that what we have here is indeed a specimen of a host-mold from the mid-fourteenth century (*de pleno siglo XIV*): the character of the letters in which persists a forthrightly Romanesque tradition (*una tradicion altamente romanica*), the extremities of several strokes ending with curves in the form of anchors, as in early fleurs-de-lys, and finally the disposition of the Crucified whose body is dangling with arms aslant and legs bent and drawn up; everything is in agreement with what we have just concluded about the date."

This could not be better said. Chronologically, we can therefore place the Vic mold towards the middle of the fourteenth century and be in complete agreement with one of Spain's most authoritative archaeologists.

Here again we have, for the iconography of the Sacred Heart, a item of uncontested date.

Mold with the insignia of Champigny-sur-Veude (Indre-et-Loire), 15th century

Around 1898, the superior of the congregational school of Champigny-sur-Veude had at his home a small plate of a black schist, similar to that of the Silurian deposits of Ille-et-Vilaine, on which a mold was hollowed out for historiated lead castings.

This outstanding religious figure has died since then; his school, closed under the confiscation laws, has undergone alternating periods of revival and dormancy, and I have sought in vain to know what has become of the mold I saw there.

Fortunately, I have several stamped impressions and lead pencil rubbings which are documents as convincing and accurate as the best photographs.

I give here an engraving of these rubbings (Fig. 8).

The hollowed out portions naturally appear in white, and the molded object is seen in reverse, that is, the spear is where the reed

Part VI: The Iconography of the Wounded Heart of Jesus

Fig. 8. — *Champigny-sur-Veude (Indre-et-Loire), 15th century.*

was and conversely, as on the wax imprints of seals.

It is easy to understand the use of this object: applied and bound to another flat part of the same size, and previously heated, the mold was set upright; molten lead or tin, poured into a funnel from above, flowed down into the whole network of contours where it was immobilized by cooling. The depth of the grooves, about 2 millimeters, gave the metal a relatively sufficient rigidity.

Large numbers of these molds are known and may be divided into two main groups: "pilgrimage insignias" and "confraternity insignias." The one that interests us should be placed in the latter category.

The heart of Jesus, crucified at the junction of the cross, is a summary of the entire divine body, while the four nails, spear, and reed form a composition around it quite in the style of the fifteenth century.

The subject is surrounded by a wire frame designed to give strength to the openwork as a whole. The rings on the perimeter served to fix the lead to clothing or a hat.

At the beginning of the sixteenth century, Champigny became the ducal residence for the Montpensiers and these princes built there a splendid palace, only a shadow of which remains, as well as a still intact Sainte-Chapelle dedicated to Saint Louis. Cardinal de Givry, who was bishop of Poitiers from 1541 to 1555, adorned this chapel with stained glass windows that are incomparable jewels. But neither the Sainte-Chapelle of Champigny nor anything else in this locality seems to have been a center of pilgrimage. While feudal and religious life, intense as it was in the fifteenth century, enables us to consider the existence of a confraternity as very possible at this time, it is just as likely that the interesting mold we have just examined was once for local use.

Confraternity mold from Rennes (Ille-et-Vilaine), 15th century

Under the signature of Bishop Barbier de Montault, one of the most qualified specialists in Christian iconography in the nineteenth century, the *Revue de l'Art Chrétien*[6] reported in 1806 a stone mold discovered at Rennes, deposited in the Museum of this city, the impressions of which Mr. Mowart presented to the Société des Antiquaires de France, June 10, 1885.

On one side, says Mgr. Barbier, were the instruments of the Passion, and on the other, a person he describes in detail.

Recalling that the learned prelate, my fellow citizen and friend, to whom I once gave an impression of the Champigny mold, told me that he owned an impression of another *quite similar* mold, I asked the directors of the Rennes Museum for a drawing of the mold in question to know whether it was the one once indicated by Mgr. Barbier.

In reply I learned from the distinguished curator of the Museum of Rennes that there is no mold fitting the description of the one reported by the *Revue de l'Art Chrétien*; and I have almost no hope now of finding its image, an image that would have been interesting to compare here with the Champigny document. Be that as it may, I thought it at least useful to point out its existence.

A cake-mold from the Rennes Museum, 16th century

When learning that the confraternity mold, which Mgr. Barbier said was deposited at the Museum of Rennes, was not there, the obliging curator of this Museum, Mr. Paul Banéat, sent me the impressions of three cake-molds, one of which bears a figure that merits studying here.

All three consist of a cylinder covered with designs in hollow relief, which, rolled on a turn of fresh dough, leave raised reliefs that remain after baking. The ends of the three cylinders also bear designs in hollow relief, intended to produce globe-shaped embellishments on the flat surface of the cakes.

On one of the cylinders can be seen thatched huts, trees, a horse harnessed with a kind of mesh-work caparison; on the second

---

6 Barbier de Montault, *Iconographie d'un moule à usage de confrérie*, in *Revue de l'Art Chrétien*, tome IV, 1st book, 1886.

Part VI: The Iconography of the Wounded Heart of Jesus

are foliage and an inscription: W. LE ROY DE F. (*Long live the King of France*); on the third, intertwining and the capital letters W L repeated and separated by simple hearts and fleur-de-lys.

It seems that one can interpret the letters W L as *Vive Louis* (Louis XII, died 1515). The shape of the Roman capitals and the general style of these molds indicates the early sixteenth century.

The last of these just mentioned molds bears at one of its ends a four-leaved floret, and at the other a symbolic figure formed by a heart supported by a crescent and surmounted by a cross (Fig 9).

How we interpret this heart should not be in doubt. It is the heart of Jesus, and this identification is further clarified by the presence of the crescent from which the heart originates.

Fig. 9. — Rennes (Ille-et-Vilaine), 16th century.

For many centuries prior to the molds of Rennes, the moon was, in Christian symbolism, one of the emblems of the Virgin Mary. "Pulchra ut luna," the liturgical books say of her: "In our sight you are, O Virgin Mary, luminous and beautiful like the moon in the dark hours of the night." And in his visions on Patmos, St. John shows her clothed with the sun and her feet resting on a crescent moon (Apoc. 12:1).

In this way then — a detail still not encountered, as far as I know, on any older or similarly stylized artifact relating to the divine heart — we have here the image of the heart of Jesus intimately united with the symbol of Mary, his mother.

Going even further, the engraver probably wanted to summarize, in the design of a single emblem, the entire human career of the Redeemer, starting in Mary's womb and ending on Calvary; for the heraldic cross pattee, which iconographically distinguishes the heart as that of Jesus, is not the only one; it bears another, a Latin cross, which brings us in thought directly back to the death of the Redeemer.

Surely those who have studied the emblems utilized from Louis XI to Henry II will not find this interpretation too forced: the secular heraldry of that time had much more complicated symbols compared with which the hieroglyph of the divine heart, exhibiting here the initial point and end of his terrestrial life, seems a quite simple idea.

Now let us see what these objects teach us. Objects of no worth in their own time, they were, first and foremost, simple ordinary things: a trinket for a shepherd or a worker, a lead seal for a country brotherhood, a mold to decorate cakes for the artisans and citizens of some fine town... but we should recognize how all these objects are full of meaning because those who made them were filled with faith. Above all we should recognize that the worship of the heart of Jesus was consequently intense, so that it could be manifested even in the most varied objects of piety and of everyday life.

And we are speaking here, do not forget, of the time between the second half of the fourteenth century and the second quarter of the sixteenth.

Another host-mold from Vic, 17th century

Earlier I recalled the very precious fourteenth-century host-mold in the collections of the Episcopal Museum of Vic, in Catalonia.

This museum also has another one, from the late seventeenth or eighteenth, the image of which we once again owe to the kindness of Don Juan Llado and which, without having the high importance of the first, is however of real interest.

From the fifteenth century, especially in France and Germany, artists began to represent the image of Jesus Christ within the setting of his own heart. Most of the time they represented him as a little child and surrounded him with the instruments of the Passion, or put them in his hands, to make it clear that from his advent in this world until the day of his death he suffered in advance in his heart the pangs of the redeeming torment.

During the sixteenth century, another subject of the same kind, but imbued with a less robust mysticism and a less clear as well as a less lofty meaning, became fashionable: on a heart with a partially open vertical wound, Jesus as a teenager or young man is resting. Father Hilaire de Barenton, of the Franciscan Order, exhibited in his work on the Sacred Heart[7] a reproduction of one of the most remarkable of these engravings, of the seventeenth century. Also, I see on the title page of a beautiful edition — the second edition I believe — of the *Treatise on the Love of God by Francis De Sales bishop of Geneva*, printed at Lyon by Rigaud in 1617, during the lifetime of the author, that the saintly founder of the Visitandines loved this subject because the same image is figured in it. In both examples, the Savior is seated on the very wound of his own heart; his feet are crossed, his head rests on his left hand, while his right hand holds on his knees the globe of the world. Jesus seems to meditate or sleep. A quadrilobate nimbus surrounds his head; his bust is radiant while his heart is surrounded by ardent flames: a dual symbol of glory and love.

Father de Barenton sees in the heart which thus serves as the Savior's throne, the Sacred Heart. I think he is right because of the injury which is difficult to attribute to another heart, although the verticality of this wound, which cleaves the heart on its median surface, is in disagreement with the tradition that always depicted it as horizontal or oblique.

And, what is more, I would stress that the flames surrounding the heart would be equally appropriate for symbolizing the ardent love of a faithful heart. Such flames are not enough to identify it as the heart of Jesus.

The engraver who executed the Vic mold which we present here (Fig. 10) was better inspired: he wanted no possible doubt on a priest's host, where the representation of a profane heart was inadmissible, as to the nature of the heart represented, and for this purpose he surrounded it not with *flames*, a symbol of love, of ardor, but with *rays*, a symbol of divine glory. And so this became the perfect touch: the circle of cherubim, forming a crown round about, could worship for the same reason both the heart and the entire person of the Savior of the world, while the images of the one and the other, at the same time as the eucharistic realities, descended into the bosom of the communicant.

---

7 *La dévotion au Sacré-Coeur* (Paris: Librairie Saint-François, 1914), p. 247.

III. REPRESENTATIONS OF THE HEART OF JESUS IN SIGILLOGRAPHY

The small seal of Estème Couret

The very rich collection of the late Count Raoul de Rochebrune contained a small seal or bronze signet, engraved with the name of Estème Couret about whom we know only, by the orbicular shape of his signet, that he was not an ecclesiastic (because no counter-seal is involved here).

We see on the field of this seal a heart that bears a cross planted in its summit and from the foot of which rays are escaping. It seems quite impossible for this cross-bearing and glorified heart to be Couret's, although his name may derive etymologically from

Fig. 10. — Host-mold, 17th–18th century. Episcopal museum of Vic. The white strokes indicate the hollow lines of the mold which, on the host, would appear in relief.

the word "heart" [in French, *coeur*]. It can only be, then, that the heart of the Savior was taken by Estème Couret as a "canting coat of arms," as an ideogram for his name (Fig. 11).

De Rochebrune, relying on the shape of the letters of this seal, dated it from the fourteenth century. This lettering is in fact closer to that of the late thirteenth century than the Gothic letters of the fifteenth. In his valuable work on the sigillography of Poitou, however, François Eygun classifies the object of our focus among the seals of the fifteenth century because its overall design is that of the seals of that time.

Fig. 11. — The seal and imprint of the seal of Estème Couret.

Be that as it may, it would not be rash to classify this document as either from the last quarter of the fourteenth century or beginning of the fifteenth.

From this date the clearly indisputable representations of the heart of Jesus, that have escaped destruction and come down to us, are extremely numerous and prove an intensity of worship of the divine heart in this locality as yet unsuspected a few years ago.

The Seal of Jacques Musekin

From our forebears prior to Caesar who covered themselves with the skins of wild beasts, from our forebears of Gallo-Roman times who, at the feast of Bacchus, were clothed with the *nebrides* (fawn skins) of the roe deer or fallow deer, to Charlemagne who, as Eginhard tells us, usually wore a waistcoat of otter skin or rat,[8] to that brilliant procession of princes and great lords, queens and high chatelaines, who the illuminators of Capetian and Valois times represented all dressed in ermine, vair, and petit-gris, to the townsfolk and peasants of that time, who wrapped themselves

---

8 Eginhard, *Vie de l'empereur Charlemagne*, French trans. L. Halphen (Paris: Champion, 1923), p. 69.

The Ancient Iconography of the Heart of Christ at the End of the Middle Ages

in winter in the skins of goats, cats, or rabbits, all Old France seems quite taken with the habitual use of furs.

So too the wealthy traders, the suppliers appointed by the sovereigns for whom they brought valuable animal furs unknown to us "from foreign lands," were esteemed persons at the court of these princes.

Such does Master Jacques Musekin, fur merchant, appear to be. He is frequently cited under the names of Copin or Iacopin Musequin in the accounts and inventories of the last hereditary dukes of Burgundy.[9]

A receipt on parchment of a payment in furs has come down to us from this person, which Dr. Jourdin, from Châlons-sur-Marne, has kindly pointed out to me through the *Intermédiaire des Chercheurs*.[10] This receipt, dated June 9, 1391, is preserved today in the Departmental Archives of Côte-d'Or at Dijon (Series B, Packet 387).

Under this date of June 9, 1391 hangs the fur-merchant's "seal" on a simple tail. I give here the reproduction according to the drawings received from Vicar General Marigny and Dr. Jourdin (Fig. 12).

From mid-seal downwards is a heart from which rises, between two stars, the shaft of a cross that ends in an eight-rayed sigil for Christ, or, if one prefers, a second cross charged with an X, the initial letter of Xhrist; around it the name of Jacques Musekin was once legible, but is now effaced from the wax.

For the learned Dr. Jourdin,[11] as well as for all those who, like him, specialize in the study of late medieval symbolic marks, the heart on Jacques Musekin's seal is surely an image of the heart of Jesus Christ.

The double cross charged with the letter X is sufficient to indicate this.

Perhaps some will say that all we have here is one of those enigmatic combinations of lines seen in commercial signs so frequently used at the end of the Middle Ages and the sixteenth century. Now, it so happens that my learned correspondent from

---

9 Cf. Henri and Bernard Prost, *Inventaires mobiliers des Ducs de Bourgogne* (Paris: Leroux, 1908), index.
10 Num. 10, 30 August 1923, col. 649.
11 Letter of Sept. 22, 1923.

Châlons-sur-Marne, Dr. Jourdin—who designated the heart in question as being indeed the divine heart—is one of the French scholars most involved with the above-mentioned commercial marks of those times. And although the plundering Germans, by transporting his Saint-Quentin library and his papers back to Germany, have deprived us of the completed study he was about to publish on *Le Symbolisme dans la Signature française*, what is left, from among other pre-war works, is a valuable study on the trinitarian "4" of traders in use until the seventeenth century.[12] I am no zealot of the "argument from authority," but I still maintain that the opinion of a

Fig. 12.—*The seal of Jacques Musekin in the Dijon archives, 1391.*

scholar, who has specialized in a particular subject and a particular era, should prevail over often improvised views to the contrary.

But, one might say, this heart does not bear the mark of the spear. Can it really be regarded as representing the heart of the Lord?

This heart was affixed to the Dijon parchment in 1391, but the heart on Estème Couret's seal, which also bears the cross and from which rays shoot forth, which is itself from the early fourteenth century if not the end of the thirteenth, does not bear the wound of the spear; the radiating heart from the graffiti of the Tower of Coudray, at Chinon, from 1309,[13] placed in direct contact with all the instruments of the Passion and under a figuration of the lateral wound of Jesus, does not bear the mark of this wound either;

12 In *Bibliographie de la France. Journal général de l'Imprimerie et de la Librairie*, 1912, fasc. 19 to 23.
13 Cf. 6th Part, Chap. 16, p. 235, Fig. 16.

neither does the heart figured on the cross, between the two other crosses of Calvary on the Vic host-mold, and beneath which one reads the name of Christ, XPS, bear the wound of the spear.[14]

And this is so for other fourteenth-century representations. It seems, then, it was the cross that was regarded as the chief feature of the divine heart; but from the beginning of the fifteenth century the artists began to represent the five wounds by the figuration of the pierced hands and feet, and placed the image of his heart opened by the spear in the middle to represent the lateral wound of Jesus.

Yet during this fifteenth century it sometimes happens that the heart of Jesus is not injured; this is because in this case its surrounding circumstances were such that the Christian of that time had no doubt about its true identity. But when the "Renaissance," in the second half of the sixteenth century, had completed the "sabotage" of true Christian symbolism, confusion was everywhere in religious art; the traditional moral or historical theological meanings of the old emblems ceased to be understood and their use was left to one's own discretion. It is then that, with respect to the heart of the Savior, the wound of the spear becomes the only characteristic that allows us to recognize it with certainty, especially since, from the beginning of this century, it became customary for the mystics to liken in several ways the heart of the fervent faithful to the One who should be their model.

Returning to the seal of Jacques Musekin, this is then, from 1391, another example of the image of the heart of Jesus used in the ordinary activities of life, because traders' seals or signets were in daily use.

IV. TRADEMARKS OF THE FIRST FRENCH PRINTERS

Since the Gallic potters of Gallo-Roman times, the first in our country to sign or mark their works, to the prestigious armorers of the late Middle Ages and Renaissance, many masters in the craft guilds had their works bear signs of their particular provenance. Thus the Merovingian "minters," responsible for the good quality

---

14 Cf. 6th Part, Chap. 17, p. 248, Fig. 7.

Part VI: The Iconography of the Wounded Heart of Jesus

of the gold and silver coins they struck nearly everywhere, and even in the quite isolated hamlets, marked them with their names, their personal acronyms, and their very effigies.

In the following centuries, a particular producer's brand was less often applied to his works, but in the latter part of the Middle Ages this practice resumed in various branches of industry, especially among the first printers who, after various hardships, published the first book printed in France, at the Sorbonne in 1469.

Very soon after this date, the printed book industry developed rapidly, and the printers soon formed — with the woodcutters, bookbinders, the last illuminators, the type foundries and booksellers — influential corporations in a large number of the kingdom's cities.

Almost from the beginning of this industry each printer had a particular mark engraved on wood, bearing his name, his monogram, his motto, emblems that reflected his tastes, his affections of a higher order, his personal wit, his professional *bona fides*, etc.

Printers usually placed these engravings in the middle of the first page, under the very title of the books originating in their workshops; others, like the Angeliers brothers of Paris, 1537, placed them at the end of the volume as a terminal motif. In both places it was a certificate of origin as much as a commercial "advertisement."

Some booksellers, not printers themselves, also had marks with their own name engraved, which they put in the same places as those of the printers on books printed at their own expense.

Because for both printers and booksellers, the book parchment or paper and the block of engraved wood lent themselves to this admirably — much better for example than the potter's clay or the armorer's metals — their professional and commercial brands were real compositions, more expressive and meaningful than any other, and many of them were reflections of the religious sentiments of those who chose them.

Among the latter we will only examine those on which the heart of Jesus appears. And we will immediately say that, sometimes sacrificing too much to a taste for the mysterious and complicated, they sometimes accompanied either the representation of the heart of the Savior, or that of their own hearts, with signs already enigmatic at their own time, and several of which have become today problems without a definite solution. This often makes their thinking quite hard to grasp, so that caution is needed, at least because of my own inadequacy.

On the other hand, certain hearts, which we will not deal with here, are impersonal, I mean purely emblematic, representing either charity or even the simple good faith of the merchant. Such quite diverse and often nebulous intentions also call for prudence in the iconographer's assessments.[15]

Antoine Vérard

Antoine Vérard, a printer in Paris from 1480 to 1530, was, in the early days of printing presses in France, one of the most famous among our printer-book sellers.

Skillful and having a sure taste in all the arts related to the book, at once printer, illuminator, calligrapher, and book-seller, in about 1485 he commenced his great luxury editions and provided a marvelous impetus for the emerging book industry.

Despite modest resources and quite primitive equipment, more than two hundred editions of French works were issued from Vérard's personal presses.

At first he lived on the Pont Nostre-Dame which collapsed in 1499, and at the Palace, then at the Saint-Séverin crossroads, then returned to the City, but always, wherever he was, he hung over his door a sign with the image of the holy protector to whom he had entrusted the success of his efforts, Saint John the Evangelist. And the books issuing from his presses say this expressly: "Cy finist le premier volume des Croniques de France, imprimé à Paris, le dixiesme iour de septembre, l'an mil iiii cens quatre vingt et treize, par Anthoine Vérard, libraire, demourant à Paris sur le Pont Nostre-Dame, à l'enseigne Saint Jehan l'Évangéliste, ou au Palais,

---

15 So as not to burden these pages with multiple references, I will only point out the following works from which I derived great benefit: Paul Lacroix, Édouard Fournier, and Ferdinand Seré: *Histoire de l'Imprimerie* (Paris: Librarie de Seré, 1852); Bouchot, *Le Livre* (Paris: Quantin, 1886); Grimouard de Saint-Laurent, *Les Images du Sacré-Coeur au point de vue de l'histoire de l'art* (Paris: Bureaux de l'oeuvre du voeu national, 1880); Louis-Catherine Silvestre, *Marques typographique* (Paris: Jannet, 1867); Anatole Claudin, *Histoire de l'Imprimerie en France* (Paris: Imprimerie nationale, 1914).

Part VI: The Iconography of the Wounded Heart of Jesus

Fig. 13. — Commercial trademark of Antoine Vérard, printer at Paris, end of the 15th century.

au premier pillier devant la chapelle ou l'en chante la messe de messeigneurs les présidens." ["Here ends the first volume of the Chronicles of France, printed at Paris, the tenth day of September, in the year 1493, by Antoine Vérard, bookseller, living at Paris on the Notre Dame Bridge,[16] at the sign of St. John the Evangelist, or at the Palace, at the first pillar in front of the chapel where the Mass of my lords the presidents is sung."]

Was it through this devotion to the beloved disciple of Jesus, who rested on the heart of the Master at the Last Supper, that Vérard was led to place on his trademark, above all else, the image

---

16 The Pont Notre-Dame was then lined with small shops on either side. Vérard could have had a shop there, but his presses would be elsewhere.

Fig. 14. — Variation on the motif of Antoine Vérard.

of the Savior's heart? One might well believe this if Vérard was the only one in his time to set it in a place of honor, but it was almost everywhere. Vérard was only following his times, when devotion to the heart of Jesus was truly popular; it had come to be recognized unanimously.

We know of two blocks of this mark of Vérard, similar in layout and motifs, but different in workmanship and design; that is, the second is copied from the first, but by a different hand (Figs. 13 and 14).

There we see: above a flower bed, Vérard's heart charged with his monogram and heraldically supported by two falcons.

Above this heart the royal crest of France, timbred with a crown and supported by two angels.

And above the two already mentioned motifs, overlaying the frame so that the entirety of a prayer runs along the edging, is the heart of Jesus, charged with his IHS, Jesus monogram. To him is addressed a prayer formulated in this way:

POR PROVOCQVER IHS TA. GRAT.
MISERICORDE. DE. TOVS. PECHEVRS.
FAIRE. GRACE. ET. PARDON. ANTHOINE.
VERARD HVMBLEMENT. TE. RECORDE. EC
QV'IL. A. IL. TIENT DE TOI. PAR. DON.
[O Jesu, to call forth thy great mercy, to grant grace and forgiveness to all sinners, Antoine Verard humbly recalls that he depends on thy forgiveness.]

There is no doubt then: two hearts are involved in this image: Vérard's, marked with his abbreviation, the other, placed within the text of a prayer and integral to it, encompassing the name of Jesus; this heart is the only religious motif in the whole composition. It can only be, then, that Vérard is asking forgiveness of all sinners by the great mercy of this heart.[17]

Pierre Le Caron

Apart from what he produced in his own workshop, Vérard also used some other good printers to supply his renowned bookstore. Thus at an early stage he used the resources of Pierre Le Caron.

Books produced by Le Caron presses are distinguished by the fact that the latter adopted one of Vérard's marks, the first of which he had engraved—and this was perhaps the occasion for

17 What is the exact scope of Vérard's public prayer? He is not asking the heart of the Redeemer to spare and forgive all sinners, but to grant grace and pardon *of* all sinners. And who can be thus forgiven out of the totality of "all sinners" if not the human race? Only too well the mysticism of his time lent this breadth to Vérard's thought, so that one might decline to recognize in his prayer what is claimed by the literal sense of his text.
   Leo XIII writing the *Consecration of the Human Race to the Heart of Jesus* and Antoine Vérard drawing up the text of his trademark have responded to the same inspiration.

Fig. 15. — *Commercial trademark of Pierre Le Caron, printer at Paris, end of the 15th century.*

producing another one — only that, in order to be able to use it in his name, a mortise cut was contrived at the bottom of the wooden block, which had no other purpose than to allow the insertion at an appropriate level of a small wooden piece engraved with the name of "Pierre le Caron." And Vérard's monogram on the heart of the latter was erased and its place left blank (Fig. 15).

I have before me a book entitled: *Les lunettes des princes cômposées p. noble Jehû Meschinot escuier en son vivant grant maistre d'hostel de la Royne de france* [*The eyeglasses of princes composed by the noble Jehu Meschinot esquire, in his lifetime grand master of the residence of the Queen of France*]. This book, printed in 1494, bears in the notch a mark with the name of Pierre Le Caron (above) in lower case Gothic.

Part VI: The Iconography of the Wounded Heart of Jesus

Fig. 16. — Commercial trademark of Pierre Levet, printer at Paris, end of the 15th century.

By thus adopting Vérard's pious mark, Le Caron made his own, by this very fact, the prayer to the divine heart that is found there. And there is nothing to suggest that he was obliged by Vérard, because Vérard had recourse, under the same conditions as with Le Caron, to several other Parisian printers, Pigouchet, Bocard, Pierre Le Rouge, for example, who never used anything but marks of a wholly secular order.

Pierre Levet

Here is another printer, Pierre Levet, who also worked to supplement the inadequacies of Vérard's personal presses.

Levet was also a neighbor of the latter since, in 1491, he lived at the bottom of the Rue Saint-Jacques, near Saint-Séverin, at the sign of the Silver Scales.

The Ancient Iconography of the Heart of Christ at the End of the Middle Ages

Three years later he settled in the Faubourg Saint-Germain des Prés, at the sign of the Golden Cross. It was probably then that he took as a commercial mark a large escutcheon with a cross on which is seen, in the place of the image of Jesus Christ crucified, that of his heart pierced by a spear, wounded by nails, and encompassed by the crown of thorns. Beside the crest, two angels hold, one the pillar of the scourging, the other the sponge (Fig. 16).

The representation of the heart of Jesus that it bears, bringing together in it all the sufferings of the Passion, is so telling that it needs no comment.

Jean Hardouin

On the *Hours of the Blessed Virgin Mary* brought out by Jean Hardouin, the vignette that stands for a professional mark, like the mark of Pierre Levet, also represents the five wounds of the Lord. The hands are at the upper corners, the feet at the corners at the bottom, the wounded heart in the middle within a double

*Fig. 17. — Professional mark of Jean Hardouin,
Paris, end of the 15th century.*

Part VI: The Iconography of the Wounded Heart of Jesus

nimbus of the crown of thorns and a rosary that six roses divide into six groups of five beads (Fig. 17).

Was Jean Hardouin a printer or simply a bookseller? Did he have a community of interest with Germain and Gilles Hardouin, printer-booksellers in Paris from 1491 to 1521, one of whom, Gilles, did not have his own name appear on any of the four different marks carried by their books?

One of these marks by Gilles Hardouin is emblazoned with the royal coat of arms of Portugal, which carries the five emblematic points of the five wounds of Christ repeated five times.[18]

Nicole de la Barre

A printer and bookseller in Paris (1497–1518), Nicole de la Barre, used two very skillfully engraved trademarks.

The first, on a "pocked" background, shows a heart surrounded by bones that are delimited by a banner with the funereal motto: *Mors omnibus equa* held by two angels. On another banner, crossed by an arrow that does not injure the heart, is the name of the master printer: *De Barra*. Each of the cherubs holding the first banner carries his family coat of arms charged with a heraldic bar.

Above the arrow and clearly separated from it is the cross of the Savior, whose shaft is adorned with the initial X of the word Xhrist, as it was sometimes written. A graceful floral decoration surrounds this part of the trademark.

Above it, the fleur-de-lys of France is surmounted by the royal crown, and on each side and above which are seen, in the center of two carnation flowers, the hearts of Jesus, I H S and Mary, M A (Fig. 18).

The funereal bones that accompany the heart of Nicole de la Barre are an allusion to his own name: "de Barra," in French "de la Barre." At that time most of the brotherhoods and major crafts corporations of Italy had their own banners, and also their *barra*, decorated with the insignia of the trade and the corporate coat of arms.

18 Cf. Part I, Chap. 2.vi.

Fig. 18. — Commercial trademark of Nicole de la Barre, printer at Paris, end of the 15th century.

The *barra* was and still is a kind of small hearse with handgrips, reserved for the members of a corporation or brotherhood. That is why, playing on the southern meaning of his name, Nicole, and his son Antoine after him, strewed their marks with funereal remains.

Nicole's other mark shows us Adam and Eve, within the enclosure of the Earthly Paradise, carrying in their hands a heart charged with the initials of the master printer and his commercial acronym. This heart is surmounted by the cross whose shaft bears the X of Xhrist, and here the Cross is set directly into the heart (Fig. 19).

Surely, the thinking is much less clearly expressed here than on the previous mark.

Two interpretations are possible. The heart represented could be Nicole's, penetrated by the cross of Jesus Christ and serving as a pedestal. But under this hypothesis how do we explain the presence of Adam and Eve? Or else it is Adam and Eve announcing to their descendants the promise of the Redeemer

Part VI: The Iconography of the Wounded Heart of Jesus

Fig. 19. — Commercial trademark of Nicole de la Barre, printer at Paris, end of the 15th century.

by showing them in advance his cross and heart. We know that the announcement of this promise was often mentioned by the ancient authors and that it was depicted by stained glass painters, miniaturists, and sculptors.

With this hypothesis, Nicole would have had the great audacity to place himself, under the emblem of his initials, in the very heart of Jesus. And yet would it be so strangely unbelievable for a pious man whose other mark ostensibly bore the hearts, designated by name, of Jesus and Mary, and who lived in the days when, in the chairs of Paris, Nicole's own city, Olivier Maillard preached and recommended this prayer to everyone: "You have willed — O Christ — that your side be opened: I beseech you, make me dwell in the midst of your heart." — *Vos voluisti latus vestrum aperire: precor in medio cordis vestri valeam habitare?*

Antoine de la Barre

Antoine de la Barre, son of Nicole, was a printer and bookseller like his father. His own mark bears a single large escutcheon, enclosed with a pennant that follows its lateral contours, and charged with the ghastly remains of the La Barre (barra), as well as the following words, which are related to the escutcheon itself: ARMA NOSTRE SALUTIS, the coat of arms of our salvation.

This is what other documents of sacred heraldry call, as we have seen in the first part of the present work, the "Coat of arms of Christ," *Arma Christi*.

On Antoine de la Barre's commercial escutcheon are the armorial charges evoking all the sufferings of the divine torture:

Around the cross, the spear and sponge; the column, whips and ropes with the rooster of Saint Peter; ladder, pincers, and hammer; the lantern, the sword of Saint Peter, and the thirty pieces of silver; the ewer of Pilate and the profiles of Caiaphas and Herod; on the cross itself, the crown of thorns, the nails, and a heart (Fig. 20).

Whose heart is this?

We see here the initials of the printer placed on the paternal banner traversed by an arrow, then the two sacred monograms,

Fig. 20. — Commercial trademark of Antoine de la Barre, printer at Paris, beginning of the 16th century.

as on the hearts of Jesus and Mary in the trademark of Nicole, his father: I H S, IHsuS and M A, MariA. The banner is interrupted and obliterated by these monograms in such a way that they rest directly on the heart.

Might it not be said that this is, by anticipation, the Eudist theory that will be publicly preached a while later: the reuniting, the fusion, of the two hearts of Jesus and Mary in a single heart?

There is something else: it is well known how the symbolists of that time liked to sometimes give two meanings to the same emblems, one obvious and common, the other secret and profound; it is also well known how occultism was in favor in the highest intellectual circles of that era, or at least in favor of what the secret sciences possessed that was compatible with orthodoxy.

Now, as for the mark that interests us here, the superimposed M and A monogram seems — much more clearly than in many other examples — apt to form the three letters M A V, which in a certain combination form an occult and mystical acronym equivalent to the *alpha and omega* of ordinary Christian iconography, and which signifies: "the beginning and end of all things."

Hence we have two possible meanings for the monograms connected with the mark of Antoine de La Barre: (1) Jesus, Mary; (2) Jesus, beginning and end of all things.

And I venture to conclude that, by reason of the sacred monograms, by reason of the position of the heart on the cross in the midst of instruments of the Passion, and presented thus as themselves, like one of the charges on the "crest of our salvation," this heart must be deemed, rather, both the heart of Jesus and that of the master-printer.

Jehan Longis

Jehan Longis, a Paris bookseller, 1528–1560, has two trademarks: one does not interest us; it represents two shepherds holding a shield charged with a heart pierced by an arrow, on a semy de larmes.

On the other, Longis, playing on the similarity of his name with that of Longinus, who was, according to tradition, that soldier who pierced the crucified Savior's heart, has taken as the subject

Fig. 21. — Professional mark of Jehan Longis, bookseller in Paris, beginning of the 16th century.

of his trademark a hand armed with a spear that pierces a heart upon which rays issuing from heaven fall (Fig. 21). Here, there is no possible doubt, this can only be the heart of Jesus. And, next to it, is to be read this motto: *Nihil in charitate violentia* [Nothing violent in charity].

Pierre Jacobi

This printer, who practiced his trade at Saint-Nicolas-du-Port and Toul from 1503 to 1521, has also used two trademarks in which appear, on or without a coat of arms, a cross into which are fixed the three nails of the crucifixion and at the bottom of which is found a heart that, with its combined proportions and position, does not seem to be compellingly indicated like the Savior's (Fig. 22).

The words from the "Pange lingua," *sola fides sufficit*, placed here as a rebus — with the two *sol*, *la* notes of plainchant and the words *fides* (suf)*ficit* — despite their liturgical origin, do not at all lead us to recognize the heart of Jesus beneath them. At that time it was a commercial rebus applicable to, with or without religious

Part VI: The Iconography of the Wounded Heart of Jesus

Fig. 22. — *Commercial trademark of Pierre Jacobi, printer at Saint-Nicolas-du-Port, beginning of the 16th century.*

accompaniment, simple professional good faith, honesty. Thus — so as not to depart from corporations of the book — Guyot Marchand, a Parisian printer-bookseller from 1483 to 1502, placed the same rebus on his three trademarks (represented exactly like those of Jacobi), beyond what is termed a "good faith" agreement, that is, beyond two hands clasping, as they will be engraved later, with a different meaning, on engagement rings.

It is possible that in the mind of Jacobi the thought of the heart of Jesus might be connected to the heart at the foot of the cross on his mark, but appearances, in my humble opinion, contradict this attribution.

Jean Corbon

With the Parisian bookseller Jean Corbon's trademark, we find ourselves once more on solid footing where there should be no room for doubt.

Corbon was in business in Paris from 1588 to 1597, a century after the first great master printers; also, his mark totally differs from their still quite medieval and marvelous style. This is an oval-shaped medallion surrounded by oak and laurel or olive branches; on the periphery of the medallion Corbon declares the meaning of his surname with a Greek inscription translated into French as: "The good hearts" (Fig. 23).

And in order to interpret this goodness of heart as perfectly as possible, Corbon placed in the middle of the medallion the very image of the Savior crowned with a halo and holding in his hand the best of all hearts, his own heart, the sanctuary of the total goodness, the infinite source of all goodness.

The Ancient Iconography of the Heart of Christ at the End of the Middle Ages

Fig. 23. — Commercial trademark of Jean Corbon, bookseller in Paris, end of the 16th century.

This genial composition is evocative of the trademark of another family of printers, contemporaries of Corbon: the La Rivière (1591-1659) of Arras, who took as emblem the Good Shepherd standing, his shoulders laden with the runaway sheep and his chest uncovered; from the wound to his heart a jet of blood spurts in a curve and falls into the bowl of a chalice placed on the earth.

Matthieu Vivian

Nor can we affirm with any confidence that the trademark of the Orléans printer Matthieu Vivian, 1490, bears the image of the heart of Jesus, despite the cross that surmounts it, despite the monograms of Jesus and Mary that accompany it (Fig. 24).

Is this heart Vivian's? Probably.

Is it that of Jesus in which, according to the devotion preached at that time, Vivian, represented by the initials of his name, has taken refuge? Perhaps.

His trademark, like Jacobi's, lacking any further details, lends itself to ambiguity.

Part VI: The Iconography of the Wounded Heart of Jesus

Fig. 24. — Commercial trademark of Matthieu Vivian, printer at Orléans, beginning of the 15th century.

Pierre Compagnon, Robert Taillandier, S. Huré & Pierre Rigaud

Now we turn to a printer's mark, or rather a title vignette, shared by several printers.

A devotional image as much as anything else, this motif was in fashion at the end of the sixteenth century and during the seventeenth. The picture represents Jesus as a child or teenager sitting in a heart, and we must seek out the main idea in these popular images of the fifteenth century depicting the Sacred Heart in the midst of which we see the child Jesus surrounded by the instruments of his Passion.

In the images that concern us, Jesus often seems to sleep, this being an obvious translation of a word of holy scriptures in the book of the *Song of Songs: Ego dormio et cor meum vigilat*, "I sleep but my heart watches." This is how we have shown it on a Spanish host mold from the Vic museum;[19] and this is how the Parisian bookseller S. Huré represents it in the second half of the 17th century (Fig. 25).

At other times Jesus is awake and seems to be the image of his own presence in the heart of the faithful one who loves him; then the heart that serves him as a throne is not radiant, but surrounded by the flames of love. But often the ignorance of the engravers at this end of the sixteenth century and the

Fig. 25. — *Commercial trademark by S. Huré, Parisian bookseller, second half of the 16th century.*

seventeenth about an accurate sacred iconography has meant that they have used characteristic features of the ancient symbolism thoughtlessly; hence the confusion in their productions, where it is sometimes quite difficult to see things clearly.

In sum, with this theme so often repeated, the surest rule is to consider the heart, whether wounded or not, as being that of Jesus when seen surrounded by rays of glory, like the person of Jesus himself. This is how it is presented on the following trademark of

19 Cf. Part 6, Chap. 17. II, p. 255, Fig. 10.

Pierre Compagnon and Robert Taillandier, associate booksellers living in Lyon, Rue Mercière, under the sign of the "Coeur bon" (1671). On the other hand, one can only recognize the heart of the faithful in the one that is shown surrounded solely by flames, which usually rise from its apex and surround it (Fig. 26).

This last composition delighted the soul of the good St. Francis de Sales who, on February 19, 1605, wrote to St. Jeanne de Chantal: "I saw one day a devout image, it was a heart on which little Jesus was sitting. O God, I say, may you also sit in the heart of this daughter whom you have given me, and to whom you have

Fig. 26. — Commercial trademark of Pierre Compagnon and Robert Taillandier, associate booksellers at Lyon, late 17th century.

given me! It pleased me in this image that Jesus was sitting and resting, a stability was represented to me by this very fact, and it pleased me that he was a child, because that is the age of perfect simplicity and sweetness, and, taking communion that day when I knew you were doing the same, I lodged with this desire that blessed guest in this place, both yours and mine."[20]

So St. Francis de Sales wanted his printer, Pierre Rigaud of Lyon, to place under the title of his *Treatise on the Love of God*

---

20 See Grimouard de Saint-Laurent, *Revue de l'Art Chrétien*, July–Sept., 1879, p. 162.

(at least for the editions of 1617 and 1620 that I have before me) the image he had described to St. Chantal.

The presence, on the one hand, of the radiant heart bearing a radiant Jesus on the Vic mold, as on the trademark of Compagnon and Taillandier, and on the other the explanation given by St. Francis de Sales of the heart surrounded by flames such as Rigaud depicted it, seem to completely endorse the differentiation explained above.

Also, what we have just explained concerning the presence of the heart of Jesus on the trademarks of French printers and booksellers could be done, not without interest, for those of the same period in other European countries, some of which had very expressive trademarks, such as, for example, Santi-Franchi, a Florence bookseller in the seventeenth century, which shows the heart of Jesus wounded and bleeding, surrounded by the crown of thorns, which supports, against the heart, the three nails of the redemptive torment (Fig. 27).

Fig. 27. — Trademark of Santi-Franchi, Florence bookseller, 17th century.

Part VI: The Iconography of the Wounded Heart of Jesus

To summarize, we see then, from the beginnings of the printing press in France until the time when the great light of Paray dawned, many printers and booksellers, some of the most important among them, placed the heart of the Savior on their trademarks.

Servants of the elite of French thought of the time, almost all of them, appear to us on the other hand as artisans of a high order and tradesmen of importance. Highly regarded by princes, high prelates, and learned men of all categories, expert artists and often quite erudite themselves, they yet worked for all classes of the nation, as for the aristocracy of intelligence, blood, or fortune.

With their books, whether costly or ordinary, their trademarks went everywhere, and we have seen that, from the fifteenth century, many of them bore the image of the heart of Jesus Christ which, with them and by them, entered fully into the social and industrial life of the nation.

A trademark was then, as today, a personal property that could not be usurped without being subject to corporate discipline, and probably, even since that time, to civil courts. It was also, as it still is today, an "advertisement" and it was so in a more or less effective way, depending on whether it was more or less striking and expressive, according to how it reflected more or less faithfully the ideas, preferences, and sympathies of the mass of the nation. However, when we examine all the many printers' and booksellers' trademarks of the time, four motifs are especially noteworthy by their frequent presence: the cross and the heart of Jesus, the fleur-de-lys of France, and the very hearts of the printers or booksellers.

In these lines we have only touched on one of the guilds of the old French industry because the marks of the old printers have preserved for us indisputable reflections of their great devotion towards the Savior's heart. What if the historiated signs, which hung by their hundreds and thousands in all our towns and villages of that very time, had been preserved for us! Would not one of them, for example, a house in Cognac of the Saintonge region, have borne the name "House of the Heart of Christ," a name given to it on a deed of that time?

The more physical documents come to me, the more convinced I am — for their number and variety begin to speak quite loudly — that the fervor towards the wounded heart of the Savior ran high in France, especially during the second part of the fifteenth century and first half of the sixteenth; religious arts of all kinds, objects of family life and, today, public documents of France's great industrial and commercial life, confirm this.

Protestantism, with its surface rigorism and theological sophisms, Jansenism, with its narrow and rigid conception of the idea of Christ, cast upon France a cold mist that obscured and weakened, though without extinguishing it, the broad piety for the heart of Jesus. After them, it would take the great breath of Paray-le-Monial to stir up the embers and kindle the flame. But two hundred years before Paray the flame had shone with a wondrous splendor that France rediscovered, thanks to Paray, only in our own time.

V. THE REPRESENTATIONS OF THE HEART OF JESUS AMONG THE CARTHUSIANS

The glorious Order of St. Bruno had a lively devotion to the heart of Jesus Christ during the time prior to the seventeenth century, which saw its liturgical worship officially sanctioned by the Church.

Next to the works composed by the famous Carthusian monks so often cited — Ludolph of Saxony from the fourteenth century, and in the two following centuries Dominic of Trier, Denys the Carthusian, and Lanspergius, who manifested so explicitly the thinking of their Order about the place of the heart of Jesus — we were most pleased to find the same fervent adoration expressed by their cloister brothers in artistic works contemporary to their writings: paintings, engravings, or sculptures, because these material artifacts are the clearest commentaries and the most indisputable of "confirmations."

The fact that these works of art are rarer than writings is self-explanatory: books were first set and multiplied by printing presses, then reissued more or less often; material artifacts are themselves almost always unique in their appearance, even when several of them interpret the same subject; but time, climate, fire, or man, all destructive agents have joined forces to annihilate them. For every one that remains perhaps fifty or more have

Part VI: The Iconography of the Wounded Heart of Jesus

disappeared; hence the importance and the value they have in the field of sacred history and archaeology.

It is first of all in the very cradle of the Order of Saint Bruno, at the Grande Chartreuse in Dauphiné, that we find the first of the artifacts we are going to study. In 1473 fire destroyed part of the great monastery, and soon after, the monks repaired the ruins. It was then that the actual old cloister was built, and at that time the heads of the Order determined that the door which opened on this cloister be adorned, on its archivolt, with what was then called the coat of arms of Jesus Christ, eternal King of souls and all else.

I have already said, in the first part of this work, that the representation on an escutcheon of the various objects that served in the tragic Passion of the Savior was called at the time *Arma Christi, Arms of Jesus Christ,* or *Crest of God.* This is the trophy of his triumph.

What do we see on this Grande Chartreuse *Arma Christi* carved in 1474?[21]

First, the cross upon which the heart of the Savior appears alone; the point of the spear penetrates half the length of its tip (Fig. 28). For the inspirers of this coat of arms, the wounded heart sums up here the Crucified as a whole; for them, as in the doctrine of Father Anizan, "it is all Jesus."

The foot of the cross plunges, not into a tomb as was wrongly said, but into what was called, at the end of the fifteenth century, the fountain of life,[22] a pool where all sinners can efficaciously wash their defilements in the purifying and redeeming blood of Christ. Even if the date of construction of the Grande Chartreuse cloister, 1473–1474, was not known to us, this detail of the fountain of life would be enough to approximately determine the time when the coat of arms that interests us was carved.

Propped against the edge of said fountain are the nails that opened the channels through which the divine blood flowed from the limbs, even before the spear opened its bodily source. Elsewhere, we see the pincers and hammer, which are notionally

---

21 I have engraved the sculptures of the Grande Chartreuse studied in these lines according to sketches communicated by the Rev. Lucien Buron of the Paris clergy, and I respectfully thank him for his great kindness.
22 Cf. 3rd Part, Chap. 7.

related to the nails, then the whips and rods of the scourging, the crown of thorns that encircled the divine brow with pain and blood, the sponge that was touched to the lips of the tortured One, and the dice of the soldiers who played for his seamless robe.

Finally, on the shield's chief part, lined up in horizontal file, the thirty disgusting pieces of silver of the false friend who sold his promise of faithful love for this price. The Carthusians who arrayed them there best understood the painful blow that the

Fig. 28. — *Escutcheon in the cloister of the Grande Chartreuse, 1474.*

betrayal of Judas bore to the heart of him who, "having loved his own, loved them to the end." And these great monks would have applauded Papini when he castigated money, the most despicable indeed of those manures that foster the worst forms of human baseness, calling it the "excrement of Satan."

Although a material representation of the heart of Jesus is not depicted there, another very expressive sculpture was inspired by Carthusian piety towards the wound in the side of Jesus long before the just studied coat of arms: it is a monogram of the name of Jesus peculiar to the Order of Saint Bruno; it evokes, at the same time as his name, the sufferings of the Redeemer.

The oldest example we know of is on a keystone of the first

chapel of the Grande Chartreuse, dating from 1375: on the field of an escutcheon, connected to the molding by two stone straps, we read the name of Jesus in its abbreviated form, I H S, in Gothic letters; but the staff of the letter h forms the cross, and the spear pierces the end of the sacred name; the end, because the spear had intervened in the drama of Calvary only after the cross (Fig. 29).

Fig. 29. — Chrismon with spear. — Keystone of an arch in the first chapel of the Grande Chartreuse, 1375.

Below the monogram, and issuing from its middle, an oak stem is probably but the emblem of the potent force and efficacious virtue of the divine name.

And this chrismon with a spear was carved in the Chartreuse three years before the death of the Carthusian Ludolph of Saxony (1378), who was one of the first to make known, through his writings, the Carthusian devotion to the heart of the Savior. For him, the lateral wound of Jesus is a blow to the heart. And for him, as later for that other Carthusian, Lanspergius, the wound of the spear is, as he expresses it, "only the door that ushers us into the heart," *Per illud vulnus, quasi per ostium in Cor introeatis.*

This suggestive monogram of the chrismon with spear was again reproduced a hundred years later, and several times, in the ornamentation for that already mentioned cloister of the Grande Chartreuse, rebuilt in 1474 after a fire. As in the old model, the spear retains the oblique position it had when it struck the sacred side (Fig. 30).

From the end of the fifteenth century also, must be dated the woodcut, which I reproduced by the same process for the very interesting article by Father Anizan: *À Paray, devant une vieille pierre* [In Paray, before an old stone].[23] We see there, held

Fig. 30. — Sculpture from the old cloister of the Grande Chartreuse, 1474.

by two angels, the heart of Jesus that the eternal Father strikes with an arrow (Fig. 31); below the wounded heart, a Carthusian monk has fallen to his knees and implores: "Miserere mei Deus!" Is this an image of the inspirer or executor of the engraving, or does it symbolize his whole Order at prayer?

At this same period the Rhinelander Lanspergius donned the habit of the monks of St. Bruno. Before dying in 1539 at the

Fig. 31. — The Eternal Father transverberating the Heart of His Son, second half of the 15th century.

23 *Regnabit*, Dec. 1921, p. 43.

Carthusian monastery of Cologne, he had become, in books of quite charming mysticism, the apostle of devotion towards the wounded side and heart of Jesus, at the same time as the propagator of images of the wounded heart; in this way he was truly only echoing his monastic family. "Place," he wrote, "in frequently passed locations, some images of this divine heart or the five wounds; they will thus often remind you to raise your affections to God."

Would it not be to support this advice and facilitate its execution that, in 1535, four years before the death of Lanspergius, the Carthusians of Cologne had engraved on wood the image reproduced by Peter Quentel in 1595?

On this wood, as on the coat of arms stone of the Grande Chartreuse, the heart pierced by a spear is placed on the cross, but surrounded by two glories, the outermost of which is cruciform. The nails are in their normal place in the sacred wood and, near them, the wounded hands and feet are each surrounded by a halo of glorious rays (Fig. 32).

Fig. 32. — Image engraved by the Carthusians of Cologne in 1535.

On the central point of the cross is fastened the spiny crown, and to each side stand the pillar of the scourging and the bitter sponge.

Clearly what we have here is the image of the "Divine Heart and Five Wounds" desired and recommended by Lanspergius; it is clearly also the repetition of the theme set in a place of honor, in 1474, on the archivolt of the Grande Chartreuse cloister in France. But, with all the artifacts we have just studied in this chapter, we have found that, even though towards the end of the Middle Ages and in the century that followed the Rhineland Carthusians, especially those of Cologne, were among the most ardent propagators of the images of the heart of Jesus, for the Carthusians of France, in the very cradle of the Order in Dauphiné, out of which came the inspirations and rules of piety for the whole of the monastic family of Saint Bruno, including monasteries of the far West, like the Charterhouse of Saint-Denis-d'Orques in the Sarthe region, the heart of Jesus was truly at the forefront of spiritual life, or, better put, it was the source from which all drew abundantly.

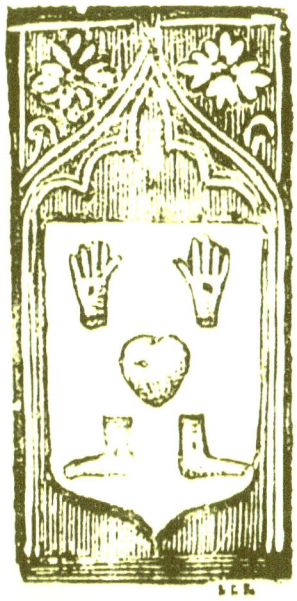

*Symbol of the five wounds, a pew panel in
St. Melanus Church in Mullion (Cornwall).
Wood engraved by the author (ed.).*

CHAPTER EIGHTEEN

The Iconography of the Heart of Christ Posterior to the Renaissance

IF THERE IS TRULY A CONFUSION IN SACRED iconography with regard to representations of the heart of Jesus Christ produced at the time of the Renaissance and in the three centuries that came after it, it seems to me this is mainly due to two causes. The first is the regrettable abandonment, by the artists of the day, of the reasoned rules established in the Middle Ages to express the full meaning of Christian iconography and emblematics. The second, as far as representations of the heart of Jesus Christ are concerned, is that current iconographers have not yet made enough connections and comparisons between the many artifacts left to us from the last four centuries.

In order to be able to look with any appreciable confidence at the pious representations of the heart produced since the end of the Middle Ages, and distinguish whether we are to see there the heart of the Lord or that of the faithful, more or less often likened to that of the divine Master, three questions need to be studied:

1st — The juxtaposition of the heart with the monogram of Jesus Christ: I H S.

2nd — The more or less immediate joining of the heart and the three emblematic nails.

3rd — The beautiful and centuries-old doctrine of a spiritual habitation in the lateral wound of the Crucified, which became, in the fifteenth century, the mystical habitation of the soul in the very heart of Jesus.

Above all, it is opportune to emphasize the following observations which, for the iconography of the heart of Jesus Christ, are strictly accurate. During the sixteenth century, artists, intoxicated by the then widespread, unfortunate enthusiasm for the old pagan art of ancient Greece and Rome, spurned the iconographic code established by the Middle Ages. However, although violated by them, the old rules of religious iconography, and especially of the heraldic nobiliary, were maintained during this century better than the others; and although in the works of religious art they were no longer regarded as imperative precepts, they still persisted more or less as workshop customs or traditions.

In the seventeenth century, forgetfulness of these rules increased, and in the eighteenth, as well as during at least three quarters of the nineteenth, there is almost complete misunderstanding and anarchy in so-called "pious" imagery. Out of this situation came works which, however well-intentioned, were nonetheless sheer nonsense, puerile and unthinking outrages on religious beauty.

I. THE HEART AND MONOGRAM OF THE NAME OF JESUS

Only a few years after the redemptive drama on Calvary, St. Paul, addressing those Philippians whom he had converted, wrote to them the inspired pages in which he so magnificently glorifies the sovereign name that reigns over Heaven, Earth, and Hell, the name of Jesus.[1] Shortly after him, St. John, in his Apocalypse, designated the same divine name as the sign of God's elect. Then, from one end of the Roman world to the other, in the nascent Christendom of Jerusalem and Damascus, Tyre and Antioch, Alexandria and Carthage, Athens, Naples, and Rome, all worship was focused on the name of Jesus, all hands were outstretched towards it in supplication; and, in the amphitheaters, arenas, and in all the places of torture, the blood of millions of martyrs flowed for it.

So to honor it everywhere, to carry it about on themselves like a divine talisman and to engrave it as well on objects for daily use, the faithful shortened it into assemblages of letters known to them. And soon, when the hour of God had come, the Emperor of Rome, Constantine, placed the monogram of the name of Jesus Christ on his banner and on the crest of his helmet. Since then it has been, and will be, so long as the race of men will last on earth, an endless hymn to the glory of the sacred name.

[1] Cf. Philippians 2.

Among those letter groupings that summarised the name of Jesus, the one most employed, from the Middle Ages down to our own day, consists of the three letters IHS from the Greek word Ἰησοῦς, Iesous.

From the second half of the fifteenth century, even though for two hundred years already artists had taken up the happy practice of representing the heart of Jesus Christ as the image of the source of the redeeming blood and as the emblem of his love that made it flow, the image of this divine heart and also of the heart of the Christian were frequently represented in juxtaposition with the monogram of Jesus Christ, but as a reflection of two very different thoughts.

Since we generally no longer know those forgotten thoughts that presided over the representation of the hearts of Jesus and the faithful near the monogram, for the uninformed the result is a complete inability to distinguish these two hearts from each other; hence some regrettable mistakes have occurred. Some very recent authors have even come to regard any heart juxtaposed with the monogram IHS as being an image of the heart of Jesus.

We will at first focus on a situational question, on the respective positions between the heart and the monogram in the composition of the motifs in which both are involved; because, as the case may be, the heart is figured *below* or *above* the monogram, or *on* the very letters that compose it; sometimes, on the contrary, the monogram is inscribed on the heart.

And remember that all the symbolism of both the fourteenth and fifteenth centuries stems, above all, from the heraldry and emblematic of the beautiful medieval period that preceded them; now, in these two branches of the great art of the Middle Ages there was, for the depicting of important persons and for the emblems charged with representing them, an attitude, a position, which might be called "the attitude, the position of homage."

It originates from those solemn ceremonies of liege-homage that vassals paid to their liege-lords, both in ecclesiastical circles and in lay feudal society: in both cases, the vassal was kneeling at the feet of his lord. The art of the illuminators and especially that of the sigillographic designers, especially the engravers of ecclesiastical seals, retained this "position of homage": although the high prelates, bishops, and great abbots had themselves represented, sitting or standing, in the double ogive of their almond-shaped [*en navette*] seals, the other ecclesiastics were most often shown kneeling at the bottom of the seal whose top is occupied by the image of their baptismal patron, or by that of their church, their priory, or simply of the place that they lived. From the beginning of the fourteenth century, and even a little earlier, this composition was modified in that the kneeling characters, hands joined and lifted — as in liege-homage — to the holy image, were replaced, represented, by their coat of arms, and thus "posed in homage."

The personal, or family, coat of arms then plays its only true and rational role, which is simply to be the sensible, visible, and quasi-hieratic sign that takes the place of someone we do not see, just as a name takes the place, at the bottom of a written document, of the signatory, or just as a candle represents and replaces one of the faithful at the foot of an altar.

I give here as an example the seal of Brother René Deblet, prior of Notre-Dame de Sales in the archdiocese of Bourges, in the fourteenth century.

Fig. 1. — Seal of the prior René Deblet, 14th century. After a wax imprint.

The shield of Deblet is seen in homage at the feet of the Virgin, patroness of his priory (Fig. 1).

Towards the end of the fifteenth century the idea arose among artists and iconographers of thus placing the heart of the faithful Christian, the mystic, as a coat of arms in homage, under the sacred name of the Redeemer. It signified not only homage, but prayer, and the ardor of love when, which is quite common, this heart is inflamed.

Also — unless traced by an unconscious hand — hearts placed under the monogram IHS never bear the wound of the spear. If it is otherwise, they obviously represent the heart of Jesus Christ, but the heart of Jesus put by ignorance in a completely unjustifiable, because irrational place. We find some rare examples at the end of the sixteenth century. But in the seventeenth, eighteenth, and nineteenth centuries the case becomes frequent because by then no one has any clear idea about these matters, and mythological attributes are better known than Christian emblematics. I saw this nonsense of the heart of Jesus *below* his monogram on many chalice patens from that sorry time in Poitou, Anjou, Touraine, Provence, and other places.

I give here as an example of the rational use of the heart of the faithful an engraved wood from the Musée des Antiquaires de l'Ouest at Poitiers: the heart wounded with nails, which we will discuss later, is seen under the seventeenth century monogram (Fig. 2).

Fig. 2. — *Proof from an engraved woodblock from the Musée des Antiquaires de l'Ouest, Poitiers, 17th century.*

Fig. 3. — *A faithful heart within the halo of the Divine Name. Musée des Antiquaires de l'Ouest.*

By contrast, there is nothing to prevent the faithful heart, placed in this way under the monogram, from being inscribed within the very halo of the divine name, because Christ, having drawn to himself the faithful soul, introduces it, so to speak, into his own radiance; and this is the reward for the soul's fidelity and fervor. This is how we see it on the frontispiece for the *Love of Jesus*, by the Recollect Barthélémy Solutive, 1623, and on another image from the same engraved Poitevin plate that bears the preceding one (Fig. 3).

When, to the contrary, the heart is placed *on* the monogram itself, or *above*, it is always, whether wounded or not — and it is so nine times out of ten — the heart of Lord, because in this case the monogram IHS is a denominative that relates to the heart and is the determining factor. It appears in this way above Janus, on an initial cartouche for the month of January on a sixteenth-century liturgical calendar (Fig. 4).

Fig. 4. — The Sacred Heart above the monogram. Miniature from the 16th century.

Still more is it always the Sacred Heart when it is one with the name of Jesus, or is attached to it, as is seen on one of the metal plates of the Hiéron of Paray[2] and on the central medallion of an embroidered chasuble from the *Musée historique des Tissus* [Historical Museum of Fabrics] in Lyon, from the period of Louis XIV, reproduced here (Fig. 5).

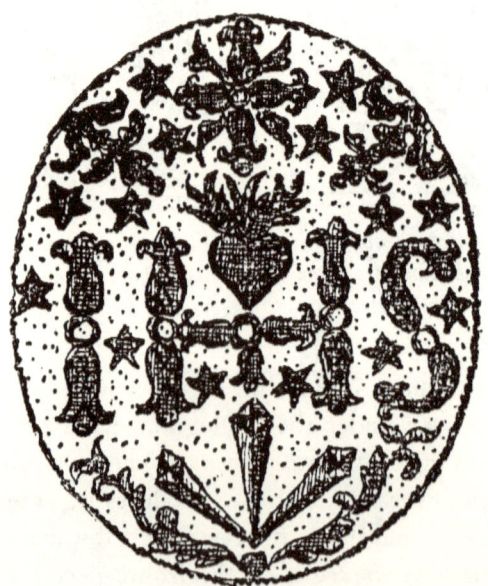

Fig. 5. — Central medallion of a Chasuble from the time of Louis XIV. 0.28 × 0.23. Musée historique des Tissus, Lyon, Num. 1376.

2 Cf. below 6th Part, Chap. 24, p. 402, Fig. 11.

Fig. 6. — Frontispiece vignette for the Paradisius animæ, *16th century.*

And no doubt should be possible as well when the heart itself bears the monogram, such as that of *Paradisus anime*, printed in the sixteenth century (Fig. 6). But sometimes, in the eighteenth century, the IHS in one heart only indicates the presence of Jesus, by his grace, in the soul of the faithful, or his intimate sovereignty over that soul that makes the sacred name its mark, its seal. This is how we should interpret the ex-libris stamp affixed to a 1709 copy of the *Ecclesiastical Conferences of the Diocese of Angers* published by order of the Most Reverend Bishop Poncet de la Rivière (Fig. 7).

The admirable and zealous movement begun at Paray, a wonderful stimulus to piety towards the heart of Jesus, did not induce, with its iconography, any return to order. At least the religious imagery posterior to this movement did not increase confusion further. Finally, the deplorable fantasies dreamt up in the nineteenth century for the populace succeeded in crossing the bounds of the ridiculous with their absurd

Fig. 7. — Stamp struck on an Angevin book of the 18th century. Musée des Antiquaires de l'Ouest, Poitiers.

compositions, where we find all mixed together: grinning angels, ecstatic urchins, any flower whatsoever, hearts without distinctive features, and flights of doves that draw on high other hearts with implausible garlands or cords; the whole arsenal of a winded and fretful art (?) that had its peak around 1880, and which is now, quite thankfully, over and done with.

II. THE IHS MONOGRAM, THE HEART AND THREE NAILS

The most well-known of these motifs that bring together at once the IHS acronym, the heart, and the three nails, is undeniably the one that served as a heraldic figure on the armorial seal for the Society of Jesus.

It consists essentially of a cartouche, variable in form, at the middle of which the monogram of the name of Jesus, IHS, placed in the center of radiant glory, is triumphant. This monogram is surmounted by the cross; and beneath it stands, in homage, an uninjured heart with three nails.

I reproduce it from the printshop woodblock entrusted, in 1761, to the Poitevin printers Jean and J. Felix Faulcon, for the frontispiece to *Principes de la Grammaire*, by Father Jean Gaudin, S. J., a work adopted in all the Society's French colleges[3] (Fig. 8).

This composition of religious heraldic art dates from the last part of the sixteenth century, but the Society's first coat of arms, determined by its founder Saint Ignatius of Loyola, included only the Monogram IHS in the midst of a glory, and, beneath, three nails, but no heart.

What, then, is the heart that appears in the arms of the Jesuits since at least 1586, since we see it on the frontispiece for the *Ratio Studiorum* then published by the Jesuits of Rome? In his *History of the Devotion to the Sacred Heart*, which has interested me lately and which contains highly valuable chapters, Father Hamon is of the opinion that this heart charged with three nails is not that of Our Lord Jesus Christ but a heart emblematic of the Jesuit.

He is absolutely right. The nails, although having served to crucify the body of the Redeemer, are not enough since the Renaissance to designate a heart as representing his own.

Since the end of the fifteenth century, the Jesuits are not, however, the only religious to use the heart charged or wounded

---

[3] The *Grammaire* of Father Gaudin had several editions prior to that of 1761. The frontispiece woodcut seems to have been engraved at the end of the sixteenth or beginning of the seventeenth century, well before the first edition of the work that bears it.

with three nails: with or without the monogram, the Carmelites, Franciscans,[4] Benedictines of Fontevrault, Visitandines, and almost all religious families have done the same. It is because this heart represented simply that of the mystic and specifically, at its origin, the monastic heart, the heart of the religious.

Let us go back to the time when this emblem originated in the last third of the fifteenth century. For two centuries already, artists of all kinds had represented the heart of Jesus Christ. Writers and preachers, especially Carthusians and Franciscans, displayed it to the elite of the faithful while repeating: Contem-

Fig. 8. — Frontispiece vignette for the Grammaire *of Rev. Gaudin, S. J., 16th–17th century.*

plate it, then model your faulty heart on that all-perfect heart. For them this was a restating of the word from the holy text: "Go, and do according to the pattern shown you." From then on iconography, like the spiritual life, recognized the theme of the faithful heart trying to assimilate itself to that of Jesus Christ, an audacious assimilation, surely, towards which the mystic could work effectively only by an ever-greater purification of his life, a constant ascent of his thoughts, a harsh labor that only an austere asceticism could sustain. And the Church did not at that time, as far as I know, in any way curb this spiritual conception, nor its interpretation by iconography.

4 By *Franciscan* I mean here all the spiritual offspring of St. Francis of Assisi.

Part VI: The Iconography of the Wounded Heart of Jesus

Even better, the Church's writers assisted it. One of their most interesting writings on this subject, and the best known since the Poitevin iconographer, Count Grimouard de Saint-Laurent, has studied the precious frontispiece vignette in the *Revue de l'Art Chrétien*,[5] is the *Exercice du Coeur Crucifié*[6] by the Cordelier Pierre Regnart of the convent of Fontenay-le-Comte, in Poitou. The author makes exhortations and sets forth methods for "crucifying" his heart in spiritual imitation of that of Jesus. In the art of the day, it was indeed common practice to represent the heart of Jesus Christ alone on the cross; as we see in the Vic host-mold of the thirteenth or fourteenth century;[7] the fifteenth-century lead-mold of the brotherhood of Champigny-sur-Veude,[8] the fifteenth-century trademark of the printer Levet,[9] and above all the carved coat of arms of the seated Christ of Venizy[10] where the sculptor, wanting to show that Christ is *all* heart and that it was the love of his heart for us that caused him to let himself be crucified, had the extraordinary idea of crucifying this sacred heart by the hands and feet that proceed directly from it without any body or head being present on the cross. One might argue about and criticize the theme of the image, but we have to recognize its strangely evocative power. This is what was being painted and sculpted shortly before the composition of the *Exercice du Coeur Crucifié*.

Regnart's book was in unison with the art and spirituality of his day. And the engraving for its title, the composition of which was very likely determined by the author himself, shows us a heart placed on a cross at the center of a frightful crown of thorns; in the middle of this heart, an indented shield bears only the monogram of the name of Jesus.[11] Three nails are plunged into this heart, the crucifixion of which is only ideal, and do not nail it there, as Father

---

5 Count Grimouard de Saint-Laurent, *Les Images du Sacré-Cœur au point de vue de l'histoire et de l'art*, in *Revue de l'Art Chrétien*, April–June 1879, p. 330.
6 Printed at Paris, on the rue Neuve-Notre Dame, at the Escu de France.
7 Cf. 6th Part, Chap. 17, p. 248, Fig. 7.
8 Cf. 6th Part, Chap. 17, p. 250, Fig. 8.
9 Cf. 6th Part, Chap. 17, p. 266, Fig. 16.
10 Cf. below 6th Part, Chap. 19, p. 337, Fig. 19.
11 And not the two monograms of Jesus and Mary, as stated by Father Hamon, op. cit., pp. 335-36.

Hamon says,[12] since their points can reach only the emptiness behind the heart, and those above are beneath the arms of the cross (Fig. 9). And these three nails are called *Povreté* (Poverty), *Chasteté* (Chastity),[13] *Obédience* (Obedience), the names of the virtues that are the object of the religious vows that St. Francis, the spiritual father of Regnart the Cordelier, has so much exalted. On the heart and around it flourish the main virtues of religious life: *Patience,*

Fig. 9. — *Engraving for the title of Regnart's* Exercice du Cœur Crucifié. *Reproduction by photographic process from Grimouard de Saint-Laurent.*

Charité (Charity),[14] *Pénitence* (Penance), *Atrempance* (Temperance), *Paix* (Peace), *Joie* (Joy), and *Longanimité* (Longanimity).

The entire meaning contained in this composition is thus dominated by the names of the three virtues that symbolize, that personify, so to say, the three nails named *Poverty, Chastity, Obedience.* Without any doubt, the inspirer of the engraving wanted

---

12 Ibid., p. 336.
13 The engraver for Father Regnart, by an obvious and incontestable absent-mindedness, has written on the lower nail: *Charity*, repeated on the top of the heart.
14 Grimouard de Saint-Laurent, repeated by Hamon, sees in the framing that bears the word *Charité* the image of the Spear. This rather questionable opinion leaves me quite sceptical.

Part VI: The Iconography of the Wounded Heart of Jesus

Fig. 10. — Coat of arms of John of Newland, Bristol (England), 15th c.

Fig. 11. — Sculpture from the Penitents' chapel at Biot, Alpes-Maritimes, 1612.

to show that, by the practice of these virtues within the setting of the religious life characterized by the three vows, this "exercise of the Crucified Heart" can best be realized. By which this heart tends to resemble, to be likened to, that of Jesus Christ.

And the names of these three nails illuminate and explain the mystery of their presence in the emblematic heart that nearly all religious orders and congregations with temporary vows have used, since the sixteenth century in varied compositions and which they have so often placed in a position of homage to the foot of the monogram of Jesus Christ, to represent their entire religious family.

Sometimes the nails make the heart bleed profusely, for which the three vows are a test, a penance, though they give both spiritual joy and security. This penitential side is one more analogy to the Master's heart. The heart of the coat of arms of John of Newland, abbot of St. Augustine at Bristol, gives us one example (Fig. 10), and Father Hamon, contrary to what he says about it,[15] can rank it among the simple faithful hearts. At the beginning of my research on the iconography of the heart of Jesus Christ in 1917, I also momentarily thought it was the image of the one before whom every knee must bend. All the iconographers affirmed it. Relationships, comparisons, and the study of the general iconography of the heart in the fifteenth century made me quickly restore it to its place within the setting of monastic hearts smitten with the ideal desire to model themselves on the suffering heart of Jesus Christ.

15 See op. cit., p. 334.

Following the example or, more exactly in this case, an overly complete imitation of religious who truly pronounced solemn vows of Poverty, Chastity and Obedience,[16] many fraternities, lay congregations, and other pious groups adopted, during the seventeenth and eighteenth centuries, the emblem of the monogram and the heart pierced with three nails; the Confraternities of Penitents, Bon-Secours, Bonne-Mort, etc., adopted it unanimously in France, Spain and Italy.

To Miss M. Berthier, the pious and zealous founder of the Beaux-Livres firm (Vichy and Cannes), I owe the ability to reproduce here the carved cartouche on the façade of the chapel of the White Penitents at Biot, near Antibes, in the diocese of Nice. Beneath the monogram, the heart of the confraternity is crossed by three mystical nails and the heart of the penitent dwells within the confraternal heart where it has found a refuge, a protective haven (Fig. 11).

It is quite evident that in the case of these pious associations, whose members were not bound by vows, the nails no longer possessed their true initial meaning; they were no more than a misunderstood tradition. The chapel of Biot is dated 1612, and in 1613 the Jesuit Nigronus, who was writing in Rome, no longer knew what the nails that St. Ignatius had brought into the coat of arms of his Company meant.[17] Saint Ignatius, who lived during the last twenty years of the fifteenth century and founded his society about the time when the Poitvin Cordelier Regnart wrote his *Exercice du Coeur Crucifié*, knew and understood the mystical iconography of his time; a hundred years later it was no longer understood.

It was clearly worse during the centuries that followed and distorted it.

What are we to conclude from this long dissertation?

This general rule is, I believe, the first to emerge: when the image of the heart of Jesus accompanies the IHS monogram, it

---

16 Vows of the lay Tertiaries of the great orders are only vows of devotion, not religious vows.
17 Cf. Hamon, op. cit., p. 337.

should normally be placed *on* or *above* it. And the proper place for the image of the faithful heart is that it be placed in homage *below* the monogram.

Many exceptions to this rule have been committed during the past three centuries, especially by ignorant people who have not known how to distinguish between the conventions relative to images of the heart of Jesus and the heart of the faithful.

Finally, the presence of the three nails on or in a heart that does not clearly bear the spear wound, designates the three main monastic virtues which are the object of the three vows of the Regulars. Sometimes, isolated from the heart as on the early seal of the Society of Jesus, the three nails have no other meaning.

And these pages would be amply justified if they but help to reserve for the representations of the heart of Jesus Christ alone some of the adoration and prayers due to it alone.

In any case, I dedicate these pages to those who imagine I am too inclined to see in every ancient figure of the heart the heart of Jesus Christ. The jewel-case of true ancient iconographic pearls of the latter in my possession is too extensive for me to be tempted to let counterfeits slip in too easily.

III. SPIRITUAL HABITATION IN THE HEART OF JESUS

The third question useful to examine in order to be able, at least more often, to distinguish the heart of Jesus from that of the faithful — sometimes likened to it by the common consent of piety and art — involves "the spiritual habitation" of the faithful heart within that of its Savior.

Originating in the Church's earliest centuries, we see this form of piety more especially favored in the cloisters of the Middle Ages, but it would be absolutely wrong to think that it was particularly intended only for the more advanced in Christian mysticism. It was always preached to all, and from the sixteenth century, at least, we find it interpreted by iconography in compositions intended to be distributed everywhere.

There are, moreover, few such purely natural forms by which the Christian soul can aspire to mentally approach his Savior, for, by having recourse to it, it is obeying what may well be called its instinct for self-preservation.

In all times and in all walks of life the Christian recognized dangers to his soul; at all times and in all places he knew them. His security was menaced on all sides: the conditions in which his life unfolded, wealth and poverty, strength and sickness, his fellow men who raised, persecuted, or humiliated him, who appealed to him, or enticed him into the forbidden territories of himself, of that dual spiritual and animal nature that had changed, as St. Paul tells us, his own mind into a battlefield. So, danger was everywhere for anyone who would keep his soul intact as much as possible while living in this world.

Faced with these multiple dangers, fear arises in the soul.

And, at all times reasoned fear was, for the human being, one of the most fortunately fruitful feelings: it made him invent the weapons for his body's defense, and the closed house for the security of his rest and well-being.

Also, the faithful soul, feeling its weakness and fearing these perils, wanted to have a refuge, but a holy and sacred refuge. And, looking to her Redeemer who died for her salvation, she saw in his side the gaping opening through which the blood of his heart flowed out for her, and she said to herself, here is my asylum!

Thus, the soul, being afraid of anyone who urges her or leads her to her loss, being afraid, too, of the One who will judge her, throws herself into the heart of its Savior and Judge.

If I were to venture here a comparison at random from memory, I would mention, as the expression of such a desire and such a need for protection, the pious feeling of that Pharaoh of the nineteenth dynasty, some twelve hundred years before our era, who, addressing the god Amon, the One god, the supreme god, desired "that he bear him in his heart."[18]

But let us stay on Christian terrain. The whole of the first millennium turned its hope towards this wound in the side of

---

18 Cf. 6th Part, Chap. 16., p. 220.

Jesus, and, although artists of the time did not show it as realistically as those who followed them in the passing centuries, they at least multiply everywhere its mysterious image at the center of the four other wounds of the divine body, representing it larger or more glorious than the others.

As early as the fourth century, the great voice of the holy bishop of Constantinople, John Chrysostom, proclaimed the explanation of this primacy of honor by which the lateral wound of Christ ought to be honored in Christian art:

> "In piercing the side of Christ, the soldier opened the entrance to the Holy of Holies..."[19]

An open door is an invitation to enter. And does not the door spoken of by the saint of Constantinople open into the most sacrosanct sanctuaries and asylums?

Iconography has proven that, even in the most troubled times of the ninth and tenth centuries, this attention of the Church to the place of the lateral wound did not dwindle; and during the following times, especially after Saint Bernard in the eleventh century had guided the thought of the mystics, not only to the approaches of the bloody wound, but even to the heart itself for which it is only the sacred way, souls, even more avidly than those who went before, sought there for their salvation a haven of safety more efficaciously protective than any other.

From then on, the spiritual writers established and maintained, one after another, the theological theory of the habitation in the wound in the side and in the heart of Jesus Christ, presented under the dual aspect of sanctuary and refuge.

To justify this assertion I must quote here some brief extracts from what they have written.

Saint Anthony of Padua (1195–1231) — "If Jesus Christ is the stone, the hollow of the stone where the religious soul must take refuge, this is the wound in the side of Jesus Christ. *Foramen istud est vulnus in latere Christi.* Is it not to this chosen refuge that

---

19 St. John Chrysostom, *Homilies*, 84, Chap. 9.

the Divine Bridegroom calls the religious soul when he says to her in the Canticle: *Arise, my dove, my friend, my spouse; hurry and come into the clefts of the rock, into the depths of the rock* (Song of Songs 2:13-14). The Divine Spouse speaks of the multiple hollows of the rock, but He also speaks of a deep cave, *caverna maceriae*. There are numerous wounds in His flesh, and there is the wound in His side; that one leads to His heart, and that is where He calls the soul whom He has made His spouse. He stretched out his arms, He opened His side and His heart so that she would come and hide there. *Christus enim non solum se, sed etiam latus, et Cor columbae aperuit, ut se ibi absconderet.* By withdrawing into the depths of the stone, the dove takes cover from the pursuit of the predatory bird; at the same time she prepares a quiet dwelling where she gently rests. And the religious soul will find in the Heart of Jesus, along with a safe haven against all the machinations of Satan, a delightful retreat... Let us not stay at the entrance to the grotto, let us go deeper, *summo ore foraminis* (the Hebrew text says: *trans os foveae*, far back into the recess). At the entrance to the grotto, at the lips of the wound, we find, it is true, the blood that has redeemed us, *foraminis os est sanguis Christi.* He speaks; He asks for mercy for us. But the religious soul must not stop there. When she has heard the voice of the divine blood, may she go to the source from whence it flows, to the innermost of the Heart of Jesus. There she will find light, consolation, peace, and ineffable delights." (*Sermo XCVIII on Psalm 54* — French trans. by Henri de Grèzes, *Le Sacré-Coeur de Jésus,* in *Études Franciscaines* [Lyon & Paris: Delhomme et Briguet, 1890], pp. 55-57.)

Saint Bonaventure (1221-1274) — "How good and pleasant it is to dwell in this Heart!... To this Temple, to this Holy of Holies... I will come to adore and to praise the Lord's name.... Admit [O Jesus] my prayer into Your holy court of audience — yes, draw my whole being within Your heart." (*Vitis mystica*, III, 3-4, in *Mystical Opuscula*, trans. José de Vinck [Quincy, IL: St. Anthony Guild Press, 1960], p. 154.)

John Tauler, Dominican (1294-1361) — He has Jesus say: "As the seal imprints its form upon the wax, so the violence of my love for man has impressed in me the image of this man; in me,

I mean in my hands, in my feet and even in my Divine Heart, so much so that I can never forget it." (*Homeliae*, p. 460, quoted by Franciosi, *Le Sacré-Coeur et la tradition*, col. 205.)

Was it possible for these holy writers to be more explicit? They repeat: it is in the sacred wound and in the heart of Christ, designated by name, that there is the happy and sure refuge of the soul.

At the time of John Tauler's life there were the first definite representations that we have so far of the heart of Jesus, of the Sacred Heart, several examples of which I have already reproduced in the preceding pages: the crucified heart on the Vic host-mold, the radiating heart that shines among the Chinon graffiti, the heart on the seal of Jacques Musekin, furrier at the court of Burgundy, and others, all previous to the beginning of fifteenth century.

It is obvious that, and I must repeat this here, in accepting, as they did, this image of the physical heart of Jesus, the theologians and spiritual writers of the day attached to the so-called image all that the teachers and sacred orators before them had said and written of the wound in the divine side. For them, heart and wound are two things that are only one, two sacred things that a single spear thrust has united for eternity.

And their successors have spoken as they did, continuing the splendid hymn that glorifies together the wound of the spear and the heart to which it leads:

Dom Henry Arnoldi, Carthusian (?-1487) — "Behold and see, says Our Lord Jesus Christ, what a painful position I am in upon the cross. My arms are extended in order to be always able to receive and embrace thee... My feet are nailed, that thou mayest know that I cannot, will not be parted from thee. My hands, since they are pierced through and through, show thee that it would be impossible for them, even when closed, to withhold the favors thou desirest from Me. But understand it is not the nails that fasten Me to the cross and keep Me there, but my love... I will never forget thee. Deeply, carefully, and lovingly have I written thee in the Wounds of My Feet and Hands; I have even gone further....
I have had My Side pierced by a soldier's spear to open wide for

thee the entrance to My Heart and to show thee how great was the love which led me to die for thee.... I have caused Blood and Water to flow from My Side after my death. Blood to pay thy ransom, Water to wash away thy sins." (*Ancient Devotions to the Sacred Heart of Jesus*, 4th ed. [London: Burns, Oates and Washbourne: 1953], pp. 24-25.)

Ludolph of Saxony, Carthusian (1295-1378) — "Arise thou, soul who is Christ's beloved. Like the dove, go make thy nest in the gaping hollow. There, like a sparrow that has found its home, keep watch; there, like the turtledove, hide the fruits of thy chaste love.... Learn to hasten to these clefts of the rock, these depths of the wall, both now and for thy final hour; go, hide thyself there; there find rich pastures, and there escape the lion's mouth." (*Vita Christi* II part C. LXIV, num. 17 — Quoted by Franciosi, *Le Sacré-Coeur et la tradition*, col. 208.)

Saint Catherine of Siena (1347-1380) often repeats that the open side of Jesus is a place of refuge, and the bridal chamber for those espoused to Christ. (*Dialogue*, chapter 20, 124, 126. *Letters* 143, 210, 270, 309, 322, 329.)

Dom Nicolas Kempf (1393-1497) — "Come, my dove, do not hover about at random, but come in the clefts of the rock, in the cavern made in the middle of the wall of dry stones. The stone is Christ himself, the hollow places of the wall of dry stones. The Rock is Jesus Christ Himself; the hole therein are His Wounds.... As to this cavern, or hollow place in the symbolic wall, it is the opening in our Lord's side. The soul that would rise and ascend to its Well-beloved when pursued by the kites, vultures and other birds of prey, figures of evil spirits, should fly away as a timid dove, and take refuge in the clefts in the rock, namely in the Wounds of Jesus Christ, and above all in the hollow place, that is to say, in the Wound in the Side of Jesus and in His Heart. There she has nothing more to dread. If she builds her nest in the Heart of Jesus...there finds shelter, there rests and takes her sleep, the spirits of evil will never attempt to set their snares for her. They dare not draw near to the Wounds and the Heart of Jesus." (*Ancient Devotions to the Sacred Heart of Jesus*, pp. 26-27.)

Saint Thomas of Villanova (1486-1554) — "The nest of the turtledove is the chest of the body, of the body, I say, of his beloved; she enters through the opening of the side, there she makes a tranquil nest, there she places her little ones in safety." (*In Ascensione Domini* II Conclusion.)

Lanspergius, the Carthusian (1489-1539) — "If devotion impels you to do this, you may also kiss this image, I mean the Heart of the Lord Jesus, a kiss bestowed with this conviction: it is this very Heart that your lips press with the desire to imprint your own heart on it, to plunge your mind into it and be absorbed there." (*Pharetra divini amoris*, "Exercita quaedam spiritus," n. 1.)

Saint Peter of Alcantara (1499-1562) — "Today think of the Savior pierced with a lance.... A soldier advances, lance in hand, and, with all his strength, plunges it into the bare breast of the Savior. The cross shakes in the air with the force of the blow, and there gush forth water and blood for the healing of the world's sin. O river flowing out from Paradise, and inundating all the earth with thy streams! O wound in the sacred side, caused by love for men rather than by the iron of the lance! O gateway of heaven, and avenue of paradise, refuge and fortified tower, sanctuary of the just... nest for the spotless doves, flowered bed of the spouse of Solomon! Hail, O wound in that precious side, which rends devout hearts; wound, which pierces the souls of the just; rose of beauty unspeakable; ruby of priceless worth; door into the heart of Jesus Christ; witness of his love and pledge of eternal life." (*Treatise on Prayer and Meditation*, trans. D. Devas, Part 1, Chap. 4 [Westminster, MD: Newman Press, 1949], pp. 74-75.)

This is the summary of the teaching of our first sixteen centuries of Christianity. And it would be wrong to think of it as a spirituality reserved for just the ascetics and mystics of the monasteries. This was spoken to the faithful from the pulpits of Italy, France, Spain, England, and Germany.

St. Anthony of Padua, from whose sermon we have just read a few lines, did not address monks alone, and I have already given[20] a passage from the sermon on the Passion of the Lord, preached to the Parisians by Father Olivier Maillard, which, translated into Latin for the learned, was printed by Jehan Petit in 1513. Maillard completes the passage relating to the spear thrust in this way: "You wanted, (Lord), that your side be open; I beseech you, make me dwell in the midst of your heart."[21]

Towards the end of this same sixteenth century, St. Francis de Sales also said in a public sermon: "The second reason why Our Lord desired that His side be opened is signified by these words of the Song of Songs, which he says to the devout soul: *Veni, columba mea, in foraminibus petrae, in caverna maceriae* (2:14). Come, my fairest one, come my well-beloved, withdraw, like a chaste dove, into the hollow places of the wall and into the clefts of the rock. Words by which he invites us to go to him with all confidence, to hide ourselves and to rest in his divine side, that is to say in his Heart which is open to receive us there with a matchless love and benignity, in order to serve as a refuge and safe retreat in all our tribulations...." (Franciosi, col. 304. — *Sermon for the feast of St. John before the Latin Gate.*)

How was this thesis of the mystical habitation in the very heart of God utilized by the figurative arts?...

Initials of baptismal names and surnames were frequently inscribed within the outline of a heart on corporate and commercial marks of the late Middle Ages and since that time, but we must recognize that it is very often impossible to say whether these hearts are an image of the heart of Jesus in which a believer has taken refuge spiritually, under the emblem of his name's initials, or if they are only the heart of the artisan or merchant, designated by these same initials; both interpretations are often equally likely.

The trademark of the wealthy John Gresham (who died in 1555), who often lent considerable sums to King Henry VIII of England,

---

20 Cf. 2nd Part, Chap. 4, Sect. 3, p. 84.
21 *Passio domini nostri Jesu Xri a reverendo p. Oliverii Maillard Parisius declamata.*

Part VI: The Iconography of the Wounded Heart of Jesus

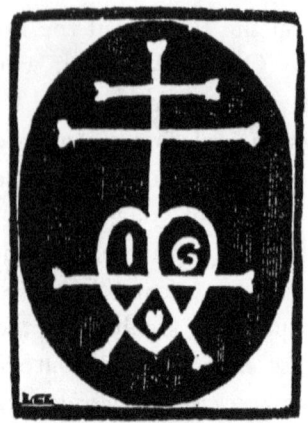

Fig. 12. — Trademark of John Gresham on stained glass, the hospital of Great Lefort (Essex), 16th century. After a sketch by Mrs. E. Wilde.

Fig. 13. — Boxwood mold with a trademark, 16th century.

seems even more expressive. It bears, in a large heart surmounted by the double cross, the initials of Iohn Gresham, accompanied by a little heart which must be his (Fig. 12).

The imprint of a boxwood mold (Fig. 13) of Spanish, Bearn, or Basque origin, which I received from Count Raoul de Rochebrune, seems to be connected to sixteenth-century artisan marks as well. The monogram S. F., or F. S., accompanies, within the heart of Jesus surmounted by the cross, a smaller heart that can only be that of the owner of the mark, who has taken refuge in the Holy of Holies, to speak as Saint John Chrysostom.

Here we have a reproduction of two woodcuts, all very popular images of the late seventeenth or eighteenth century; the original woodcuts are in the Musée des Antiquaires de l'Ouest, at Poitiers. Both show us the faithful heart within that of its Savior. On the first the faithful heart is at the foot of the IHS monogram and within the radiance that illuminates the interior of Christ's heart (Fig. 14). The Sacred Heart, which carries the cross, the spear, and the sponge, radiates in its turn into an oval that is cantoned by various motives relating to the redeeming torment.

The second image simply shows the faithful heart in a position of homage beneath the monogram of Jesus and within the

Fig. 14 & 15. — Wood engraved for popular images, eighteenth century. Musée des Antiquaires de l'Ouest, Poitiers.

framework of his Sacred Heart surrounded by the crown of thorns (Fig. 15).

The singular embossed copper medal, collected by the Father Georges Goyet in Saint-Loup-sur-Thouet (Deux-Sèvres), seems to me, now, connected to the theme of the habitation of the human heart in the heart of Jesus (Fig 16).

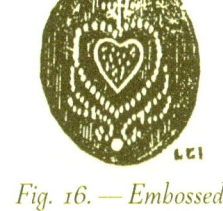

Fig. 16. — Embossed copper medal originally from Saint-Loup-sur-Thouet.

In recent centuries, we have sometimes had the idea of representing the heart of Jesus in his Mother's, but then both of them were sufficiently characterized so that we could recognize them.

Another way to depict this recourse to the protective hospitality of the heart of Jesus known in the eighteenth century, and used in the nineteenth in compositions that were often lamentable in their affectation, was to represent a bird, and more specifically a dove (one, not a whole volley), arriving in full flight to the gaping wound of the Sacred Heart. This is the interpretation of the words of the Song of Songs that inspired St. Anthony of Padua in the above-mentioned text. There was a beautiful artistic motif to be developed, but the draughtsmen of the last century approached it with a complete lack of hieratic sense and thus spoiled the expression of a beautiful thought.

In summary, it would appear then, as a general rule, that even though the theme of the spiritual habitation of the faithful heart in that of Jesus Christ is not, usually, clearly shown in iconography by the initials of human names placed alone on a heart, we can also regard, with a sufficiently justified certainty, those pious compositions that bear in themselves, with or without initials, small hearts devoid of particular characters as being images of the heart of the Lord.

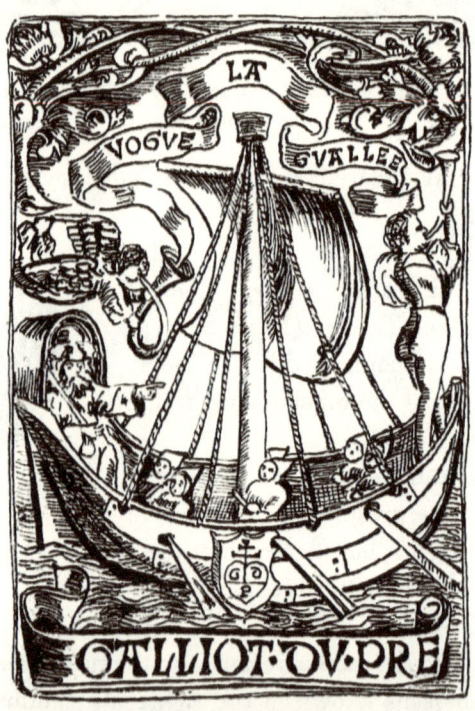

Ink drawing, copied from the Chronicle of Anjou, *1529, and sent to the author by a correspondent. Charbonneau-Lassay Archives (ed.).*

CHAPTER NINETEEN

Ancient Testimonies of Piety in Small Provincial Towns

TO THOSE OF OUR READERS WHO RECOGnize a certain interest in our search for ancient documents relating to the cult of the heart of Jesus, and who wish to continue to find these very old testimonies of a form of piety that many still believe to be relatively new in the Church, a piety which is, in fact, many hundreds of years old, we answer: Start by looking around you, in the old churches, ancient monasteries, old castles, old houses, dilapidated alleys. And, if you live in the least old small provincial town, worthwhile artifacts will certainly emerge from obscurity. Every day material evidence, kept in public museums, in private collections, or having remained so far without attracting attention in poor or splendid churches, comes out of oblivion and proclaims to us how much the truly ardent prayerful thought of our Fathers had ascended to the Savior's heart.

In this chapter we will give some examples of these ancient testimonies of piety. The first comer among these small French towns, the one where I write these lines, is Loudun, in the diocese of Poitiers.

I. ANCIENT ICONOGRAPHY OF THE HEART OF JESUS AT LOUDUN

The ancient capital of the Pays Loudunois, a small independent province wedged between Poitou, Touraine, and Anjou, and which, like these three large provinces, had its special legislation and particular government, Loudun, from the Gallic period to the end of the Middle Ages, wrote a glorious and very separate history.

In the religious domain, Loudun had, over the ages, two parishes with four parish churches, two collegiate churches, one Carmelite and three Benedictine Priories, monasteries of the

Cordeliers and Capuchins, a commandery of Malta, houses of Augustinians, Mathurins, and Jesuits, convents of Fontevrist Benedictines, Benedictines of Calvary, Ursulines, Visitandines, Hospitalers of Mercy, to speak only of establishments that have disappeared with the Revolution.

This is to say that the religious life was intense, even for the civil sector in daily contact with monks, priests, or nuns.

In the fifteenth and sixteenth century, Loudun, which now has only five thousand inhabitants, harbored thirteen or fourteen thousand.

The oldest testimony I have ever known of the cult of the heart of Jesus in Loudun can be attributed to the third quarter of the fifteenth century. It existed in a very interesting house of that time, all in wood and slates with timber joists crossed externally; it was at the corner of the rue de la Poulaillerie and the rue de la Boucherie, facing the rue de la Porte de Chinon, and regrettably was demolished about 1900 to make way for a commonplace modern store!

On the wooden casing of its spiral staircase, two carved panels were decorated, within a rectangular frame, with a lozenge cantoned by four Gothic trefoil ornaments; one of these lozenges bore a cross made of four hammers joined by their handle to a central medallion on which two Gothic letters, 𝔭𝔫, were legible, a craftsman's monogram.

On the other panel, the diamond contained, at the center of a cross, a heart in flat relief on which were traced the Gothic cipher for "Jesus" (Fig. 1):

I𝔥S

It is shown here according to the sketch, found in his papers, that a Loudun archaeologist, Dr. Gilles de La Tourette, made on the reverse of a letter addressed to him and stamped with a

Fig. 1. Panelling, Loudun, 15th century.

postmark of May 26, 1867. Beyond a doubt, in the fifteenth century, a heart placed on the cross and charged with the monogram of the name of Jesus was intended to represent the heart of the Lord.

It is probably necessary to ascribe to the next century the quite singular outline of an image of the wounded heart which, while being no exquisite work of art, nonetheless remains an expressive act of faith.

Quite a while ago, our Saint-Pierre du Marché church owned, in its immediate neighborhood, two or three vicarages; one of them was externally embedded in a recess formed by a large organ-loft and the baptismal fonts; it was the home of the vicar-guardian, which explains why a window, blocked today, overlooked the inside of the church from the main bedroom of this house, thus ensuring a night-watch.

Another vicarage was on the small Place Saint-Pierre, a few steps and to the left of the main entry to the church. This house has an extremely deep cellar cut into the unbroken secondary turonian limestone massif that underlies the city. Descent is by a steep and very long staircase on which vaults open halfway to the right and left. Now, in the right wall, going down to the middle of the stairs, a large heart about 80 centimeters high was "drawn" by pickaxe (Fig. 2); the lower part of its outline is formed by a furrow with an average width of 10 centimeters and about as deep; the upper part of the outline is incomplete and is indicated only by a much less accentuated stroke; the curving segment at the top of the heart reaches just under a large pebble of ferruginous sandstone out of which the nodules in this terrain and relief on the wall is composed; the wound to the heart is very clearly indicated, and a precise feature suggests that the "sculptor" intended to represent the spear; two strokes form a cross above the wound.

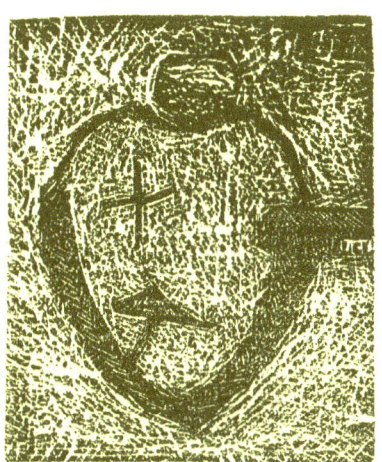

Fig. 2. Rock-work, Loudun, probably 16th century.

Subsequent to this unfinished work, a framing that encroaches on it was contrived for the laying of a plank, no doubt intended to facilitate the difficult descent of wine barrels on the stairs.

As rough as this large image may be, it leaves no doubt as to its identification; the initial letters G and S in rather decadent Gothic cursive of the sixteenth century, engraved a few steps lower, were probably cut out at the same time as the heart.

On several occasions at that time, the Protestants were masters in Loudun, molesting the secular clergy, killing the religious whose houses they devastated or burned, seizing churches and forbidding Catholic worship. I would not be surprised if the vicar who then occupied this house withdrew into his cellar to celebrate Mass, as we know from contemporary writings that the two cults thus had to alternately hide underground for the Mass and for the Lord's Supper.

Loudun possessed, as I said above, Fontevrist Benedictine nuns, and Madame de Fontevrault, the "Grand Abbess," as she was called at court, had inside our ramparts, not far from its priory of Asnerie and its seigniory of Saint-Mathurin (not counting its lodgings in the suburbs), a house that still bears the arms of the Abbess Jeanne-Baptiste de Bourbon, daughter of Henry IV. Now, we know from documents that devotion to the place of the wounded and bleeding heart of Jesus was lively, since the fifteenth century, in the Fontevrist Order.

From this beautiful tree, a branch, which retained all the spirit of piety, was detached in the time of King Louis XIII in the person of Mother Antoinette d'Orléans (followed by some companions), and transplanted to Poitiers, under the name of the Benedictine Congregation of Our Lady of Calvary, under the charge of the Capuchin Brother Joseph du Tremblay, "the Grey Eminence." In 1623 Father Joseph, while in Loudun, founded a convent of Calvarian nuns, and this house flourished until the Revolution. It was demolished around 1830, except for the vaulted rooms on the ground floor, which were used by the Confex-Lachambre family in the construction of a turreted castle with romantic pretensions. In the service area of this dwelling, which is still called *Le Calvaire*, "Calvary," there was in 1911 an old furniture door, from the end of the seventeenth or eighteenth

Ancient Testimonies of Piety in Small Provincial Towns

century, used to close another old chest. This panel, which certainly came from the furniture of the Calvarians, bore in the middle of its lower portion a suggestive carving: a lyre 15 centimeters in height inwardly formed of the heart of Jesus surmounted by the cross (Fig. 3).

Clearly, this is one of those mystical inspirations that are the poetry and charm of those peaceful hours in the pious silence of the cloisters and in the presence of which souls nourished by God are uplifted to thoughts that simple Christians do not even suspect. I remember from some twenty-five years ago an old hymn that spoke of some very lofty things quite naively, a hymn that was still sung in country churches of the Poitou valley of Sèvre-Nantaise. It began as follows:

Fig. 3. — Panelling from the monastery of the Calvarians, Loudun, 17th century.

Chante, chante, ô ma lyre,	(Sing, sing, oh my lyre,
L'amour de mon sauveur:	The love of my Savior:
Que tout ce qui respire	Let all that has breath
Lui consacre son coeur	Pledge its heart to Him)

Most likely it too dates back to the eighteenth century, and if I had to illustrate the text, it would be the mystic lyre of the Loudun Calvarians that I would reproduce as a frontispiece: is it not at once the emblem of religious melody and that of "the love of our Savior"?[1]

The Benedictine priory of Notre-Dame du Château, a dependency of the Tournus abbey in Burgundy, was founded within the enclosure of the Loudun fortress, which dates from that time, by Charlemagne as a favor to Alcuin, abbot of Saint Martin of Tours, a charter for which we have the text; it is the sacrosanct ground of the Loudun people: a council was held there; later a pope celebrated there; a saint died there and other saints prayed there, and ten kings, from Guesclin and Clisson, came there to kneel. In 1606

[1] If I had to create a banner for a Catholic musical society, I would utilize the design of this lyre as well.

the Tournus abbey yielded this house to the Jesuits of Poitiers who tore down the venerable monastery to build in its place a kind of mediocre house, become today the archpriest's residence. In the eighteenth century they also replaced the Romanesque entrance to the old chapel of Notre-Dame with a square door surmounted by a hideous triangular tympanum, and later they cut into the top of this tympanum to embed a stone laden with an image of the Sacred Heart (Fig. 4). Although situated in this way on the street, the Revolution that razed the chapel to five or six meters in height respected this image that only bad weather has regrettably altered.

Fig. 4. — Entrance to the old church of Notre-Dame du Château, Loudun, 17th century.

It was not, however, through the Jesuits that Loudun became, in the eighteenth century and soon after the events in Paray-le-Monial, a true center of regional renewal of devotion to the wounded heart of Jesus, and spread of its images; this honor accrues to the nuns of the Visitation.

They settled in Loudun in 1648, and a few years later built there, for 68,000 livres, one of the most beautiful monasteries of their order. At the time of St. Margaret Mary, this house harbored fifty-three choir nuns, and it was especially from this time that the Visitandines of Loudun became active propagandists for devotion to the heart of Jesus. To serve this apostolate, they worked actively with their hands, and among the many objects of piety they made and spread throughout the countryside, many reproduced the Sacred Heart.

Bishop Barbier de Montault gave the Museum of Poitiers a whole lot of images, made by them, in parchment cut into lacy open-work and painted with religious motifs; more than sixty represent the heart of Jesus or the heart of the faithful made to resemble It.

Some of these small mystical compositions show us the Sacred Heart raised on a cross, or placed on the spear and sponge, and topped with more or less regular heraldic crowns.

In the chapel of the Visitandines even nails attached to hangings or furniture ended with heart-shaped heads, and in the sacristy an iron peg, stuck in the wall near the door that opens under the cloister carries at its vertical end the Sacred Heart shown here (Fig. 5). The middle of the cross that surmounts it has a star-shaped perforation, and, on the heart itself, the following inscription is struck with a chisel in the metal: divine heart of Jesus.

Roger Drotiault, the Loudun scholar from whom I received one of the nails mentioned above, also introduced me to an old marking-iron originally from the Visitation of Loudun: it carries, within a crown of thorns, the heart of Jesus charged with a monogram that joins those of the names of Jesus and Mary. As a

Fig. 5. — Iron peg, chapel of the Visitandines, Loudun.

result of a probable distraction of the engraver the spearhead is inscribed, on the imprint, at the heart's left side (Fig. 6).

Since the Revolution, the former Visitandine convent has become the municipal hospice and, for the greater benefit of all, has the good fortune to be still held by the nuns of the Presentation of Tours, who faithfully kept all that still remained of objects that belonged to the Visitandines.

Also worthy of note is the stained glass window placed late in a fifteenth century crossing of the Chapel of Our Lady of Recovery in the church of Martray, a former monastery of the Carmelites; the two hearts of Jesus and of Mary are seen in deep violet on a deep blue background (Fig. 7).

Part VI: The Iconography of the Wounded Heart of Jesus

Fig. 6. — *Branding iron of the monastery of the Visitation, Loudun, 18th century.*

Fig. 7. — *Stained glass window from the church of Martray, Loudun.*

Naturally the fervor manifested in this way for the place of the heart of Jesus in religious houses of a small town could not fail to have happy repercussions on the piety of its civilian populace; that is why there are so many items of personal property that still testify to this. I have already reproduced a holy water stoup popular at that time, where the basin is formed by the heart of the Savior[2] (Fig. 8); then there is an emblazoned seal where the trickle of blood that issues from the wounded heart is prolonged into an enormous drop (Fig. 9). I also know of several interesting engravings or paintings that were held in honor in local houses, and before which our fathers prayed.

In this class of idea more particularly, I have collected a large watercolor with this theme: upon a rectangular base a cylindrical fluted pedestal supports a vaguely Louis XVI bowl filled with a spray of roses, carnations, and various smaller flowers; from the midst of these blossoms rises a large cross enhaloed with the crown of thorns, a cross that bears

Fig. 8. — *Rural holy water stoup, Loudun, 17th or 18th century.*

2 Cf. 3rd part, chap. 7, p. 106, Fig. 5.

320

Fig. 9. — Silver seal of the 17th century, Loudun.

in the middle of its shaft the wounded heart behind which spear and sponge cross in saltire. The heart is flesh-colored but veined all over with blue streaks; the wound is also blue and, to make it more impressive, surely, and to make it actually gape, the paper was incised with a penknife.

Below this composition is this inscription: *Dedicated to Madame Bérault, born Marie Moulier.*

I will end this review of the Loudun artifacts I have on hand without including those from the suburbs. They form enough of a sequence to show that here, as almost everywhere in France, the heart of Jesus Christ was really, from the middle of the fifteenth century at least until the Revolution, the object of veneration and the spiritual recourse of the faithful.

II. THE WOUNDED HEART OF THE CHURCH OF LANGEAC

Langeac is a large canton of the Haute-Loire, located on the course of the Allier. Its church is the seat of one of the archpriests of the present-day diocese of Puy, but was formerly part of the Saint-Flour diocese of Auvergne.

This church, built in the fifteenth century, is a beautiful building of Gothic style thronged with works of art, fifteen of which have been classified by the Fine Arts Council as historical monuments.

Among them, in the first rank, is a beautiful painted triptych on wood and silver, carved groups from the Rosary and the Placing in the Tomb.

At the time when the church of Langeac was built and enriched with its valuable masterpieces, the civil lordship of Langeac belonged to the noble family of this name, an old illustrious race, issued from the kings of Sicily, and at the time represented by Tristan de Langeac and Marie d'Alègre, his wife. Foremost among their children stands Jean de Langeac, the stately Bishop of Limoges to whom Francis I later confided important diplomatic missions, and who

Part VI: The Iconography of the Wounded Heart of Jesus

was one of the most titled and most opulent prelates of the realm.

Surely the church of Langeac, seat of a college of canons, the chapter of Saint-Gal, was favored with the generosity of lords of the place, whose family spirit of liberality became famous especially with Bishop Jean de Langeac and his brother, François de Langeac, commendatory abbot of Chézy. However, it is not to their munificence that the collegiate church owes its possession of the very beautiful stalls in its sanctuary, the work of art that will occupy us here, because the chapter of the canons of St. Gal alone paid for it, as the following inscription carved in splendid ornate Gothic characters on the wooden stalls attests, an inscription that tells us both the stalls' origin and exact date:

VT GLORIA XPI DIETIM EXALTETVR DIVINV̄ EXERCENDO OEFICIV̄ VENERABILE LANGIACI CAPITVLVM MOTVM DEVOTIONE FECIT HVNC ERIGERE CHORVM ANNO DOMINI 1526	IN ORDER TO EXALT CHRIST'S GLORY DAILY IN ACCOMPLISHING THE DIVINE OFFICE, THE VENERABLE CHAPTER OF LANGEAC, MOVED BY ITS DEVOTION, HAD THIS CHOIR ERECTED IN THE YEAR OF THE LORD 1526

On the wood of these stalls, four carvings evoke, in a linear language of the most beautiful heraldic and mystical allure, the final sufferings of the Savior Jesus; they are presented as in the order of the Gospel narratives:

1st — A kneeling angel holds obliquely, on his two unevenly extended arms, the pillar of the scourging.

2nd — A bust of an angel whose face, wings, and hands alone are visible, holds straight on his chest an ogival-shaped shield charged with a whip of three braided cords (Fig. 10).

Fig. 10. — *Shield containing a whip with three braided cords, Langeac.*

The angel thus employed as the heraldic "supporter" of the escutcheon was a much favored motif in the coat of arms of France and England in the fourteenth and fifteenth century; and we must congratulate the

Langeac carver for knowing how to thus retain in his work the traditional and national forms of the noble art in his own day when so many blazons became complex Italian cartouches which, especially outside of those lands, are pitiful.

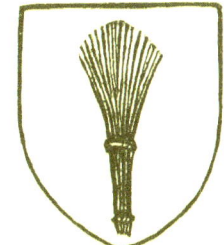

Fig. 11. — Shield containing a bundle of rods, Langeac.

3rd — An angel, similar to the one who carries the shield with the whip, holds in his turn, but obliquely, an escutcheon where a bundle of rods is spread out (Fig. 11).

Before going any further, I would like to point out the very great analogy between the drawing of the whip and rods on the Langeac shields and those same flogging instruments on the fresco of the Saint-Jean-Baptiste church in Chaumont (Haute-Marne), 1471 (Fig. 12).

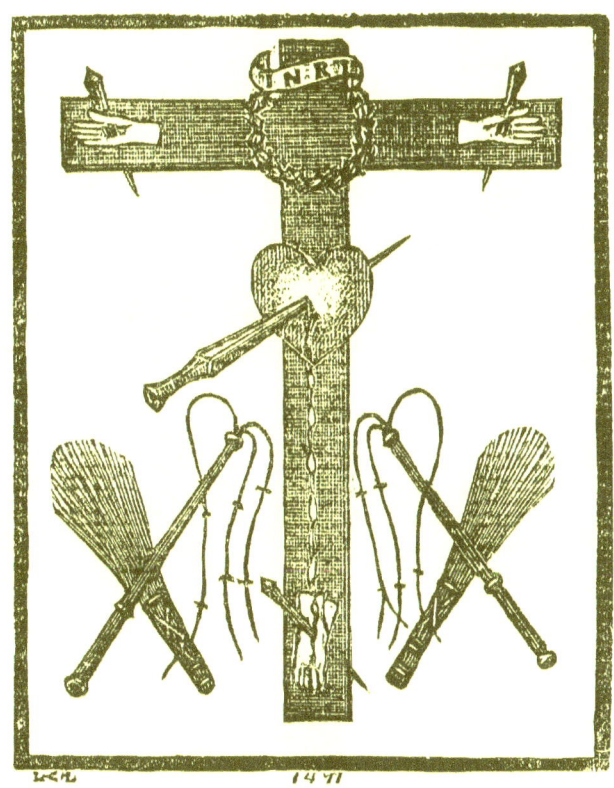

Fig. 12. — Fresco in the Sepulchre Chapel of the Saint-Jean-Baptiste church, Chaumont, 1471.

4th — If the first three carvings on the Langeac stalls evoke, by the pillar, whip, and rods, only the sufferings from the scourging, the fourth alone, on the other hand, sums up the other tortures of the Passion: the crowning with thorns, the crucifixion, the opening of the heart of Jesus by the spear; it is one of the most beautiful examples of what was then called the "Coat of Arms of the Passion," or the "Blazon of Jesus Christ," and sometimes the "Five Wounds Shield."

I reproduce here this superb carving from the drawing that was most kindly sent to me, as well as those of the other two shields, by Canon Ollier, archpriest of Langeac (Fig. 13).

Fig. 13. — *Angel holding a coat of arms with the wounded Heart, or Blazon of Jesus Christ, Langeac.*

As with the crest with a whip, the shield-bearing angel holds on his chest a large upright coat of arms. The whole field of this shield is furnished with a stout crown of thorns of two intertwined scions, in the middle of which the divine heart is shown pierced with the nails that caused the limbs of Jesus crucified to bleed accompanied by the spear that opened his side. Is not the heart the core of our humanity where all the pains, all the sufferings of our souls and our affections, our minds and thoughts, our bodies and their sensitivities end up at last? — This is a summary of the whole Man.

And that is why, God having been made man to save man, a man one day dared to summarize God. God died for us, and the infinity of his suffering from all injuries of his body... is summarized in just the drawing of his wounded heart.

The sculptor of Langeac, even though he had to kneel to chisel his work, was not that man; even though he surpassed him in his mastery of the art, he was, however, only a late imitator.

For centuries, the Christian hand engraved, chiseled, painted the adored heart of Jesus Christ; for quite a long time blazons carved on the walls of cloisters and churches, on tombs and furniture, bore the pierced hands and feet of the Savior around his wounded heart.

Forty years before the Langeac chapter of Saint-Gal had the stalls of its collegiate church carved, a Parisian printer, Pierre Levet (1487–1491), took for his trademark and commercial firm a large escutcheon that also centralized in the very heart of Jesus, in the middle of his dolorous crown, the instruments of his five chief wounds (Fig. 14).

I have already given Levet's mark in the previous chapter, but it is, for the subject under consideration, a document too expressive for it not to be referred to here.

And even though the art of blazonry can grant perhaps a superiority to the crest of Langeac over that of Pierre Levet, both are to be set in tandem as heraldic expressions of the same pious thinking, with the same manner of representing the heart of the Savior as that source of our redemption and that sensible recipient of the infinite sufferings of Jesus dead for us.

Part VI: The Iconography of the Wounded Heart of Jesus

Fig. 14. — Trademark of Pierre Levet, printer in Paris, end of the 15th century.

III. THE FORMER BENEDICTINE ABBEY OF THE TRINITY AT VENDÔME

One Sunday evening, the Count of Anjou Geoffroy-Martel, who ruled from 1040 to 1060, was gazing from the top of the towers of the Vendôme castle on the beauty of a resplendent sky when three dazzling stars stretched out and lengthened, each "like the spear of a knight," and then fell, one after the other, into a fountain before the church of Saint-Martin.

At that time, the count had built in this place a monastery that he endowed and populated with Benedictine monks provided by the large abbey of Marmoutiers, near Tours.

The new foundation, dedicated to the Holy Trinity because of the three streaks of fire fallen from the sky, quickly became one

Ancient Testimonies of Piety in Small Provincial Towns

of the most powerful monastic houses in France, yet, despite time and the outrages of men, it still retains its imposing grandeur. The nave of its church is immense and divided into sections built at the end of the twelfth, fourteenth, and fifteenth centuries. Its early ornamentation was extremely rich according to the custom of all the important monasteries of the Order of St. Benedict. "Poverty for the monk and luxury for God," was an adage among those Benedictines of the Middle Ages, whose piety, I am told, was too male, too exclusively set and entrenched on the theological summits, for it to be able to welcome at an early date a devotion as sentimental as one that has the heart of Jesus for object.

The truth is that at first, in its origins and until the sixteenth century, devotion towards the heart of Jesus was no more sentimental than was the one that prostrated the world before the true cross, before the precious blood, before the five wounds of Jesus, and especially before the open wound in his side, of which the image of his transpierced heart is only the divinely wonderful and triumphant flower; the truth again is that this devotion flourished among the Benedictines as soon as in the other great Orders, just as soon as in the Church of God, of which they were always the most learned and most docile offspring.

At La Trinité of Vendôme, at least one testimony remains of this ancient Benedictine piety to the place of the Sacred Heart. In the chapel where the baptismal fonts are today is one of the precious stained glass windows that the edifice still holds in such large numbers. It is composed of two parts from different time periods: the lower one, from the sixteenth century, was given to the abbey church by Jean Galloys, cellarer of the monastery, and it bears his *à enquerre*[3] coat of arms, emblazoned: *d'argent au fraisier d'or, tigé, feuillé et fruité du même* (*argent* with strawberry *or*, slipped, leaved, and fructed of the same). Jean Galloys, whose gravestone is in this same chapel, died on September 21, 1546. The top of the stained glass window, including all the floral mullion-work, is fifteenth-century. On each side it bears the repeated coat of arms of Dom Aimery de Coudun, abbot of La Trinité from 1470

---

3 That is, not in a routine shape.

to 1492, *gules* a saltire *or*. In the middle of the stained glass are the royal arms of France, and above them, in the *jour* [daylight], the highest pane, is what was then called the "Coat of Arms of Jesus Christ," that is, emblems recalling the mortal sufferings of the Passion. And on the stained glass window of Aimery de Coudun, it is the very heart of Jesus, placed on the cross, pierced with three nails, wounded by the spear, and surrounded by a large spiny crown (Fig. 15).

But why is the shaft of the cross, below the heart, oblique in the dexter part of the escutcheon? I confess I do not understand the meaning of this surely intentional detail.

The escutcheon is *argent*, the cross and crown of thorns are *or*, and the heart is greyish white. I think it was originally flesh-colored but has since deteriorated. In other stained glass windows of the same period, people's faces have also become almost white.

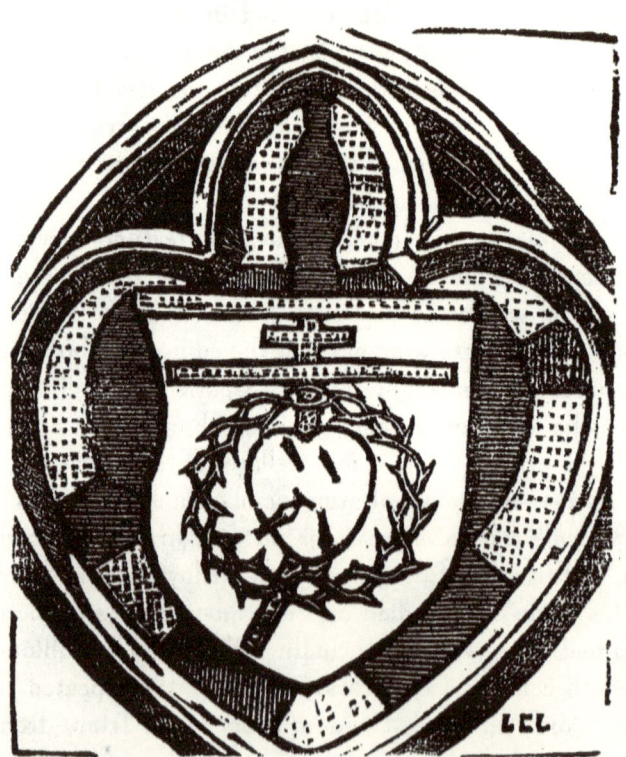

Fig. 15. — Stained glass window from the Church of the Trinity at Vendôme, 15th century.

Fig. 16. — Carving on the entablature of an altar in La Trinité Church, Vendôme, 16th century.

As for the date of execution of this part of the stained glass window, I believe it attributable to the time of King Charles VIII, the second of the two rulers during whose reigns Aimery de Coudun carried the abbatial crosier of La Trinité. The particular forms of the coat of arms of France and the "Coats of arms of Jesus Christ" compel, it seems to me, this attribution.

And the scalloped coat of arms on the dexter side only, of interest to us, would also suggest that the glass painter who drew it was from the east or north of France, rather than from the interior or other ends of the kingdom.

In this same church of La Trinité at Vendôme, one of the chapels of the ambulatory is dedicated to the Sacred Heart.

The altar reredos found there dates from the middle of the sixteenth century; it consists of a stone background in front of which detached columns support an entablature adorned with a carved frieze. In the middle of this frieze is, very prominently, a large flattened heart surrounded by fanciful foliage (Fig. 16).

What does this heart represent? That of Jesus, or that of the donor placed in homage, as was quite often done? Or is it, following the same and very lofty thought, the emblematic heart of the convent, that is, of the conventual assembly of the La Trinité monks?

A carved motif placed above the heart and which, most likely, would have removed any hesitations, was mutilated. In the shadow of the immense building, enshrouded on the day I was there by a dark stormy sky, I could not perceive anything on the stone surface crushed by a vandal's hammer. What was the object removed: crown, monogram, sheaf of flames, radiant cross, or unusual heraldic motif?

I give the image of this heart here, but with all due caution, recalling that only a century before it was carved, the image of the Sorrowful Heart of Jesus triumphed a few bays away, in Aimery de Coudun's stained glass window, and since the altar that bears this enigmatic heart is in the chapel of the Sacred Heart.[4]

IV. THE CHURCH OF TAVERNY (SEINE-ET-OISE)

The present church of Taverny, built by the glorious House of Montmorency, was started in 1230, the year of the death of Matthew II of Montmorency, Matthew the Great, Constable of France, one of the most valiant auxiliaries of Philip Augustus in his work of bringing the provinces together in national unity, and one of the most invaluable supporters of Queen Blanche when she, in turn, assisted the Capetian Monarchy's effort towards the same goal.

Located only a few leagues west of Montmorency, the church of Taverny often benefited through the centuries from the munificent piety of these very great lords who, more than all their other titles, took the one reserved for them alone, that of "first Christian barons."

The most illustrious of them, the Constable Anne de Montmorency, first Duke of that name, favored in his turn the humble country church that his loved ones had loved. We know his feelings of piety, and history itself tells of his chivalrous valor at the battles of Marignan and Pavia, his glory as victor at Metz, Toul, and Verdun against the Imperial forces, then against the Protestants at

---

4 I most respectfully and warmly thank the canon Renvoisé, Archpriest of Vendôme and Rev. Plat, President of the Archaeological Society of the Vendôme area, to whom I owe the knowledge of the just mentioned documents. And the same thanks also go to Dom Séjourné, to Father Anizan, and to the Rev. Roux, parish priest of Taverny, with respect to the sculptures of the Anne de Montmorency altar.

Dreux and Saint-Denis, in 1567, where he was mortally wounded.

Fifteen years earlier, in 1552, he had donated to the church of Taverny the beautiful altar of the Blessed Virgin which remains a perfect example of what was, in the taste of that time, a most sumptuous decoration for an altar. On the whole it is dull and graceless, but very rich; and the details of carved ornamentation are of a consummate perfection, worthy of the chisel of Jean Bullant, to whom it is attributed.

Like the altar of the Sacred Heart, in the abbey church of Vendôme, the reredos for the one at Taverny is composed, in its lower part, of a colonnade supporting an entablature on the frieze of which twines an ornamentation of oak and laurel branches. In the windings of these branches, emblems occupy the points where triglyphs are usually found in Doric decoration; we see in particular the pillar of the scourging with whips and ropes, the lantern, the veil of Veronica with the Holy Face, and above all a cross before which we will pause.

Fig. 17. — *Carving from the church of Tarverny, 16th century. After a drawing sent by Dom Séjourné, O. S. B.*

The three nails of the crucifixion are in their normal places on its shaft, and in the center of its arms is depicted only the heart of Jesus, against which leans an inclined spear whose stem starts from the same horizontal line as the foot of the cross (Fig. 17). The latter is only 15 centimeters high.

Is not this, once again, the grand idea that the artists of the late Middle Ages and sixteenth century have so often symbolized: the suffering body of the Redeemer entirely summarized on the instrument of his torture with just the image of his transpierced heart?

Above the first just mentioned entablature, caryatids, which separate curved niches where saints are placed, support a second entablature. A heart appears in the middle of its frieze, alone, in the middle of a very stylized crown of thorns (Fig. 18). On each side of this crown, and a little beneath it, are two long branches of vine, laden with vine leaves and grapes.

Despite the crown and despite the garland of vine, a eucharistic plant, the heart that occupies the central point seems, in its present form, to demand as much caution as that of the altar of La Trinité at Vendôme.

Perhaps the artist had intended to represent the heart of Jesus here, but, several times over the centuries and especially in the early nineteenth, his carving was covered with thick layers of plaster and paint; it may be that the mark of the wound of the spear, necessarily apparent — since the crown itself is only 12 centimeters in diameter — has remained coated to the point of no longer being apparent.

Fig. 18. — Carving from the church of Taverny (S.-et-O.), 16th century. After a drawing sent by Dom Séjourné, O. S. B.

As it stands today, it lacks distinguishing features and raises strong doubts; the crown of thorns, which would, before the end of the third quarter of the fifteenth century, indicate that a carved or painted heart is the Savior's, is, in my humble opinion, insufficient for a heart produced after that date, because at that time an iconographic practice about which we have precise data is disseminated: the likening of the heart of the fervent faithful, or that of the religious, to the very heart of Jesus.

It is from this bold idea that the image of the *"heart crucified in imitation of the heart of Jesus Christ"* has come, where each nail that fixes it to the cross bears on its iron the name of one of the three monastic vows;[5] hence we also have many iconic hearts in several religious families, where the crown of thorns that surrounds them seems to be only a hieroglyph for the monastic rule, a barrier and rampart for the religious heart.

5 Cf. 6th Part, Chap. 18, ii, p. 299, Fig. 9. — Frontispiece engraving for *L'Exercice du Cœur crucifié*, by Pierre Regnart, Franciscan of Fontenay-le-Comte, 1525.

Such, for example, is the heart of the Benedictines of Fontevrault that I find in the sixteenth, seventeenth, and eighteenth centuries, always surrounded by the crown of thorns and never wounded. This does not mean that devotion to the Sacred Heart was not practiced in this illustrious house that was the most important women's monastery in France, but when it was represented there, it was sufficiently characterized so that there could be no confusion with the one that only a crown of thorns surrounded.

And the simple faithful, too, sometimes symbolized, during the last centuries, the trials of a lifetime's sorrows with an encircling crown of thorns.

Usually, these diverse ideas are clearly indicated by circumstances of place or accompanying details. This is no longer the case on the altar of Vendôme, and neither is this so on the upper part of the Taverny altar.

Nevertheless, these two churches provide two very fine artifacts for our research; these, like so many others, are pearls retrieved from the oblivion of the past. Let us ever so carefully gather others wherever they are: they will one day enable us, God willing, to go back at least in part, perhaps enough to gain a fair idea of the richness of its totality, of the magnificent adornment that the imploring piety of the past devoted to the heart of Jesus, at a time when, even quite recently, we were told that this devotion was unknown.

V. THE SEATED CHRIST OF VENIZY AND ITS COAT OF ARMS

The last three centuries of the Middle Ages were truly a very strange and a quite powerfully expressive world. At no time in its life has mankind, as much as at that time, felt his soul vibrate in his hands under the great inspirations of faith.

That is why the artists of the time were so personal in their designs, without any of them appearing to have violated the at once broad and precise discipline of art, which imposed general forms on each of these three admirable centuries.

The artists of France, relieved of all the old influences of dead paganism, creators of the most beautiful, the most ethereal, art that ever was, held at the time first rank in the world; and because they were sincere and deep probers of the soul, they excelled at creating remarkably impressive attitudes.

Thoroughly imbued with a Christian spirit, and often even with a true spiritual science, they bowed low their finest talents above all before two of the great dogmas of the Christian faith: to the mystery of the Eucharist they raised incomparable churches; for the mystery of the Redemption, they populated them with marvels of art that remain among the most telling and most moving works of human genius.

The arts of eleventh and twelfth centuries had only shown God on the cross in triumph through it; the thirteenth placed there "The Man of Sorrows" and glorified the instruments of his torture; the fourteenth conceived a Christ convulsed and twisted by suffering, and crowned with thorns; the fifteenth showed him, to the contrary, hanging lamentably on the cross, bloodless and straight, almost spectral.

Heir to the enthusiastic worship of previous generations for the blood of the Savior, for that purple ransom paid to Justice in humanity's name, thus ransomed, this fifteenth century knew how to make astonishingly touching creations spring from its faith.

Thus in honor of this sacred blood, and to show the effective virtue of purification and redemption, he invented those impressive *fountains of life* where a whole throng of sinners sometimes bathes in deep basins filled with the divine blood fallen from the wounds of the Crucified One.

What is more, he imagined those troubling *divine winepresses* where the very body of Christ replaces the vat full of the trampled grape harvest and from which the blood issues in torrents. He emblazoned on large purple crests, not only the emblematic image of the holy wounds, but the heart, hands and feet, pierced with the spear and nails. And, as incomparable "monstrances" for these same redemptive wounds, he created the so-called Christs and Virgins of pity.

This was to exalt, to magnify, the bodily sufferings of Jesus, and to proclaim by this a touching recognition of the world's redemption.

But he wanted to go even further. He wanted to also show the intimate pangs of the very heart of the Redeemer during his Passion.

And then one day, in the land of France, a humble artist found himself daring to approach with serenity this confusing problem. And from his prayer and his chisel a new sculptural type was born, the most poignant perhaps ever created in the field of Christian art. So beautiful was his work found to be that immediately, from one end of the kingdom to the other, reproductions were made.

To situate his theme, the artist chose the moment of the Passion immediately preceding the crucifixion: Jesus has arrived at the uttermost limit of human strength. Already, the day before, in the pangs of the garden, his body was soaked with an exhausting sweat of blood; and since then his nerves have become tense with the sarcasm, spitting, buffetings, and the nameless brutality of the mob that pursued him from Annas to Caiaphas, from there to Pilate, then to Herod, and again to Pilate.

In this terrible journey, his blood flowed superabundantly under the prickings of the diadem of thorns, above all under the rods and whips of a terrifying flogging. Three times he fell under the weight of the gibbet that he was made to lift up from below, on his swollen shoulders.

Finally, here he is!...

Here he is, where he must die. This is the tragic moment captured by the medieval artist: seated on a block of stone, and, in this relative cessation of the external tortures of his body, we are presented with this scene to show what is happening within him.

Unclothed and bound with ropes, retaining only his lacerating crown, all his wounds reopened by the pitiless wrenching off of his garment, his blood falls freely all along his body, and, slowly, his life is beading and dripping through all his pores.

Now, with his human eyes, he looks at the executioners who bustle about with his cross and cast before him the terrifying nails and hammers, while his divine eyes are afflicted by visions of the spiritual and prophetic kind: the heaping up of human and future culpabilities, and, among those who will commit them, the uselessness of his sacrifice for legions of souls.... Dread for the flesh that shudders to the heart, and, even more inexorable, terror for the mind.

And in all the bitterness of this agony brought to its climax, the condemned man is alone in the midst of his persecutors. His dearest friends have abandoned him; the first among them has denied him, and he knows it; Mary, his mother, and John the beloved, and the compassionate saints who dared to approach him during the painful ascent have been pushed away; the Cyrene himself is gone.

Jesus is alone.

Is this not the *Vae soli!* from the Book of Ecclesiastes (4:10), in all its cold and inexorable cruelty? Woe to the man who is alone when pain grips his heart and churns through his body!

This is the stage, the often unnoticed moment of the Savior's Passion evoked by the seated Christ of fifteenth century artists. And this image aroused, from its creation, such a devotional fervor that the sculptors from that time carved it in profusion.

I have known some such in painted wood, for which their authors have asked for only a posture, since they have known how to be infinitely moving while asking the forms of human anatomy to be only a point of departure sufficient for their poem. Others, chiseled in stone with admirable mastery, are true masterpieces in the full sense of the word.

Here I want to describe only the one in the small rustic church of Venizy, in the Yonne, because of a particularity of the ornamentation on its base.

The seated Christ of Venizy is fixed in the pose common to all statues of this kind. At his feet, a human skull testifies that the rock on which it rests belongs to the summit of Golgotha, which is called in Latin *Calvarius mons*: the Mount of the Skull. A circle made of a single thorny branch encloses the divine forehead, and the hair is unkempt, its long locks heavy with glaucous and congealed blood. A rope goes down the neck between his torso and right arm; it is doubly tied at the wrists that it binds together and fetters the two legs halfway between feet and knees (Fig. 19). This is indeed the great sacrifice, in all the anguish of supreme expectation. Soon they will seize him because, so bound, he cannot walk; he will be thrown on

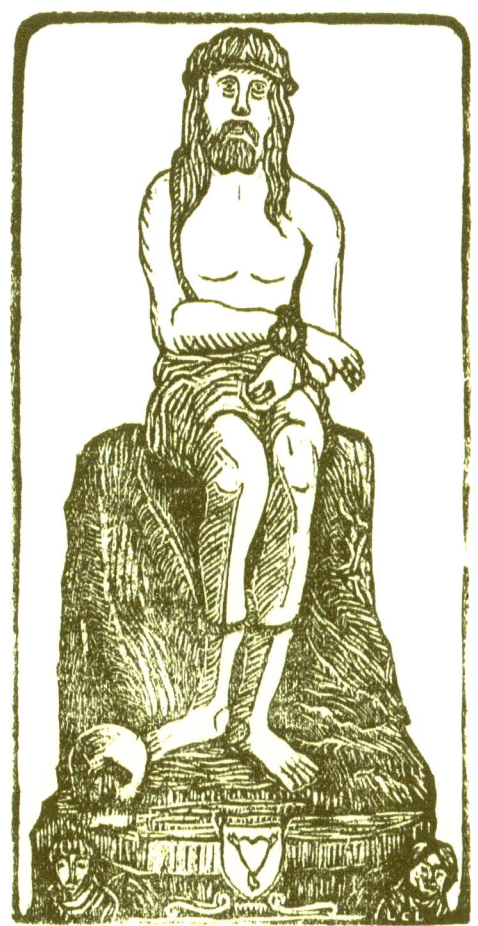

Fig. 19. — The Seated Christ of Venizy (Yonne), end of the 15th century.

the cross lying on the ground, and the nails will grate against, one by one, the bones of his four limbs, while disjoining them under the repeated blows of the hammers.

But, as I said before, at the precise moment when the sculptor brings this scene before us to contemplate, it is only the heart that suffers, but frightfully!

And while carving in stone his pious and tragic work, the old image-maker, thinking of the statues of sovereigns and grandees of his time, said to himself that for this king of sorrows, too, a blazon was necessary. So, on a beautiful escutcheon he chiseled this strange, but how significant pattern:

The heart of Jesus, membered with two hands and two feet pierced by Passion-nails.

The heart itself is unwounded, it is the heart of the Redeemer nailed to the cross, but still physically alive.

Surely, such depictions astonish and shock today's eyes, still too accustomed to the nonsense of the sanctimonious, so-called pious imagery of the nineteenth century. The old artists of the centuries of living faith carved in stone or wood as the authors of that time wrote on rough parchment, and the realism, of one and the other, was overflowing with meaning and life.

The preachers repeated that the Savior of men allowed himself to be "nail-fastened to a cross" only out of the immensity of his love, that he was all love, all heart! And in the rightness of his quite unpretentious thinking, the image-maker represented the divine Crucified One just as he heard it said: all heart.

Only, such is the potential superiority of an image stabilized before our eyes over a word that "strikes the air for half a second and flies away," a word we hear without it hardly describing anything, a word that, once materialized before our eyes, offends and baffles our present refinements. Our fifteenth-century French artists, without having been as realistic as those of England and Germany, would not have had pity on such refinements. In their religious symbolism they sought before and above all else the power of expression. To appeal to them, emblems had to express, even to the extent of shouting aloud, the truths or the things they had to openly represent. And, for as strangely bizarre as this might seem to our eyes, we are forced to recognize that the image of the crucified heart of Venizy has to its credit this complete fullness of expression.

I do not think it would have been possible to affirm more explicitly by sculpture that the heart of Jesus was both the principle and the starting point of our redemption, the physical and sensible point where the unheard-of sufferings of the Redeemer came to an end, and also the natural and primary source that provides the wounds of torture with the blood they shed before "all was consummated."

Now, I will borrow the last word to close this chapter from the eminent master Émile Mâle. Speaking in one of his books of the most pathetic works inspired by piety among fifteenth-century artists, he rightly states that "what they wanted to glorify was not suffering, but love; for what they show us is the suffering of a God who died for us. Suffering, therefore, has no meaning unless it is accepted with love, transfigured into love: 'love' remains the final lesson of Christian art in the fifteenth century, just as it is in the thirteenth."[6]

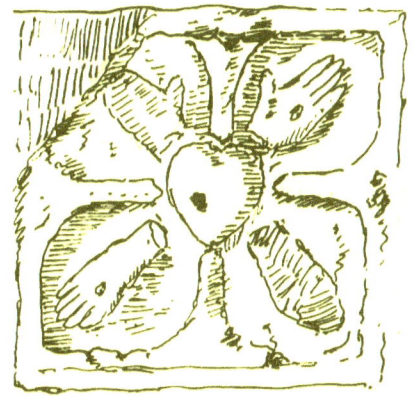

Sketch by the author of the Central panel of a tomb in the Church of St. Dubricius in Porlock (Somerset) based on a drawing of Sir Carruthers Gould transmitted by Mrs. Edith Wilde in 1923. Charbonneau-Lassay Archives (ed.).

---

6 E. Mâle, *Religious Art in France: The Late Middle Ages*, p. 93.

CHAPTER TWENTY

The Image of the Sacred Heart and the Coats of Arms of Sovereigns

SINCE SOMEONE HAD THE AUDACIOUS and providential idea to summarize the whole person of the Son of God made Man by representing his heart alone, it has happened several times that, in order to honor this divine image, sovereigns have taken it for an emblem or associated it with the insignia of their supreme dignity; and sometimes subjects have also arrayed themselves with it as a distinctive mark of royalty, or brought it into contact with the coat of arms of their princes, either to place these under its protection, or else to unite in a common and greater homage the heart of the Lord of Kings with their own sovereign here below.

Of these forms of glorification — from the highest glorification on earth after the act of worship — some rare testimonies are left to us. But also at this time when, from various sides, Rome is being solicited to establish a special feast for the Social Reign of Jesus Christ, it seems appropriate to group here some images prior to the Revolution that I have been able to find and that others have already pointed out, which show the heart of Our Lord Jesus Christ in contact with the idea of earthly royalty and the emblems of the sovereigns of old.

I. THE ROYAL ARMS OF PORTUGAL

One of the earliest authors who, on the other side of the Pyrenees, busy with the meaning of the coat of arms of Portugal, Anton Ginther, priest of the Holy Cross of Biberach (Würtemberg), is strangely mistaken about it.

Part VI: The Iconography of the Wounded Heart of Jesus

This coat of arms must be read in this way in normal heraldic language: "Argent five shields azure placed crosswise, each charged with five roundels argent placed in saltire; bordure gules charged with seven Castillian castles argent, masoned sable."[1]

And here is what Ginther wrote: "Alfonso I, King of Portugal, at the command of Jesus Christ who appeared to him during the night, had painted and carved, not only on the flags and banners of his army, but also on his coat of arms, the five sacred wounds of his Redeemer, and he placed in the middle the most sacred heart of Jesus, transpierced by the spear; and on the morrow, having raised this shield during the battle against the Moors, the king saw his enemies terrified, scattered, and destroyed in a wondrous way. Since that day the Kings of Portugal wear this sacred shield as a blazon."[2]

Ginther is alluding here to the battle of Ourique, where in 1139 Count Alfonso Henriquez defeated five Moorish kings, and was proclaimed King of Portugal on the battlefield. With the morning he had indeed told his troops how the previous night Jesus Christ had promised him victory, telling him to take as a sign the image of his five wounds. And this is how he arranged them on the royal escutcheon that became a kind of solemn ex-voto: on each of the five blue shields of the conquered kings, which he placed in a cross as a monument of his quintuple victory, he placed the sign, already many centuries old, of the five wounds, that is, five silver rounds in saltire that are only

---

[1] Cf. M. L[emoine], *Nouvelle Méthode raisonnée du blason ou de l'Art Héraldique du P. Ménestrier*, Lyon, Bruysset-Ponthus, 1770; p. 394. — We should add that, since the beginning of the seventeenth century, the Castilian castles of the royal crest of Portugal have been simplified into seven separate towers; the earliest documents bear the most numerous castles: thus the Portuguese coat of arms on the fourth mark of the Parisian printer Gilles Hardouin (1491–1521) bears a dozen turreted castles. — The Castilian castles on the coat of arms of the county of Poitou have, during the same period, undergone a similar simplification.

[2] Ginther, *Speculum amoris et doloris in sacratissimo ac divinissimo Corde Iesu* (Augsbourg: J. J. Lotteri, 1731), p. 68.

the stylization of the five wounds[3] (Fig. 1). But Ginther goes beyond the truth by adding that the new king also placed there the image of the heart of Jesus.

I know that spirituality, mysticism, pious literature can say, often with good reason, that the wound in the side of Jesus is his very heart. But iconography does not admit this kind of interpretation, nor does heraldry; for them, the wound in the side is the natural or stylized representation of the

Fig. 1. — Coat of Arms of the Kings of Portugal.

wound *on the surface* of the body of the Savior, and nothing more; it is neither the wound to the heart or the heart itself; it is only the external opening of the way of grace opened by the soldier's spearhead and though it can lead our thought as far as the heart, it does not represent it. King Alfonso did not put the heart of Jesus on his crest as wrongly repeated, after Ginther, by several French authors.[4]

Certainly, the notion of worshiping the Sacred Heart could not be all that foreign to the piety of the victor of Ourique: of French race through his grandfather, Duke Henry of Burgundy, great-grandson of King Robert of France, he was in correspondence with the first of the great apostles of the cult of the heart of Jesus, that other illustrious Burgundian, Saint Bernard; and the latter sent him, when he founded his Abbey of Alcobaca, some of his own Cîteaux monks to populate it. But even if we should learn that the King prayed with them to the heart of the Savior by name, that would not change anything in the heraldic correction I have just made to Ginther's text.

---

3 And not *bezants* (pieces of Eastern money) as treatises on blazonry from the last three centuries state.
4 Cf. Grimouard de Saint-Laurent, in *Revue de l'Art Chrétien*, April-June 1879, p. 318; Hilaire de Barenton, op. cit., p. 137.

Part VI: The Iconography of the Wounded Heart of Jesus

II. THE EMBLEM OF KING FERDINAND OF PORTUGAL

In the same work mentioned above, Ginther speaks also of a heraldic emblem adopted by the King of Portugal, Don Fernando, who reigned from 1367 to 1383: "Formerly, Ferdinand, King of Portugal," he states, "took as a family symbol (according to the testimony of Typotius[5]) two hearts: the most sacred heart of Jesus, wounded and cruelly pierced by the point of the spear, and, placed next to this divine heart and to its left, his own heart without wound, with these words: *Cur non utrumque*. Why not both of them!" Iconographers and mystics have translated this: why would not both be wounded?

Fig. 2. — The personal emblem of King Don Ferdinand of Portugal.

I reproduce here the very image of Ginther's book, according to a sketch by Father Buron (Fig. 2). And I must point out that there is disagreement between the author's text and the engraving that accompanies it: the royal emblem, composed in the fourteenth century, is treated in a quite seventeenth-century style, and I do not see the spear, but a sword; plus, the second heart is wounded like the other; the first is glorified with a crown of roses, flowers of the

---

5 Jacobus Typotius, *Symbola Divina et Humana Pontificum Imperatorum Regum* (Prague, 1601), plate L.

Passion, the second bears ripe ears of wheat; this is the moment to recall that wheat has sometimes symbolized the earth of which it is a fruit precious above all others.

The Portuguese symbolists and authors clearly recognize in the first of these two hearts that of the Savior and in the other that of King Ferdinand, and despite the enigmatic character of the emblem in question, I do not quite see what major reason might compel us to reject their opinion. Some see, in the juxtaposition of the royal heart with the divine heart, along with the motto, an expression of the king's desire to participate mystically in the wound of the heart of Jesus; others see it as the symbol of the heart of Jesus "penetrating the heart of the Portuguese ruler, even to its thoughts and most secret recesses."[6]

We know that the heart of Jesus was represented in the Iberian peninsula before the reign of Ferdinand, who died on October 22, 1383, and so the Gothic host-mold reminiscent of Romanesque art at the Episcopal Museum of Vic, where it appears alone on the cross of Calvary, should be an indisputable testimony of this.[7]

III. THE MYSTICAL COAT OF ARMS OF THE BLESSED JEANNE DE VALOIS

A century after King Ferdinand of Portugal left this world, it was the noblest daughter of the land of France who in turn took the material image of the heart of Jesus and joined it in a veritable union with her own family coat of arms.

Jeanne de France, of the Valois branch, daughter of King Louis XI and sister of King Charles VIII, had been married to her cousin the Duke of Orléans, who in turn became King of France in 1498, on the death of Charles VIII. This prince then had his marriage annulled in the court of Rome, because of close kinship, on the one hand, and, on the other, as having contracted it under duress, under the formidable pressure of King Louis XI. Jeanne

---

6 Cf. Antonio Cactano de Souza, *Historia genealogica da casa real Portugueza*, (Lisbon: J. A. de Sylva, 1735), tome 1, p. 429.

7 Cf. 6th Part, Chap. 17, ii, p. 1, Fig. 7 — Iron host-mold, from Vic, fourteenth century.

Part VI: The Iconography of the Wounded Heart of Jesus

de France then received the Duchy of Berry and took the name of Jeanne de Valois.

Heartbroken, because she loved her husband and was never reconciled to her disgrace, Jeanne withdrew to her city of Bourges, where she founded in 1501, to live with her in prayer and austerities, the Annunciation order.

As long as Jeanne de Valois was Duchess of Orléans and during the short while she was Queen by right, she bore as arms of alliance two shields azure with three fleur-de-lys or, supporting a floretty crown, one from the chief of her father, the other from that of her husband Louis de Valois, Duke of Orléans, when, repudiated, she lived at Bourges and gave herself entirely to God, she replaced the shield of the King, her husband, with that of the King of Heaven, Jesus Christ: "*Parted, dexter argent with the Heart of Jesus Christ gules, rent with an open wound in fess and cantoned with four other wounds in saltire, also gules and bleeding; sinister, gules with a Host argent issuing from a chalice or.*"[8]

The old magazine *L'Art Catholique* has reproduced in miniature Claude Gellé's beautiful seventeenth-century engraving that represents the blessed Jeanne. The mystical shield of the Sacred Heart and the chalice is depicted there to her right, and the shield of France to her left. Rather than these two separated shields, I preferred to give here the true arms of alliance of interest to us from an old woodcut, formerly with the late Guy Jouanneaux, a most considerate Poitevin scholar (Fig. 3); it too probably dates from the seventeenth century, but the two joined coats of arms were certainly copied by the engraver from a document of the previous century.

Fig. 3. — The mystical coats of arms of Jeanne de Valois.

---

8 One knows that the expression "gules" in blazonry indicates the color red, just as "azure" designates blue.

Under the same and common fleur-de-lysed crown, the two coats of arms are juxtaposed in a veritable arms of alliance between Jesus Christ and the House of France in the person of Jeanne de France, the husband on the right, the wife on the left.

IV. THE SACRED HEART OF THE ROYAL STALL AT WINDSOR (ENGLAND)

In the choir of St. George Chapel in the royal castle at Windsor, at the top of the English Sovereign's stall, which is early sixteenth-century, and above the Queen's place, the heart of Jesus, surrounded by the crown of thorns and rent by a wound from which issues an outpouring of blood, is shown glorious between the Lamb immolated on the Apocalyptic Book with seven seals, and the Divine Hand which appoints it for the adoration of all.

Fig. 4. — The Sacred Heart on the royal stall at Windsor.

I give here its representation from the work of Father Alet, S. J., *La France et le Sacré-Coeur* (p. 261). Not intending to explain this emblem from a strictly archaeological and chronological point of view, I only want to emphasize this fact: even though the Sacred Heart is not surrounded there by the scepter, the crown, or any other insignia of royalty, the hand that wanted it here has placed

Part VI: The Iconography of the Wounded Heart of Jesus

it above all the supreme attributes over which this heart holds sway, at the very summit of the throne occupied by the royal majesty in prayer before the almighty Divine Majesty (Fig. 4).

For the record, I recall only one other English iconographic document where royal tribute is somehow also rendered to the blood of Jesus Christ issued from his heart; it is a fifteenth-century stained glass window in the Sidmouth Church, on which the five bleeding wounds are all crowned with golden coronets.[9]

V. THE INITIAL IN THE TITLE OF "TREASURY OF THE POOR," 1527

There was also, about the same time, a modest artist in France who placed the golden crown of kings over the heart of the Lord: "On the 18th of August, 1527," *The treasure of the Poor according to Master Arnoult de Villenove, Master Bérard de Solo and several other Doctors of Medicine at Montpellier* was printed at Lyon, from the press of "Claude Mourry, dit Le Prince," residing "next to Our Lady of Comfort." The first page of this work entirely engraved on wood was adorned with the image of a doctor installed in front of his "desk" laden with books, and whose name an angel displays on a banner: "Maistre Arnoult de Villenove." Above this composition is the aforementioned title whose first letter, a capital L, is accompanied by a crest charged with a heart surmounted by a crown (Fig. 5).

Fig. 5. — *The initial of the "Treasure of the Poor."*

Certainly, a more adroit engraver might have better located and better marked the wound to the heart, but today's rare artists who engrave wood with the simple tools of Renaissance engravers

---

9 Cf. 3rd Part, Chap. 8, p. 1, Fig. 3—The "Springs of the Savior" on a shield with the five wounds at Sidmouth Church (Devonshire), England, fifteenth century.

know how easy it is, even with skill, to miss a stroke in such small subjects: a defect in the wood, a slight movement, almost anything is enough.

Because the "Treasury of the Poor" is involved here, I know some will say that this heart is only an emblem of Charity. I do not disagree that this might be so, and we have the liturgical Litany of the Sacred Heart to answer them: "Cor Jesu fornax ardens caritatis," the Heart of Jesus is a fiery furnace of charity. Charity of a God for men, of a man for his suffering brethren, therefore find here an emblem, better than the Heart of Jesus, to happily and fully symbolize this.[10]

VI. BLAZON OF A BIBLE OF LA ROCHE-CLERMAULT (INDRE-ET-LOIRE)

I noticed some twenty years ago on a quarto Bible in the rectory of La Roche Clermault, near Chinon, the colored drawing here (Fig. 6).

On the reverse of the tawny leather cover a blue orbicular crest, or rounded shield, bears a flesh-colored Sacred Heart, above three royal fleur-de-lys; around the escutcheon two green palms. And everything is drawn in that particularly heavy style of the second half of Louis XIV's reign.

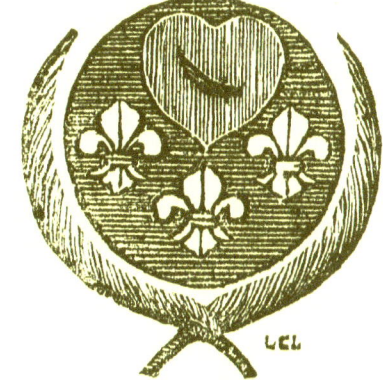

Fig. 6. — *The Roche-Clermault Bible (I.-&-L.).*

We saw, a few years ago, a descendant of the so-called Louis XVII — Naundorf — adopt a similar arrangement for the "new coat of arms for the House of Bourbon," with the difference that two lilies were placed in chief on the shield, the Sacred Heart in the center, and a lily in base.

---

10 I owe the knowledge of this artifact, and much other intellectual aid in the work I am pursuing, to Miss Madeleine Berthier, director and founder of the Firme des Beaux-Livres. — Most respectful and heartfelt thanks.

Part VI: The Iconography of the Wounded Heart of Jesus

The Roche-Clermault coat of arms on which the heart of Jesus appears clearly seems but a mark of devotion from a particular inspiration, an inspiration due to the same sentiment that gave rise to the drawing the Abbess Flandrine of Nassau (1579–1640) had applied to all the manuscript books of her Benedictine abbey of Sainte-Croix at Poitiers;[11] that is, unless the Roche-Clermault Bible is a remnant from the great monastery of the Visitation at Loudun, located barely five leagues away and whose library and numerous pious objects were scattered throughout the region during the Revolution.

Founded in 1648, this monastery was an early and ardent center for the distribution throughout the country of images of the Sacred Heart; but I emphasize that I am suggesting this hypothetical origin for the Roche-Clermault coat of arms only as a possibility, devoid at the moment of any documentary support.

VII. SCULPTURE OF THE RUE DE LA JUIVERIE, FRÉJUS

It was again thanks to Miss Berthier, from Cannes, that I was able to find in the little street of Juiverie near the market square in Fréjus a very pretty wooden medallion carved in the early eighteenth century, and then inlaid on a curious older door. It shows a raised heart, surmounted by the cross, on the surface of which are the three fleur-de-lys of France. From the foot of the cross issue two vegetal garlands; everything is somewhat corroded by time (Fig. 7).

Fig. 7. — Door medallion, Rue de la Juiverie, Fréjus.

11 Cf. Mgr Barbier de Montault, *Pays et Monuments du Poitou* (Paris: May et Motteroz, 1890), tome I, p. 167.

The Image of the Sacred Heart and the Coats of Arms of Sovereigns

What interpretation to give to this motif?

Either this is the image of the heart of whomever had it carved and who wished in this way to proclaim his dual and ardent love for religion, symbolized by the cross, and for the Royal House of France; or else it is the heart of Jesus — even though it does not bear any trace of the spear wound — and, looking at it through the eyes of the times that produced it, this is even the first thought that comes to mind: the heart of Jesus, under whose protection a faithful subject has confided the person of his king, a kind of *Domine salvum fac Regem* sung by the chisel. "May God have you in His holy keeping," our ancient kings always wrote to their subjects when ending their letters, and "May God keep our King in His heart!" the Fréjus notable who stamped this pretty medallion upon his door seems to reply...

CHAPTER TWENTY-ONE

The Astronomical Marble from the Charterhouse of Saint-Denis-d'Orques

I HAVE FROM MRS. CL. CHARRIER, TO WHOM I wish to express my most sincere gratitude, a small bas-relief in black marble, from the second half of the sixteenth century, which is, it seems to me, the most magnificent hymn one can sing on a theme in honor of the glorious heart of Jesus Christ. The back of this marble plaque bears a label on which is written, "This stone was collected, before 1875, at the abbey of Saint-Denis-d'Orques, department of Sarthe." I would like to immediately rectify a slight error in this text: there never was an abbey in Saint-Denis-d'Orques—I mean a religious house with a prelate monk having the title of *abbot* for superior—but there are still the remains of what was once a Carthusian monastery. It was founded, around 1234, by the blessed Geoffroy de Loudun, bishop of Mans, and continued to thrive until the Revolution, which destroyed it almost entirely, leaving only farm buildings and a small chapel once reserved for women.[1]

Our readers know how lively was the devotion to the heart of Jesus at the end of the Middle Ages in the Order of St. Bruno,[2] and with what fervor this Order propagated its worship by writings of Ludolph of Saxony especially, from the middle of the fourteenth century, then by those of Dominic of Trier, Denys the Carthusian, Lanspergius, and others.

The sculpture of Saint-Denis-d'Orques is even more evocative than the very beautiful keystone set by the monks of St. Bruno in their cloister of the Grande Chartreuse in 1474, and

---

1 Information kindly communicated by the pastor of Saint-Denis.
2 Cf. Part 6, Chap. 17, p. 281.

Part VI: The Iconography of the Wounded Heart of Jesus

Fig. 1. — The astronomical Marble from the Charterhouse of Saint-Denis-d'Orques (Sarthe).

which represents the heart of Jesus on the cross, pierced with the spear and surrounded by the various objects cited in the Gospel accounts of the Lord's Passion.

The hollowed-out parts of the marble that interest us are covered with a kind of matte white patina that quite forcefully underscores the ornamental assemblage as a whole. This has made me decide, in carving the wood engraving included in this text, to represent, contrary to usual practice, the relief-work in black and the hollow-work in white (Fig. 1).

The heart of Jesus is triumphant at the center of the composition, rent by a long double-curved wound that cuts through it obliquely. It is raised, in high relief, from the bottom of a kind of shallow basin lined with rays that ascend from the periphery of the heart to the surface level of the marble. These twenty-eight radii are an iconographic feature of "the glorious state."

The heart and its irradiation are circumscribed, first by the planetary circle, then by that of the zodiac; at the four corners of the marble, the spandrels are decorated with ornamental palmettes.

Given its place of origin, it is quite evident that this object could have been inspired only by a Carthusian monk; very probably it is even the work of his own hands: we know that the Carthusians have the obligation to divide their time, every day, in the eremitic isolation of their cell, between study and manual work, which vary according to the tastes and aptitudes of each. This marble is, then, most likely the work of one of them.

We will study successively the date, the two bands laden with astronomical signs that direct our thoughts to the most distant infinities, then look into the problematic use of the object itself.

I. THE DATE

The overall arrangement of the composition might leave one undecided between the second half of the sixteenth century and the threshold of the seventeenth. However the examination of a whole series of sundials dated from 1600 to 1638, and for reasons to be explained below, obliges me to fix the date of the Saint-Denis-d'Orques sculpture between 1550 and about 1575:

Palmettes. — Each marble spandrel is decorated with double palmette foliage composed of a central point and two long leaves. This ornamentation — whose lines recall those of the symbol of the winged sun, or god of the air, on the monuments of the Egyptians[3] — was especially favored by us at the end of the fifteenth century. At this time there are many examples in the works of the wood engravers who served the first printers, as well as in the works of carpenters, sculptors, metal carvers, etc.

For book corporations, for example, palmettes similar in all respects to those of our marble appear at the angles of the

---

3 Cf. Noël-Antoine Pluche, *Histoire du Ciel*, Tome I (Paris: Estienne, 1739), p. 42, fig. 3.

engravings for the *Danse macabre*, printed by Guyot Marchand, in 1486 (Num. II of the terminal engraving, p. 224) and on the plates of *Tristan* published at the same time by Antoine Vérard (Num. I of the aforementioned engraving). Similar motifs also adorn the top corners of the trademark of Philippe Pigouchet, who printed for this same Vérard; and the same palmettes are still visible, at the end of the fifteenth century, on the *Encomium trium Mariarum*; also on the *Shepherds' Calendar*, of the same date, and which was in favor until the end of the sixteenth century, etc....

Thus, to consider only the decorative part of the work we are studying, it should be dated to the end of the fifteenth century, or a little after.

Irradiation of the Heart. — On this subject we will only note that the alternating straight and undulating, or so-called flamboyant, rays, by no means dictate, as one of my friends believes, a late date: on the beautiful "fountain of life" fresco in Chinon's Saint-Mesme, 15th century, all the rays of the sun are flamboyant, and on an engraving from the same period of the *Song of Songs* — one of the most beautiful blockbooks of the fifteenth century[4] — the Virgin is encompassed by a halo made of alternating straight and undulating rays. We could mention fifty examples...

The astronomical signs. — Everyone knows more or less these conventional signs, adopted by the science of yesteryear, astronomy, astrology, alchemy, kabbalah, etc., to symbolize the various stars of our firmament; they are called kabbalistic, hermetic, esoteric — that is, "secret" — because they were specific to the above-mentioned sciences, then reserved for quite rare initiates. From their use on the planetary circle and on the zodiac of our marble, the learned Rev. Moreux, writing to me, would fix the date for the sculpture that bears them as "close to two centuries ago." However, comparing the shapes of these signs on the marble and those of these same signs on the seventeenth-century works that I have here, especially the *Works* of J. Belot, pastor

---

4 Cf. Émile Mâle, *Religious Art in France: The Late Middle Ages*, p. 203.

of Milmont, professor of divine and heavenly sciences,[5] I have noticed that those executed on the marble are more archaic than those in Belot's book, especially the planetary signs for Mercury, Jupiter and the Sun; the latter is featured with its human face and its curved rays slanted in the same direction as those borne by the sun on the Tielman Kerver *Hours* for use at Rome, 1505; and, on the seal of the thirteenth-century Cathedral Chapter of Waterford, in England, the sun and moon bear similarly curved rays, symbol of the astral circuit through space.[6]

On our zodiac, the sign of Virgo is made of the tiny conjoined Gothic letters, m and r (Maria), which is typical of the fifteenth century.

One might add that the system of cosmogony that presides over this marble is still the one known throughout the Middle Ages, a system in which the earth is the center of the universe. On the planetary circle we read only the signs of the seven satellite planets which, accompanied by the sun, it was believed, revolved around it. From 1507, it is true, Copernicus realized the true order of our solar constellation: the sun in the center, the earth, a simple planet like the others, tracing out along with them and around the sun the same procession of vassalage. But Copernicus did not publish his discovery until 1543, and even in the next century, in Galileo's time, his system was still contested by Scholastics. The inspirer of the Saint-Denis Charterhouse sculpture, then, might very well serenely believe as yet, in the middle of the sixteenth century, in the old system of the ancient astronomers.

Because of what we have just examined, I do not think, therefore, it would be rash to assign about the third quarter of the sixteenth century as a date for this marble that so magnificently glorifies the Savior's heart in a way which remains to be told.

---

5 Lyon, Claude La Rivière, 1654.
6 Cf. Richard Caulfield, *The Episcopal and Capitular Seals of the Irish Cathedral Churches Illustrated*, Part II (Dublin: J. M'Glashan, 1853), p. 18 and p. III, Num. 3.

Part VI: The Iconography of the Wounded Heart of Jesus

II. THE PLANETARY CIRCLE

On the marble of Saint-Denis-d'Orques, the heart of Jesus is therefore in the middle of the planetary circle, that median place given to the earth in the cosmogony of the ancients. It is presented here as the center and pivot of the worlds that make up our solar constellation first, then, with the second circle, as the center of the zodiac's constellations, and, by extension, the nebulae of the extra-zodiacal vastness; finally, as the soul and the center too of innumerable invisible stars: "suns already grown old, dying suns, dead stars that have populated the vast cemeteries of the heavens for millions of years."[7]

In a word, to the eyes of the Le Mans Carthusian, contemporary of Erasmus and Rabelais, the Sacred Heart of Christ turns out to be really, in the divine plan, the vital point of the absolute infinity of spaces, the heart of this immensity whose limitless deployment is, for our minds, such a formidable mystery.

It is equally, in the thought of the monk, the Source; because of the ancient place which this heart has conquered on the reverse side of the earth, it does not receive, quite the contrary, it bestows, and that with a sovereign liberality.

Let me explain: One of the most prolific authors of the Middle Ages, who dealt not only with astronomy, but also — to contradict their fallacious elements — with astrology and alchemy, Blessed Raymond Llull studied, through the entire length of the ninth book of his *Tree of Knowledge*, how "the impression that heavenly bodies imprint on earthly bodies and the nature that these latter receive from them" was understood at the time (1247).[8] Four hundred years later, J. Belot, pastor of Milmont, in the chapters of his work quoted above dealing with "chiromancy" and "physiognomy" and, after him, our modern astrologers, repeat the same theories. Now, on our marble it is not the heart-center that receives and absorbs, for its benefit, the emanations of the stars; quite the contrary, it is this heart that projects towards

---

7 Théophile Moreux, op. cit., p. 213.
8 Cf. Marius André, *Le Bienheureux Raymond Lulle* (Paris: Lecoffre, 1900), p. 64.

them, irradiates them, vivifies them, and reigns over them. It is the Munificent that gives, divinely.

For greater clarity in the rest of our examination, I will repeat here the planetary band:

First of all, the cross, which never represented any star in our Western hermeticism, and which is there as a kind of sacred sphinx whose enigma we will try to pierce later.

Then come the seven classical planets:

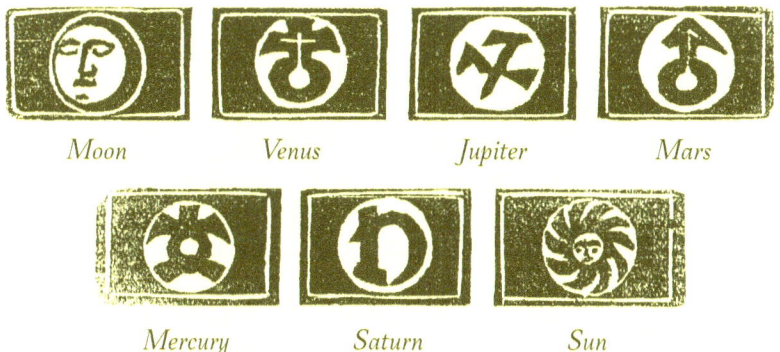

There they are, the seven radiant stars, first in rank of the great and luminous army of the Infinite, like the first great heavenly vassals of the Heart of the Word, Creator and Sovereign.

Now what does the presence of the cross mean at the point of departure, at the summit of the circle of the planets?

Since Christianity's early centuries, religious inquiries have been made into this question: if living, conscious, and responsible beings, composed of bodies and souls of the same nature as ours, exist on the surface of the planetary worlds that encompass us, and if these beings have had need of redemption, has the redemption merited for Earthlings by the death of Christ Jesus on the cross had an efficacious impact even on them?

And they concluded in the affirmative.

Part VI: The Iconography of the Wounded Heart of Jesus

Is not an echo of this response to be found in this passage from the hymn *Crux fidelis*, composed in the sixth century by the poet-bishop of Poitiers, St. Fortunatus,[9] and which the Church sings at the Lauds of the Precious Blood and Good Friday, during the Adoration of the Cross:

Spina, clavi, lancea	The thorns, the nails, the spear
Mite corpus perforarunt;	His tender body have pierced;
Unda manat et cruor:	Water has poured out with the blood:
Terra, pontus, astra, mundus	The earth, the sea, the stars, the world
Quo lavantur flumine!	Are bathed in this sacred flood.

And what makes me believe even more that this thought of redemptive efficacy, conveyed as far as the stars, had in all likelihood engaged the mind of the inspirer of the Carthusian marble is a detail such as this:

On all the representations of the planetary circle, in the works on alchemy, astronomy, astrology, and occultism prior to the Renaissance, the order of the planets is this one: 1st the Sun, 2nd the Moon, 3rd Venus, 4th Jupiter, 5th Mars, 6th Mercury, and 7th Saturn. Now on our marble, to the contrary, after the cross, the planetary series begins with the Moon, which thus assumes 1st place instead of 2nd, and ends with the Sun, which goes from first place to last.

Such an anomaly is obviously intentional, and can have as a deciding factor only the unusual presence of the cross on the circle. This arrangement seems solely the result of the sculptor's wish to place the redemptive cross between the ancient sacred sigil of "Sol et Luna," just as it is in nearly all the crucifixions by artists up until the thirteenth century, where, on each side of Jesus crucified, is seen the disks with human faces of the Sun, to his right, and the Moon to his left.

Notice how, by so placing them, the sculptor was not being blindly obedient to a practice of his own times: the custom of placing, as in the above-mentioned centuries, the two stars on each side of the cross as a symbol of eternity and glorification, already rarer in the

---

9 Also the author of *Vexilla Regis*.

fourteenth and fifteenth centuries, was completely abandoned[10] by the middle of the sixteenth; but here we are indisputably in the presence of a work by an artist of considerable knowledge, an artist who wanted to situate the heart of Jesus Christ within the most extensive and impressive of glorifications.

To solely keep to what we have just examined is already immense, but there is still more: after the homage of the infinity of spaces, here is the homage of the infinity of times.

III. THE ZODIAC

Above the planetary circle cross begins the series of zodiacal constellations that divide our years into four seasons and twelve months.

Here they are, represented by their kabbalistic signs and in concordance with the monthly period specific to each of them.[11]

Sagittarius	*Capricorn*	*Aquarius*	*Pisces*
November	December	January	February
Leo	*Virgo*	*Libra*	*Scorpio*
July	August	September	October
Aries	*Taurus*	*Gemini*	*Cancer*
March	April	May	June

10 I do not think that one can see in the presence of the cross on the planetary circle an allusion to the Carthusian motto: *Stat Crux dum volvitur orbis*, "The cross stands while the world turns," for there is nothing here to distinguish the stability of the cross from the mobility of the planets.
11 The astronomical signs are represented here just as they are on the sculpted marble.

From the origins of Catholic worship, the Church did not fear to borrow from the practices of pagan cults the hallowed images of the zodiac and have them represented in the ornamentation of the first basilicas. The Romanesque and Gothic periods often placed them on the main door of the churches by attaching to them symbolic meanings that would take too long to explain here; we will just note that the idea of having the year begin — as on our sculpture — with March, that is to say, with Spring, instead of January, is not encountered on the churches of the thirteenth, fourteenth, and fifteenth centuries; only the arts of the Romanesque period offer an example of this.[12] And let us also underscore this surprising singularity of a sixteenth-century sculptor who, in his series of months as in the employment of "Sol and Luna," returns to traditions of national origin abandoned for three centuries, while at the same time his contemporaries prostituted French religious art to the craze for a bastardized and ridiculous neo-paganism.

Another idea, which would not have escaped him, finds its place here: the grouping into twelve constellations of the stars of the zodiac, whose movements delimit our months and years, date from some five thousand years ago,[13] and originates with the surprising and quite perfect astronomical work of the Chaldeans, though the name of this arrangement is Greek. In the sixteenth century as in the seventeenth, it was explained as follows: "The Greeks say Zodiacos, which is to say Life-Bearer, in this respect, that the life of all animals depends on this circle because the Sun rises towards us along it, brings us the generation of things, and, by going down, corruption."[14]

If then, in the thinking of the time, the Zodiac brought Life to all living beings, we see from which center, from which radiant and generous divine source, the author of the Saint-Denis-d'Orques marble drew, for, unlike God, in order to be able to give, something must first receive. But the stars are not gods, and that is why the author has them draw the gifts of life from the very heart

---

12 Cf. Émile Mâle, *Religious Art in France: the Thirteenth Century*, p. 426, note 18.
13 Cf. T. Moreux, op. cit., p. 108.
14 J. Belot, *Œuvres* (Rouen: Pierre Amiot, 1688), p. 2.

of God, which they then distribute, according to His providential plan, to animated beings.

And this heart appears to us now, not only as the radiant ruler and the All of the worlds in their boundless immensity, but still more as the center of the infinity of duration, of these two eternities that are only one: the past and the future; at the same time it is affirmed as the creative and redeeming core of all life on the Earth and in the universality of the stars: *Cor universi*! This is what the monk's planetary circle and zodiac proclaim!

I do not think it possible for human thought to imagine a more complete apotheosis for the heart of Jesus Christ, or likewise to give rise to a concept whose range can ascend higher and trajectory reach further, since, in whatever direction we gaze, we see this concept reach infinity and, with that, plunge towards the reserved domains of God and His secrets. The intelligence of man stops and staggers at their threshold, and his tongue has no more words to solicit for these "unrevealed mysteries," often mentioned by Fr. Faber,[15] the appeasing of man's thirst for knowledge and his need for love; there is no longer anything left to do but to fall back to the center of all things where the soldier's spear opened with its depredations a refuge, a source, a home.

Let nobody tell me that no author prior to the seventeenth century speaks of the heart of Jesus as the center of the universe. I would respond that, for the marble of the unknown Carthusian, as for the radiant heart of castle-keep of Chinon, a man always has the right to be ahead of others, and that, if the marble I received is ahead of the texts — even assuming we know all of them — this proves once more that, in religious iconography, such old images are often prior to the texts that speak of them or the thoughts they convey, because the written dissertation dealt with one or the other only when they were already known.

The seventeenth century, as well as those that followed, actually spoke of the Universal Heart. They have even conveyed this grandiose idea through engravings, and we have already given

---

15 Cf. Ernest Hello, "Le Coeur humain," in *Revue du monde catholique*, tome 44 (Paris: Victor Palmé, 1875), p. 759. — *Trans.*

several examples, but on a much smaller scale, in fact, than that of the composition of the Le Mans Carthusian.

On one of these engravings, dated 1708 and kept in the Library of the Hiéron of Paray, the inscription: *Cor Jesu, Cor universi* unfurls above the wounded and flaming heart on the surface of which is inscribed the map of the five parts of the Earth (Fig. 2). That is, our planet and not, strictly speaking, the universe.

Fig. 2. — Engraving from 1708, Bibliothèque du Hiéron de Paray.

Another engraving from the same period, by Klauber,[16] bears at its center the heart of Jesus wounded and placed on the trinitarian triangle with the inscription: *Centrum universi*. It is surrounded by glory and a crown made of hearts flaming like itself; from it to them, and from them to it, flaming arrows come and go (Fig. 3). These hearts obviously represent those of all departed, living and future men. This is the universality of human hearts.

16 Cf. *Revue de l'Art chrétien*, July, 1879, p. 101.

In both of these engravings the idea lacks neither grandeur nor beauty, but it remains far, however, from the total breadth given by the monk to his composition!

Surely the thought of likening in a certain manner the entire person of Christ to the stars, and above all to the Sun by reason of its brightness, warmth, and other benefits, was not new to the Middle Ages. And the Church, which has us glorify it each morning under the vocables of Purity of eternal brightness, Sun of

Fig. 3. — *Engraving by Klauber, 18th century.*

Justice and the True Light,[17] is simply echoing its past: does not the Nicene Creed, which dates from 325, call "the very essence of all light, 'Lumen de lumine'"? And, a short while after Constantine, "Christians, thanks to the interpretations they bestowed on the old emblems, imposed a new meaning and baptized the most venerable pagan types; for example, the god Sol became Christ who rises above the earth with the brightness of the sun."[18] From this came

17 *Litany of the Holy Name of Jesus*: Jesu candor lucis aeternae... Sol justitiae... Lux vera...
18 Dom H. Leclercq, Bénédictin de Fomborough, *Manuel d'archéologie chrétienne* (Paris: Letouzey et Ané, 1907), tome. II, Ch. XIII, p. 579.

a whole magnificent flowering in Christian rites, sacred writings and arts.

I have had the occasion to study from one end of Poitou to the other some twenty cemeteries from the first ten Christian centuries, and leaning over these long dead people, who had possessed my faith and my hope, to gather testimonies of what, while alive, they believed and hoped. I have rather often recovered, from above their chest or near their hand, small disks of stone or terracotta which appear to be nothing but religious emblems of the solar idea. I am depicting one of them here, collected in 1912 during my excavations at Mouterre-Silly, near Loudun (Vienne), on the chest of a skeleton. It bears a central hole for suspension from which twenty-six rays issue (Fig. 4). Now, those buried at Mouterre had been there since the sixth century, around the first place of deposition for the venerated body of St. Maximin, bishop of Trier, born at Mouterre. These were clearly pious Christians, then, and the rayed disk taken by one of them to the grave, suspended from his neck, is, to my eyes, only an image of Christ Jesus, source of that divine light whose revivifying rays the Church invokes upon her dead children.... *Et lux perpetua luceat eis!*

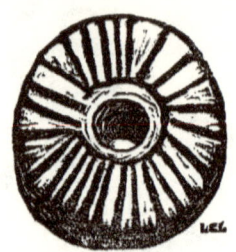

Fig. 4. — Limestone disk, cemetery of Mouterre-Silly, 6th century. Musée des Antiq. de l'Ouest.

Let no one cry out against the unlikelihood of this interpretation: at Saint-Just-sur-Dive,[19] another burial contained one of those patens in glazed greyish-black clay upon which the faithful sometimes sent each other "eulogies," that is, blessed foods, and which are included in the category of those dishes that St. Fortunatus of Poitiers, writing to St. Radegonde, designated under the name of Marmorean plates, "marmoreus discus." In the churches of the West — Poitiers, Angers, Nantes, Saintes, Bordeaux — these patens were often decorated with the mystical pursuit of the stag. An image of the Christian soul pursued during earthly life by the passions,

---

19 In the former lands of the Loudunais, today in Maine-et-Loire.

symbolized by dogs; the stag, to escape them, flees towards a cross behind which is found the palm of ultimate triumph.

Now, on the Saint-Just plate, above the stag and dogs, above the obstacles over which it leaps, above the cross and palm towards which it bounds, hovers a Sun the center of which, the heart of which is made of the Constantinian monogram of Christ, the two superimposed Greek letters X and P (XPistus) (Fig. 5).

Have we not here, then, that Christ-Sun about which the Latin liturgy speaks in the Holy Saturday office at the blessing of the Paschal candle: "May the morning star find its flame alive; that star which knows no setting, that star which returning from hell, shone serenely upon mankind"? And here the liturgy is only the echo of St. John's Apocalypse: "I, Jesus... I am the root and stock of David, the bright and morning star" (22:16).

Fig. 5. — *The Christ-Sun, Saint-Just-sur-Dive.*

But how far we are, some will say, from the Saint-Denis-d'Orques marble! Most definitely not! From the Christ-Heart of the Sun on the Saint-Just plate, left under the hand of a dead man for fourteen hundred years, to the radiant and wounded heart, the center of all suns on the Carthusian marble, there is truly, by eternity's measure, only the distance of a fleeting instant, and, with regard to the Faith, only a difference in expressing two alike and magnificent homages, two similar acts of adoration. The Carthusian's thought is only the grown-up sister of those of our Merovingians of the West, and the Christians of Rome at the time of Constantine. In Catholic piety everything stands together, everything is connected.

IV. THE USE OF THE CARVED MARBLE

Above the radiant heart a hole was made after the completion of the sculpture, and a metallic object, the upper part of which was larger than the diameter of the hole, has left its trace.

Was it a peg or just a nail?

I have questioned astronomers, specialists in gnomonics, archaeologists, and nobody could find a practical use for this marble that is neither a sundial nor anything like it.

I am left to assume that it was executed to be simply the ornamental and symmetrical counterpart of a sundial, either horizontal or vertical, placed on each side of an entry for example, and that its ornamentation was dictated solely by the idea of a glorification as expressive as possible of the heart of Jesus.

Especially understood as he knew how to express it, it is quite beautiful, by itself, so that the monk has imposed the long work of his transcription on the hard and beautiful marble at his disposal.

He alone, who felt this inspiration arise and take shape in the soaring flight of his prayer, could have worthily spoken of it, and perhaps have all these suns open as of themselves, like overripe fruits, and have them sing before us, in honor of the Heart of God, the inaudible hymns of those worlds treading the pathways of heaven! But, only in their ecstasies can the saints and predestined ones have, here below, as if the semblance of the slightest perception of this.

For us, falling back on ourselves with humility, we have only the right to implore: O Heart! who are the center of the Universe, the seat of the Infinite, and our Redeemer, have mercy on the dust of atoms that we are, be our Light and our Life now and at the moment we enter real life through Death's dark door.

N° 1. — *Palmettes appearing on the plates of* Tristan, *published by Antoine Vérard.*

N° 2. — *Palmettes appearing at the angles of the engravings for the* Danse macabre, *printed by Guyot Marchand.*

CHAPTER TWENTY-TWO

Heart-Shaped Sundials

I. THE SUNDIAL OF MARIGNY-BRIZAY (VIENNE)

IN THE PREVIOUS CHAPTER I MENTIONED, when speaking of the astronomical marble of the Saint-Denis-d'Orques Charterhouse, that my research into the times that saw it carved has led me to examine quite a number of sundials dating from the end of the sixteenth century and the first part of the seventeenth.

Among the latter I noticed at the Musée des Augustins in Poitiers, which belongs to the Société des Antiquaires de l'Ouest, the drawing of one that used to tell the hours at the castle of Marigny-Brizay (Vienne) and which was given to the learned Poitevin society in 1918 by Mr. Cesbron, Lord of Marigny.

It is a slate plaque, almost square, 37 centimeters in length, dated 1637 (Fig. 1); it bears, around the graduated hour-lines, an ornamentation that derives from two sources of inspiration: a) Above, a utilitarian part, astronomical and chronometric in nature. b) Below, a part relating to the personality of the first possessor of the dial and his religious sentiments.

Let us now examine each of these two areas of the Marigny sundial:

a) The middle of the first part is occupied by a solar chronometer; a heart represents the sun from which rays issue whose ends touch on the hour-markings. These markings are on a double graduated curve the projected upper parts of which would trace the outline of an oval with a wide base.

From a hole, made above the elliptical medallion where the heart-sun is to be found, issues an oblique peg that bends at an angle above the heart (I have not represented this on the engraving so as not to complicate the drawing of the central medallion). It is the shadow of the angular tip of this peg which, projected by the sun, crossed the graduated line and thus marked the hours.

Part VI: The Iconography of the Wounded Heart of Jesus

Fig. 1. — *The former sundial from the castle of Marigny-Brizay (Vienne). Musée des Ant. de l'Ouest, Poitiers.*

Three angels indicate the three cardinal points of the horizon whence sunlight comes to us daily: east, south, and west. The angel of the north does not appear because the sun never visits the point he occupies; in its place is the family shield of whoever had this sundial engraved in 1637.

We find here the practice dear to old Christian ornament makers of depicting the four main points of the rose of the winds as angels, and the origin of the choice of this motif is clearly situated in the very depths of Christian times since it is derived from this verse of the Apocalypse, written by St. John around the year 96: "I saw four angels standing on the four corners of the earth, holding the four winds of the earth, that they should not blow upon the earth nor upon the sea nor on any tree" (7:1).

These angels, by the way, are all that christianizes — and how little — the time-measure part of this sundial, which in this respect remains far from many others, such as the one in the old Poitevin collection of the Marquis de la Sayette, whose Christ-Sun occupies the center and the twelve apostles the points of the hours.[1]

On each side of the hour-register on the Marigny sundial, two stars remind us that time also regulates astral conjunctions and revolutions, and these symbolize space.

b) The zone relating to the first owner of the Marigny sundial is very simple. It only has his coat of arms and two pious medallions; only the zone on the lower part is obviously due to the sentiments of the person who ordered it for his family home, while the ornamentation of the chronometric part comes from a specialist in sundial-making responsible for executing an hour-dial on the slate.

In the middle is a coat of arms supported by two greyhounds. I think I can recognize in this shield that of the De la Lande family,[2] ennobled in 1594, and to which the *Armorial des Maires de Poitiers*, and Poitevin heraldists, attribute a blazon of *Argent with an oak vert on a hillock of the same, chief azure charged with a crescent argent*.

On the sundial that concerns us, the one who bore this escutcheon in 1637 placed it therefore as the emblem of his lineage and his person between the heavenly protection, thus solicited, of the hearts of Jesus and Mary, to which by this very gesture, he consecrated the hours that govern family life in his home. And the reach of such a thought is already great since it fills the whole intimate setting of human life.

In the medallion on the right, the eastern side, the heart of Jesus is marked by its abbreviative sign, IHS, composed of the consonants of the name of IHESVS, with the cross rising above.

In the western medallion, on the left, the heart of Mary bears her name, reduced to its first two letters MA(*ria*). Above it is

---

1 Cf. Mgr Barbier de Montault, op. cit., tome I, p. 103.
2 Not to be confused with the Goudon de la Lande, Counts of Héraudière, Poitevins, who have different arms.

a recumbent S-shaped sign, whose true meaning remains problematic for me.

This S-shaped sign, which had various very precise meanings in the symbolism of ancient times and the High Middle Ages, has since then received and long preserved the sense of being an emblem of the serpent, the very image of Satan and evil (on the monogram of the name of Jesus, said to be of King Henry III, the letter S of the initials IHS ends at both ends in two snake heads).

And that sense is the only one that seems acceptable to me here, because the serpent has always been, and remains, one of the iconographic attributes of the Virgin Mary in which the Church recognizes that woman predicted in the Book of Genesis (2:15), whose task it was to crush the head of the serpent.

So then, the pious part of the Marigny sundial would seem to be as if the consecration of a family to the united hearts of Jesus and Mary, under whose protection its shield's chief places it by the figure of its coat of arms, that is to say, with the emblem of lineage personified by it. And that in 1637.

What is interesting to note again, after the examples already given in this book, is this pervasiveness of the idea of the Sacred Heart and the spontaneous use of its image at this time in the habits of intimate family life where no ecclesiastic authority could have imposed it.

II. THE SUNDIAL OF THE CHARTERHOUSE OF LUGNY

From Mrs. A. Chégut, of Paray le Monial, I have the drawing of another sundial set up in the northern part of the diocese of Dijon, where, within the contemplative setting of great curtains of evergreen trees, between Recey-sur-Ource and Leuglay, the ancient Charterhouse of Lugny is still hidden beneath the tall mansard roofs with which the monks of Saint Bruno covered it in the time of Louis XIV. In the nineteenth century, it belonged to Dr. Lacordaire, father of the illustrious restorer of the Dominican Order in France, who was born in the village of Recey. Mr. Hubert Landel and Mrs. Landel, Mrs. Chégut's sister, lived in the beautiful building of the monastery's former inn upon which the sundial was erected in 1614 and about which I will now speak.

I reproduce it here according to an excellent copy made by Mr. Landel, despite the place it occupies (Fig. 2).

Located on the southern facade of the house, above a large arched portal, it covers a square area, a half-meter per side, in the middle of which the outline of a kind of large shield encloses the outline of a heart on which the chronometric rays lead to figures indicating the hours; they tell the hours from four in the morning to eight in the evening.

Fig. 2. — *Sundial from the Charterhouse of Lugny (Côte-d'Or).*

In the middle of the heart is a small cartouche that frames the date of the dial, 1614, surmounted by the abbreviated monogram of the name of Jesus: I H S. Below, and from each side of the ensemble, two laurel branches spread apart.

Whose is the heart thus placed as a setting for the hours: that of our Lord Jesus Christ, or that of the faithful?

At first glance, this heart's position under the monogram could lead us to see there only a simple human heart placed in homage under the divine name, since this was still — with or without the iconic nails — the generally observed rule. But, contrary to this opinion, we must take into account three features worth noting: the first is that here the heart is united with the sacred name by the line that surrounds them; the second, that it is not the heart that is accessory to the monogram here, but, quite the contrary, this acronym seems related to the heart. Finally, this image was drawn by Carthusians, and we know, through the writings and the works of art that they have left us, how lively was the piety towards the heart of Jesus Christ in the monks of Saint Bruno, at least since the beginning of the fifteenth century.

III. THE SUNDIAL OF SAINT-GENIS-LAVAL

Another sundial, said to be of the same date as or shortly after that of Lugny, is certainly related to it by the design of its layout, and even by the arrangement of its decoration. It was sold in Lyon only a short time ago, and I was able to garner only a single, rather imprecise indication of its origin: the vicinity of Saint-Genis-Laval, a few leagues south of Lyon.

It is engraved on slate, and was used, not vertically as that of Lugny, but horizontally, on a stone pedestal. Its outline shows us a large heart divided up into hourly zones, numbers of which, ranging from six in the morning to six in the evening, are elegantly indicated on a band parallel to its lower contour.

No doubt is possible here: the heart thus represented in the same manner as the one at Lugny, bears the Name of Jesus *on itself*, and the cross surmounts it within the halo of a crown of thorns framed by two supple olive sprigs (Fig. 3); it is then the image of the heart of Jesus Christ.

Thus, the two sundials complement each other: that of Lugny makes it possible to date that of Saint-Genis-Laval, and the latter indicates the religious character of the first and clarifies it. With these two images of the Sacred Heart that entirely fill the hours of each day we are therefore, even more than with the Marigny-Brizay dial, in the presence of this affirmation that all the moments of our days are from God and that, consequently, we owe them back to Him.

*Fig. 3. — Sundial from Saint-Genis-Laval
(Rhône), 17th century.*

In their life so seriously oriented towards Christian horizons, our fathers of that time, more than many of us, were attentive to the lofty lesson of hours passing and years lapsing, one after the other, into the bottomless abyss of the past, an irresistible and fast current that the stable Majesty of God Eternal governs from on high.

IV. A FORMER EMBLEM FOR THE MONTH OF JANUARY

To this same idea of time passing, I will add here the reproduction of a drawing received from the learned Poitevin collector, Count Raoul de Rochebrune, whose recent death is mourned by French archaeology; it is a cartouche painted on a detached page of a church manuscript book, which would have terminated the leaf for the month of January on this book's introductory calendar. The copy of this cartouche was made by Rochebrune at Luchon.

At the top of the inner medallion, the abbreviative monogram IHS is surmounted by the spear-thrust wounded heart, and the rest of the orbicular space is occupied by the bust of Janus Bifrons, the dual-faced god of Roman mythology.

Surely, the whole composition is intended to allegorically represent the month of January; now, on the first day of this month, the Feast of the Circumcision, the Church has us read, at Mass, a passage from the Gospels where it says, "And after eight days were accomplished, that the child should be circumcised, his *name was called Jesus...*" (Luke 2:21). The Catholic liturgy therefore begins, so to speak, January and the year with the proclamation

Fig. 4.—Allegorical representation of the month of January. Illumination, 16th century, Luchon (Haute-Garonne).

of the Savior's earthly name, hence the perfectly justified presence of the monogram at the top of the cartouche (Fig. 4).

The presence of the divine heart is certainly harder to explain; this can be understood, however, through the quite frequent practice they had in the sixteenth century of adding it, by tradition moreover, to the sacred monogram with the idea of a habitual gaze towards it; perhaps also by the very likely intention, with the artist, of associating it with the entire cycle of the year of which January is only the threshold.

This month takes its name from the Roman god Janus, it is the "Januarius mensis," and congratulations follow from what there is thus to be found of good fortune under the sponsorship of one of the quite rare fictitious personalities of mythology who are somewhat decent.

It seems to me that Janus could be regarded as one of the pagan "figures" of Christ, as was Orpheus for example:

In the religious fiction of ancient Rome we are told that, having helped Saturn, Janus received in return full knowledge of the mysteries of the past and future; that is why the ancients represented him with two faces, that of an elderly man turned towards time passed, the other, younger man, gaze riveted on the future. As god of time, he presided over the closing and opening of successive years, and the first month of each of them was devoted to him.

On the monuments of that time he is shown, as on the Luchon cartouche, with a crown on his head and a *scepter* in his right hand, because he is a king; in the other hand he holds a *key* because he opens and closes time periods; that is why, by an expansion of the idea, the Romans dedicated the doors of houses and the gates of cities to him.

No longer according to the illusory realm of fiction, but according to most certain realities, Christ, too, governs past and future. Co-eternal with his Father, he is like Him "the Ancient of days"; "in the beginning was the Word," says St. John. He is also the father and the master of the age to come, "Jesu pater futuri seculi," the Roman Church repeats every day, and he has proclaimed himself the beginning and end of everything: "I am the Alpha and Omega, the beginning and the end." He is the Lord of Eternity.

Like the Janus of old, he bears the royal *scepter* to which he is entitled by his Father in heaven and his ancestors here below; and his other hand holds the *key* to eternal secrets, the key dyed with his blood, which opened to lost humanity the door of life. This is why, in the fourth of the great antiphons before Christmas, the sacred liturgy thus acclaims him: "O Clavis David, et sceptrum domus Israel! You are, O Christ the Expected One, the Key of David and the Scepter of the House of Israel. You open, and no one can shut; and you shut and no one can open."[3]

The illuminator of the Luchon page was thus quite inspired by showing Janus in profile under the liturgical calendar for January, as also, with or without intention, but effectively, by placing the

---

3 *Roman Breviary*, Office of the 20th of December.

images of the heart and of the name of Jesus above the pagan god of years gone by and years to come. He utilized the same truth as those who composed, some fifty years later, the sundials of Lugny and Saint-Genis-Laval: one after the other they have proclaimed that the passage of time is a thing of Christ and that, for his faithful, it is especially with his heart that he holds sway over it and governs it.

Merovingian heart. Fibula from Jouy-le-Comte, Saint-Germain-en-Laye Museum. Ink drawing by the author. Charbonneau-Lassay Archives (ed.).

CHAPTER TWENTY-THREE

Reliquary Hearts

THROUGHOUT THE MIDDLE AGES, RELIquary art was the triumph of French goldsmithing; from the first, most solemn of acts of the monarchy, in the text of the Salic Law, the Franks already evinced great merit, before Christ to whom they had given themselves, in that they covered with precious silver, gold, and gems the bones of the martyrs whom the Romans had put to death.

These reliquaries of the saints have taken every form over the course of the centuries: shrines fashioned like churches, chests, tombs, busts, and heads of saints, blessing arms, monstrances or openwork pyxides, medallions of all sizes, etc. The relics of the Savior's Passion were also kept in custodials of quite varied forms. Only the True Cross quite often received, for its innumerable fragments, two types of reliquaries that were specific to it. First, and this is quite natural, its tiny parcels were enclosed in precious metal crosses from the sixth century onwards, as is proven by the splendid golden cross with two branches sent for the royal nun of Poitiers, Saint Radegonde, by the Emperor Justinian II. Then, starting with the last centuries of the Middle Ages, the True Cross of the Savior was sometimes enclosed in the very image of his heart.

Among reliquaries, only the latter ones interest us here, and, however rare, they are only the more interesting to study.

I. SACRED HEART RELIQUARY FROM THE CASTLE OF OYSONVILLE (EURE-ET-LOIR), SEVENTEENTH CENTURY

I owe to the obliging friendship of the owner of this most interesting object, Count François de Rilly, a fine watercolor that, reduced to a tracing, enables us to study it here.

The exterior consists of a thick etched crystal plate. It is placed on the front of one of those small furnishings usually

Part VI: The Iconography of the Wounded Heart of Jesus

Fig. 1. Crystal reliquary and embroidery from the castle of Oysonville (Eure-et-Loir).

called "corner-pieces" because, built on a triangular plan, they are intended to furnish the angles of an apartment.

This one, from the castle of Oysonville, is in rosewood marquetry and probably of Lombard origin (Fig. 1). Several scholars attribute it to the middle of the seventeenth century.

It is hard for me to see its original place anywhere else than in the private oratory of a prelate, an abbess, or some high-ranking lady.

The plate of glass covers a Sacred Heart painted in flesh-tones, on white silk and from which is emitted a glory made of nineteen bundles of rays composed of braided gold wire. From the top of the heart issue purple flames, in the midst of which stands a silk cross containing a fragment of the True Cross. Above this is the inscription:

Sanctae Crucis Christi

Around the heart of Jesus are these other words:

Peccatorum doloribus oppressum Cor Jesu
Amore nostri in cruce mortuum Cor Jesu

The garlands of flowers, as well as the instruments of the Passion, carried in baskets by naive cherubs, are painted on the silk; the horns of plenty and the acorns at the top are in threads of braided gold, as well as the monogram of the name of Jhesus, IHS, at the foot of which a small, inflamed and faithful heart stands in homage.

All the rest of the decor is very finely engraved on crystal glass encompassed by a dark thread.

The total height of the whole reaches o m. 42 and the width at the base is o m. 34.

Surely, the height of Italian fashion that presided over the decoration of this reliquary can be disputed; its love of the complicated, the "finicky," to speak like Huysmans, its mannerism, are definitely inartistic. Only the radiant, quite stylized heart of Jesus is remarkably treated; we feel that the whole idea is concentrated in it; also the hand of the artist, at the service of a rather childish concept in the ornamental frame, suddenly evinces a more forthright design once it begins to trace the contours of the divine object.

The fact remains that the whole is very rich and that the reliquary of the Count de Rilly is a valuable document for the time to which it belongs. We will see, going back a little in time, that in France and England the same quite logical thought of uniting the True Cross to the Savior's heart had occurred much earlier in remarkable works of art.

II. PECTORAL CROSS OF AN ABBESS OF FONTEVRAULT, DIOCESE OF POITIERS, 16TH CENTURY

This silver cross, of local provenance, belonged, at the end of the nineteenth century, to the parish priest of Lencloître (Vienne), who then gave it to the Poitevin collector, the canon Ripault, at whose home I made the drawing (Fig. 2).

Lencloître-en-Gironde, a large village placed between Loudun and Châtellerault, was, from the twelfth century until the Revolution, one of the most important priories of the famous Royal Benedictine Abbey of Fontevrault, situated seven leagues distant. It is extremely likely that the pectoral cross pictured here was that of one of the abbesses of this great abbey.

Its mid-sixteenth-century date coincides with the beginning of this illustrious series of seven great abbesses, all from the House of France, who successively and most worthily held the crosier of Fontevrault; and the fleur-de-lys at the foot of the cross inclines us, by itself and in all likelihood, to attribute it to one of them.[1] At the center, a medallion depicting the heart of Jesus contained the relic; round about, the crown of thorns intertwines its branches and once more identifies the heart depicted. On the arms of the cross we read the words of the *Vexilla Regis* by Saint Fortunatus of Poitiers: *O crux ave, spes unica.*

If we did not know that the abbesses — as most superiors of congregations who are not priests still do today — blessed their subjects with a relic of the True Cross, the inscription of the cross of Lencloître would suffice to inform us about the nature of the relic once contained in it.

At its base, a small tenon that descends from a Renaissance-style cartouche would have allowed the cross to be erected on a tabor or pedestal pierced with a hole, to expose it to veneration.

So here is a second example of a heart of Jesus reliquary of the True Cross.

[1] Either to Renée de Bourbon (1491–1534) or Louise de Bourbon (1534–1575).

III. PECTORAL CROSS OF THE LAST ABBOT OF COLCHESTER, 15TH–16TH CENTURY

The Most Reverend Benedictine Abbot of Buckfast, England, received from Lord Clifford's son an old pectoral cross on which the chiseled ornamentation is, of itself, most interesting.[2] Furthermore, it is a real relic since it was once worn by Thomas Beche, last abbot of Saint John the Baptist of Colchester, put to death, in December 1539, for refusing the schismatic oath of supremacy demanded by King Henry VIII.

Fig. 2. — Lencloître pectoral cross (Vienne), 16th century.

Fig. 3. — Pectoral Cross of the last abbot of Colchester, 16th century.

On the main face, which I reproduce here (Fig. 3), the center of the cross is occupied, as on that of Lencloître, by a heart surrounded by the crown of thorns; at both ends of the transverse

---

2 This interesting jewel was first reported to me by the Rev. Lagrillère, of Bourges, and, due to the obliging kindness of Dom J. Stephan, director of the magazine *Chimes*, I am able to reproduce it here.

branch, two medallions contain the image of the pierced hands; the monogram IHS occupies the place of the divine body and the two wounded feet are, like the hands, in their normal place on the cross.

On the other side of the jewel are all the other emblems of the Passion: the pillar and ropes, nails, pincer and hammer, rooster and dice.

Thus, on the abbey cross of Colchester, as in quite numerous sculptures or English paintings from 1480 to 1530, the heart of Jesus appears as the center, not only of the five wounds, but of all the sufferings of the Redeemer in his dolorous Passion.

IV. 15TH CENTURY RELIQUARY HEART FROM THE FORMER FILLON COLLECTION (VENDÉE)

Fig. 4. — Reliquary heart from the former Fillon collection, 15th century.

I present here the image of a quite lovely jewel from the fifteenth century, but which, to be frank from the outset, does not bear precise enough markings.

It was shown in 1878 at the Paris World's Fair, and, in an article in the *Gazette des Beaux Arts* (October 1878, p. 561), Alfred Darcel gave a description of it in these terms:

"A jewel exhibited by Gabrielle Fillon, a small heart surrounded by the philosophical inscription in fifteenth century lettering: *Ubi amor ibi frequens cogita*[*tio*], and bearing the monogram LR at its point."

To read these lines, one might think it simply a secular jewel, and immediately deem it similar to those quite numerous hearts worn today with the image or hair of someone departed and more or less deeply missed. Yet there is nothing to assure us that we are in the presence of a belted medallion of a widow's cordelière rather than the pious reliquary of a member of a third order Franciscan set with the knotted cord of the sons and daughters of

Saint Francis, and we know that a very great number of high lords and noble ladies of that time were members of this third order.

I even think that the *cordelière*, as a heraldic insignia for widowhood, was adopted somewhat later than the Fillon reliquary (Fig. 4); and as to "the philosophical inscription," which assures us that "wherever your love is, there are your frequent thoughts," this could have had, in the spirit of the times, a religious just as well as a profane meaning; at that time both spiritual love and human love quite frequently made use of the same emblems and the same vocabulary.

In the next chapter, I will show the image of the central motif on the banner of the Brotherhood of the Black Christ of Cartagena, in Spain. There we see a large image of the heart of Jesus, surmounted by the crown of thorns and within which are contained the hearts of the thirty-three members of the brotherhood. Around the divine heart, and bordering it just as on the Fillon jewel, we read an inscription; it declares: *Ubi enim thesaurus vester est, ibi et cor vestrum erit.* Where your treasure is, there too will be your heart.

And these words are so similar to those on the Fillon reliquary that they enable us to think, and almost believe, that the two hearts that they surround are both of the same and of a divine nature.

To suppose the worst, I will add that even though the heart-shaped medallion that interests us might have an undeniably secular meaning, it was worth publishing here by way of artistic comparison with the preceding undisputed reliquaries.

V. HEART-RELIQUARY FROM THE INVENTORY OF CHARLES V, 14TH CENTURY

What now are these hearts, these exceedingly precious jewels, mentioned at the end of the fourteenth century in the 1379 inventory of the treasure of Charles V, King of France?

> 2.500 — *Item, ung cueur d'or esmaillé de rouge cler: ou dedens est crucifiement de Nostre Dame.* [Item, a golden heart with light red enameling: within which is the crucifying of Our Lady.]
> . . . .

> 2.930 — *Item ung autre reliquiaire ou il y a ung roi et une royne qui soustiennent un ballay en façon d'ung cueur ou il y a une croisette en laquelle il y a du fust de la Vraye Croix, et au dessoulx une grosse perle et deux esmeraudes pesant deux onces.* [Item, another reliquary where there is a king and a queen who support a ballay (a light red or purplish pink ruby) in the fashion of a heart where there is a crosslet in which there is some wood of the True Cross, and below a large pearl and two emeralds weighing two ounces.]

It is possible that the first of these hearts was a representation of the heart of Mary, and that, bearing her image placed on the cross, it was already ideationally related to what fifteenth-century art will popularize soon after under the name of "Passion of Our Lady." But what of the second?

This one is expressly a reliquary of the True Cross. It was made with a very expensive stone, a ruby laden with a crosslet in which rests the sacred relic, and towards which "a large pearl and two emeralds weighing two ounces (!)" form a procession.

And the king and the queen of France, performing in this way an act of subjection, raise aloft in triumph this very costly heart within which, as in those of Oysonville and the abbatial crosses mentioned above, the cross of the Savior is enclosed.

Might this not also be an image of the heart of Jesus?

I do not see to which other heart the king and the queen of the "most beautiful kingdom after that of heaven" could thus, without stepping down, serve as "tenants" in the chapel of their own palace; because, in such a case, it would not represent their own heart or any emblematic heart whatsoever: which heart would have been worthy, in their own eyes, to serve as a setting for the adorable cross?

We no longer possess, we will never possess, the image of the wonderful jewel of King Charles V, and its loss is exceedingly regrettable, but the description of the Inventory of 1379 is such, or so it seems to me, that in contemplating it through the old words of the text, those who know what the first representations of the heart of Jesus were, will sense words similar to the apostle Peter's coming quite naturally to their lips: "You are truly the Christ, Son of the living God!"

And now, what is there to be said about this idea of thus choosing as a form for a reliquary of the True Cross of Jesus Christ that of his heart? What to say, if not admire how our old goldsmiths have happily symbolized by this the effectual love of Christ the Savior, which, starting from his heart, "for us men, and for our salvation," has led him to death on the cross! And also how they knew, so to speak, how to give substance to this truth: the True Cross has become for us worthy of worship only by absorbing into itself the precious blood come from the heart of Jesus, the blood poured forth on it by all the wounds of the Crucified One.

Like the *Vexilla Regis*, it is a kind of epithalamium of this union, both material and mystical, of sacred blood and redeeming cross that gives the latter access to a god-like station before which heads bow down in worship.

VI. RELIQUARY CROSS FROM CHISSEY (JURA)

Fig. 5. — Copper reliquary cross.

On the subject of our study in the first part of this book on the *Signaculum Domini* and the archaeological artifacts relating to the emblematic of the five wounds of Jesus, we received from our distinguished colleague at *Rayonnement Intellectuel*, Mr. Pidoux de la Maduère, the sketch (Fig. 5) and note we reproduce here. We respectfully thank him for this interesting communication:

"Copper reliquary cross, now empty but probably having served as a reliquary for a thorn of the Holy Crown described by Pouillés and missing; this cross belongs to the church Saint-Christophe de Chissey, diocese of Saint-Claude. The settings for the cabochons are finely carved, the central stone and one cabochon are missing. The two stones on the shaft are of an almond shape, one purplish, the other limpid, almost white (could this be blood and water?). That of the right arm is purple. The four branches are equal (0 m. 058 in all). Thickness 0 m. 005. This cross opens by a hinge at the bottom. The closing key at the top is missing. This cross was entrusted to me for study and expertise by the Rev. Thevenin, parish priest of Chissey. It seems to date back to the thirteenth century, when Jean de Chalon the Elder, uncle of Joinville, and his relatives had obtained several thorns of the Holy Crown. There is one at Château-Chalon, one at Raynans, and six that Jean de Chalon had in his treasure and which I was able to rediscover and follow in all their vicissitudes. They are now with the uncloistered Ursulines at Dole." — Pidoux de la Maduère.

German wood-engraving from the fifteenth century communicated by Rev. Richstaetter. Photo Regnabit. Charbonneau-Lassay Archives (ed.).

CHAPTER TWENTY-FOUR

The Iconography of the Heart of Christ Abroad

JUST YESTERDAY NEARLY ALL CATHOLICS still regarded piety towards the heart of Jesus as an innovation of the seventeenth century, whereas, as early as the eleventh, Saint Bernard already hymned it, theologians and mystics of the following centuries glorified it, and, from the threshold of the fourteenth century, and perhaps earlier, artists of all kinds multiplied images of it. In much the same way, devotion to the eucharistic heart of Jesus is still generally viewed today as a fairly new aspect of contemporary piety.

This is a second error similar to the first; and the truth is that, even though the expression "eucharistic heart" is indeed rather recent,[1] the idea that it represents and the worship it designates are already, in sacred iconography, at least six centuries old.

The realm of the question of Christ's eucharistic heart extends to everything that, in the liturgy, theological or historical studies, in sacred literature, in all the representative arts, relates the idea of the wounded heart or side of Jesus closer to that of the matter of the sacrament of the Eucharist, under its double aspect of bread and wine, flesh and blood.

Like almost all particular forms of Christian piety, the worship of the heart of Jesus Christ, as the source of the redemptive blood that the Eucharist offers us under the guise of transubstantiated wine, has had a period of preparation, of formation that one might call "the prehistory of the eucharistic heart of Jesus": to this period belong the words of fervent adoration written by the

---

1 It is found however, as early as 1705, in this title of a book by Ginther: *Speculum amoris et doloris in sacratissimo ac divinissimo Corde Jesu incarnati, eucharistici et crucifixi orbi Christiano propositum,* "Mirror of love and suffering presented to the Christian universe in the most sacred and most divine Heart, eucharistic and crucified, of Jesus Incarnate."

Fathers and Doctors of the first millennium in honor of the open wound in the divine side; to it also belongs the story of the Holy Grail, written between 1168 and 1191 by Chrétien de Troyes, then his continuator Robert de Boron, and in which, knowingly or not, they adapted ancient traditions and old Celtic myths from before our era to the Gospel information about the Passion, showing us Joseph of Arimathea collecting in the cup of the Lord's Supper the blood and water from the source opened by the spear-thrust to the Redeemer's side. Add to this as well the painted or carved works of Giotto, of the others primitives of Italy, and of our own amazing Gothic masters, during the thirteenth and fourteenth centuries, where weeping angels collect in marvelous chalices the blood of the Crucified, where we see it spurt in a curve from his side and fall into a cup placed on the ground before him. All this is not yet a juxtaposition within the same artistic composition of visible heart and Eucharist, but the idea is there; because the thought of the simple Christian of that time, and so much the more the thought of intellectuals and mystics, went of itself, by the crimson pathway made by the spear, from the fallen spurt of blood back to the inner source that formed it, and from which it departed to come to us.

And all the more naturally since, from the end of the thirteenth or the dawn of the following century, artists, moreover, deliberately represented the image of the fleshly heart of Jesus, the physical crucible wherein the human blood that was his bodily life was wrought for thirty years and, ultimately, the matter for the supreme and divine gift he gave to us at the Last Supper and the ransom he paid for us on the tragic wood.

It was the providential lot of fifteenth-century artists, especially in France, England, and Germany, to connect the visible image of the open heart to emblems of the sacrament of his love.

With regard to Germany, the former journal *Regnabit* exhibited several fifteenth- and sixteenth-century engravings that show this connection in a striking manner; one especially, despite being bereft of all artistic qualities and its oddness that lays it open to criticism. Two angels raise a chalice to the crucified heart of Jesus, and, to one side, this same heart is repeated and crowned with a host while, from the wound it bears, another host emerges (Fig. 1).

Fig. 1. — German wood engraving of the 15th century, communicated by the Rev. Richstaetter, S.J.

This is one of those outrageous and complicated fantasies in which mystics from Germany and the artists who served them — Dürer not excepted — once delighted without sufficient moderation (see also Plate 30).

In France, England, and Flanders it was generally enough to simply juxtapose, either with the group of five wounds or, by itself, the wounded heart and one of the emblems dedicated to the Eucharist.

I will start by bringing together here only a few of these compositions preserved from before Protestantism by our neighbors across the Channel.

Part VI: The Iconography of the Wounded Heart of Jesus

I. DOCUMENTS FROM ENGLAND IN THE 15TH AND 16TH CENTURIES

Crest from St. Meriadoc's Church, Camborne (Cornwall)

This heraldic composition was already reproduced in the chapter on the Springs of the Savior.[2]

As in many similar English sculptures, and its fifteenth-century contemporaries, the wounds to the divine members are here called wells of *pity, comfort, grace,* and *mercy,* that is to say fountains or sources of pity, comfort, grace, and mercy, and the heart: *everlasting life,* fountain of life eternal.

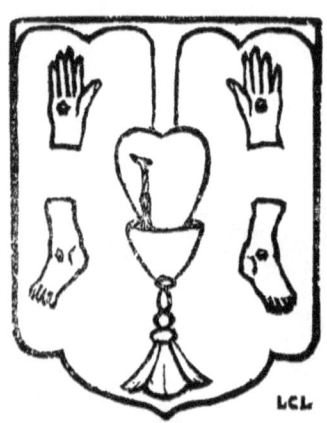

Fig. 2. — St. Meriadoc's, Camborne.

And this source feeds the eucharistic chalice, the vessel of life about which we must speak as St. Thomas Aquinas does of the Host in *Lauda Sion*: "*Panis vivus et vitalis,*" he says. The blood of Christ which falls from his heart is also "the living wine that gives life," *everlasting life,* life for eternity! (Fig. 2)

I owe this document, as well as nearly all those that follow, to the great kindness of the learned curator of the Archaeological Museum of Winchester, Mrs. Edith E. Wilde.

Bishop Fox's Chantry Crest (Winchester)

A eucharistic meaning can also be found on this crest of the chantry, or funerary chapel, of Bishop Fox of Winchester, in the cathedral of this city.

It is a parted per pale shield, charged dexter with the spear and sponge tied together in saltire (Fig. 3), sinister with a chalice surmounted by a host. It is obvious that the sponge is only represented here, as in many religious motifs of the same inspiration, to form a symmetrical counterpart to the spear; and the relationship of the latter with the host and chalice is an evocation

[2] Cf. Part 3, Chap. 8, p. 117, Fig. 5.

of the blood that has flowed through the wound that it opened, and which became, or rather which was already, since the Last Supper, part of the eucharistic reality.

On the chantry frieze of Bishop Fox this crest forms part of a succession of personal or mystical heraldic shields that angels separate and support; as a whole this makes for a most beautiful decorative effect.

Fig. 3. — Winchester. Chantry of Bishop Fox.

The Insignia and Signs of the "Pilgrimage of Grace" and the Western Rebellion

At the beginning of the reign of Edward VI, who bore the English crown from 1549 to 1553, the discontent caused in several provinces by the establishment of Protestantism, a consequence of the unfortunate break of King Henry VIII from the Roman Church, increased. Groups of Catholics armed themselves to defend their faith, and various rebellions were organized, quite analogous in principle to the heroic revolt of our Vendée against the French Revolution.

These troubles began in 1536. They had as main centers of rebellion the counties of Devon, Oxford, and York, but lacked cohesion and, despite Constable's heroism, despite J. Rose Tromp, Arundel, and other valiant leaders, the hoped-for results were not achieved. They gave rise above all to two important movements: the "Pilgrimage of Grace" and the "Western Rebellion."

At first the insurgents victoriously defied the Protestants troops commanded by the Marquis of Northampton, but were then vanquished, at the end of the reign of Edward VI, by the Earl of Warwick.

As our Vendeans did, two hundred and fifty years later, the Catholic insurgents of England adopted a religious emblem as a rallying sign: the Sacred Heart occupied the central part, surrounded by a retinue, very much in favor with English Catholic piety at the time, of images or emblems of the four other major wounds of Jesus.

Part VI: The Iconography of the Wounded Heart of Jesus

The Badge worn by Sir R. Constable at "Pilgrimage of Grace"

The Duchess of Norfolk retains as a heroic and very precious family relic the badge worn, from 1537 and during the Pilgrimage of Grace, by her ancestor Sir R. Constable.

It is a rectangle of fabric on which was embroidered a shield bearing a chalice surmounted by a host charged with the image of the wounded heart of Jesus Christ from which blood flows. At the four corners of the escutcheon, the Savior's feet and hands are fixed by the nails of the crucifixion and, above the eucharistic emblem, we find the abbreviation for the name of Jesus surmounted by the crown of thorns. Asterisks dot the surface of the badge at the bottom of which two letters, I and G, are embroidered, initials for the "Pilgrimage of Grace," *Itinerarium Gratiæ* in Latin (Fig. 4).

Fig. 4. — *The insurrectional badge of Sir R. Constable.*

Some thought that the disc that carries the heart of the Lord above the chalice here represents the paten rather than the host, probably because this disc is embroidered by concentric threads that give the illusion of a circle formed by the fold at the edge of a paten; but other representations on the badges of sixteenth-century English Catholic insurgents clearly bear the host, which is often radiant; it is therefore permissible to recognize it on Sir Constable's badge as well. Besides, with the paten the eucharistic character of the heart bleeding into the chalice would be as real, but it still seems strengthened by the association of the image of the heart with that of the eucharistic bread at the same time as with that of the cup.

The Kingerley Badge

In 1889 the *Catholic Times* described, in this way, in connection with the Tudor Exhibition, a liturgical purse in use at the castle chapel of Kingerley, Lincolnshire:

> Among the exhibits, one of the most interesting for the Catholic visitor is an image from the "Pilgrimage of Grace," that armed uprising of northerners for the defense of the Faith of their fathers. It is a piece of red velvet embroidered with gold and representing the five wounds, the ancient emblem of Catholic England. The insurgents carried it on their banners (Fig 5).

Fig. 5. — Printed vignette bearing the badge of the Itinerarium Gratiæ.

In the middle is seen the Sacred Heart wounded and shedding blood; this heart is shown in the center of a host placed above the chalice. At the four corners, we see the feet and hands of Our Lord pierced with nails and shedding blood and giving off golden rays, while below are the letters "I H S," and at the bottom the initials I and G, that is to say "*Itinerarium Gratiæ*," "Pilgrimage of Grace."

Someone has made a purse from this image for the Kingerley castle chapel.

Part VI: The Iconography of the Wounded Heart of Jesus

The *Catholic Times* is right: the Kingerley badge was not one of those the insurgents wore on their arm or hat, it could only have adorned a standard, since it is large enough to cover a liturgical purse, that is to say a square and rigid sheath in which one encloses the corporal and with which the priest covers the chalice to transport it, before and after Mass.

The Stamped Copper of Mr. Smith, from London

Reproduced here is the image of a small stamped copper that should find a place in this study (Fig. 6).

It belonged in 1885 to Mr. Th. S. Smith, of London. By the chalice surmounted by a host marked with the Sacred Heart, by the nails evocative of the divine wounds, it is akin to the ordinary badges of Catholic insurgents in England; it seems, though, to be one from the Western Rebellion rather than those of the Pilgrimage of Grace, since it does not bear the initial letters I and G.

Fig. 6. — Stamped copper, London.

Be that as it may, the heart that is there, on the host, is clearly eucharistic in character since it is in contact with both perceptible elements that constitute the material of the sacrament.

Graffiti from the Tower of London

A great many of the Pilgrimage of Grace and Western Rebellion insurgents, as well as other Catholics of the time, taken on the battlefield or elsewhere, were imprisoned in the Tower of London, as under Henry VIII were Bishop John Fisher and Chancellor Thomas More.

With the prolonged inactivity of their detention, these prisoners covered the walls with inscriptions and various drawings, a number of which repeated, especially, I was assured, the venerable image of the heart of Jesus Christ accompanied by eucharistic emblems in the Salt and Beauchamp towers.

Despite repeated attempts I have not been able to obtain a copy of these impressive testimonies of courageous Catholics who defended their faith to the death.

Carved panel in St. Petrock, Padston (Cornwall)

Under the reign of Mary I, Tudor, who reigned after Edward VI, from 1553 to 1558, English Catholics found peace.

Teams of foreign sculptors, many of whom had come from France, traveled at that time about the country decorating the last Catholic churches that were completed, or were in need of embellishment. To the chisels of these skillful artists are due some very beautiful works, many of which are of interest to the iconography of the heart of Jesus Christ, including a panel attributed to them on the pulpit of Saint Petrock's in Padston, Cornwall (Fig. 7).

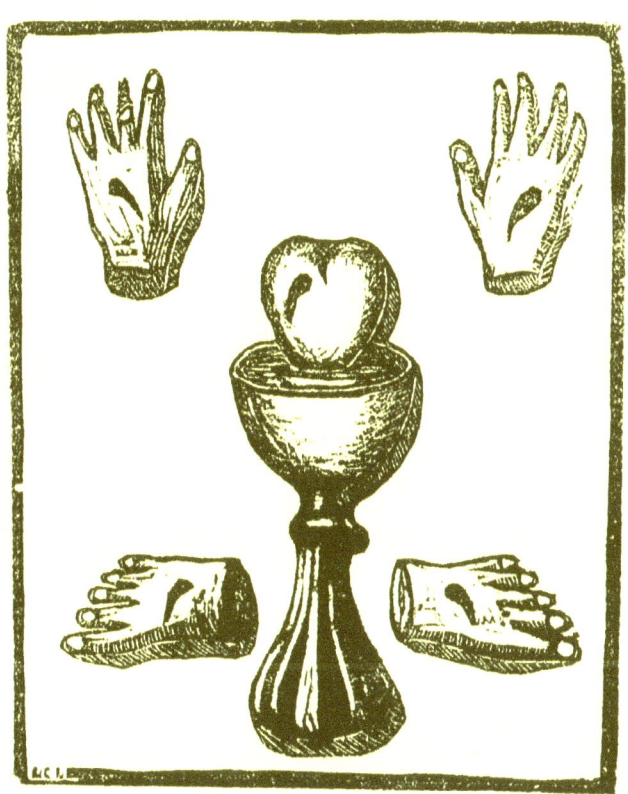

Fig. 7. — Pulpit panel at St. Petrock's, Padston (Cornwall).

We see there the wounded heart placed between the other four wounds of Jesus, and this heart plunges its apex into the depths of a chalice. The wound is gaping and no longer bleeding: all that the source of life contained of blood and water has been collected in the nourishing cup where, now, the very life-blood of the Heart of God is waiting for souls to come and drink. Was this not at once a happier and simpler way to convey, through sculpture, that the eucharistic cup is indeed the Vessel of Life? And what the liturgical text says of the heart of Jesus itself can likewise be said of the cup: the "Fountain of Life and Holiness."

II. SPANISH ARTIFACTS OF THE SEVENTEENTH CENTURY

We dedicate this section to some old representations of the heart of Jesus, sent from Spain by devoted friends.

All are of the seventeenth century or verging on it quite closely, but this does not mean that the heart of Jesus the Savior was not depicted in Spanish art prior to this time.

We have already presented the image of a host-iron or mold from the fourteenth century, possessed today by the important Episcopal Museum of Vic.[3] It bears the Sacred Heart placed on the cross of Calvary. And this beautiful object, of incontestable date, remains one of the most valuable artifacts we have, from that distant time, with regard to Spanish piety.

On the other hand, the Canon Don Juan Llado, of Vic, has kindly pointed out to us, with R. P. Capuano, O.M.I., that the catalog of the former Francesco Miguel y Badia collection contains, under number 98, the representation of a fabric, from the fifteenth or early sixteenth century, in silk and thread, black and white, adorned "with an image of the heart of Jesus with flames and the wound of the spear, above are the letters I H S." Having no representation of it, I wanted to note its existence on the threshold of these lines.

---

3 Cf. Part 6, Chap. 17, ii, pp. 247-48.

Brotherhood Banner of the Black Christ of Cartagena

To the kindness of Fr. Capuano I also owe an image of the heart depicted on the banner of the Black Christ of Cartagena.

The "Brotherhood of the Black Christ," also called "the Most Holy Christ of Succour," is comprised of only thirty-three members, probably in honor of thirty-three years that Jesus spent on earth.

Its official emblem is a heart crowned with a braid of thorns in which are included thirty-three small hearts representing those of the members of this "fraternity" (Fig. 8).

Fig. 8. — Heart-emblem of the Brotherhood of the Black Christ of Cartagena.

In the nineteenth chapter of the *Constitutions* of the Christ of Succour, approved in 1697, we read:

> "The goods that the Brotherhood must possess:
> "... A banner of violet color, with a large heart in the middle, surmounted by a crown of thorns. In this heart, thirty-three small hearts, and this inscription around: *Ubi enim thesaurus vester est, ibi et cor vestrum erit.*"

It is this motto, taken from the Gospel of St. Matthew (6:22): "Where your treasure is, there too will be your heart," which I have previously related[4] to a small French reliquary of the fifteenth century around which is written, "Wherever your love is, there your frequent thoughts." This is the same idea endowed with slightly different terms.

On the banner of the Black Christ, the heart is surmounted in the manner of a heraldic diadem by the crown of thorns that personalizes it as being that of the Savior. The necklace of the Order of Knights of the Golden Fleece, the Grand Masters of which are the Kings of Spain, surrounds the heart and ends up giving to the whole its character and clearly heraldic meaning. This is surely a reminder of the special affection of a Spanish sovereign for the Brotherhood of the Black Christ.

Around the heart a banderole that follows its contours exactly bears the motto of the Brotherhood mentioned above. Notice the distorted and pointed form of the heart, which is a frequent feature in trans-pyrennean iconography, but rarer elsewhere.

The Sacred Heart of the San Clemente Church in Seville

Seville, that wonderful city legendary for its beauty, also has an old representation of the Sacred Heart, which the Very Reverend Gonzalez y Gea, S. J. has most kindly brought to our attention.

It is to be seen, in the San Clemente church, at the top of a large altarpiece the center of which is occupied by a painting of the Holy Face, and which is entirely decorated with an elaborate ornamentation of columns, niches, pediments, arabesques, tracery, moldings, and small angels. This heart appears in high relief at the center of a medallion forming a crown and emitting a glory of rays. The summit of the heart supports a high cross that dominates the whole ensemble, and is itself girt by a thick spiny crown (Fig. 9).

I do not know if this heart is absolutely contemporary with the altar that bears it, but its more anatomical appearance than that of the Cartagena heart would lead me to attribute it, especially if it were French, only to the first part of the eighteenth century.

---

4 Cf. Part 6, Chap. 23. iv, pp. 384–85.

Fig. 9. — Sacred Heart, at the top of the altarpiece in the church of San Clemente, Seville.

Spanish metal plaques from the Musée du Hiéron

Georges de Noaillat, head of the Musée du Hiéron, in Paray-le-Monial, had the kindness to send to Father Anizan, the devoted head of the former *Regnabit* magazine, drawings of two metal plaques. In the absence of any indication of origin, and solely on the evidence of the drawings sent, I think I can connect these plaques to seventeenth-century Spanish art.

These two plaques were obtained by a process common, since the the Middle Ages, to all the "pilgrimage leads" and "confraternity badges," that is, molten metal was cast into a stone mold where it solidified by taking the shape in relief of all the hollow parts of the mold.

The first of these objects offers us an image of the Holy Trinity represented in the middle of a set of clouds populated by small angels. The Father, characterized by the symbolic triangular nimbus, presides at the top of the composition; the Son is figured by the monogram of his name, I H S, *Ihesus* and by a heart — his heart — which is fixed there, which forms a part of it, and from which descends a glory that serves as a halo for a dove, the usual emblem for the Holy Spirit.

At the bottom of the plaque hangs another little heart connected by three rings to the whole (Fig. 10).

It seems to me that here the two hearts are perfectly identifiable: the first, that of Jesus, is the one with the divine name; it occupies the central point of the trinitarian motif, and glorious rays shine down from it. The second can only be the image of a heart of the faithful, the plaque's bearer, attached with sure faith to the great Christian dogma of the Trinity.

Fig. 10. — Metalic plaque from the Musée du Hiéron, in Paray-le-Monial (Saône-et-Loire).

Fig. 11. — Another plaque from the Hiéron in Paray-le-Monial.

The second of the Hiéron plaques is simply the abbreviated monogram of the holy name with a flaming heart beneath. This heart lacks sufficient precision; compared to the other plate one is inclined to see in it that of Jesus, but the fact that the height of its flames is attached to the monogram says nothing, since a channel would be required for the liquid metal to circulate in the mold: the bands connecting the arms of the cross to the uprights of the letter H have no other purpose (Fig. 11). But is the relief that girts the heart a crown of thorns or a blood vessel? One sure fact is that the place it occupies, at the bottom of the monogram, makes it rather the heart of one of the faithful, and this is the moment to recall a general rule valid in 90 per cent of cases:

a) When a heart, whether glowing or not, is placed above the I H S monogram or an art motif of a sacred nature: host, chalice, cross, or trophy of the instruments of the Passion, etc., or when *intimately united with it*, this is almost always a sure image of the heart of Jesus.

b) When a heart is placed below the same motifs, it is then said to be "placed in adoration or homage," and it is almost always an image of the Christian heart expressing its love, ardor, or fidelity.

The Sacred Heart on the Cross of Caravaca

Pictured here are the images of two Spanish crosses, badges for the grand and centuries-old pilgrimage to Caravaca — Spain's most frequented after Santiago de Compostela and Montserrat — which, in the seventeenth century, were sometimes decorated at their center with an image of the Sacred Heart (Figs. 12 & 13).

Because the general shape of these crosses, with two horizontal branches and expanded ends, has not varied since the fourteenth century, one of them was cited, some thirty years ago, as one of the most ancient European artifacts relating to the cult of the heart of Jesus. But there is nothing to this.

This cross, in the middle of which is seen the divine heart, also bears inscriptions which are in roman capital letters, whereas in the fourteenth century only lower case Gothic script was usual. But there is more: the said cross is also adorned, on its reverse side, with a reproduction of the St. Benedict Medal; now, we

Part VI: The Iconography of the Wounded Heart of Jesus

Fig. 12 and 13. — Examples of double crosses for the pilgrimage to Caravaca in Spain, 17th century.

know historically that this medal was struck and propagated only after the sensational witchcraft trial adjudicated in 1647 at Nattremberg, in Bavaria, and reproduces a sculpture from the Benedictine Abbey of Metten, a sculpture that had attracted no attention, even in the immediate neighborhood, before that time.

As a result, we are forced to remove from the iconography of the heart of Jesus an artifact that would have been highly significant if it were truly attributable, archaeologically, to the fourteenth century. I might regret that this is not so, but there is really no regret that can stand before the truth.

CHAPTER TWENTY-FIVE

Varied Representations of the Heart of Jesus

I. ENIGMATIC HEART OF THE EIGHTEENTH CENTURY AT THE CLUNY MUSEUM

SINCE THE SAINT-DENIS-D'ORQUES MARble and the Marigny sundial led us into the field of astronomy,[1] I will add a few lines here about an enigmatic object at least one detail of which also evokes, in symbol or rather in rebus, the idea of celestial spaces, these too understood moreover as an image of the blessed abode of souls.

Thanks to the great kindness of Father Lucien Buron I have an excellent photograph from which I have engraved the image on the following page (Fig. 1).

It is a heart made of wood or a composition that imitates it. Its almost circular periphery is set with a metal frame supported above the base by a richly wrought foot. Above it stands the cross surmounted by a small celestial sphere. The whole measures 16 centimeters in height.

This object of French workmanship dates from the sixteenth century. It belongs to the Cluny Museum, where it bears the number 5031.

On the heart itself two capital 'A's are linked together, while the cross that surmounts the celestial sphere is charged with six 'L's. We are obviously in the presence of a double rebus formed on the one hand by the heart itself and, on the other, by the heart's attributes.

Around the pedestal an inscription gives us a clue to the first part of the mystery:

---

[1] Cf. Part 6, Chaps. 21 and 22.

Part VI: The Iconography of the Wounded Heart of Jesus

Fig. 1. — Enigmatic heart at the Cluny Museum.

VNG CVEVR CRUCIFIE TIENT DEVLX AMYS ENSEMBLE
A crucified heart holds (reunites) two friends together

This is what the "deux A mis ensemble" ["two 'A's put together"] on the heart symbolize, where they are as if bound by the most tender yoke of friendship.

On the circle of metal that winds round and frames the heart we read these other words:

CE N'EST QUE' VNG CVEVR ET VNE AME
This is only one heart and one soul

Quite undeniably, this inscription does not relate to the material heart it surrounds but to the two friends it brings together and who are but one. This is the biblical expression we read in the *Acts of the Apostles* (4:32), where the author tells us that the union of those who first believed was such that "they had only one heart and one soul."

On the reverse side, opposite the two 'A's, the heart bears an M that seems to be the initial of a first name or a surname common to both friends.

The second part tells us that this union of the two friends must end in heaven, and that is where the rebus ends:

On the cross, the letter L, repeated six times, is only a hieroglyph for the word *Ciel*, that is to say: six 'L's, which must be read: *Ci-el* (i.e., as a homophone: *si*[x]-*el*). And this meaning is specified further, at the top, by a small *celestial sphere* of the starry sky, image of the abode of the blessed.

Thus it seems the sum total can be interpreted as follows:

"Ung coeur crucifié tient deulx amys ensemble,
au ciel," or "pour ciel."
*"A crucified heart holds two friends together,
in heaven" or "for heaven."*

Quite obviously the expression "crucified heart" leads us to consider the cross as splitting its thickness at the top of the heart, encompassing it, and recovering its unity right down to the flower-work that rejoins the supporting rampants above the base.

When I stated in a previous chapter, speaking of the first French printers[2] at the end of the fifteenth and sixteenth centuries,

---

2 Cf. Part 6, Chap. 17, iv, p. 260.

that, in the choice of their emblematic motifs, the people of that time sacrificed much, often much too much, to a taste for the complicated, the mysterious, the enigmatic, was I wrong?

Now, what is this crucified heart that reunites two friends in heaven, or for heaven?

Two opinions are possible:

One is to see in the object presented to us only the profane emblem of a profane friendship, although very pious, cemented by a trial common to the two friends and which, so to speak, crucifies them. And this is a thesis that can be upheld.

The other leads us to regard the crucified heart as the image of the heart of Jesus Christ, in which, in the love of which, if one likes, two friends will take refuge, and who, through it, hope to remain united all the way to heaven.

It must be recognized that this interpretation has strong arguments for it: first, it corresponds to the character and to one of the pious forms of those days, because this object dates back to the very time when the eloquent Olivier Maillard,[3] in the pulpits of Paris, Poitiers, and elsewhere, the Carthusian Lanspergius[4] in his writings, and other masters of spirituality advised souls to establish themselves in the heart of Jesus Christ as in a mystical refuge, as in a dwelling.

Next, also at that time — numerous material proofs are provided in earlier chapters — when artists of all kinds wanted to represent the carnal heart of Jesus Christ, six or seven times out of ten they placed it, alone or with the other holy wounds, on the shaft of the cross, thus creating in this way a "crucified heart" without any metaphor. Now, everyday expressions almost always point to those reoccurring visual impressions that have given rise to them; this makes me think that in the sixteenth century the expression "crucified heart" would have turned, of itself, all thoughts to the wounded heart of Jesus. The title for the book, *The Exercise of the Crucified Heart*, written about 1530

---

3 Cf. Part 6, Chap. 17, iv, p. 270.
4 Cf. Part 6, Chap. 17, v, p. 284.

by the Franciscan Poitevin, Pierre Regnart in Fontenay-le-Comte, is in no way opposed to this view, since the author assimilates, in its pages and even in the ornamental engraving of its title, the heart of the Franciscan ascetic to the "crucified heart" of Jesus Christ.

It seems to me, therefore, that the second of the two possible interpretations of the object in one of Cluny's display cases is more satisfactory than the other, and should be preferred. This is why, however enigmatic the appearance intentionally imposed on it by its creators, I regard this small monument to friendship as offering us an image, veiled it is true, but real and of particular interest, of the heart of Jesus Christ.

With its secular medals, tokens, and heraldic emblems, does not the decorative art of the same period display a variety of other far more bizarre rebuses? And so it comes as no surprise that, since the sixteenth century, individuals have chosen, as a precious jewel or invincible stronghold for their mutual affection, the heart towards which the adoring and trusting thought of the Christian people turned then and for quite a while afterwards.

II. THE DIVINE MUSIC OF THE WORD

Heart & Lyre

Some moving pages from Germaine Maillet[5] have recently spoken of the real torment of talented poets, sincere seekers of a divine ideal. She showed us how, in stanzas bright with flame and sometimes tearfully sad, they have feverishly sung the agony of their thoughts and the suffering of their souls.

This distress is, alas, incurable because these poor hearts throb too far from Christ; because they do not draw near enough to the lyre that is the Heart of the Word of God with its consoling harmonies, to this divinely attuned lyre that the ever so wonderfully inspired pen of Father Anizan compared to the harp of the

---

[5] "Le Sacré-Coeur et les Poètes," *Regnabit*, 5th year, num. 7, tome X, Dec. 1925, pp. 30–37. Laforgue and Beaudelaire are among the poets discussed. — *Trans.*

bard, in the fiction of Taliessin, which, on a desolate lake, seemed to be the living heart of things.

This comparison, between the heart from which springs the words of life that have regenerated the world and the instrument whose strings vibrate in such perfect accord with the emotions of the human voice and heart, is an especially happy one.

Heart and word are but one same continuous thing; the voice is the resonance of the heart; they are like spring-head and torrent, a wound and the shedding of blood, a rose and its perfume, a tree and its fruit, a fire and its heat: as Jesus says: "Out of the abundance of the heart the mouth speaks" (Matt. 12:34).

In God, as in His image man, the word is the heart's bursting forth from the person. It is the heart, through speech, that makes contact with the outside. The tongue is its organ and the lips its jewel-case.

This is why the Egyptians, who, more than other pagans of former times, had astounding views on the divine, sang "the Mystery of the Creative Word" while they bowed down before the Heart of God and everything good that the human heart contains.

And this is the reason for the veneration they had for the *persea*, that symbolic shrub which they consecrated to Isis "because its fruit resembled a heart and its leaf a tongue."[6]

The wise of Egypt regarded the heart not only as the affective organ of man, but also as the true source of his intellect; for them, thought sprang from a movement of the heart and was externalized by speech; the brain was only deemed a way-station where a word might come to rest, but was often bypassed with a spontaneous outburst.

Song is only the blossoming of the word. When the heart is bursting with intense emotion, when it vibrates not only on the surface but in the very depths of its fibers, speech becomes then insufficient, and man sings. He sings with joy or sorrow, for the sob is only a song from his anguished heart. The first human music sprang from the first great joy or the first great sorrow.

---

6 Plutarch, *Isis and Osiris*, c. 68.—The *persea* of the Egyptians was one of the thirty or so varieties of "Mango Tree," the fruit of which are cordiform and the leaves lanceolate.

Soon his God-given voice was no longer enough to ease the weight of his happiness or distress: that was when he invented musical instruments.

The first one, they say, was the reed flute that sings like a bird; and the second was a lyre that sings and cries like the human voice, the lyre whose charms the Pythagoreans had recourse to before giving themselves up to sleep, "so as to appease and enchant their souls' instinctive and passionate elements."[7]

How many times has ancient art celebrated the musical contest of Pan and Apollo! Pan, the sylvan and sensual god bound to the earth by the split hooves of a herbivore, challenged, with his flute of joined pipes; Apollo, the god of light, and his lyre. Both played with great talent, but such beautiful harmonies took flight from the lyre that, next to it, the flute seemed only to stutter. However, King Midas, the arbiter of this melodious contest, oddly imperceptive, decided in favor of Pan and against Apollo. And the latter, to chastise him, inflicted on him a pair of donkey ears.

This is just a fable to show us at what point passions and prejudices can warp the clear-sightedness and impartiality of a judge. But the Christian mystics of past centuries have seen in this fiction, by analogy, something quite different: the very voice of Christ who sings of the salutary law, the voice of the true god of light contending with the enemy's voice that also calls out to us.[8]

Some very ancient songs, composed by the Greek *rhapsodes* and *aedes* long before the coming of the Savior, also glorified the combat of Apollo, son of the supreme god, against the injurious reptile. One such example is this hymn, the text of which, discovered on the marbles of the temple at Delphi in 1894, begins in this way: "God with golden lyre, Son of great Zeus, on the peak of these snowy mountains, you who spread among mortals

---

[7] Plutarch, *Isis and Osiris*, c. 79.
[8] And this connection could also be established with what Egyptian mythologists say about Hermes, who, after having stolen the evil spirit Typhon's nerves, made strings for his lyre from them. — See Plutarch, *Isis and Osiris*, c. 55.

immortal oracles, I will tell how you conquered the prophetic tripod guarded by the dragon, when, with your darts, you put the hideous monster with twisting coils to flight!"[9]

This lyre of Apollo, musician and god, and the lyre of Orpheus, the divinized poet, both emblems of the superhuman Word, have found a most favorable welcome among ancient Christian symbolists: although certain aspects of the fiction of Apollo, the pagan god of light, harmony, eloquence, and beauty, seemed acceptable to them as material for emblematic analogies to the realities of Christ, the Orpheus myth lends itself even more to such happy comparisons.

What the Greek legend relates about Orpheus is well known:

Son of Apollo himself and Clio, say some, of King Oeagrus of Thrace and Calliope (in reality, a priestess of Apollo), say others, Orpheus had learned at a very early age, from the celebrated Linus, how to join his voice, which was of an unequalled beauty, with the harmonies of his lyre. And soon, with his talent ever improving, he attained a consummate mastery of this art. Thus, at times, the least docile and most dreadful creatures, and even inert matter, were subject to him. When the ineffable harmonies took flight from his lyre and lips, birds came to join in his concerts, the most ferocious wild beasts became attentive, gentle, and lay down at his feet to listen. Bare trees covered themselves in verdure and opened their trembling buds when he sang. Wind, hail, and lightning storms were stilled, and ships beached in the sand went of themselves into open water when the enchanting voice of Orpheus soared from his heart and hovered over things...

Orpheus, who had followed the Argonauts in the conquest of the golden fleece, next returned to Thrace, his native land. And there one day, O mournful day, the Thracian women, enraged by the indifference shown them by the poet, faithful to the memory of Eurydice, killed him and threw his torn remains into the Hebrus. But, not wishing to engulf them, the river gently bore his head with its inspired lips and his lyre that floated nearby to Lesbos.

---

9 From Reinach and d'Eichthal's French translation.

This legend of Orpheus continued to grow. It was related that, at Lesbos, his head and lyre produced oracles, and the Greeks spoke only of the "divine Orpheus."

Mysterious rites of heavenly origin, they said, were brought by him from Thrace into Greece, and the wise esteemed that they contained the secrets of efficacious purification, the only means of access to a happy immortality.

These Orphic mysteries were based on the fable of Dionysius-Zagreus: by Zeus, the supreme God, Kore, daughter of Ceres, engendered a child named Zagreus; jealous of Kore, Hera[10] had the newborn torn to pieces by the Titans; but wise Athena[11] saved the heart of Zagreus, and the child was reborn from his own heart under the name of Dionysius.

The goal of these religious rites based on this mysterious fable was to assure the faithful initiate or *myst* of eternal felicity. To attain this, man could aspire to — and should — divinize himself, that is to say be purified by sufferings and die to what is so as to be resurrected in a new soul. The sufferings of Zagreus, his death and rebirth, were the allegory of the stages of this palingenesis, that is, of this regeneration of the human soul with a view to its admittance to eternal and supreme happiness.

Orpheus seemed, then, to the Greek initiates of the Dionysius-Zagreus mysteries as a kind of Savior who had brought them the key to a happy life beyond the grave. And the written poetry attributed to him prolonged the magic power of his talent and kept the marvelous aura of the early days about his name.

Of all the fables invented by the exuberant imagination of the poets and mystics prior to our times to glorify the human word, none impressed the Christians of the early centuries more than that of Orpheus. And among the great many mystery rites and cults mingling the sublime and the abominable known to ancient paganism, none, except perhaps certain Egyptian concepts, have come as near to Christian truths as the Orphic theories.

10 Among the Greeks, Zeus, Korah, and Hera were the same myths as Jupiter, Proserpine, and Juno among the Romans.
11 Athena is Minerva, goddess of wisdom.

Part VI: The Iconography of the Wounded Heart of Jesus

This is why the first Christian teachers of Greece and Rome saw, in the legends relating to the sublime artist of Thrace who charmed the wild beasts with his voice and made them follow of themselves, a providential image of the blessed Christ calling people of all races to the new faith. Doubtless, they also saw in the Orphic rites of purification an anticipatory glimmer of Christian spirituality, arising later from the teachings of Jesus.

Moreover, for a whole segment of pagan society, "Orpheus represented," says Heussner,[12] "the idea of immortality, and as such was admitted by the first Christians as an ancient witness to their own hopes."

This interpretation may perhaps be seen as a variation of Schultze's, who sees in the Orpheus of the catacombs "a pagan prophet of Christianity,"[13] an opinion supported by the eminent authority of Dom Leclercq.[14]

For, in the holy catacombs of Rome, the image of Orpheus with his lyre and his retinue of animals is side by side with images of our religion's founders in the impressive decoration of these underground chambers where our great martyrs were buried. We see it thus in the catacombs of Domitillus, St. Callixtus, and elsewhere.

It is possible that, in some of these venerable paintings, Orpheus may be depicted, as Schultze says, only as a pagan prophet of Christianity, but it remains certain that he was sometimes the image of the Lord Jesus Christ himself, of the Divine Word, painted with his features.

And here is, perhaps, one of the most curious testimonies: a little before 1900, laborers, digging up the ground to lay a wall in the ancient Gaulish town of Loudun (Vienne), found, in the midst of charcoal, ashes, and ceramic fragments, a calcarious stone carved with a knife, and which they brought a few hours later to the learned archaeologist of the town, Joseph Moreau de la Ronde. This latter person returned to the discovery site and recognized, having previously studied a good number of them in

---

12 See Heussner, *Die altchristlichen Orpheusdarstellungen* (Cassel: Druck von Baier & Lewalter, 1893).
13 Cf. *Revue de l'Histoire des Religions*, 1894, p. 243.
14 *Manuel d'Archéologie Chrétienne*, tome I, p. 128.

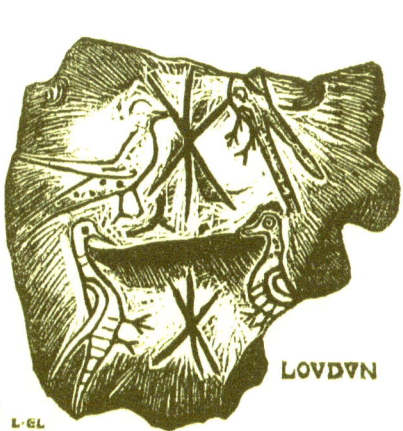 

Fig. 2. — *Carved limestone, 3rd to 4th centuries, Loudun.*

Fig. 3. — *Carved limestone, 2nd to 4th centuries, Loudun.*

this same terrain, that the sculpted stone came from the firepit of a cremation burial. This enabled him to date it from the end of the third or beginning of the fourth century of our era. This was the period when, a hundred meters above the place where it was found, Sts. Claire and Lucian were decapitated, according to local tradition, victims of the Maximian persecution (296–305).

On one side (Fig. 2) the stone bears the cipher for Iesus Xrist, an I on an X, and two doves adore this divine monogram. This twice-repeated motif is an undeniable proof of the stone's Christian character. Upon its other side (Fig. 3) is a person draped in the ancient manner holding a lyre with his left arm, and two birds sing on either side of him. In appearance, then, this is clearly an image of Orpheus; but, at his feet, one of the faithful prays kneeling, and next to each of the birds is found, similar to those seen in the catacombs, the representation of a eucharistic bread. In this most Christian decoration, in such perfect accord with the cipher for Jesus Christ engraved on the other side, the Savior of the world, the divine enchanter of souls, appears under the poetic image of Orpheus.[15]

15 I owe the possession of this interesting document to the great kindness of André Moreau de La Ronde, son of the archaeologist, who has obligingly offered it to me for the pursuit of my studies.

Part VI: The Iconography of the Wounded Heart of Jesus

The presence at Loudun of this icon of Christ-Orpheus can be explained in this way: immediately above the plot of land that has produced it is the ancient Roman fortress of Lugdunum, the walls and towers of which are still two or three meters high at certain points. This enclosure which comprises twelve acres of land, with praetorium and buildings over hypocausts, would have lodged, with its permanent garrison, legions on the march. It is therefore quite likely that, among those legionnaires passing through or in residence, were some knowledgeable Christians from Rome, and one of them died in the course of his stay. His cremation, in this instance, would have been ordered automatically, but the Orpheus stone undoubtedly placed with his ashes by the hand of a coreligionist testifies that his faith had become our faith.

I know of only one other depiction of Christ-Orpheus found on French soil from those distant times: it is carved on a Christian sarcophagus discovered at Cacarens (Gers). It represents Orpheus playing the lyre in the midst of faithful sheep (Fig 4). In studying this sarcophagus at the Academy of Inscriptions on April 13th, 1894, E. Le Blant declared that this was the only monument of this kind to be found in Gaul. The stone from Loudun that came to light about this same time is older than the Cacarens sarcophagus.

Fig. 4. — Orpheus, in the posture of Mithra (with broken lyre), on an early Christian sarcophagus in the Vatican Museum.

In Italy the image of Opheus was rather frequently adopted as decoration for Christian tombs of the first centuries; and this choice, like its presence in the Loudun cremation burial, can be explained by the fact that the ancient world regarded Orpheus as personifying the idea of immortality.

The art of the Middle Ages, at least in France, was wrong to relinquish the image of Orpheus as an emblem of the Savior's word.

Varied Representations of the Heart of Jesus

Fig. 5. — *Orpheus on a sculpture from the Abbey of Cluny, 11th century.*

Nevertheless, we find it again among the Benedictine carvings of the grand abbey at Cluny in the eleventh century; there the poet was representing Gregorian chant in its third tone (Fig. 5). He is likewise featured as representing music on twelfth-century sculptures at Rheims cathedral, in the company of Arion and Pythagoras.[16]

The lyre was also employed alone to symbolize harmony, and until recent centuries even preserved its meaning as a direct emblem of the Savior.

When, in 1648, the Cistercian monks of Pin-en-Béruges Abbey, in the diocese of Poitiers, had their abbey restored, they covered it with long flat tiles ornamented with etchings of religious emblems: there we see the Christ-Lyre marked at its center with the monogram of Jesus, IHS (Fig. 6).

Fig. 6. — *Flat roofing-tile bearing the Mystical Lyre. Pin-en-Béruges Abbey, 1648. Musée des Antiq. de l'Ouest, Poitiers.*

I have previously reproduced,[17] and I repeat it here (Fig. 7), the lyre-heart of Jesus carved on an old piece of furniture from the monastery of the Benedictines of Calvary at Loudun (seventeenth to eighteenth century), and this carving, to conclude, leads me back to the principal theme of the present work.

Have I then finished with the old pagan fictions of Apollo and Orpheus? I think much less in reality than in appearance.

Fig. 7. — *The Mystical Lyre, wood carving from the former monastery of the Calvarians of Loudun, 17th–18th century.*

16 Barbier de Montault, *Traité d'iconographie chrétienne*, tome I, p. 307 and plate XVII.
17 Cf. Part 6, Chap. 19, i, p. 317, Fig. 3.

417

Does not this lyre of Christ-Orpheus, image of the Word sprung from the divine heart, recall the visions that ravished St. Gertrude in the fourteenth century of our era?

"Sometimes the heart of Jesus appeared to her as an harmonious lyre toward which the Holy Trinity, that rejoiced in the sweet melodies of this instrument, gently inclined itself. The adorable Trinity set three strings therein, the pleasant harmony of which had to supply what was lacking in Gertrude, and these three strings are the power of the Father, the wisdom of the Son, and the love of the Holy Spirit."[18]

Does not this singing together of the divine perfections through the lyre-heart of Jesus seem to be as if the blossoming, the Christian flowering of this splendid and great concept already enunciated by the Pythagorean school six centuries before the night in Bethlehem: "Make of the seven planetary orbs a celestial lyre giving the seven notes of the scale by the proportion of their respective distances,"[19] and doing so the whole immensity of space vibrates at a touch with a matchless hymn to the glory of the divinity.

God has willed that the ray of His sun illuminate the paganisms, because in all of them very beautiful souls have served Him in all uprightness of heart, without however knowing Him; thus, now and then, inspired individuals have arisen to acclaim in their fashion the divine Word which spoke within them amidst a tumult of errors. All believed in their own way that they knew God, the true God, and looking closely we can discern, in the outline of the ancient myths, that they have created those lightly sketched features that we rediscover, dazzlingly bright, in the person of the Savior.

Who, then, knows if, enlightened by traditions of many millennia, or by divine inner lights, the sages of Asia have presented Him under the emblematic figure of Indra; Zoroaster, under the blazing halo of the fiery-hearted Ormuzd; Hermes, under

---

18 Dom Berlière, *La Dévotion au Sacré-Cœur dans l'Ordre de saint Benoît* (Paris: Lethielleux, Desclée de Brouwer, 1923), p. 32.

19 Bouché-Leclercq, *Les Précurseurs de l'Astrologie Grecque* (Paris: E. Leroux, 1897), I.

the tiara of Osiris, when the mystery of the creative Word was chanted before the pyramids and the sphinx; Orpheus, perhaps under the features of Zagreus reborn from his own heart, and Pythagoras, under the name of the divine Logos, the creative and lifegiving Word?

To all these thirstings, to all these unsuspecting aspirations of the old humanity toward the One who must come, it was John the beloved who poured forth the quenching word after Jesus had completed his work: "The Word of God was made flesh, and dwelt among us."

If the blood that issued, on the day of his death, from his half-opened breast is truly the very life-sap of his heart, then his Word, his Speech, is its flower.

And how profound is the thought that carved the heart of Christ — image of his love, the source of his blood — and the lyre — image of his Word, the flower of his heart — as one emblematic whole.

III. A HYMN-BOOK OF THE WHITE PENITENTS OF MARSEILLES

A young and skillful artist, Miss Rossollin, of Marseilles, and Mrs. Rossollin, her mother, were kind enough to send me, with ample historical notes that I am unable to give in full here, some very beautiful watercolors reproducing illuminations from a large lectern book of the White Penitents of Marseilles.

This brotherhood, also called *Penitents of Trinité-Vieille*, was founded, according to some, as early as 1306, or, according to other local historians, in 1514, to help the Trinitarian monks in their most excellent work of ransoming Christian slaves held captive by pirates on the African coast.

Dissolved by the Revolution, the White Penitents of Trinité-Vieille were reconstituted in 1817 and were then able to recover, with some of their ecclesiastical privileges, their habit, the customs so peculiar to their brotherhood, and even many material objects that had belonged to their fellow-members of previous centuries.

And so they still possess today an old large lectern-book that contains, first, an Office of the feast of the Sacred Heart of Jesus, next, Offices for the feasts of King St. Louis of France, St. John the Evangelist, and some others.

This undated hymn-book seems attributable to the time when Mgr. De Belsunce, who was bishop of Marseilles from 1710 to 1755, and Mother Anne de Rémuzat, ardently propagated the cult of the Sacred Heart in this city; and if it is anterior to them, it cannot be by more than a very little — not more in any case than the initiatives of the Mother De Capel, superior of the Visitation nuns at Marseilles, in 1691 and 1696,[20] which were, under Louis XIV, the first manifestations of the cult of the Sacred Heart in the great Phocaean city.

The book opens with the OFFICIUM S.S. CORDIS DNI NTRI JESU CHRISTI, and under this title stands a large red heart, surmounted by a cross of the same color at the foot of which the three nails of the crucifixion are stitched in the heart, whose central part is open with a large gold wound through which an azure arrow passes.

And everything in these colors is symbolic: the heart is red because it is physically flesh and source of the precious blood. Does not the prose of the old Parisian rite's *In capite libri* Mass tell us that "it is in it that is wrought and colored the purple with which the martyrs are clothed and dyed"? The wound is of gold because it is the divine coffer for the treasure of graces, and the arrow is azure because it comes from heaven (Fig. 8).

Fig. 8. — Heart transpierced by an arrow. Hymn-book of the Penitents of Marseille.

In his excellent article, *At Paray, before an old stone*,[21] Father Anizan tells us the meaning that must be attached to this bolt shot

---

20 Cf. Abbé Buron, *La vénérable Rémuzat*, in *Regnabit*, Oct. 1922.
21 In *Regnabit*, December 1921.

from on high into the Savior's heart and shown by a fifteenth-century wood engraving as leaving from the hand of the eternal Father, a bolt that wounds in this way the heart of His Son,[22] that is, which allows our redemption by the mortal sufferings of the Passion, summed up in the wound that the arrow makes to the heart.

Fig. 9. — *Letter C containing a Heart. Hymn-book of the Penitents of Marseille.*

In the book of the Penitents of Marseilles, the ornate letter that begins the musical notation for the vespers hymn, *Cor Jesu melle dulcius*, a crescent-shaped "C," contains another image of the heart of Jesus nearly similar to that of the title for the Office, but this one is crowned with a bouquet of flames (Fig. 9). Like the first, it assumes a contorted and pointed form that was in favor, from the sixteenth century to the present century, in southern regions: northern Italy, Provence, eastern Languedoc, Roussillon, and Spain; we have already noticed this singular form on the banner of the Brotherhood of the Black Christ of Cartagena (Spain).[23]

It is probably still the heart of Jesus that the illuminator of the Marseilles book wanted to depict at the head of the Lauds text for the same Office (Fig. 10); the gold that covers it corresponds well to an intention of glorification, but it must be confessed that it is also completely lacking in identifying features, and that, placed elsewhere than in an Office of the Sacred Heart, one could see in it just about anyone's ardent heart and nothing more.

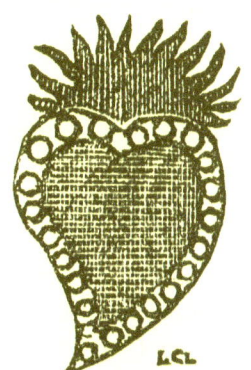

Fig. 10. — *Heart ablaze. Hymn-book of the Penitents of Marseille.*

22 Cf. Part 6, Chap. 16.v, p. 285, Fig. 31.
23 Cf. Part 6, Chap. 24, ii, p. 399, Fig. 8. — Heart-emblem of the Brotherhood of the Black Christ of Cartagena.

And the Office ends with a lovely pink or brick-red cartouche that holds in its center the monogram of the divine name, Jesus, IHS, *below* which burns an adoring heart which, in that placement, can be only the image of a believer, and in the circumstances, a heart emblematic of the Trinité-Vieille Brotherhood; the monogram, heart, and border of the cartouche are deep red. On either side of the cartouche two White Penitents are kneeling.

All these emblems of the heart of Jesus in the book of the ancient brotherhood of Marseilles, so full of regional flavor, seem to admirably complete the illustration of the studies included in this work, and we respectfully thank Madam and Miss Rossollin for having brought them to our attention.

IV. VOTIVE HEARTS ON WAYSIDE AND MISSION CROSSES

I could have begun these lines with this title: "On an irrational use of the image of the Sacred Heart," for even though God may be, in the words of the good knight Jean de Joinville, "so good a thing that better cannot be," yet one must not make true nonsense of images and emblems by placing them without reflection no matter where.

Yet this is what has so often happened for three quarters of a century in the case of wayside crosses or simple crucifixes frequently erected at the crossroads of highways, in city squares, sometimes inside churches, and which a piety, more sincere than enlightened, covers the shaft and arms with a strewing of little Sacred Hearts in gilded metal.

Let us go back and place ourselves at the origin of this use, at the end of the seventeenth century and during the eighteenth.

This epoch, a period of moral corruption and, above all, intellectual perversion for the high society of the great cities, was, on the other hand, in almost all France, a period of active religious life for rural communities and small towns, thanks to the missions, the Advents and Lents preached everywhere by the religious of the great Orders, and by ardent societies of diocesan or regional missionaries.

Beside the "sacred orators" who aimed at an academic style and preached in the classical manner, there also appeared Bridaine, who alone gave two hundred and forty-six missions and preached as a doctor; then Father Maunoir in Brittany, the Blessed Louis Grignion de Montfort and his company of Missionaries in Poitou, Saintonge, Nantais, and Anjou, and the venerable and awe-inspiring Antoine Receveur in Franche-Comte, all of whom preached as apostles; then Jesuits, like Fathers Gros and Caussade; Capuchins, like Father Ambroise de Lombez, who preached as mystics, and many others.

Almost every one of these sermons, preached in this way throughout the kingdom, ended with the erection of a Calvary of remembrance; and from that time a touching custom was established.

Small pewter or lead hearts were melted, or they were made of sheet metal or wood, and often they carried on their reverse side a formula of homage. Heads of pious families bought them, inscribed their names, and then those hearts were nailed to the cross around the crucified Redeemer.

Fig. 11. — Saint-Aubin-Baubigné (D.-S.) from the Rev. Gabard.

We will see that sometimes, in some very Christian provinces, the affixing of these hearts also corresponded to family events, and therefore was done in isolated units.

The Revolution, by tearing down the Calvaries on the roadsides and public squares, has eradicated almost all the hearts of the Calvaries that dated from before the Revolution; only exceptionally are they found today.

Father Gabard, parish priest of Saint-Aubin-Baubigné (Deux-Sèvres), had collected one of them on the estate of the Durbelière castle where the heroic, young leader of the Vendean insurgents, Henri de la Rochejaquelin, lived. I am presenting a half-size image of it here (Fig. 11); it bears only a cluster of flames at its summit and, on its inner, concave surface, the inscription represented below (Fig. 12), which should be read: to [Jesus] my [heart] and my life.

Part VI: The Iconography of the Wounded Heart of Jesus

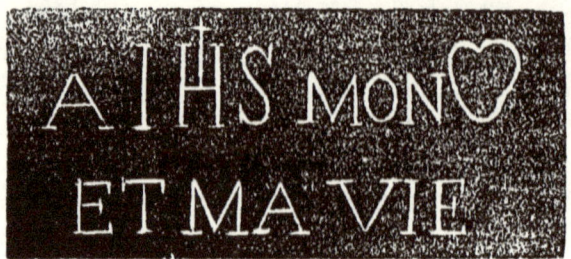

*Fig. 12. — Saint-Aubin-Baubigné (D.-S.).
Inner inscription on a votive heart.*

This seems a faithful echo of the prayer so popular in the Christian families of Poitou in the time of our grandfathers:

> Heart of Jesus, Heart of Mary,
> I give you my Heart, my spirit and my life;
> Heart of Jesus, Heart of Mary,
> Help me during my last agony;
> Heart of Jesus, Heart of Mary,
> Make me die in your company.

After the Revolution, especially during the first years of the royal Restoration, the missions resumed in almost all France, and large crosses were erected again at road corners, in the public places, and against the walls of churches; for example, in 1817 in Bordeaux, in 1819 or 1821 in the church of Saint-Jean d'Angely, and around the same time, in the old cathedral of Grasse, in Provence.

The Bordeaux cross is quite beautiful: spear and sponge are placed on each side of Christ, with the ends of their shafts crossing under the Savior's feet and their tops passing beyond his hands. Behind his head a large heart, placed at the meeting of the arms of the cross, bears a cluster of flames and the crown of thorns, clearly the image of his own heart. But the shaft of the cross is adorned with much smaller hearts that have only the cluster of flames and are simply votive human hearts, emblems of their donors' hearts. Besides, the inscription at the base attests to this; it reads: "Mission of 1817. — This cross adorned with gilded hearts in which are inscribed the names of the faithful was solemnly blessed by Bishop d'Aviau on the public square of Rohan"; and the rest of the text indicates that it has been harbored in the cathedral since 1830.

The cross in the church of Grasse is also studded with small hearts and its ends bear four large ones, the larger dimensions of which correspond only to decorative concerns; all are just images of the hearts of the faithful.

The hearts decorating the cross of Saint-Jean d'Angely are in gold plate; those that adorn the sides of the cross are a third smaller than those in front.

Through the obliging intermediary of Abbé Dougny, the Archpriest of Saint-Jean has kindly sent me three of the little squares of paper from the inside of all these hearts that bear the names of donors. On one we read: *Aglaé de...*; on the other, *Le Bar... Louis d'... aie*; the third is totally illegible. As we can see, these are the names of donors and the hearts that contain them can only be emblematic of their own hearts. All are surmounted by the cross.

About nearly the same time, the use of lead and pewter hearts, which do not oxidize, and the outer face of which was almost always gilded, was resumed on crosses exposed to the weather. The Poitevin collection of my good friend, François Eygun, of the École des Chartes, includes a mold used to manufacture these hearts.

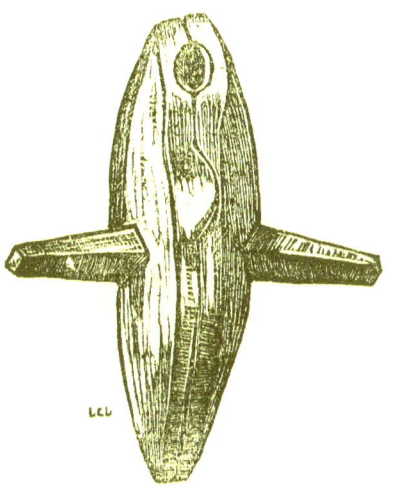

Fig. 13. — Poitiers. — Mold for casting hearts (closed). Fr. Eygun Collection.

It consists of two plates that fit together, leaving a heart-shaped gap where the molten metal penetrates and solidifies. Here these two plates are shown juxtaposed, that is, with the mold closed (Fig. 13); the lateral projections it bears were driven in for wooden handles that allowed an operator to keep the two plates in contact while another poured the molten metal into the upper orifice.

The engraving below represents, in its actual size, one of the hearts thus obtained, seen from the inner and concave side (Fig. 14). The inscription reads: I offer my (heart) to J. C.

This heart bears both the cluster of flames of the older heart of Saint-Aubin-Baubigné and the cross with hearts of Saint-Jean d'Angely.

I received from Dr. Fiévé, from Jallais (Maine-et-Loire), a tin heart from an old Calvary of this locality and which seems attributable to the 1830–1840 period, shortly after François Eygun's mold. It is more comparable than the previous examples to the

Fig. 14. — Poitiers. — One of the hearts produced by the mold from the Eygun collection. Inward side.

Fig. 15. — Jallais (Maine-et-Loire). Collection of the author.

current "Sacred Heart" type, since it is surrounded by the crown of thorns (Fig. 15); it is, however, only a votive human heart, and on its interior we read in relief the ordinary formula: I offer my [heart] to Jesus Christ (Fig. 16).

Dr. Fiévé, who is a learned traditionist, kindly gave me, together with this heart, the following information, precious testimonies of the spirit of faith that animated and sanctified the family life of former times and by which a greater part of his native region of Anjou still abides: "Our old crosses, our old wooden Calvaries,

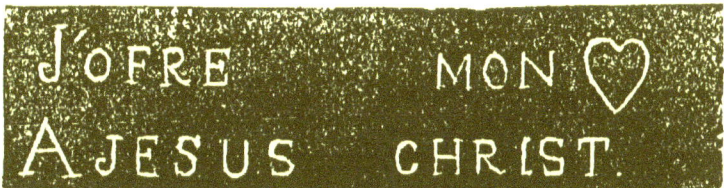

Fig. 16. — Jallais (M. et L.). Inner inscription of a votive heart.

were for the most part formerly covered with these hearts in pewter, lead, or any other metal; I have seen about fifty bearing them.

"It was customary in our country, as soon as a child came into the world, to attach to the cross of the nearby crossroads a heart within which the name of the newborn was often written."[24]

In other parts of western France, it was on the day of their marriage that new husbands affixed their votive hearts to the wood of the cross at the crossroad, in front of which the bridal procession would pass returning from the church; just as — alas! — a small wooden cross would be deposited at its foot when a coffin was passing, carrying to the altar the cloak of flesh left by a soul upon its summons from God.

It is therefore well understood, let us repeat, that the hearts thus presented to Jesus Crucified for a birth, a marriage, or offered in thanksgiving of a Mission, and each of these as material testimonies of love, fidelity, or gratitude, can only be symbols of the hearts of those who "offered them to Jesus Christ."

Now, we see that the manufacturers who poured these hearts gradually brought them closer to the "Sacred Heart of Jesus" type: the Jallais heart lacks only the characteristic spear wound for it to be truly an image of the divine heart.

Since the first years of the Second Empire, this step will be briskly taken by the misunderstanding of manufacturers — one may judge for oneself by the image below (Fig. 17) — and the piety of this time, ignorant and naive as well as sincere, will welcome these objects without hesitation to assign them to the same votive use as traditional human hearts.

---

24 Letter of September 27.

Part VI: The Iconography of the Wounded Heart of Jesus

Fig. 17. — Loudun (Vienne). Collection of the author.

As a result, the Christian who, in order to affirm his heart's belief, piety, fidelity, or gratitude, nails the image of the heart of Jesus to the shaft of the cross, offers up a perfect intention with a gesture devoid of aptness and meaning: he offers to Jesus Christ the heart of Jesus Christ.

I am well aware that a complicated, highly refined mysticism can justify a gift of his own heart made to the Savior and extol it as the most marvelous gift and the only one worthy of him that can be made to him. But this is a subtle idea perfectly inaccessible to the average Catholic, and the use of a traditional human heart with the words "To Jesus my heart and my life," or "I offer my heart to Jesus Christ," answered perfectly to the custom for which it was intended, and which alone had given birth to the simplest and most straightforward popular piety.

Let us recall that in the seventeenth and eighteenth century it was not the orators preaching "in the classical style" that brought into vogue the naive and touching use of small votive hearts, but the missionaries who were praying then for the bountiful goodness of the soil and the people in the fields.

With regard to pious practices, we must always go back to the origins of local customs; and the clergy, who have the mission of explaining them and keeping their original meaning intact, can never know them too thoroughly.

On all of our French soil we have traditional customs, we repeat ancestral and age-old gestures, even often practiced by a number of the indifferent — gestures full of admirable and wonderful Christian meanings. There is in this heritage a store of nourishment and *soul*, a hundred times more invigorating than all

Varied Representations of the Heart of Jesus

Plate 30. — Hosts fall from the Wound of Christ. Engraving from the Basel Museum, 15th century. Heitz Collection, Strasbourg; xi, No. 6. Regnabit Journal *archives, 1921–1929 (ed.).*

the short or long devotions of recent invention, many of which are only faddish.

Even among the practices that are today actually in the realm of superstition, several have a quite lofty origin, with their deviation or falsification due only to the forgetfulness of the thinking that had created them. But, setting aside regret for this forgetfulness, to return to the just-mentioned objects, I will venture to say this:

That the image of the heart of Jesus Christ, the divine crucible where our redemption was wrought, is multiplied everywhere, this is splendid; but let the votive hearts of our large crucifixes retain their human character. To the flame that symbolizes their ardent throbbing, add, if you will, the cross by which they were redeemed, but please let us not substitute for them the image adopted and dedicated to represent the Lord's heart. The idea that created them is lofty enough to be interpreted in all the fullness of its meaning, and our poor human heart, despite — alas! — what we do sometimes, is still precious enough to be offered to God, since it is, after His own, the most marvelous of the fruits of flesh to which His goodness has given the gift of life.

SEVENTH PART

The Iconography of the Heart of Jesus
IN THE COUNTER-REVOLUTIONARY ARMIES OF THE VENDÉE

CHAPTER TWENTY-SIX

Rally-badges, Also Called "Scapulars," with the Image of the Sacred Heart

I. THE BEGINNINGS OF THE INSURRECTION IN POITOU AND ANJOU, THE FIRST BADGES

ALREADY FOR THREE YEARS THE REVOlutionary ferment had thrown France into disorder, and, under the pretext of establishing freedom there, oppressed the countryside with an odious tyranny that became more crushing with every passing day. The Terror was approaching.

The lands of the West, Poitou, Brittany and Anjou, were not unaware that social reforms were useful, but they wanted to see them accomplished peacefully, with respect for necessary order and authority, with full freedom of conscience and personal liberty.

In these regions more than elsewhere the clergy exerted, with dignity, an influence highly appreciated by everyone; with rare exceptions, the nobles lived there less remote from the people than elsewhere, without foolish arrogance, and many of them regarded themselves as the first among the peasants for whom they were most often benefactors and respected friends.

Also the first vexatious measures that caused the first threatened emigrés to depart abroad, that first harassed, then soon persecuted the priests in the most essential functions of their pastorate, gave rise to violent murmurs, the first rumblings of a thunder which would soon explode into a terrible storm.

It expanded especially on the present territories of the four bishoprics of Poitiers, Angers, Luzon, and Nantes, which it was to ravage and depopulate frightfully. This was what was called the *militarized Vendée*, an area much larger than the department of Vendée.

By early 1792, groups of dissatisfied people had gathered at various points of Deux-Sèvres and the Vendée, and openly expressed their disapproval of the persecutory measures officially promulgated and increasingly implemented.

Especially in the Bressuirais the decree of May 27, 1792, condemning to deportation any priests who refused to take the schismatic oath, caused the first noisy disturbances.

Finally, on the following 27th of July, the day when the fair of Saint-Jacques was held at Bressuire, the "patriots" of the city wanted to force the peasants in the vicinity to wear the tricolor cockade. As a result, that day and the days following, bloody fights that could not be pacified broke out and the mayor of Bressuire, Joseph Delouche, had to abandon the city and take refuge in the village of Moncoutant.

On the following 19th of August, the young men of the twelve neighboring communes, who had come to this last mentioned locality for recruitment purposes, grouped themselves around Delouche and called for all men to take up arms against a government of tyrants that they refused to serve, calling for the King to be restored to his full authority as the only way to return to social order and religious freedom.

The insurgents immediately went to the castle of Pugny, residence of the Marquis of Mauroy, former colonel of the Médoc regiment, to make the latter their chief, and defend themselves at his residence. They did not find him there, but obtained from his steward the flag of his old regiment: a white silk strewn with golden fleur-de-lys with the royal arms in the center. The acclamation "Vive le Roi" [Long live the King!], written in large capital letters, was added, it is believed, during the war.

This was the first standard for those giantic struggles known as the "Wars of Vendée."

From Pugny, the troop went to the home of Brachain, to Gabriel Baudry d'Asson, a former officer too, who accepted the command of the 2,000 men already present and returned with them to Moncoutant. There, someone named Micheneau was in charge of organizing the armament, while Bazin was in charge of making and distributing *white cockades* to the insurgents as a *rallying sign*. The first ones were cut from a bed blanket.

It is therefore not correct to write, as several authors have done, that "from the first day of the insurrection, the Sacred Heart was adopted as a rallying-sign by all the Vendeans." The first official insignia was the royal cockade, under the folds of the royal flag. That is the truth.

Five days later, when the troop, 6,000 strong, was preparing to attack Bressuire, M. de Hanne, of Moncoutant, came to join it bringing victuals and *white cockades* and they marched on Bressuire with some hunting rifles, iron-tipped poles, old pikes, pitchforks and other makeshift weapons. But there had just arrived two companies of naval infantry, hastily summoned from Rochefort since the early hours of the uprising, also the national guard of Niort, La Mothe-Saint-Héraye, Saint-Maixent and Parthenay who, well-armed with war-rifles and supported by cannon, fired on the peasants and dispersed them.

The Averti's *Journal des Deux-Sèvres* wrote at the time that 118 insurgents were left on the ground, and he adds that they "were covered with crosses and rosaries."

So they wore religious emblems of their choice at the same time as the royal cockade, and, although Averti does not speak of it, it is quite likely that images of the Heart of Jesus were also to be found there — later we shall see what makes us think so — but in a rather limited number so that they did not attract attention.[1]

A kind of lull followed this first uprising, but from time to time, at various junctures, isolated acts of violence showed what fire was burning beneath the ashes. In this way the winter months passed painfully. On the 21st of January of the following year, in 1793, Louis XVI attained on the scaffold what Pope Pius VI so rightly called "his martyrdom"; and before this insane parricide committed by France in revolt the whole of the West was stupefied, and more than ever abhorred this anarchy, which, after having legally assassinated the King, made the worship due to God impossible.

[1] See C. Puichaud, *L'Histoire d'un drapeau vendéen. L'insurrection d'août, 1792*, in *Revue du Bas-Poitou*, ann. 1899 — and H. Baguenier Desormeaux, *Le Premier Drapeau de la Vendée Catholique et Royaliste*, in *Revue du Bas-Poitou*, ann. 1921, num. 2.

Only two months after the death of the King, on March 13th, a peasant from a very small village in Anjou, Jacques Cathelineau, of Pin-en-Mauges, gathered in his cottage the twenty-seven "young lads" of his parish that military law called up, and made them swear to die rather than serve the persecuting Republic. They greeted this with cheers, then, like him, passed a rosary around the neck and stitched a "*Sacred Heart*" on the back of their jackets.

Leaving immediately, they went to the villages of Jallais and Chemillé, whose able-bodied men joined up with them, and now they were five hundred! And, like the first group, everyone was decorated with "rosaries and Sacred Hearts." We shall see how these last insignia came so easily to hand, ready-made.

The next day they were twelve hundred, "all bearing," says a document from the Archives of Angers, "white cockades, and decorated with a *small square cloth medallion* on the which (*sic*) were embroidered different figures of *small stitched hearts* and other signs of this ilk."[2]

From that day, and for the whole course of the "Great War," as well as during the 1815 taking up of arms, and the Chouan insurgency of 1830, the white cockade and the "Sacred Heart" were the distinctive and inseparable signs of the Vendée fighter. The leaders usually wore a white belt or scarf. Shortly thereafter, the whole country, from Angers to the ocean, from Parthenay to Nantes and from Bressuire to Luzon, was under arms, and Jacques Cathelineau, acclaimed commander-in-chief of the "Catholic and Royal Armies" by both great lords and peasants, saw indisputably accepted everywhere the pious image which had become in his cottage the official badge of the uprising, at least equal to that of the royal cockade.

And then this remarkable coincidence: at nearly the same time, March 15, 1793, more than twenty leagues from Pin-en-Mauges, in Poitou, the Chevalier de Saint-Laurent de la Cassaigne sent to Mademoiselle de la Rochejaquelein a dozen Sacred Hearts painted by him. The letter which accompanied this packet contained these words: "I am sending you a small provision of Sacred Hearts

[2] E. Boisseleau, *Le Sacré-Cœur des Vendéens* (Luzon: Bideaux, 1910), p. 4.

which I have drawn for your intention. You know that people who believe in this devotion succeed in all their endeavors.... It is a very solid devotion and has been practiced for many centuries."[3]

II. THE VENDEAN BADGES KNOWN AS "SCAPULARS OF THE SACRED HEART"

No kind of uniformity was imposed on these pieces of cloth, improperly called "scapulars." One was simply asked to wear the image of the Heart of Jesus.

The greatest number were of white or black cloth, with a heart in the middle, the divine character of which is specified by the

---

[3] Canon Uzureau, director of *Anjou Historique*, has sent us a very interesting note concerning this letter:

"The day after the capture of Cholet by the Catholic army, March 14, the knight de Saint-Laurent de la Cassaigne wrote to his cousin, Miss de la Rochejaquelein: 'I am sending you a small collection of Sacred Hearts of Jesus which I had put aside for your sake, and which I had kept in the hope of paying you homage. It is a very sound devotion and has been practiced for many centuries. It has never been more necessary than in our present unfortunate circumstances; I cannot recommend it enough for all the great benefits derived from it by those who have devoted themselves to it with that confidence that one ought to have in the kindness and mercy of the best of all fathers.'

"This letter, as indicated in the copy sent to the superintendents of Maine-et-Loire, was 'seized on Saturday the 16th, on a servant of Sire Lescure, by patriots who stopped him on the road to Chatillon-sur-Sevre.'

"We find mention of this incident in the *Memoirs* of the Marquis de la Rochejaquelein: 'M. La Rochejaquelein sent his servant on horseback to his aunt's house, which was only four or five leagues from Herbiers. This servant was arrested at Bressuire, and a letter was found on him from M. de la Cassaigne to Mademoiselle de la Rochejaquelein, a relative and friend of his, and a dozen Sacred Hearts painted on paper. The letter was very short and contained only this sentence: *I send you, Mademoiselle, a small supply of Sacred Hearts which I have made for you. Please note that anyone relying on this devotion succeeds in all their endeavors.* Word for word, this was what it said; as a matter of fact, the rebels had all attached a Sacred Heart to their clothing; we do not know the whole of it.' (*Memoirs*, first edition, pages 103-4)" lateral wound, by the cross at its summit, and often by these two distinguishing features at once.

The "Sacred Heart" of Father Guignard, of Voultegon (Deux-Sèvres), one of the followers of the Marquis de Lescure, then of La Rochejaquelein, is in dark green cloth with a large heart made of a sort of yellow plush; the wound is represented by three long and parallel "stitches" in red wool (Fig. 1).

Yellow, the color of gold, when bestowed by peasants of the West on an object, is a kind of glorification of this object, gold being the king of metals and its color, in their eyes, the most prized of colors.

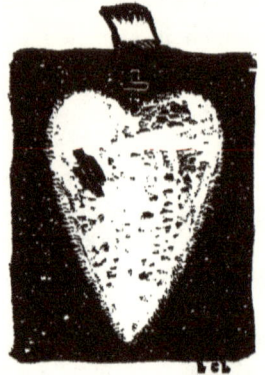 

Fig. 1.—*The Sacred Heart of Guignard de Voultegon, (Deux-Sèvres), unpublished.*

Fig. 2.—*Sacred Heart "preserved" at Jallais (Maine-et-Loire), unpublished.*

A bit of white lace made it possible to hang it on the jacket by a pin or a needle point.

The Archive of the Prefecture of Laval preserves several "scapulars" of the Sacred Heart, taken from the prisoners and the Vendean dead during the expedition beyond the Loire; all but one, to be discussed below, are as simple as Guignard's: a red heart on a black or white cloth, and nothing more.

To the kindness of Dr. G. Fieve, of Jallais (Maine-et-Loire), I owe an unpublished drawing of a "Sacred Heart" preserved in his neighborhood and consisting of a square of white cloth with a red heart surmounted by a brown cross. Around the heart, the inscription "God and the King" affirms the religious and monarchist character of the heroic Vendée revolt (Fig. 2).

The same outcry of the soul can also be read on a "Sacred Heart" from the F. Parenteau collection, today at the Musée Archéologique of Nantes.

In a study published under the title *Médailles Vendéennes*,[4] Parenteau has dedicated a remark to it: "Everybody knows these squares of white or green fabric, whether cloth or silk, bearing, whether painted or embroidered, one or two inflamed hearts which the Vendeans fastened onto their chest."

And he adds that the one he shows an image of is "a piece of brocaded satin having, drawn in red, a heart bleeding and

Fig. 3. — Sacred Heart from Château-Thébaud (Loire Inférieure). Parenteau Collection.

Fig. 4. — The Sacred Heart of Lhuillier de la Chapelle.

aflame, and the legend *God and the King*, written in black ink. It comes from Château-Thébaud," near Vertou (Loire-Inférieure) (Fig. 3).

The "Sacred Heart" of Lhuillier de la Chapelle, an Angevin officer who distinguished himself especially in the uprising of 1815 and took a glorious part in the battle of Rocheservière, consists of a rectangle of white velvet on which was sewn a heart aflame and surmounted by a cross, cut out in one piece with its frame from a kind of red flannel or fleece. On the left of the heart, the wound of the spear is set in black (Fig. 4).

---

4 Fortuné Parenteau, *Médailles Vendéennes*, in *Revue des Provinces de l'Ouest*, 1856-57, offprint, p. 8.

On each side of the cross that carries the heart, two long fleur-de-lys in yellow wool embroidery complete the ensemble which, once more, is an interpretation of the Vendean motto: *God and the King.*

This badge, piously kept by Mademoiselle Marie L'Huillier, at Gesté (Maine-et-Loire), was placed side by side at her home with old Vendean jewels, the white cockade of the old leader, her grandfather, and his personal sealing-stamp with his arms *azure two lions or affrontant and together holding a sword palewise.*

The departmental archives of Mayenne have another rather curious "Sacred Heart" the knowledge of which I owe to the scholarly Vendean historian, H. Baguenier Desormeaux, and which

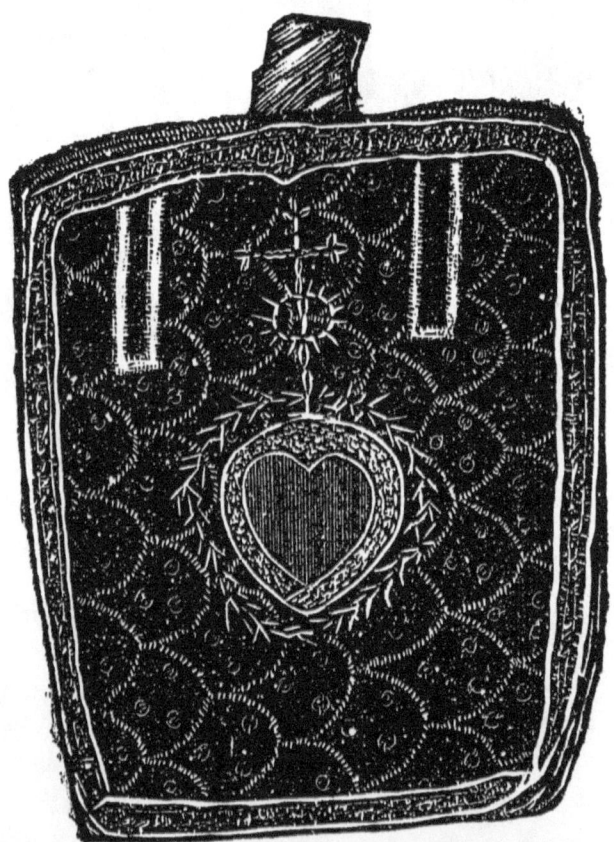

Fig. 5. — *The Sacred Heart of "Silver-Leg" the Chouan at the Departmental Archives of Mayenne, unpublished.*

I reproduce here according to a watercolor that I owe to the great goodness of Mr. Laurain, the learned archivist of the Prefecture of Laval. It is that of the famous Chouan Bergère, nicknamed Silver-Leg, made prisoner on the 5th Frimaire, year VI (Fig. 5).

The material, writes Mr. Laurain, "is a kind of black satin, lined with white silk, on which has been sewn a red woolen heart surrounded by a yellowish edging, which must have once had a golden color. The background is decorated with half-circle netting throughout the length of the object in the form of a mesh strewn with sequins."

I will add that the heart is surrounded by a crown of thorns in stitched yarn surmounted by a cross and a radiant host (?).

The "Sacred Heart" worn by the Vendean general Stofflet deviates, too, from the ordinary type and calls for some iconographic observations (Fig. 6).

Here is what Parenteau wrote in the *Inventory* for his collection:

Fig. 6. — The Pseudo "Sacred Heart" worn by the Vendean general Stofflet.

> A Sacred Heart in white fabric set on black cloth with colored silk embroidery. Within the field Christ on the cross with two Sacred Hearts aflame, embroidered in red silk. Legend: The zeal of the Lord devours you. Above, a white silk ribbon for suspension.
>
> This embroidered heart is the one worn by Stofflet on the day he was arrested by the Republicans. It was given to me by A. Dupuy-Vaillant, Deputy Attorney General at the Poitiers Court of Appeal, who had received it from Mr. Alain Targé, then Attorney General of the aforesaid Court of Appeal. The latter had collected it at Angers in 1847. — Signed: B. Fillon
>
> This note was written by B. Fillon upon giving me the Sacred Heart described above.

All this gives us serious probabilities, if not sure guaranties of authenticity, but the object described demands another explanation: in reality neither of the hearts seen here can be an image of the Savior's heart. In adopting it, Stofflet certainly saw there the hearts of Jesus and Mary, which were indeed embroidered, both together, on a few badges. Stofflet was wrong.

These burning hearts are simply those of the faithful devoured by zeal for Christ Jesus, embroidered above them, on the Cross, whose flank bleeds profusely; they are only the pictorial translation of the motto that accompanies them: *The zeal of the Lord consumes you* and that is why they are consumed by flames.

I believe this image is older than the Vendean uprising, and I would readily suppose for it a Carmelite origin; whether it was made in a Carmel of the region, or came from the monastery Carmes de La Flocellière, adjacent to the region controlled by Stofflet. The motto it bears seems an abbreviation of the one for the same great Order of Carmel: *Zelo zelatus sum pro Domino Deo exercituum*, I have been devoured with zeal for the Lord God of Hosts. Stofflet would not have disavowed it in its full form.

The illustrious House of Charette has treasured the "Sacred Heart" of the great Vendean knight. It is a rectangle of serrated black cloth that carries another smaller rectangle, in white cloth, in the middle of which triumphs a simple red heart surmounted by the cross.

I wanted to reproduce with it the frame that serves as a case for this heroic relic because it serves as a hymn written by the Catholic and Royalist Vendée, with all its blood, to the Sacred Heart from 1792 until recently (Plate 31).

At the top of the frame is the Charette coat of arms: "Argent with lion sable between three canets also sable"; stamped overall with the crown of a marquis and framed by royal flags. On the top and bottom of the frame are monograms for the great leader of 1793, Athanasius de Charette, with the 'A's and 'C's joined at their centers by the Sacred Heart. At the top of the two uprights, the image of the Pontifical Zouave standard at the Battle of Patay, in 1870, with the supplicating inscription: Heart of Jesus, save France! Below are the two glorious Swords, that of Athanasius, who did

Rally-badges, Also Called "Scapulars," with the Image of the Sacred Heart

*Plate 31. — The Sacred Heart of the Vendean
General Athanasius Charette de la Contrie.*

marvelous deeds against the Revolution, and the other, that of the last general of Charette, the magnificent hero of Mentana, Castelfidardo, and Patay. About the Swords is the proud motto of the Charettes: I never give way!

Lower down is the Vendean double heart, which will be discussed later. At the four corners of the frame and on its uprights is the fleur-de-lys of France which was, on the chests of the Vendeans of old, the royal and faithful companion to the heart of Jesus.

And, at the very bottom, in a cartouche set with oak branches, is the inscription: "Sacred Heart and facsimile of the door against which the general Athanase Charette de la Contrie was shot, March 15 [in fact: 26], 1796."

His blood was but one drop in the terrible holocaust of all the people of Vendée, who offered themselves spontaneously to death for the liberating and avenging work, but from this shed blood sprouted first of all religious tolerance and, soon after, freedom.

Fig. 7. — Commemorative cross raised near the château of La Chabotterie, in Saint-Sulpice-le-Verdon (Vendée) at the place where Charette, wounded, was taken prisoner by the Revolutionaries. On its pedestal: "Here the Vendean general François-Athanase Charette de la Contrie was seized by General Travot, on 23 March 1796."

III. THE MARTYRS

Many were those in the West who suffered the glorious death of martyrs for simply wearing or making badges with the image of the heart of Jesus.

Such was, for example, Miss d'Aux, condemned to death in Bas-Poitou by the Revolutionary Committee "for having embroidered Sacred Hearts."

Such was the La Billiais family, father, mother and daughters, arrested in their castle of Saint-Etienne-de-Montluc (Loire-Inferieure). The main charge, which sentenced them to the scaffold, was that the La Billiais ladies were seen embroidering and distributing "Hearts of Jesus." They confessed to it.

In Brittany, the same sentence overtook Victoire de Saint-Luc, then Jean Benard, former chaplain of the Rennes general hospital, who had also distributed "the badge of rebellion."

The report of the arrest of Count Geslin de Villeneuve, arrested at Tillers (Maine-et-Loire) on 2 Nivose, year IV, and condemned to death, informs us that he was a former émigré and that he "was found carrying several signs of royalism, including an emblem in pencil representing a cross on a heart supported by two swords in saltire; two armed men, one with a spear, the other with a club, supported a royal crown above the heart surmounted by the motto: *Vive le Roi* [*Long live the King*]."

The "Sacred Heart" that sentenced Catherine Joussemet to death is part of the Parenteau collection. It seems to have been engraved on wood, printed on paper and painted by hand. Within a green circle and with a red frame, it contains the invocation: *Sacred Heart have mercy on us*.

I only represent here the central part, actual size, according to Parenteau (Fig. 8).

In giving it to the latter, B. Fillon accompanied it with the following words:

"A Vendean heart seized, after the battle of Savenay, from Catherine Joussemet, a former nun of the order of Notre-Dame, my maternal grand-aunt, who had followed the Catholic army beyond the Loire.

Fig. 8. –Central part of the Sacred Heart of Catherine Joussemet de la Longeais.

"Over two hundred hearts, also drawn by her, were found on her. Arraigned for this fact before the Military Commission of Nantes, she was sentenced to death and shot.

"Catherine Joussemet de la Longeais was born at La Roche-sur-Yon; she was fifty-seven years old when she died."

And there is a whole host of holy victims sacrificed for the Image of the Heart of Jesus that the Vendean historian could further name, while saying with the Office of the Martyrs: "Isti sunt Sancti qui pro testamento Dei sua corpora tradiderunt..." Here are the Saints who delivered their bodies for the testament of God and who entered into his glory, dressed in their robes dyed in the blood of the Heart of his Christ!

IV. CONCERNING THE ORIGIN OF THE BADGE CALLED "SCAPULAR OF THE SACRED HEART"

Indisputably, and whatever else may have been written about it, the invention of these squares of cloth bearing the heart of Jesus, intended to be worn ostensibly on one's clothing, is not due to the great piety of Jacques Cathelineau. The "Saint of Anjou" was only heir to an ardent, long-enjoyed worship of the Sacred Heart in the regions of the West, the most indefatigable sower of which was the blessed Louis Grignion de Montfort. On the day of the beatification of this ardent apostle, the illustrious Bishop of Angers, Mgr. Freppel, solemnly proclaimed it, in front of 20,000 Vendeans, at Saint-Laurent-sur-Sèvre, where the remains of this extraordinary stirrer of souls rest. It was through Montfort and his spiritual sons, the Missionaries of Saint-Laurent, that the fertile tide of Christian life-blood flowed over the western countryside throughout the eighteenth century.

That century, even though it was elsewhere a time of moral decadence, was to the contrary in the West, except in the large cities, an era of Christian vivification during which the people of this region, says Mgr. Freppel, "were as if molded by two feelings equally apt to engender heroism: religious faith and fidelity to legitimate power. So when, in a day of hatred and blindness, they came to attack the anointed of the Lord, of all that represented Christ in the State and in the Church, this people shuddered in their groves and at the bottom of its ravines. They arose to defend everything they loved, everything they respected, and the world witnessed a struggle such as it had not seen since the Maccabean era."

And this is what the mystified Barère called, at a meeting of the Convention on October 1, 1793, "the inexplicable Vendée."

For a century then, at the very least, "scapulars" of the Sacred Heart had been in use. At Beaufou, diocese of Luzon, "as early as 1705, a white square cloth with perforated circumference was venerated in the church; at its center was a small heart of red cloth surmounted by a cross. This heart was surrounded by a semblance of the crown of thorns and a few drops of blood flowed from it." "At that time, all the parishioners of Beaufou wore a heart similar to the one in their church on their chests, over their hearts. Later, many people replaced the heart of fabric with a leaden heart. We often find this leaden heart with the bones of the dead."[5]

Shortly thereafter, in 1726, the Missionaries of Saint-Laurent, preaching a mission to Brézé, in the former Loudunois country, today of the diocese of Angers, distributed "small Sacred Hearts" which they combined *"with other Scapulars."*[6] In fact, at the very time of the Revolution, the Sacred Heart on fabric existed in almost every house and this explains how Cathelineau and his first companions at arms, and the five hundred men who joined them the day after they took up arms, were able to wear — immediately — a badge to be found everywhere. And that is why I am convinced that it must also be among the religious objects that covered the peasants who fell in the attack at Bressuire on the 24th of August, 1792, during the first Poitevin uprising.

Thus it was not, as is so often repeated, the vow made by Louis XVI, shortly before the day of August 10th, 1791, on the advice of Fr. Hébert, superior general of the Eudists and his confessor, to consecrate his kingdom and his family to the Divine Heart, which gave rise in the West to the spread of the image of the Sacred Heart.

5 Canon Huet, Letter of October 4, 1921, and the *Chroniques Paroissiales du diocèse de Luçon*, tome VI, p. 531 and following.
6 François-Constant Uzureau, *Origine du culte du Sacré-Cœur en Anjou*, in *Regnabit*, Nov. 1921, Num. 6, p. 450.

Part VII: The Iconography of the Heart of Jesus

V. THE CATHELINEAU COAT OF ARMS

From the time he ascended the restored throne, Louis XVIII turned to the Vendée, and although he could not do for the region all that he would have liked, he insisted on showing his admiration and gratitude.[7]

And one of the first royal acts was to surround the poor family and the name of Jacques Cathelineau with honor.... The hero of Pin-en-Mauges had died of the glorious wound that had struck him down at the battle of Tremblaye, near Cholet, June 29th, 1793; Royal letters gave the son of the heroic peasant a rank of honor in the nobility of the kingdom, as well as the coat of arms of a true knight.

And what a coat of arms!

"*Azure fleur-de-lysed staff in bend, with* flamme *banner argent charged with a Sacred Heart gules supporting a cross of the same,*" the whole accompanied by a motto from the cry of the mortally wounded Jacques Cathelineau: God and King! To summarize: that time's white flag of France charged with the Sacred Heart (Fig. 9).

And this splendid coat of arms of the most noble race of the Counts of Cathelineau will be there for as long as France and History endure.

Fig. 9. — Coat of arms conceded by Louis XVIII to the descendants of Jacques Cathelineau.

Then there is this curious relationship: when, in 1870, coming to the aid of France in distress, the glorious papal Zouave regiment transformed itself into the regiment of Volunteers of the West, under the command of Baron de Charette and Count Henri de Cathelineau, in the shadow of their cloister the hands of the nuns embroidered an oriflamme banner for the new regiment. And this

---

7 Cf. Émile Gabory, Archivist of the Lower Loire, *Les Bourbons et la Vendée*, in *Revue du Bas-Poitou*, year 1921-23, num. 2, p. 149.

new flag, which would become red with the noblest blood of France at the epic battle of Patay, was a white *flamme* bearing the Sacred Heart — the same standard as the Cathelineau coat of arms — with the supplicating invocation: Heart of Jesus, save France!

Louis XVIII died in 1824; and on the 6th of July, 1826, the Duchess of Berry, visiting the Vendée in the name of Charles X, came to kneel with emotion in the humble Pin-en-Mauges cottage, in that poor room where, on March 13, 1793, Jacques Cathelineau had pinned the white cockade to the hats and the Heart of Jesus on the hearts of his twenty-seven first comrades-in-arms (Fig. 10).

It must have been these two badges, placed like this, that inspired a few days later this superb reply by a Vendéen from Maulévrier that one of the Duchess of Berry's officers found short in stature: "In Vendée, Sir, men are measured from head to heart..."

In all its upsurge of heroism and in its sublime testing, the ardent cult of the Heart of Jesus was for the Vendée the great refuge and the great spur to action. We will see that the wearing of the official badge with which we have just dealt was not its only external and material manifestation, but that a whole series of quite local objects sprang from that ardent piety of a people who gave its blood to keep its God, to keep its Kings.

Fig. 10. — Pin-en-Mauges (Maine-et-Loire). The house of Jacques Cathelineau is the one whose door is surmounted by a small cross. According to an old drawing kindly sent by Father Madiot, parish priest of Pin.

VI. ON THE USE OF "SCAPULAR OF THE SACRED HEART" AFTER THE VENDÉE WARS

After the counter-revolutionary wars, even more so than in the eighteenth century, the use of the Heart of Jesus on a cloth remained a beloved emblem in Vendean popular piety.

During the nineteenth century, as still today, it was the badge of Vendean pilgrimage and pilgrims. In many parishes the custom was to place it on the heart of the dying as a preservative against last temptations and so that the heart of the Christian might cease its beating beneath an image of the Savior's own heart. Elsewhere, it was put in a place of honor in houses; I even saw it in the barn of a farm in the parish of Largeasse (Deux-Sèvres) with the penciled inscription: *Mon Dieu protégés nous et nos affere* [*My God protect us and our affairs*]; a naive prayer which the liturgy expresses more learnedly, but no less clearly, in the supplications of the Litany of the Saints.

A special kind of badge was created for home use and put on the market. It displays, on a serrated white fabric, a Sacred Heart printed in red, surrounded by a crown of thorns forming an oval frame, and accompanied by the imperative command: Halt, the Heart of Jesus is here.

Several of these badges were collected on the battlefields of 1870, and some have since been placed in the Paris School of Anthropology's collections, in the amulet section, under the name: "Preservative against bullets"[8] (!!), the organizers not having understood that the inscription, in the thought of its inventor, was not addressed to Prussian or other projectiles, but to the Spirit of Evil!

Although more straightforward and telling with its formula of exorcism, this type of "scapular of the Sacred Heart" should not make us forget the old badge where everyone put a bit of oneself, a bit of one's at times political affections, but especially much of one's trust and faith.

In June 1888, at the triumphant celebrations of the beatification of Father de Montfort, the great promoter of piety towards the

---

[8] Cf. *La Société: l'École et le Laboratoire d'Anthropologie de Paris à l'Exposition universelle de 1889.* — Chap. IV, 308-29.

heart of Jesus in the West at the time of Louis XIV, almost all of the 25,000 faithful who came to Saint-Laurent-sur-Sèvre (Vendée), especially all the former Vendée military, wore the traditional badge.

I have in my possession the one worn on Roman purple by his Eminence the Archbishop of Rennes, Cardinal Place. It is a large rectangle of fine white fabric, with serrated edges, twelve and a half by eleven centimeters; in the middle, an oval of purple velvet with shimmering reflections, bears an unusually protruding golden heart, wounded in red, surmounted by flames embroidered with gold lace and a cross formed of five small gold plates; drops of scarlet silk fall from the heart (Fig. 11).

Fig. 11. — Sacred Heart worn by his Eminence Cardinal Place, Archbishop of Rennes.

Framing the heart is a crown of thorns, in fine gold lace, which follows the contour of the serrated purple oval. It is the most sumptuous badge of the Sacred Heart that I have known, and even if my poor engraving faithfully renders the lines, it is very far indeed from giving any idea of its magnificence.

VII. OTHER ITEMS MARKED WITH THE IMAGE OF THE DIVINE HEART

We have previously seen how the heroic revolt of the western countries, under badges associated with the Sacred Heart of Jesus and the royal cockade, had begun against the persecution by which the Revolution was oppressing France.

Soon after Cathelineau's taking up of arms at Pin-en-Mauges, the whole region that was to form the Vendée military, Poitou, Anjou and the Nantais country, was mobilized. With Cathelineau proclaimed commander-in-chief, d'Elbée, Bonchamp, and Stofflet led the Angevins; the Marquis de Lescure and Henri de la Rochejaquelein, along with Marigny, Baudry d'Asson, Sapinaud, Royrand, Beauvollier, La Ville-Beauge, commanded the Poitevins in the regions of Bressuire and Parthenay; young men from Bocage, from Marais of Lower Poitou and from the Nantais marched with Essarts, Nouhes, Béjarry, the epic knight Charette de la Contrie, and the prince of Talmont.

On May 2nd, 1793, the city of Bressuire was taken; then it was Thouars, Fontenay-le-Comte, Cholet, Saumur, and Chinon.

On October 18th, the "Catholic and Royal Armies" crossed the Loire and were successively at Angers, Laval, and Dol. Against the Vendeans, victorious with local troops, the Revolution sent its best generals at the head of armies who had proven themselves against foreigners. And yet, during the entire time the Terror oppressed France, the Vendée fought day and night, until finally its first great leaders having died in the struggle and setbacks having come, the region accepted the amnesty with religious toleration offered it by the Revolution.

But later when, in 1815, Napoleon, on his return from the island of Elba, made the legitimate king, after the Hundred Days, go back into exile, the Vendée, which had acclaimed the restoration of the throne of Saint Louis, stood once more arms in hand under the orders of Louis de la Rochejaquelein, Suzannet, d'Autichamp and children of the first great leaders.

And these two levies of arms were the most nobly disinterested, the most chivalrous epic that any province of France has ever written with its blood in honor of fidelity to God and the King, God's representative. And these years of heroic struggles, Mgr. Pie declares,[9] were filled "with two hundred seizures and take-overs of cities, seven hundred private skirmishes, seventeen major pitched battles," with the burning of hundreds of villages, and with the frightful holocaust of thousands of combatants and thousands of martyrs.

We have seen that the efficacious piety which supported above all the extraordinary courage of these peasant heroes and the gentlemen whom they themselves placed at their head, was a fervent worship of the wounded heart of the Savior, the heart of the expiatory victim whose image they bore as an ostensible rallying sign on their chest. In addition to this insignia, having become official, the cult of the Sacred Heart was also expressed among themselves by the wearing of a multitude of objects marked in the image of the Divine Heart.

And here are some of those that are left to us:

From the beginning of the Revolution, two years before the military uprising, when religious objects were already no longer manufactured anywhere and no longer sold openly, there clandestinely circulated, in the Vendée, lead medals bearing the Heart of Jesus, with the inscription: *Ego dilexi vos in finem*, I have loved you unto the end, and the date: 1791 (Fig. 12); on the reverse side, the Heart of Mary with words from the Stabat Mater: *Doloris pertransivit gladius*.

Fig. 12. — Medal in lead or tin and silver, 1791.

---

9 Monsignor Pie, funeral prayer for the Marquise de la Rochejaquelein.

Part VII: The Iconography of the Heart of Jesus

A copy of this lead medal was in the Parenteau collection, from Pouzauges, and is now in the Nantes Archaeological Museum; another in silver and tin alloy belonged in 1898 to Brother Fulgent, director of the Congregational School of Châtillon-sur-Sèvre (Deux-Sèvres). I would not be surprised if these medals were cast at Saint-Laurent-sur-Sèvre, the religious center of the Vendée, during the Revolution.

Here is a small Sacred Heart in melted and hammered copper, intended to be worn as a medal, collected near Saint-Amand-sur-Sèvre (Deux-Sèvres). It is thick, but completely flat, and the spear-wound is not depicted (Fig. 13). However, one should not be hesitatant either about its religious character or its date. It reminds one of those small lead hearts that the people of Beaufou substituted, in the late eighteenth century, for the heart of fabric they wore on the back of their jacket as we saw in the previous chapter: this is clearly a peasant's pious trinket as well.

Fig. 13. — Small copper heart; thickness: 2 millimeters.

Here is another medal, which comes from this village of Moncoutant (Deux-Sèvres), where the first armed uprising of the counter-revolutionary Vendée was fomented. One day a Vendean found this token, already nearly two hundred years old; he saw two hearts beneath the royal crown of France, two royal hearts, and the happy thought came to make it an object of devotion by transforming these profane hearts into images of those of Jesus and Mary, and, quite simply with the help of a hammer and a piece of steel, he struck in hollow relief on the right the abbreviation for the Name of Jesus: I. H. S., and on the other the initial M of the name of Mary. A hole drilled in the top of the crown allowed the suspension ring to pass through, and in this way was the medal finished (Fig. 14).

But if we look at the reverse, we see two figures in profile, superimposed in perspective, wearing ruffed collars and crowns on their heads; and the Latin legend that accompanies them tells us that these are the faces of "Louis XIII by the grace of God King of France and Navarre and Anne of Austria-Spain."

And we might well believe that the Vendean who wore this old token of the royal marriage on his chest, perhaps on the eve of giving his life for his God and for the son of his Kings, was certainly quite happy to display his ingenious badge where the

Fig. 14. — Medal in lead or tin and silver, 1791.

two self-same hearts summed up his two heroic fidelities: both Jesus and Mary, and the King and Queen of France!

On this souvenir of the 1615 royal marriage, the two hearts are united by three banners where we read the names of the three theological virtues: *caritas, spes, fides*; and, lower down, a lily (poorly represented) with the two initials: L (Louis) and A (Anne). Below is the name of the engraver: Hans Laufer. — The Laufers were Nuremberg medalists who struck a profusion of medals in honor of the kings of France, Henry IV, Louis XIII and Louis XIV.

I owe to my most distinguished colleague of the Antiquaires de l'Ouest, Max Deloche, the imprint of a counter-revolutionary Vendean seal from his rich collection.

In the center of the oblong dish of this seal, the Bourbon crest is surmounted by a royal crown; all about, two oak and laurel branches accompany it and are united, I was going to say knotted together, by the unambiguous image of the Heart of Jesus, as if to say to the defenders of God and the King that all strength and all victory can only come to them through the Heart of the Almighty Savior (Fig. 15).

Around the seal unfolds the Vendean acclamation: Religion and the King!

The Vendean combatants were not always content to wear the adored image of the Divine Heart on their chest, they sometimes marked their very weapons with it as well; witness this flintlock, a big short and stocky weapon of English manufacture, knowledge of which I owe to Father Courteaud, a priest of Adilly, and which comes from Neuvy-Bouin (Deux-Sèvres).

Fig. 15. — Vendean counter-revolutionary signet from the Deloche collection.

Fig. 16. — Engraving on flintlock gun. Neuvy-Bouin (Deux-Sèvres).

On its stock, the Chouan who used it engraved two hearts with the point of a knife; one, marked with a cross and rent by a wound is undeniably the Heart of Jesus, and the other, surmounted by a clumsily carved fleur-de-lys, the Heart of Mary (Fig. 16).

In depicting them thus, one in the center of the other, the hand which engraved them was able to approximate, by the straightforwardness of its faith, the great theological thesis dear to Father de Montfort: coming to Jesus by passing through Mary — and, practically, the representation in this way of the two hearts one within the other had the advantage of taking up little space on the arched top of the weapon's stock.

In the next chapter, we will see these two hearts of the Virgin and her divine Son, associated in more artistic forms, more heraldic, but not more clearly comprehensible.

As a heart fixed on weaponry, I figure here a copper heart, flat and slightly bevelled on its edges, which was collected by Madame de la Rochebrochard-Tinguy, during repairs to the old castle of Cerizay (Deux-Sèvres), an exact drawing of which Mr. Gobillaud, mayor of Moulins, was good enough to send me (Fig. 17).

Fig. 17. — *Heart-shaped copper plaque coming from the old Cerizay Château (Deux-Sèvres).*

Six points riveted into the copper plate were used to affix it to the leather of a saber baldric. I certainly do not see in this object an image of the Heart of Jesus, I even think it detached from a harness belonging to the revolutionary army, so striking is its resemblance to the heart-shaped "retroussis" [turned-back uniform facings] of Nantes manufacture which bear the inscription: *République française*.[10] But the fact that it was found in the castle of Cerizay occupied by the Vendeans, hidden with a large octagonal medal representing the Annunciation, makes me regard it as a trophy picked up probably on the battlefield by a Vendean who, misunderstanding the origin and the profane character of this heart, will have concealed it for the same reason and with the same feeling of piety as the medal of the Blessed Virgin found with it.

Is this not an instance for recalling that a good and right intention purifies everything, divinizes everything?

---

10 Cf. Parenteau, *Inventaire Archéologique*, p. 99, plate 46, nums. 8 and 9.

Scapular carried by M. Lhuillier de la Chapelle during the Wars of 1793. Penknife engraving by the author (ed.).

CHAPTER TWENTY-SEVEN

The Order of St. Michael of the Chouans

THE GREAT KINDNESS OF COUNT JEAN Villoutreys has enabled me to present here a document, both unpublished and of the very first order, which reveals as certain the existence, hitherto scarcely suspected, of a kind of order or society, somewhat secret perhaps, among the Catholic and Royalist insurgents, the order of Saint Michael of the Chouans (we know that the name of Chouans—a modification of the word "chat-huant" [wood-owl]—was given to the insurgents of the West, in 1793, because they recognized and communicated with each other at night, remotely, imitating certain variations of the hooting of owls).

The curious document from Count Villoutreys is a copy of this order's very diploma: under the royal coat of arms accompanied by the Vendean motto: God and the King, it bears the following text:

BY THE KING OF FRANCE AND NAVARRE

GREETINGS *to you Brothers of the Royal Order of St. Michael, nicknamed* CHOUANS, *supporters of Religion and the Throne.*

WE, Members of the Council, in correspondence with the powerful Concurators, have issued and will issue by this present letter to .... a propagandist patent of the Order of Royalists CHOUANS, in testimony of which we have signed the present letter.

I will multiply your race like the Stars that are in the Firmament, like the grains of sand that are on the seashore.

DONE at the Council on .... the year of grace 179...

Part VII: The Iconography of the Heart of Jesus

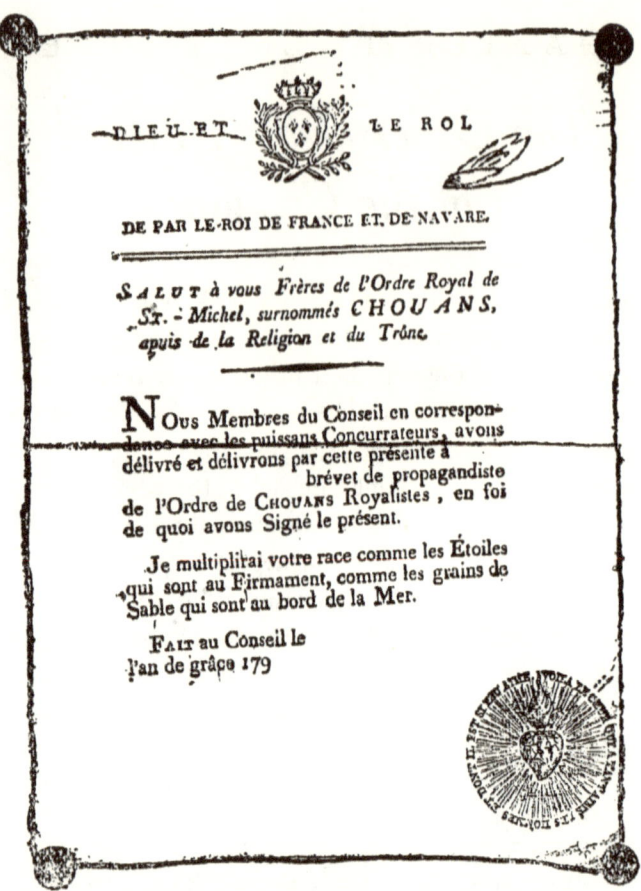

Fig. 1. — *Patent of the order of St. Michael of the Chouans.*

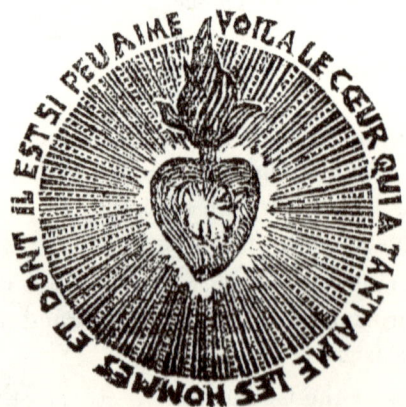

Fig. 2. — *Stamp of the order of St. Michael of the Chouans.*

The Order of St. Michael of the Chouans

And below, as the seal of the Order (Fig. 2), is the heart of Jesus within the flashings of a glory surrounded by these words: This is the heart that has so loved men, and by whom he is so little loved.

This is an abridgement of the very text given by St. Margaret Mary, which is literally: "Behold this heart which has so loved men that it has spared nothing, even to exhausting and consuming itself, in order to testify its love. In return, I receive from the greater part only ingratitude, by their irreverence and sacrilege, and by the coldness and contempt they have for Me in this sacrament of love."[1]

There is no doubt that the creators of the order of Saint Michael of the Chouans knew this text, and the stamp on their diploma, which I reproduce here, remains the most precise and most telling document of the cult of the heart of Jesus from the counter-revolutionary armies of the West.

Thus far we are without any information concerning this organization of Saint Michael, which seems to have been quite mysterious and whose creation, I imagine, may have followed very closely the apparent pacification of the Vendée, about 1795.

Also, I suspect that this order must be connected to the lead and tin shells cast in the Vendée, either in the very last years of the eighteenth century, or during the uprisings of 1815 and the *chouannerie* of 1830. I offer here a reproduction of two different types of these shells. One of them (Fig. 4) represents in my eyes the initial model, and I owe it to Canon Pierre Charbonneau, a former priest of Bressuire. The Sacred Heart alone appears in the center of the shell's concavity.

The other one (Fig. 3) is in the Parenteau collection. This is of the 1830 type; the initial of the Count of Chambord, Henry V of France, serves there as guard — I was going to say custodian — for the heart of Jesus, and all around a banner carries these words: *Our Lady and St. Michael pray for us.*

The invocation to the victorious Archangel is here doubly mentioned, first because he was the official protector of the French Monarchy, and next because the Count of Chambord was born on the feast day of Saint Michael, the 29th of September.

---

[1] Rt. Rev. Émile Bougaud, *The Life of Saint Margaret Mary Alacoque*, trans. A Visitandine of Baltimore (Rockford, IL: Tan Books, 1990), p. 176.

Part VII: The Iconography of the Heart of Jesus

Fig. 3   Fig. 4
Tin and lead shells of Vendean origin.

The mold used to cast this shell comes from the castle of Angebaudière in the municipality of La Gaubretière (Vendée). In 1898 it belonged to the Saint-André family.[2]

The nobility of Poitou, under Louis XV and Louis XVI, included a certain number of knights of the former grand Royal Order of Saint Michael, founded by Louis XI at the illustrious abbey of Mont. I would not be surprised if the Order of St. Michael of the Chouans was organized more or less directly by one of them.

We know that the necklace of the Order founded by Louis XI was formed of intertwined cords and golden shells, and that one of the main insignia of pilgrims to the Abbey of Mont was, from the Middle Ages, the lead shell in the center of which the conquering Archangel, sword raised and wings open, ready for glorious flight, tramples on the vanquished Dragon.

The fact that our Vendée shells bear the Sacred Heart instead of the archangelic image is not enough to destroy the hypothesis of a relationship between them and the order of Saint Michael of the Chouans, since the diploma of this society that we owe to the Count of Villoutreys itself bears, as a seal, the heart of Jesus instead of the seal of the old order of Louis XI where the fight of the Archangel and Satan were depicted.

2 Parenteau, *Inventaire Archéologique*, p. 94, plate 46, num. 10.

The Order of St. Michael of the Chouans

*Vendean badge from Cholet. The four drops
that fall from the heart are each made of wool
stitching: two of red wool (to represent the blood);
two of white wool (to represent the water).
Penknife engraving by the author (ed.).*

CHAPTER TWENTY-EIGHT

Old Vendean Jewelry

INSTEAD OF BEING ALMOST ALWAYS INSIGnificant like those in the trade today, jewels of old often had a meaning that their forms and decoration manifested at first glance, or, at the very least, a soul able to be divined by perceptive eyes.

And if this is absolutely true for ancient civil jewelry, it can be more rightly said of religious jewelry; for, although our ancestors often used them as pious talismans, although they were in their eyes like prayers that art had had the gift of materializing, of rendering motionless in the beauty of the lines, they also often bore

them as outward manifestations of faith, piety, spiritual affections, or the hopes of their souls. Clearly, this was, in the highest degree, the character of the quite crude, quite rough, or quite delightfully naive jewels that were created during the counter-revolutionary wars in our western provinces.

We have already seen that the greater number of these pious objects affirmed and glorified at the same time an indomitable attachment to God and the legitimate king of France. They were dynamic professions of faith, eloquent declarations.

Because the religious persecution, with which the Revolution from its very beginnings battered France, had impelled the Vendée to produce, two years before the military uprising, lead medals and other paltry jewels in honor of the Sacred Heart, we can without hesitation conclude that all the older local jewels, representing the same divine image, were also worn with fervor during this frightful torment that a whole people proudly braved.

I. THE POITEVIN HEART, DATE AND VARIOUS KINDS

Now, for at least two centuries, Poitou was in possession of a local gem, unique within the national jewel-case of France's provinces; this is the single or double Poitevin heart, known today under the faulty name of "Vendean heart." I say *faulty* because this jewel is older than the creation of the geographical word "Vendée," and on the other hand it was formerly worn as much in the diocese of Poitiers as in the current territory of Luzon.

This jewel is essentially composed, for the simple Poitevin heart, of a heart formed by a flat and narrow metal strip in the shape of a heart, leaving a hollow space in the center. Behind, a hinged pin, the point of which catches on a hook, was used to fasten it either to a garment or hat.

In double Poitevin hearts, two hearts of the same shape as the simple heart blend the curves of their lines harmoniously while intermingling.

Generally the jewel is surmounted by a crown or undulated headband dominated by the cross.

Before the Revolution, these hearts were usually made of silver, sometimes of copper, exceptionally of gold. Their surface is almost always decorated with a pattern of etched broken lines.

Fig. 1. — Poitvin heart on the bezel of a copper ring.

The earliest type of Poitevin heart I know is deeply engraved on the bezel of a massive copper ring at the Musée des Antiquaires de l'Ouest in Poitiers and of local provenance (Fig. 1). I studied this ring with the learned archaeologist and sigillographer Max Deloche, and we believe it to be at least from the seventeenth century.

I assign a great double heart in the collection of Count Raoul de Rochebrune to the end of Louis XIV's reign or the first part of Louis XV's (Fig. 2). The crown that surmounts it is decorated with seven pearls, each bearing a starry ornamentation. By its extraordinarily arched shape, this crown validates my chronological attribution because it is found in the lapidary heraldry of the same period in Poitou. One might say it is notably copied on the crown that surmounts the shield of Pierre de Mondion in the church of Chasseignes, near Loudun (Vienne), in 1733.

Fig. 2. — *Double heart decorated with seven pearls.*

We should immediately say that, on the subject of the crowns that surmount the old Poitevin hearts, they almost never had the

Fig. 3. — *Ancient Poitevin heart.*   Fig. 4. — *Ancient heart (Deux-Sèvres).*   Fig. 5. — *Ancient heart (Deux-Sèvres).*

same number of pearls as the noble crowns of count and viscount which, in French heraldry, bear nine and five respectively; the crowns of Poitevin hearts generally have seven or six and, exceptionally, three florets (Figs. 1 and 3).

When the heart bears a pearlless crown, the undulations are of no set number and can vary from three to seven: here are two ancient hearts from Deux-Sèvres (Figs. 4 and 5) that have beheld that heroic era. The eighteenth century can also lay claim to a charming brooch composed of a circle of silver decorated by three small double hearts, crowned like the large ones (Fig. 6).

This same period also knew a type of simple, contorted, and pointed heart, crossed by a horizontal or oblique arrow. It was worn on the ribbon of a man's hat.

In an article entitled "The Vendean Heart," published in 1904 in the *Revue du Bas-Poitou*, Baudouin and Lacouloumère have thus described the Poitevin heart that "the famous Vendean leader La Rochejaquelein" wore on his hat. "This oval heart, with its tip slanting to the right, possessed a crown with nine peaks or pearls, which was surmounted by an ornamented Latin cross; moreover, it bore an almost horizontal arrow with a left-pointing tip."[1]

Fig. 6. — Brooch with three double hearts.

Count Raoul Rochebrune has in his rich collection, not this historical heart, but the one borne, also on his hat, by the nephew of the great La Rochejaquelein, General Marquis Louis de La Rochejaquelein, killed on the seacoast in the Mattes battle during the second Vendée uprising in 1815 (Fig. 7). It is the same jewel that was worn by his uncle, according to the above authors, with the difference that, on the 1815 jewel, the crown is surmounted not by pearls but by flames, while the arrow is quite oblique instead of horizontal, and the heart bears the Vendean acclamation: God and the King! written in that wavering and fanciful Gothic style from the beginnings of Romanticism.

Fig. 7. — Jewel with a heart crossed by an arrow.

I also deem the old hearts whose center is adorned with a fleur-de-lys to be post-Revolutionary. It is of the type issued under Louis XVIII and Charles X, which was very much in vogue during the Chouannerie of 1830.

---

[1] Tome XVI, 15th year, 1904, pp. 389-90.

Old Vendean Jewelry

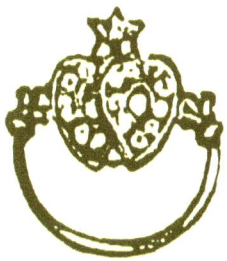

Fig. 8. — Poitevin ring, 19th century.

I think a magnificent ring of Poitevin manufacture, belonging to Madame Lartigue of Loudun (Fig. 8), should likewise be assigned to the first quarter of the nineteenth century, or else more surely perhaps to the reign of Louis XVI. On a gold setting, its double Poitevin heart is decorated with a bright diamond sash that goes along its entire periphery. At the center of the heart the coloring is visible in the almost mauve reflections of a ruby, and the traditional crown is replaced here by a goldsmith motif enhanced by three small diamonds. The gold ring is attached to the hearts by a floret, frequently used by the Poitou goldsmiths of old.

Carried far from its origins by happenstances that will remain obscure, this charming and sumptuous jewel was found, about 1857, on the island of Cuba.

Modern industry has resumed the manufacture of the Poitevin heart, an industry that has too often adorned this heart's center with various motifs: crucifixes, flecks of ermine, stars, deplorably misshapen fleur-de-lys, flames, etc. Many of these creations are regrettable alterations of the secular type, but rising above them all are the delightful productions from the workshop of Gérard Levrier, of Niort, who has attempted to bring popular taste back to the traditional jewels of the West. The double Poitevin heart opposite (Fig. 9) is but the strict facsimile of an authentic old heart on which the lily of the Restoration had been added. There is something else in Monsieur Levrier's artistic enterprise besides mercantilism.

Fig. 9. — Double Poitevin heart with fleur-de-lys.

II. RELIGIOUS MEANING OF THE POITEVIN HEART

Thus, Poitou has then a typical ancestral gem, with very particular features, very heraldic in form, and which became traditional only because it had a profound meaning.

Those who view things superficially see a Poitou double heart only as an emblem of conjugal love, even when they do not know what plausible meaning to assign to the single heart. Yet the single heart has clearly sprung from the same idea that gave rise to the double one.

In the article quoted above, Baudouin and Lacouloumère recognize, however, that Poitevin hearts are the product of "an unknown influence, probably religious and of foreign origin, perhaps Spanish." I absolutely contest the validity of this hypothesis because Poitevin hearts are not restricted to the seacoast where, in fact, a column of Spanish troops had settled prior to the second half of the seventeenth century: the area of discovery of the oldest of these jewels involves the regions of Bressuire, Parthenay, and Niort much more than coastal Vendée; some — the oldest but rare — even come from around Thouars, Loudun, and Poitiers. In the nineteenth century their manufacturing centers were Niort, Bressuire, and Les Sables d'Olonne.

As for the real and primary meaning of the Poitevin heart, I believe I am absolutely right in designating the simple heart as one of the most hieratic, the most stylized, the most heraldic figures of the heart of Jesus, and the double heart as that of the combined hearts of Jesus and Mary.

I find a clear confirmation, it seems to me, of this interpretation in the composition of a mold from Poitou engraved with care on "island wood,"[2] a wood used, in 1710, at Migné near Poitiers, in the manufacture of melted wax objects "by Sir François Courbe, master chandler" (Fig. 10).

This mold, which belongs to Mr. Houdaille, the notary, was published by my learned colleague of the Société des Antiquaires de l'Ouest, Émile Ginot, who has enabled me to reproduce the imprint here.

[2] A general term for a variety of tropical woods. — *Trans.*

Fig. 10. — Mold from a Poitou wax-works, engraved on wood, 1710.

The central motif of this mold reproduces exactly the design of a double Poitevin heart, minus the two interior segments that were elided to make room for two monograms of an early form: IHS, *Ihesus*, and MRA, *Maria*. By amplification, each of the two hearts is again designated, that of Jesus by the sun and that of Mary by the moon, old symbols whose meaning leaves no room here for equivocation.

Beneath the Sacred Hearts is a heart of a believer set on fire by the ardor of his piety.

Part VII: The Iconography of the Heart of Jesus

The meaning of the single Poitevin heart flows naturally from the one revealed by the wax mold for the double heart: it can only be the image of the heart of Jesus, alone.

I will add this comparison: In the seventeenth and eighteenth centuries, the nuns of the monastery of the Loudun Visitation actively engaged in the manufacture of small objects of piety, including miniatures painted in the center of vellum leaves with finely cut openwork.

A large number of these images have been preserved in the region, and the Loudun expert archaeologist Mgr Barbier de Montault has given a lot of 315 to the Museum of Poitiers. About sixty represent either the divine heart or the hearts of the pious faithful, and some of these small mystical compositions show us quite explicitly the heart of Jesus surmounted by a more or less regular crown of a count or viscount; this is the theme of the single Poitevin heart. How could the meaning not be the same?

So it is really to the heart of Jesus that our ancestors wanted to pay homage by the most noble and most characteristic of their jewelry, because it is the noblest part of the body of God made Man, and the material source of the blood he shed for the salvation of the world.

III. A PROFANE POITEVIN HEART?

Simply for the record, I would like to compare here the traditional and catholic Poitevin heart with a type of quite rare, more sober, more unadorned heart. The one I am depicting here comes from Ardin (Deux-Sèvres). Its only ornamentation is a slight relief on its edges (Fig. 11). Baudouin and Lacouloumère have published one that does not even have this slight decoration.

I do not think I am mistaken in attributing these cold and severe

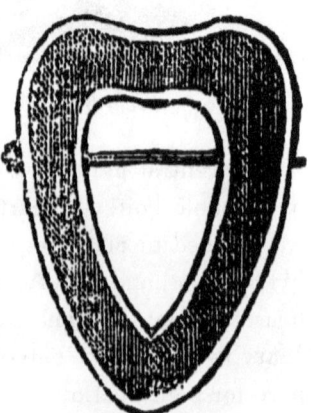

Fig. 11. — A profane Poitevin heart.

jewels to the Protestant groups of Poitou and regarding them as from the seventeenth century.

In another of his studies (which I do not have at hand) Baudouin states that the Protestants of Bas-Poitou had adopted the *Heart* as a rallying sign at the end of the religious wars of the sixteenth century. Even today, at the Protestant cemetery of Pouzauges (Vendée), most of the tombs are surmounted by a small low stone pedestal from which a long iron rod issues, on the top of which a large flat heart bears the epitaph of the deceased. I did not encounter this particular feature in other Protestant cemeteries of Poitou.

It would be interesting to know if the Reformed people of the past attached a religious idea to their emblematic hearts, and which one.

IV. POPULAR RINGS WITH THE IMAGE OF THE SACRED HEART

The museums and collections of Poitou, Anjou, and Nantais contain enough eighteenth-century rings adorned with the image of the hearts of Jesus and Mary that we can be assured that these popular jewels, like the Poitevin hearts, were favored by the combatants of the Vendée Militaire.

One model especially seems to have been quite common in the West. This is the so-called "Holy Family" ring, on the bezel of which three hearts, engraved in relief or hollow relief, appear in various combinations. I know several of them and reproduce here one of those in Count Raoul de Rochebrune's collection (Fig. 12).

Fig. 12. — Ring with the image of the Sacred Heart.

These rings might well be, as well as rings of the same kind that are their contemporaries, the reflection of one of the favorite apostolates of the Sulpicians who, at this same time, brought into vogue a pious monogram, hitherto unusual, which combines the three initials of the names of Jesus, Mary, and Joseph.

Moreover, there was an iconographic theme then in favor of representing, as on the altarpiece in the chapel of the Beaugé hospital for example, "the Trinity on Earth" in parallel with "the Trinity in Heaven." And Mgr. Barbier de Montault,[3] who pointed out this practice, noted that, on numerous paintings of that time representing the Holy Family, painters never failed to irradiate the sky above it. The idea of this emblem of glory seems not to have been forgotten on the pretty ring of Mr. de Rochebrune. It likewise appears around the trinitarian triangle placed above the hearts of Jesus, Mary, and Joseph on the eighteenth-century seal of the Saint-Jean d'Angely Benedictines.

Fig. 13. — *Ring with two Sacred Hearts.*

Max Deloche conveyed to me another ring from his collection, of the same period as the preceding one, and of Vendean origin. It bears a large arched oval on the outside of which are the two Sacred Hearts, oddly shaped, surrounded by the inscription: To the glory of the hearts of Jesus and M. (Fig. 13).

The cult of the heart of Jesus entering by half or as a third into the decorative composition of these rings, it seemed that a description of them should be given here.

V. THE HEART OF JESUS AND THE JEWELS OF THE LAST VENDÉE UPRISINGS

The second call to arms of the Vendée Militaire, against Napoleon returned from the island of Elba, did not last long, since the new exile of King Louis XVIII was this time only a hundred days,

---

3 *Traité d'iconographie chrétienne*, tome 2, p. 126.

from March 20 to June 20, 1815. Shortly after his return, some new jewels were distributed in the West, jewels that glorified the great and double cause served by the Vendée since 1793, that of God and King.

On some of these jewels the religious character is manifested by the image of the heart of Jesus. This is the case for this very pretty small silver cross, originating in the Cholet region, the ends of which blossom in fleurs-de-lys (Fig. 14).

The Chouannerie of 1832 also had its flowering of religious-political jewels, manufactured, I believe, in England.

What this movement was is known: In 1826, in the name of King Charles X, the Duchess of Berry paid a marvelous triumphal visit to the Vendée. Four years later, overthrown by his cousin Louis-Philippe d'Orléans, Charles X abdicated in favor of the young Henry of France, Duke of Bordeaux and Earl of Chambord, son of the late Duke and Duchess of Berry, and took with him the path of exile.

Fig. 14. — Small silver cross.

Two years later, the young prince's mother remembered the reception of Vendeans and, in spite of the decree of banishment that had struck her along with her son, braving all the dangers with true knightly daring, she went to the Vendée to militarily organize the defense of the legitimate rights of the young Henry V.

There were, most certainly, nobles and peasants warmly devoted to the princess. However, there were isolated groups of insurgents who organized, but no army; there were shots fired through the hedges on the Orleanist soldiers, but no battles.

The Vendée looked upon Louis Philippe as a usurper, and he was; but he was not a tyrant. His troops in the Vendée were opposed to the ventures of the Legitimists, but, outside of that, did not persecute priests, nobles, or peasants who remained faithful to the fallen king. The knightly enterprise of the Duchess of Berry could not succeed.

Soon hounded on all sides, hiding under the name of "Petit-Pierre," the princess wanted to join her son in exile and had clandestinely already arrived at Nantes so as to go, from there, to sea. It was in this city that she was betrayed and handed over for a price by Deutz. She was immediately shut up in the citadel of Blaye.

Connected to these insurrectionary disturbances of 1832 are the silver pendants made with an image of the heart of Jesus supported by a small chain and surmounted by a crown of flames and a cross; on the heart itself is an inscription engraved at its tip: GOD AND THE KING, HENRY V OR DEATH, or some other acclamation of the same inspiration (Fig. 15). Underneath hangs a small medal with the effigy of the young pretender. De Rochebrune's collection contains a very fine specimen of this jewel.

Until his death, the Count of Chambord retained the fidelity of large numbers throughout the West. I have seen or collected in various places of the old Vendée Militaire a considerable variety of medals or small jewels struck in his honor. On some, the hearts of Jesus and Mary evoke the great Vendean devotion. One medal, for example, bears on one side the royal numeral surrounded by four crowns and, on the other, the heart of Jesus with the year 1792, date of the vow to the Sacred Heart of Louis XVI while in the tower of the Temple, next the heart of Mary over the year 1636 in which, on August 15, the King of France instituted the votive ceremony which still bears the name "Procession of the Vow of Louis XIII."

Fig. 15. — *Silver pendant with an effigy of the Heart of Jesus.*

This series of relatively recent objects could be further lengthened, but I end the series with a medal common in the Vendée, the meaning of which is open to discussion. On one side is the effigy of the Count of Chambord; on the other, a superimposed anchor, heart, and cross symbolize respectively Hope, Charity, and

Faith (Fig. 16). This interpretation is all the more certain because other medals of the same prince designate these same theological virtues by their written names, but do not represent them with the emblems of anchor, heart, and cross.

It is therefore quite likely wrong to have wanted to see on the medal that concerns us the image of the heart of Jesus figured as the only hope of the royalist party. At the very least, it must be said that if this idea was implied, it was certainly not expressed explicitly.

Fig. 16. — Medal with an anchor, heart and cross superimposed.

Badge of the Marquis de Razilly, a Le Mans chouan. Penknife engraving by the author (ed.).

CHAPTER TWENTY-NINE

The "Cross of Father de Montfort"

I. FATHER DE MONTFORT

IN EARLIER CHAPTERS, I REPRODUCED A large number of iconographic artifacts related to Poitevin devotion to the heart of Jesus, including objects connected to the great religious and royalist insurrection of the Vendée against the Revolution.

And, in several passages of my text, I spoke of the distant, but very real and great part, which was, among the efficient causes of the heroic revolt, that of the activity, outlasting himself, of the Blessed de Montfort.

This extraordinary missionary, a strangely original man, the saint that was Louis Grignion de la Bachellerie, the so-called "Father de Montfort," evangelized by himself from 1700 to 1716 the dioceses of Poitiers, Luzon, la Rochelle, Angers, and Nantes. During these apostolic labors, he formed the first nucleus of the congregation of the Missionaries of the Society of Mary who continued, especially in the same field of activity, the work of their founder.

The populations of the West were thus, at the time of the Revolution, as if "kneaded" with the teachings and the Christian spirit cast in such an abundant sowing by Montfort and his heirs over three of their generations. And, under the scorching breath of persecution, these seeds sprang up to produce a magnificent flowering. And one sees the soul of a country people, the simplest of France, rouse itself to take on great responsibilities, rise to a height of supernatural feeling, material disinterestedness, and an unequaled abnegation of earthly life.

All the historical evidence is there to proclaim that this outburst of heroism first manifested itself and reached its peak in the countries that today form the northwestern Vendée, the northeast of Deux-Sèvres, the southwest of Maine-et-Loire, the southeast of Loire-Inferieure. That is, in the area that forms an immediate circle around, as a central point, the village of Saint-Laurent-sur-Sèvre, where Louis Grignion de Montfort died, where we find his now glorified tomb and the mother-houses of the religious families he founded.

II. FATHER DE MONTFORT'S DEVOTION TO THE HEART OF JESUS

Father A. David, who knew Montfort's soul so well, has marvelously shown us the large share that the worship of the heart of Jesus held in the personal piety and the apostolate of the powerful missionary.[1]

This apostolate was exercised on the crowds by the most diverse means, in the first rank of which we must place, on the same level as his sermons, the hymns he composed and had sung to the crowds, the great Calvaries he erected at the end of his missions, as well as the crucifixes and crosses he distributed as souvenirs to the faithful.

Montfort, in his songs, knew how to direct the attention and prayer of souls to the heart of Jesus as towards that point where everything begins and ends that can go from Christ to man, and from man to his Savior. These canticles have come down to us because they were written, and printed at an early date; the Calvaries, raised in the open air, have deteriorated under the action of time and weather, and the few descriptions that remain of some of them are not sufficiently detailed for us to know what part the Sacred Heart would have had in their ornamentation. By contrast, in rather numerous Christian families of the regions he evangelized, there are still preserved, under the name of "Crucifix of Father Montfort," crosses that would have been distributed by him during his preaching.

I know of no old descriptive text about these crucifixes—which does not mean that there is none! But all the historians of the

---

[1] A. David, *Le Bx Louis Marie Grignion de Montfort, chantre du Sacré-Cœur,* in *Regnabit,* April and May 1923, pp. 453-64.

blessed[2] tell us that the distributions of these pious objects entered into his apostolic practices. Moreover, at the very beginning of his work, when, prostrate at his feet, he received from Pope Clement XI the title of Apostolic Missionary, he asked the Pope for, and at once obtained, the Indulgence of a Good Death for the ivory crucifix to be used in his sermons. At the same time, probably with the same privilege for them, he asked for the power to distribute, at the end of each mission and to whomever of the faithful had attended thirty-three sermons, small paper or cloth crosses bearing the names of Jesus and Mary.[3]

It is possible that during his apostolate Father Montfort replaced these fragile crosses with some more durable than those attributed to him by tradition.

These last are, to my knowledge, of two kinds:

1. — Large wooden crosses adorned with a Christ and various subjects nailed to the cross.

2. — Small copper crosses cast in one piece.

III. THE WOODEN CRUCIFIXES

In his *Revue d'Archéologie Poitevine* (August 1898, p. 240), Mgr. Barbier de Montault exhibited the entire image of one of these wooden crucifixes collected in Doué, in Maine-et-Loire, by his sister. "Objects of this kind," the learned prelate writes, "pass in Poitou — as in Anjou — for having been distributed to the faithful, during his very popular preaching, by the Blessed Louis Grignion de Montfort, founder of the Daughters of Wisdom at Saint-Laurent-sur-Sèvre, where his tomb is venerated."

This cross, which is of blackened wood, measures 34 centimeters in height and rises on a flight of steps; it is covered with tin subjects independent of each other and nailed to the wood of the cross. They represent, around the body of Jesus crucified in the center, the pillar of the scourging, the rooster of Saint Peter,

---

[2] Beatified by Leo XIII on January 22, 1888; canonized by Pius XII on July 20, 1947. — *Trans.*

[3] Cf. Charles Pauvert, *Vie du vénérable L. M. Grignion de Montfort* (Poitiers: Oudin, 1876), p. 202.

the symbolic and legendary death's-head, the sponge and spear, the pincers, the nails and hammer, the sword of St. Peter that cut off the ear of Malchus, the crown of thorns, and the titulus of the cross. A cabled tin wire follows the contours of the cross, whose ends are adorned with trilobed florets.

The Sacred Heart is absent from the ornamentation of this cross.

It is also the same for the ornamentation on another crucifix of the same kind owned, in 1898, by a priest of Varennes (Vienne) to which is attached the same traditional origin, and that Mgr. Barbier describes at the same time as that of its sibling.

But it is not the same for several others:

One of them was shown to me in 1917[4] by Father Davin, the priest of Sigournais (Vendée) who had collected it in his parish.

Above the crucified Christ, the Sacred Heart, in tin, applied to the upper branch of the cross, occupies its full height; as a divine proclamation of supreme love, it dominates the standard of human royalty: INRI, *Jesus of Nazareth, King of the Jews.*

Fig. 1. — *Sigournais (Vendée).*

The wound of this heart is strongly accentuated and — by a singularity that alone persuaded me, when shown the Sigournais cross, to make an exact drawing of it (Fig. 1) — the spear completely traverses the heart and comes out behind. Surely, the tinsmith did not think that the heart of the Savior was thus truly, dare I say, "skewered" by the legionnaire's spear. But perhaps this was done to make the weapon and wound more apparent to the eyes of the simple, or perhaps only from mere slip of the hand that

4 On the occasion of an article I published at that time in the *Revue du Bas-Poitou* (1917, 3rd issue) on *Anciens emblèmes bas-poitevins du Sacré-Cœur.*

cut out the stone mold into which the tin was to be poured; and so the artisan, having prolonged more than was appropriate, even onto the surface of the already carved-out heart, the groove that would, at the pouring, show the shaft of the spear in relief, did not want to break its mold and to take the trouble to cut a new one.

On the Sigournais cross, as around Mgr Barbier's cross, a tin thread decorates the edges of the wood and ends at the extremities in trilobed florets. The hammer, pincers, and bundle of rods were still on what was left of the cross in 1917. The other detached subjects were lost, and the cross itself, whose base was already broken, was no more than a fragile remnant.

Another crucifix, in good condition, belongs to my excellent and distinguished friend, René Vallette, director of the *Revue du Bas-Poitou*, who collected it in Fontenay-le-Comte, his native town.

Like the ones just mentioned, Fontenay's crucifix is composed of a black wooden cross on a stoop and decorated with tin subjects: at mid-height is Jesus nailed to the cross and, at his feet, the Virgin Mary stands in accordance with the text of the Office of her Sorrows:

> "*Stabat Mater dolorosa...*"
> "The grieving Mother stood weeping beside
> the cross where her Son was hanging"!

On the rest of the Fontenay cross are also fixed the skull, the ewer of Pilate, the rooster of St. Peter and, beneath the I N R I titulus of the cross, above the head of the Crucified and right at the intersecting arms of the sacred wood, a broad crown of thorns surrounds the inflamed and wounded heart.

A second crown of thorns, unfortunately half-erased today but still quite visible, surrounds the heart itself above the wound (Fig. 2). I do not understand why the image of the thorny diadem was repeated in this way.

Fig. 2. — Fontenay-le-Comte (Vendée).

Three large fleur-de-lys adorn the ends of this crucifix, which thus combines the emblem of the heraldry of France with the images of the three great devotions of Montfort: Jesus crucified, the wounded heart, and the Virgin Mary. This is the symbol of all that the Vendée, eighty years later, will defend with all its strength, all its possessions, all its blood.

On one of the pieces of tin, at the casting itself, the date of the Fontenay crucifix was marked: 1716. It was on the 18th day of April of that year that Louis Grignion de Montfort delivered up his ardent soul to God.

IV. THE CROSSES OF FATHER DE MONTFORT

The crosses of the second of these two categories indicated above, also known as "the Cross of Father de Montfort" in the western countryside, are small in size and their height varies between five and ten centimeters. They are copper or bronze and cast in one piece. Of those that I have had in my hands, the center is occupied either by the wounded heart or by the monogram of the name of Jesus, IHS, surrounded by a glory; the instruments of the Passion are distributed differently on the cross itself: some have a loop at their apex, others are raised on two or three small steps that make them stand up in a rather insecure equilibrium; but these steps clearly belong with the crucifixes described above.

One of them, which bears the Sacred Heart, was formerly shown to me by Madame Plumant, of Saint-Amand-sur-Sèvre (Deux-Sèvres), who owned and dwelt on the very site of the house where Father de Montfort lived during the long and fruitful mission he preached in this excellent parish. It is one of those crucifixes which, with the greatest likelihood, could justify the tradition of a link of origin connecting it to the holy missionary. I regret today that I did not draw it when it was easy to do so.

I offer here the reproduction of another cross, almost completely similar to that of Saint-Amand-sur-Sèvre, but smaller, it seems to me. It is situated in one of the display cases of the Musée des Augustins owned by the Société des Antiquaires de l'Ouest at Poitiers (Fig. 3).

Fig. 3. — Musée des Augustins at Poitiers.

The image spares me from giving any description here, but I emphasize the great similarity that exists between the ornamentation of this object and that of the pectoral cross given by the Pope to Mgr. De Belsunce, a cross made known by Father Buron in a very interesting historical study he devoted to the illustrious bishop of Marseilles in the former journal *Regnabit*.[5]

By this precious jewel of a prelate contemporary to Father de Montfort, we see that the crosses with which we are concerned here were of a type relatively common in their time; but this type was not the only one then in common use, and for the name of "Cross of Father de Montfort" to be attached exclusively in the West to these crosses, to these crucifixes adorned with evocative images of the sufferings of the Savior in his Passion, this type must have been favored by the powerful apostle. I will

5   Lucien Buron, *Monseigneur de Belsunce*, April, pp. 397-417 and May, pp. 478-82.

add and stress that for popular opinion, still vibrant after two hundred and seven years in the four neighboring dioceses evangelized by Montfort, to attach his name to these crosses, there must indeed have been, at the source of this tradition, an ample share of truth that would only be superseded by the attributing of similar objects actually distributed by the holy missionary's initial successors.

And if, more precisely than other objects of the same kind, these crosses were kept with the memory of the great missionary, this is, Mgr. Barbier states, because Montfort had blessed them and had attached to them the Indulgence of the Good Death, a precious favor he held from the Pope and for which the rural clergy did not have the same privilege at that time. This spiritual advantage had made these objects the quintessential family crucifix, the one utilized at the most solemn hours of existence and especially at the awe-inspiring hour of death.

That is why I have never touched these venerable objects without great respect, thinking of those Christian hearts whose final breath was exhaled on the very image of the Savior's heart and wounds, in the union of their dying lips with the assured pledge of salvation that the Church thus appointed for the last agony and the total hope of her children:

> "*Cor Jesu, pax et reconciliatio nostra,*
> *Cor Jesu, spes in Te morientium.*"
> "Heart of Jesus, our peace and reconciliation,
> Heart of Jesus, the hope of those who die in You!"

I will stop here this comprehensive study on the iconography of the heart of Jesus in lands of the West in rebellion against the Revolution.

I have told what trials, what terrible sufferings, what real disasters this uprising of a whole people, for the defense of the most sacred rights, drew on themselves and their countryside, and how the ardent worship of the divine heart was for these so simple and so great heroes a most powerful driving force and supreme consolation.

Old scapulars of fighters; old jewelry melted or forged in the secrecy of hamlets; old Poitevin hearts of the elderly, made sacred in torment by the heroism and blood of their sons; rings or medals in the image of the adored heart where fidelity to the king unites with fidelity to God; poor and holy relics of a Faith that would brook neither capitulation nor compromise, these are the jewels from the epic jewel-case of the Poitevin, Angevin and Nantaise Vendée.

And does not this array suffuse a deeply penetrating perfume of sacred poetry and heroism? Even though some of these witnesses to a struggle incomparable in its beauty are industrial products — and many of lofty inspiration — most of them remain creations of individual and spontaneous feelings. And together they sing, it seems to me, as well as any hymn composed of words, the virtues of this race that was able to translate in its own way, with the superabundantly shed blood of its own people, the word of the Maccabees: it is better for us to die in our simplicity than to abandon the Law of our God and the cause of our King.

EIGHTH PART

Diverse Representations

RELATING TO OR FOREIGN TO THE CULT OF THE HEART OF JESUS

CHAPTER THIRTY

Representations Relating to the Worship of the Sacred Heart

I. LOVE-RINGS OF POITOU

FIRST WE HAVE POITEVIN RINGS WHOSE meaning is but barely understood. Was their quite particular type created in this same Poitou that had conceived the noble and beautiful jewel called the "Poitevin heart"? I think so, because they are—and by far—more numerous than in the other neighboring provinces.

The ones I depict here represent the three main known varieties. The first is a woman's ring adorned with an L and a heart; it is in low-karat gold, "pauper's gold," as our forefathers would have said in their frank language. The second is a large silver man's ring of the same ornamental type as the first. The third, also in silver, for man or woman, has a heart in the widening out of a V (Fig. 1).

Fig. 1. — Love-Rings of Poitou, 17th century.

These jewels are absolutely foreign to any religious idea, but they remain one of the most dignified and graceful emblems of human love.

The rebuses engraved on them must be interpreted as follows:

For the ring for feminine use, the heart placed in the letter L meant: *My heart in him.* On the man's ring, it meant: *My heart in her*; and the one who offered the third meant in presenting it: *My heart is in you.*

Is this not the echo, very nicely naive, of the old Poitevin song whose refrain said:

> "*J'ay revê qu'il estoit oiseau*
> *Et que mon coeur estoit sa cage*"
> "I dreamed he was a bird
> and that my heart was his cage."

These three rings, which belong to me, are of the seventeenth century. We know of them from the end of the fifteenth and the end of the eighteenth. On the most recent as on the oldest the letters have remained, as if crystallized in their form, what they were in the time of King Louis XII.

II. POITEVIN MEDAL WITH THE HEARTS OF JESUS AND MARY

This singular medal comes from Saint-Loup-sur-Thouet (Deux-Sèvres) (Fig. 2).

It is clearly akin to the two hearts engraved with a knife, one within the other, on the stock of a flintlock pistol of the revolutionary era, also from the Deux-Sèvres (Neuvy-Bouin is not far from Saint-Loup), whose image I have already reproduced (Fig. 3).

The hearts of Jesus and Mary are distinguished, one by the cross, the other by a fleur-de-lys roughly carved in the stock's hard wood.

On the medal I have before me, the cross and symbolic stars also seem to indicate the hearts of Jesus and his Mother; it is made of a very thin stamped brass plate; that is to say, the hearts, done with

Fig. 2. — Medal from Saint-Loup-sur-Thouet (Deux-Sèvres).

Fig. 3. — Hearts engraved on a pistol stock (Neuvy-Bouin, D.-S.).

Representations Relating to the Worship of the Sacred Heart

Fig. 4. — *Breton cross and heart 18th century.*

Fig. 5. — *Reverse of Breton Heart.*

"embossing," are seen on one side in relief and on the other in hollow relief.

The two figurations of nearby provenance on the Neuvy pistol and the Saint-Loup medal complement each other. They are the illustration of the peculiar form of piety dear to Blessed Louis Grignion de Montfort and preached tirelessly, for three centuries in Poitou, by his spiritual sons, the Missionaries of Saint-Laurent-sur-Sèvre: "Go to Jesus through Mary."

III. BRETON CROSSES AND HEARTS

Ancient Breton hearts completely differ from Poitevin hearts by their form and meaning. While the latter, whether single or double, are formed of flat sections that leave the middle of the heart in openwork, Breton hearts are extraordinarily convex on both sides.

The side in back is fenestrated with three openings; the two ends of a ribbon are inserted into those at the top, emerge jointly from the one at the bottom, and support a terminal cross a little below the heart. The whole forms what was once called a "pend-à-col" (neck-pendant), and this name alone speaks to its use (Figs 4 & 5).

Traditional Breton crosses are always decorated with flowers in their center and at their extremities. The heart that brings together the two slips of ribbon can only be a human heart, an earthly heart being always characterized by the most graceful of what the earth produces: flowers.

It is the emblem of the Christian soul attached to the cross, not by bonds of suffering, like crucified hearts, but by bonds of affection. The Breton woman who wore it — for these are essentially feminine jewels — seemed to say to God: my whole heart binds me to you.

IV. SAVOYARD CROSSES AND HEARTS

Nothing resembles the general form of the Breton neck-pendants more than that of the hearts and crosses of Savoy.

In the second as in the first, the heart serves as "slider" to the two strands of traditional black ribbon that support the cross.

Savoyard crosses also differ from Breton crosses, and even differ from one region to another. Those of the Chambery region terminate in flow-

Fig. 6. — Cross peculiar to La Maurienne region (Savoy).

ered arrangements and usually bear the crucifix on one side and, on the other, the Virgin at the foot of the Cross; those of the Tarentaise, which are more like Breton crosses, have their center adorned with a Holy Spirit dove; those of La Maurienne are totally different from the others and recall certain decorations of a chivalric order (Fig. 6).

Of course, like Breton neck-pendants, Savoyard jewels relate to the affectionate feelings of the soul for the mystery of Calvary, and not to the worship of the heart of Jesus.

I owe to the learned Émile Ginot, of Poitiers, former President of the Société des Antiquaires de l'Ouest, knowledge of these traditional jewels of Savoy, and respectfully thank him.

V. THE SECULAR HEARTS OF NORTHERN ITALY

The sumptuous neck-pendant hearts of northern Italy are, I think, of Venetian manufacture. Like our rebus rings from Poitou, these hearts are altogether secular and have only a kind of diadem that surmounts them in common with our Poitevin hearts.[1] They are certainly not, as one of my friends thought, their prototype.

The one I present here dates from the eighteenth century. This solid silver heart is surrounded and crowned with openwork filigree ornaments, also of silver. It comes from the south of France (Fig. 7).

Fig. 7. — *Heart of possible Venetian origin, in silver.*

I know another jewel of the same kind, perhaps less elegant, but richer: in gold and likewise filigreed, it was formerly to be seen in the window of the Arman-Demeyer goldsmith shop in Vichy.

Why are our Christian artists no longer inspired by these ancient models, whether secular or not, for magnificently glorifying the divine heart? Women's jewelery especially lends itself to marvelous combinations, and the art of goldsmiths, chasers, jewelers, and enamellers can also sing its hymn, and more marvelously than many others, in a concert of homage that art itself now sends up, each day more ardently, to the glorified heart of Jesus Christ.

---

[1] See Part 7, Chap. 27, p. 467, Fig. 3.

Part VIII: Diverse Representations of the Heart of Jesus

VI. SEAL WITH THE "CRUCIFIED HEART" AND ANGEVIN BOOKPLATES

Colonel Picard, of Saumur, has recently communicated to me, and without mistaking its true meaning, the most beautiful seal below, preserved for generations in the family of Colonel Picard's wife (Fig. 8).

It is of the seventeenth century. The inscription that surrounds it specifies its exact meaning. CONFIXVS.SVM.CRVCI, "I am fastened, nailed [with him] to the cross." It is the melancholy and resigned emblem of a Christian well tested by life and who, meritorious, joins his sufferings to those of the Savior.

Fig. 8. — *Seal of the 17th century of the crucified Heart type.*

Fig. 9. — *Ex-libris given by Mgr Barbier de Montault to the Musée des Antiquaires de l'Ouest, at Poitiers.*

In the iconography of the heart of Jesus, the difference between time periods imposes differences of interpretation on data that are linearly the same, for example: whereas, prior to the last quarter of the fifteenth century, a cross marked in any way whatsoever with a heart seems sufficient, by itself, to designate it as that of the Savior; it is no longer so in later times. In the seventeenth and eighteenth centuries the singular and often confused fantasies of mystical iconographers force us to take into account all the relativities: the object that bears the heart and its normal use or destination, the decor that surrounds the heart, the time and the very country where the representation of the heart was carried out; and it is a great joy when an inscription happens to specify the idea that presided over these compositions.

Thus, a heart occupying the center of an ex-libris stamp, struck on the title of a 1710 Angevin ecclesiastical book, is only a believer's heart, even though it bears the acronym of the name of Jesus, IHS, joined to the cross, since the legend that surrounds it speaks these words from a Psalm of David to the book's owner: SIGNACULUM CORDIS MEI DEUS, "God is the seal on my heart"[2] (Fig. 9).

And there is another human heart, one on a small copper seal found in the Carmel of Loudun[3] that bears a Christ on the cross within itself, a Christ who, from the inscription, speaks to the heart whose entire interior he occupies: IL N'Y A PLACE QUE POVR MOY (17th c.), "there is room only for Me."

VII. MONETARY ENGRAVING: CAROLINA (UNITED STATES)

The heart in the engraving on here, collected in the Vendée, whose twelve other hearts proclaim that they will never be separated: QUIS SEPARABIT? (Fig. 10), is also only a human heart, despite its radiating halo.

But no, these are not the hearts of the twelve apostles arranged in a nimbus around that of the divine Master: this

Fig. 10. — Monetary vignette from South Carolina.

---

2 Cf. Psalm 72:26.
3 *Confréries ecclésiastiques du diocèse d'Angers sur le Sacrement de l'Ordre*, Angers, Olivier MDCCX (my collection).

vignette is of a civil and wholly secular order; it is the reproduction of the central motif of the paper money issued in 1776 by the state of South Carolina. These hearts are simply those of the 13 founding states of the American Union.

Two years later, Carolina and Georgia together adopted another symbol of the *American Union*, a quadrangular pyramid of thirteen stages.

It should be noted, however, that the quite tender emblem of those hearts entwined with verdure contrasts sharply with the aridity, the cold stiffness, of ordinary Protestant emblems, which were then official in the United States; which makes it necessary to remember that at the time, in various countries such as Spain, Portugal, and Mexico (with which the South of North America was in frequent contact), the hearts of the members of the same community, monastery, chapter, college, or brotherhood were often represented arranged around the radiant heart of Jesus or even grouped within this heart, for example, on the banner of the Brotherhood of the Black Christ, in the Cathedral of Cartagena (Spain), where the hearts of the thirty-three members of the brotherhood are represented within the heart of Jesus.[4]

I would be not at all surprised, then, if the author of the Carolinian emblem from the United States, if he was Protestant like the mass of his compatriots, had come under the influence of Catholic art in composing it, especially since, in the subject he had to symbolize, the radiation that surrounds the central heart is hardly justified. But the sole and weak link which, perhaps, remotely ties his work to the thought of the Sacred Heart, surely ends there.

---

4 To be compared also with the Carolinian vignette of Klauber (18th century) presented in a most beautiful article by Father Anizan on *Quelques témoignages sur le Centre du Plan divin*, "Some Testimonies on the Center of the Divine Plan" (*Regnabit*, Sept. 1922, p. 293), which we have reproduced on p. 365, Fig. 3. The heart of the Savior is surrounded by the hearts of the whole of humanity also arranged in a nimbus.

VIII. AN OLD MEDAL WITH THE IMAGE OF THE RADIANT HEART

In closing, we will turn to an old coin where the heart, the heart alone, without wound or dolorous crown, is the very center of a dazzling sun that dominates the cross (Fig. 11). No human heart, were it incandescent with love for its fellows or for God himself, were it even that of the glorious Virgin, would be in its place.

Seeing it, there comes to mind the Sun-God, the victorious and succoring Christ whom our fathers of the first Merovingian times represented by the Constantinian interlacing of the Greek X and P, at the center of a radiant sun.[5]

Fig. 11. — Medal from the 18th century.

Thus, from the sixth to the eighteenth century, the thought is the same, and likewise the symbol; only, throughout the centuries, not a more beautiful, but a more affective piety has produced this iconography, and the Constantinian acronym of the Labarum has given way, in the center of the divine Sun, to the heart wholly composed of welcoming mercy, gentle goodness and radiant beauty.

IX. PECTORAL CROSS OF A BENEDICTINE NUN FROM CRAON

Thanks to the obliging kindness of Count François de Rilly, I have received an elegant cross from the period of Louis XIII, in copper, beneath the foot of which is a heart, deeply engraved, accompanied by two very small stars (Fig. 12).

The image of the Savior and various ornaments that decorated the shaft and arms of the cross have fallen away.

---

5 Tray for eulogies from Saint-Just-sur-Dive, near Loudun; cf. 6th Part, Chap. 21.iii, Fig. 5, p. 367.

Part VIII: Diverse Representations of the Heart of Jesus

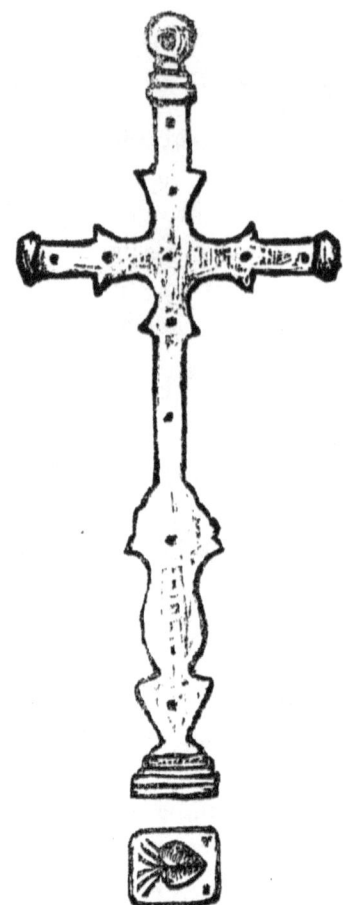

Fig. 12. — Pectoral cross with heart-shaped stamp.

Designed to be worn on the chest, ostensibly or not, this cross could have also served as a seal for correspondence. It comes from the Benedictine monastery of Craon (Mayenne).

The heart that has been engraved there is certainly a human heart, a heart ardently in love since it is aflame, and the fact that it is placed beneath the cross tells us that this ardor can only have its source in a very keenly felt love for the cross, for Jesus the Savior whose sufferings unto death and eternal triumph it symbolizes at the very same time in our eyes.

CHAPTER THIRTY-ONE

Blasphemous Representations of the Heart of Jesus

PARODY, PROVOCATIVE USE, IRONIC OR grotesque representation of divine emblems by impiety, or of those emblems of human authority by their enemies, have occurred in every age. These were always gestures of blind hatred, the affirmation of a triumph, the manifestation of a contemptuous mockery or the expression of a challenge.

In the religious realm, the representations of the Circumcision, the Eucharist, the Crucifixion, the image of the Cross, the Trinitarian Triangle, the Pelican and other emblems, were in turn ridiculed, or shown with slightly differentiating features, to express feelings or thoughts, or symbolize beliefs in opposition to those out of which orthodox Christian iconography has fashioned consecrated emblems.

The representation of the heart of the Lord, the most plenary, the most representative of all the divine emblems, often even having become the abbreviated image of his whole person, could not escape the insult of those astray who serve the "Other." Among these, the Masonic groups above all have produced, in recent years in particular, some fairly successful types of blasphemous Sacred Hearts.

Has the pseudo-Renaissance of the sixteenth century perhaps produced some too, having left us heart-pendants whose true meaning is as obscure as their obscenity is shamelessly patent? I must confess, though, I know of no representation of a derisive or impious heart of Jesus that predates the revolutionary period.

I. MASONIC JEWEL FROM MACHECOUL

From the Revolutionary era, I have the tracing of a copper heart that carries in its center the letters I H S, an abbreviated monogram for the name of Ihesus, and, at its summit, three flames.

Part VIII: Diverse Representations of the Heart of Jesus

The shape of this heart, bent and pointed, is exactly that of the large hearts figured on the red cloth "facings" of old revolutionary cavalry uniforms found in Nantes, by the collector F. Parenteau, hearts on which are embroidered in yellow, with flags and Phrygian caps, the words: République Française.[1] (Today in the Parenteau Collection at the Musée de Nantes.)

On the jewel that interests us, the heart is inscribed within an inverted triangle, a feature that is surely not justified only by the greater graphic ease of thus inscribing a heart in a triangle (Fig. 1). We will encounter a use with an actual motive later.

Fig. 1. — Jewel in copper. Machecoul (L.-Inf.).

This jewel was collected at Machecoul (Loire-Inferieure) by a leading citizen of Saint-Jean-de-Monts, who gave it to Father Chevalier, deceased pastor of Mortagne (Vendée). Machecoul is a locality that was made infamous in the West, in the fifteenth century, by the crimes of alchemy and satanic magic of Gilles de Rais, the Blue Beard of the tales of Perrault. During the Revolution, the "lads" of the Pays de Retz, of which Machecoul was the capital, joined with those of the Vendée's northern Marais under the command of the epic knight Athanase de Charette, took an active and glorious part in the counter-revolutionary wars of the Vendée, and like the heroic peasants of Cathelineau, Rochejaquelein, Lescure, and Bonchamp, their brothers in arms, they sported the image of the Sacred Heart in their hats and on their chests.

There was also at Machecoul — and since that time, I am assured — an organized Masonic lodge whose stamp-seal was in the possession of the aforementioned collector Parenteau. I very much suspect it of being the creator of the pendant figurine above, where the Sacred Heart is the prisoner of the triangle; it would probably be an obscure retort to the Sacred Hearts of Vendée soldiers.

---

1 Cf. Fortuné Parenteau, *Inventaire archéologique* (Nantes: Forest and Grimaud, 1878), p. 98, Pl. 48.

II. THE SACRED HEART BOUND WITH ROPE

Three quarters of a century later, during the War of 1870, the Sacred Heart was still gloriously raised on the battlefield by the Papal Zouaves, having become, again under the command of a Charette and a Cathelineau, the regiment of the Volunteers of the West; and, on the heroic day at Patay, the blood of the counts of Bouille, both father and son, and Verthamon reddened, in mortal homage, the white pennant that bore It.

I do not know if this deed, and the national homage which the French Parliament paid three years later, on July 24, 1873, to the heart of Jesus Christ by voting 382 to 138 for the erection of the sanctuary of Montmartre, gave birth to any sacrilegious imitation of the image of Jesus Christ.

But the war of 1914–1918 brought us, on the other hand, during its all too lengthy span, a rather large variety of images of the Sacred Heart drawn under the direct inspiration of Masonic centers or, beyond that, more intermediate but nevertheless real works under their influence.

From the beginning of the war, thousands of mobilized Catholics put on themselves either the medal or the image of the heart of Jesus, not only, as has been said, as a talisman or pious amulet against danger, but especially so as not to die, if they were struck down, without having with them the most expressive sign of the love and merciful pity of their Savior.

Considerable quantities of images printed on fabric or paper and medals were sent to the combatants by French piety, and especially three points of the territory, the Lyonnais, Poitou and Paris-Montmartre, became at once ardent centers of prayer and sources for the diffusion of images of the heart of Jesus.

The Masonic reply to this apostolate was not long in coming: images of the Sacred Heart, also printed on fabric or paper, were soon appearing in the trenches of the front, although in smaller numbers. The heart is set off above the inscription: Heart of Jesus, save France; it is magnificently radiant, its flaming summit bears the cross, and the traditional crown embraces it. But when

Part VIII: Diverse Representations of the Heart of Jesus

we look closely we see that this crown is not braided with thorny branches, but...with ropes!

The heart of Jesus was tied up in effigy! "Heart of Jesus, save France," now that you are bound!

It is the echo of a nineteen-hundred-year-old blasphemy:

Reread the first three Evangelists and their accounts of the Passion: Jesus is nailed by the hands and feet to his gibbet, quite soon he will die. Before him his enemies defy and taunt him: "You who wanted to save others, save yourself then, if you can, and come down from the cross!..."

I reproduce here the image of one of these blasphemous hearts collected in 1917, in Champagne (Fig. 2). Below it was the ordinary inscription: Heart of Jesus save France. Take it for granted that ninety-eight out of one hundred of our soldiers would have seen nothing but the heart of the Almighty Lord, the emblem of his love and goodness.

Fig. 2. — *Sacred Heart bound with ropes. War of 1914–1918.*

Often even, to imitate more completely the type consecrated by Catholic piety, frayings of the rope imitated the spines of the ordinary crown. What we have, then, is a God well-secured by a rope that frays of itself in twenty places!

Thus, and very similar to the preceding engraving, with its radiance and its cross in addition to its form, but finer in artistic expression, the heart of Jesus appears on the cover of a periodical entitled *Littérature*, a Dadaist mouthpiece whose text[2] refers to both the Salpêtrière[3] and a house of debauchery. By the place it occupies there, the Most Holy Heart is not only

---

2 September 19, 1922.
3 *Trans.* — A women's asylum in Paris.

the object of a blasphemy, as made explicit by the ligature that binds it; it also serves as a recklessly unfair trap for souls.

It should be pointed out that this same issue of *Littérature* protests (p. 23) against the rejoining of Alsace-Lorraine to France. Would not that be a mark of its origin?

III. THE SACRED HEART BOUND WITH A CHAIN

At the same time as the cloth and paper insignia, Catholic soldiers of the Great War also wore small enamelled orbicular medallions where, on three blue, white and red circles or vertical bands, the heart of Jesus was depicted with various formulas: *Heart of Jesus, save France*; or: *Hope and salvation of France*, etc.

Fig. 3. — *Heart bound with a chain. War of 1914-1918.*

Freemasonry responded by having a star-shaped medallion manufactured in Bordeaux and sent to the front in large numbers (Fig. 3).

In the center of the star, on a circumference of white enamel, a red heart, uninjured, is surmounted by a flame and a cross; it is encompassed by a chain, the "fraternal chain" of the Masons, no doubt. Around it are to be read these words: Psychology-Science.

Going down, from top to bottom and from left to right, the points of the star are successively gold, red, green, blue, red. I must admit I do not understand the symbolism of these colors that "harlequinize" the jewel in a more gaudy than harmonious way.[4]

Another variety of the same starry and variegated medallion shows us the heart belted not with a chain, but with flowers, and

---

4 The Russian Soviets have also taken a star as their emblem.

surrounded by foliage still with the two words: Psychology–Science, and, in addition: God–Country.

It has been said that the hearts of these medallions do not represent the heart of Jesus, but the heart of humanity, set thus in opposition to the heart of the Savior adored by Catholics. I wish the "heart of humanity" well, but, being in the intention, the blasphemy remains nonetheless real. Perhaps I am wrong but I cannot persuade myself that this apostolate in favor of the heart of humanity has caused, among the combatants, a very serious injury to the worship of the heart of Jesus.

Heart of Humanity... However, this is not what the Masonic magazine *L'Echo de l'Invisible* of January–March 1917 says about the emblem of interest to us: "In the inner circle of the multicolored star, the divine heart (the *divine* heart...) is surrounded by palms of laurel and olive. This heart is crowned with forget-me-nots and thorns, which tells us: by this all-powerful science, no more suffering in truth; this heart symbolizes the heart of the human homeland, of the holy covenant. Yes, by this science, no more misery, no more plagues that wilt human dignity...,"[5] etc.

Do these people know what they are saying? The heart of their star has only one goal, only one *raison d'être*: to parody the Catholic medals of the Sacred Heart, and that's all; the rest is just verbiage.

IV. THE TRICOLOR FLAG DECORATED WITH THE SACRED HEART

Desiring more than the personal homage of all, both soldiers and civilians, French devotion solicited during the war, and by eloquent voices, a national tribute to the heart of Christ by placing the image of his heart on the flag.

This desire, very praiseworthy in itself, was based on an interpretation of what was called the "Message" of Saint Margaret Mary to Louis XIV, a message that, according to the authoritative

---

5 Cf. Bishop Jouin and Canon Gaudeau, *Le Sacré-Cœur de Jésus et le cœur maçonnique* (Tours: Cattier, 1918), p. 28.

opinion of Father Jean-Vincent Bainvel, S. J., had asked the king for several acts of *personal* devotion, but did intend to bring about a national tribute, in the sense we understand it today, obligatory either for him or for France as a nation.[6]

Be that as it may, many flags were made with the heart of Jesus on their middle band, and several were deployed under the firing of the Germans.

And quite soon a blasphemous counterfeit appeared. In the booklet already quoted, Mgr. Jouin, the parish priest of Saint-Augustin in Paris, and Canon Gaudeau spoke at length about it, and, on this topic, they quote from this passage from *L'Echo de l'Invisible* which seems written by the inventor of one of the types of these flags:

"The tricolor flag adorned with the symbol of the Sacred Heart of Jesus, branches of mistletoe, vine, oak, wheat, palms of laurel, olive, cross; on the reverse side the heart of Mary symbolizing the maternal heart of the human homeland, the feminine heart, and the heart of Jesus symbolizing the paternal heart of humanity, the masculine heart; the heart of man, the heart of woman, both *divine* in their spiritual and natural principle. On this solemn flag shone in gold letters these words: 'Glory to the Most High! Honor and country! Heart of Jesus, save France! Love, solidarity, peace to men of good will, 1914, 1915, 1916. Bordeaux-Montmartre, Sacred Heart...'"[7]

And here is the Sacred Heart, tied up by some, which would be for others the symbol of the paternal heart of humanity... In fact all these war insignias, whether directly or indirectly Masonic — wearable hearts, medallions, stars and pseudo-religious flags — are only parodies, intellectually quite poverty-stricken, of Catholic tokens.

---

6 Cf. J.V. Bainvel, *La Dévotion au Sacré-Coeur de Jésus* (Paris: Beauchesne, 1921); on the precise meaning of the Message, pp. 589-96.
7 Op. cit., p. 23.

Part VIII: Diverse Representations of the Heart of Jesus

V. THE FLAG OF THE LEAGUE OF NATIONS

Impiety would go even further. When the League of Nations was organized, the creation of a flag was proposed for this contrivance, a new flag that Jean Hennessy asked to be all blue, "the color of the sky and sea," in which no one would see, I think, any major drawbacks. But the newspaper *The League of Nations* wanted it to be stamped in the middle "with a golden disc, an image of the sun, and with a triangle pointing downward to signify the emancipation of humanity, whereas the upward pointing triangle is an emblem of autocracy and divinity." But as the people would not grasp the contributions of freedom, fraternity, and democratic sovereignty contained in this inverted triangle, the proposal was completed as follows: "By inserting in the center of the triangle the image of a heart, we would give to this symbol a tangible expression more within reach of the masses."[8]

And here we are back to the old revolutionary jewel of Machecoul, which also has a heart within its inverted triangle, a triangle that I found, also overturned, on the crest of the Rose Cross Chapter of Heredum Kilwining, founded at Paris in 1776 by Freemasons of the Scottish Rite.[9]

Another proposal for the central motif of the same flag has been communicated to me, which appears opposite and corresponds exactly to what was stated in the anonymous pamphlet (Fig. 4). *The Flag of the League of Nations*,[10] which bears on its cover a red and blue banner charged in the middle with a design substantially similar to the one I reproduce here: a heart, the aforesaid brochure explains, encircled with thorns and pierced from top to bottom with a sword, the image of suffering humanity, placed in an overturned triangle at the center of a sun; this signifies the suppression of God and the march of humanity towards the sun by its own strength...[11]

8 Jouin and Gaudeau, op. cit., p. 11.
9 Cf. De Gassicourt and du Roure de Paulin, *L'Hermétisme dans l'Art Héraldique* (Paris: Dragon, 1907), p. 143.
10 Paris, 1921.
11 I will be more severe with regard to the lodge whose seal is owned by

Blasphemous Representations of the Heart of Jesus

Fig. 4. — Motif proposed for the flag of the League of Nations, 1921.

Once again, here we have the good God prisoner of a triangle... He must be very worried... In short, all the insignias we have seen, like everything that comes from the Lodges, are but impotent cries of revolt against a God whom they insult but do not reach.

Should I have some reservations when speaking of the Lodges? I will make the following clarification about "that comes from the Masonic lodges," because I am assured that "a small, very secretive group" (perhaps not the only one in the world) formed in the manner of a Lodge and recently organized in Paris, would be as far removed as ourselves from the spirit of impiety of the true Masonic lodges, and would have no hostility against the Catholic religion, quite the contrary; and, while standing on her fringes, would adore Christ in a kind of Manichaeism, where the Person of Jesus alone would be the Trinity, and his heart

---

my colleague in heraldry, Joseph Pallu Du Bellay. This seal bears on a heart-shaped cartouche three small flaming hearts accompanied by compass, set-square, level, plumb-bob, calibrated protractor, etc., all between two branches of acacia. At the top, the motto: Virtuti, silentio, concordiae, and at the bottom: L. D. S. C., which some translate: Loge des Sacrés Cœurs, Loge des Saints Cœurs [Lodge of the Sacred Hearts, Lodge of the Holy Hearts].

the only good principle, dualistically opposed to the evil principle, Satan. Hence Christ would be on this count the effective source of all justice, all goodness, all devotion, as well as the only source of grace.

This group therefore, in our eyes, accepts a false concept born of religious ignorance, and not of a perversion of the will. Good faith, both genuine and sincere, can unwittingly bring its members into touch with the "Soul of the Church," which will grant them, on the day they ask for it, the light they seek.

And now what is to be said, if not to observe that, to the extent that the magnificent cult of the heart of Jesus Christ grows, with the multiplication of its images and the part given to it in Catholic life, to the same extent the anger of the Counter-Church mounts, along with its efforts to associate, as a symbol, the image of the Sacred Heart, or the parody of this image, with everything that it can undertake against this heart.

This is a war between the two cities, a battle between two camps and two standards, about which St. Augustine and St. Ignatius wrote in their time. Others more qualified will probably speak of Satan's eternal struggle against Christ, against the heart of Jesus Christ; in these lines I only wanted to situate beforehand some of the most recent artifacts in order to highlight Masonic texts to come.

But let us kneel before these images of the heart of Jesus entwined with ropes, with impotent chains or hemmed in by enclosures that will never imprison it, just as we do before the paintings of artists who would have us adore the blood-stained Redeemer, bound against the pillar, where his torturers of yesteryear bound him to scourge him. Addressing those people today who would join their rabble, Moreno's[12] last words alone are fitting: "No, God does not die!"

---

12 Gabriel Garcia Moreno, president of Peru, assassinated on August 6, 1875. — *Trans.*

CHAPTER THIRTY-TWO

Hearts of Bewitchment

THE EMINENT DIRECTOR OF *ÆSCULAPE*, Dr. Bord, published a very interesting article in this review on "A scene of bewitchment of the heart" painted in the fifteenth century by, it is thought, Jan Van Eyck.[1]

The painting in question, known as *Sortilège d'Amour* [*The Curse of Love*], and which is in the Leipzig Museum, depicts a naked woman whose feet tread magic flowers (Plate 32). "To her right," Dr. Bord says, "in an open coffer borne by a stool is a heart—we mean the image of a heart—made of wax or of some quite different material. She holds in her right hand a flint stone and a piece of tinder, in her left hand a lighter. By the attitude of her folded left arm, we judge that she has just struck the flint with the lighter to make the sparks fly to warm the heart lying below, and therefore the heart of the young man she loves and by whom she wishes to be loved..."

This is indeed a scene of a love spell, but magical operations of this kind were done for many other purposes, and at all times: from prehistoric times, at the very time when primitive man crawled into the long underground caves or hid in rock shelters, he cast spells on wild beasts and big game so that they would be easier to capture; hence the rhinoceros pierced with arrows from the cave at Colombier (Ain), the cat in reindeer horn, and the sandstone bison found in Isturitz by the learned speleologist René de Saint-Périer, the bear riddled with stones and arrows, and the amazing clay bison from the Cave of the Three Brothers, discovered by Count Bégouën and his sons.

And this hunting magic brings us back to the bewitchment of the heart with the Aurignacian cave painting at Pindal, near Oviedo (Spain), which represents an elephant marked at the site of its heart with a red representation of this vital organ. In the province of

---

1 *Æsculape*, March 1926, pp. 94–95.

Malaga, a large black doe at Ardales presents the same peculiarity. In these two cases, the heart does not appear as a center and source of love, but as a vulnerable point accessible to magic incantations.

Prehistoric man also bewitched his human enemies, hence the image of the wounded man of Saltadora.

At all times since then, and in all civilizations, we encounter spells in an all too well-supplied succession of human vileness and malice: Egypt, Babylonia, ancient Persia, and the old Greco-Roman world practiced it according to quite diverse rites.

After the establishment of Christianity, the depraved who used the spell brought into their rites two of this religion's sacraments, Baptism and the Eucharist: a statuette of wax, resin, or other material was first baptized in the name of the person to be bewitched, so that, by substitution, the statuette took the person's place. Sometimes it was a heart of wax or flesh instead of a complete effigy.

Ordinarily, holy water was used for these sacrilegious baptisms, and sometimes the Eucharist entered into this diabolical liturgy by having a consecrated host kneaded into wax, or dissolved in baptismal water.

More often than being made of wax, hearts of bewitchment were natural hearts of he-goats, she-goats, black cats, crows, and especially black hens — the ritual hen of black magic and low sorcery. When one wanted to preserve these hearts of flesh, they were rendered rot-proof by alum, salt, alcohol, or aromatics.

I have before my eyes two of these hearts of bewitchment: one, having become dry and hard as wood, was provided with a large bronze buckle, so it was intended to be worn. Two pins cross it obliquely from top to bottom, and thus intersect in the middle; their points are bent into hooks, as used in crochet, and in this way seem like fasteners to secure the heart in place. By the shape of their heads, these pins are recognized as dating back to the eighteenth century.

This heart, which belongs to me, was found in the double bottom of an old buffet cast into the bonfire of a country house in Haut-Poitou.

The second heart was pointed out to me by the archpriest of a small town of the West. It was found in a deposit of fine, dry sand under the flooring of a closet. I drew it while it still had the normal shape of a heart; since then, it has changed considerably. It was, at the time of the incantation, pierced with twelve needles which are surely of the nineteenth century. I do not think that this heart is to be classified among the artifacts relating to love enchantments: enchantments are also performed from hate, revenge, ambition, or jealousy to bring down on the person enchanted reversals of fortune, general bad luck, and physical or moral suffering capable of causing wasting, helplessness, mental debility, or death.

To serve these evil purposes, and during an incantation, hearts and statuettes would be abused with iron or fire while ritual curses were uttered against the bewitched, whose name these objects bore. It is in this evil and abominable line that must be ranked the second of the two hearts mentioned above. It was not intended to be worn.

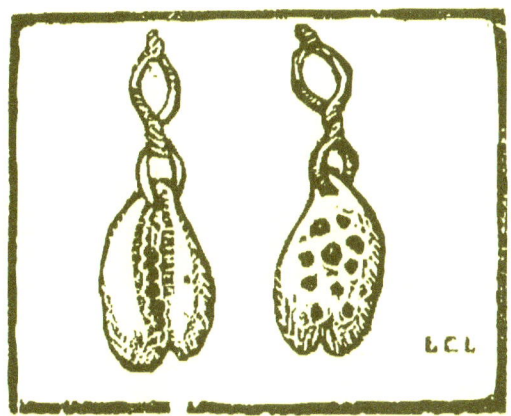

Fig. 1. — *Cypraea shell, reversed emblems of female genitals and the heart, 17th or 18th century.*

There is another very different object related to this magical liturgy of this heart, but which, although it proceeds from human depravity, has however no mark of cruelty: it is the shell of the shellfish called *cowry* or *cypraea*, from the name Cypris, the Greek goddess of love. The shape of this shell, when seen point down and from the back, is that of a heart, also the opening on its underside was, from the time of the ancient Greeks, one of

Part VIII: Diverse Representations of the Heart of Jesus

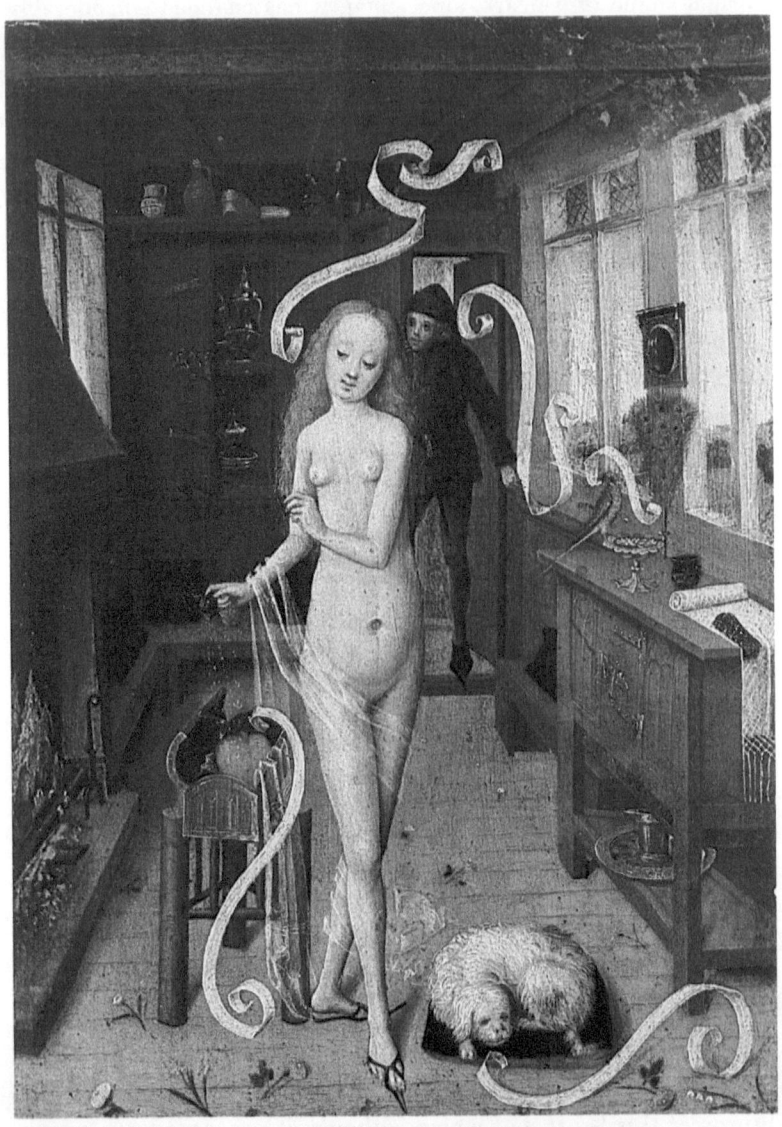

Plate 32. — The painting called "Sortilège d'Amour" by Jan Van Eyck, 15th century. Leipzig Museum (ed.).

the emblems of the female genitals. Consecrated magically and ritually like the hearts of bewitchment, this shell was worn by superstitious lovers for the same purpose as the first of the hearts mentioned above in these lines, that is, to influence the feelings of the woman in whose name it was baptized. I depict here one of those magical and documentary objects which, supported by a very old, bronze fastener, is hung with the point up (Fig. 1), and, in this position, pertains to the rite of "reversal of symbols" so important in all ancient symbolisms.

This artifact comes from the same region as the previous ones.

In ending our considerations of these magical hearts, about which much more could be said, I will reproduce an image of the heart preserved by André Moreau de la Ronde. This object was found by his father, the erudite Loudun archaeologist Joseph Moreau, in the masonry at the base of the fortified entry gate, at the great round castle-keep of Loudun, ruined in 1636. On the back, non-visible side of one of the stones of this portal, two cavities had been made during its construction by the architects of King Philip Augustus in 1206; one contained nothing; in the other was a little heart carved out of the dome of a skull; it bears, at the top, a trace of a suspension hole, and its shape was that of the old heraldic heart, but the left atrium and the right side were altered by disintegration of the osseous material (Fig. 2).

Fig. 2. — Heart in bone, immured in the base of fortified entry to the citadel of the Château of Loudun, built in 1206. (Moreau de La Ronde Collection)

It is difficult to know what thinking went into the immuring of this object which, I think, must be ranked among the series of benefic amulets... But nonetheless it has its place in the succession of human aberrations, aberrations which we cannot say were the exclusive lot of our fathers, since our contemporaries still practice them.

CHAPTER THIRTY-THREE

Epilogue and Refutation of Some Criticisms

STUDIES OF SACRED ARCHAEOLOGY INI-tiated, then methodically conducted during the last century and continued since then, have led to some quite interesting discoveries: gratuitous assertions, presented up to that point as certainties, have departed, fleeing before them, and have been dispatched to that cemetery where, alas! many old errors of human knowledge lie. Dispatched along with them, too, was the strange historical school of the first half of the nineteenth century, the principle of which was—surely a convenient principle for authors—that history is made to tell a story, not to prove what it tells. The last roots of this noxious plant still remain, moreover, all too full of sap, in the textbooks of schools and colleges.

Nevertheless, an effective work of shedding light on these matters has transpired for eighty years, which is a happy advance of the human spirit towards the truth.

In the considerable sum of ancient iconographic monuments studied during this period, archaeologists' research has revealed some that are undeniably associated with the iconography of the heart of Jesus Christ, and which, by their date, have shown that the piety and the arts of yesteryear dealt with it during times that were said not to have known about it.

Scholars like Mgr. Barbier de Montault, Cloquet, and Grimouard de Saint-Laurent, studied and reproduced these artifacts in their books; other experts spoke of them in articles published by various periodicals: they were few in number, but, because of their value, raised questions, established realities that deserved... some to be examined, others to be exposed.

The historians of the Sacred Heart, and those who at that time wrote works relative to the people connected to the history of its worship, did not favorably receive the artifacts presented by iconographic archaeology: these old witnesses to a forgotten piety disturbed and demolished ideas accepted and taught for two centuries, and reared up against carefully constructed systems. It was painful for some to have to be contradicted, others to leave the beaten path followed by everyone until then. And authors continued to say that, before the events of Paray-le-Monial, devotion to the place of the Lord's heart did not exist; that St. Margaret Mary was the first to reveal the Sacred Heart to the Church.

The Eudists replied that their founder, Father John Eudes, had composed, before there was any question of Sister Margaret Mary, a Mass of the Sacred Heart; the Carthusians noted, in the writings of their fifteenth-century brothers, a real and very pious devotion towards the Sacred Heart and its images; the Franciscans, Benedictines, and Cistercians also affirmed that the history of their orders revealed that they had formerly known and loved the heart of Jesus Christ. Christian archaeologists insisted: we have all possible veneration for the marvelous sanctity of Margaret Mary; we recognize that in the Catholic propagation of the cult of the Sacred Heart, her role was of the highest order, but we have, in Langeac, for example, and elsewhere, beautiful sculptures of the sixteenth century that represent the heart of Jesus pierced by the spear; similar sculptures, undoubtedly of the fifteenth century, are known in France, England, and Germany; we are certain that the heart of the Redeemer was represented on the trademarks of those times; so we maintain that Christian thought had turned to it many centuries before the admirable movement of faith for which Paray was, in the late seventeenth century, the radiant center.

How could one answer to that? Some replied that the artifacts brought forward did not appear to them sufficiently identifiable; others that these were isolated cases that only indicated the personal fantasies of artists; most of the authors adopted that which was for them the most convenient attitude: they put the light under a bushel and placidly repeated their old thesis, especially in those writings intended for the mass of Catholics.

However, some writers judiciously saw the various disadvantages that would arise from their predecessors' way of proceeding. Even though all too often there was still a tendency to minimize the efforts that preceded the Paray movement, books became more welcoming to iconographic material. In his book *France and the Sacred Heart*, Father Victor Alet, a Jesuit, reproduces a good number of them, and shows, in particular, the Queen of England's stall at Windsor Chapel; it is a very beautiful piece of furniture in flamboyant Gothic style, carved at the beginning of the sixteenth century, above which appears the Sacred Heart with its bleeding wound.[1]

Jean-Vincent Bainvel, S. J., whose work, *The Devotion to the Sacred Heart of Jesus*, had great success, does not grant to the ancient iconography of the divine heart the place it deserves in a work as considerable as his. Yet in the 1921 edition, and for the first time then in a three-page appendix, he points out several items painted or carved in the fifteenth and sixteenth centuries.[2]

The book by Fr. Hilaire de Barenton, a Franciscan religious, *The Devotion to the Sacred Heart*,[3] is far more explicit: it establishes the existence of a true piety with respect to the heart of Jesus during the Middle Ages and reproduces about a dozen French and German depictions of the Sacred Heart from the fifteenth and sixteenth centuries. This is a fine work in which the author deals mainly with the role, actually quite considerable, which was that of his Order during the second part of the Middle Ages, with regard to the spread of the form of piety that interests us here, and, although we can underscore slight misunderstandings of details, we must thank the author for having represented in his pages a body of figurative documents likely

---

1 Victor Alet, *La France et le Sacré-Cœur* (Paris: Lethielleux et Demoulin, 1905), p. 377. It is true that, while attributing the whole of this document to the sixteenth century, the section that depicts the heart of Jesus, which we have reproduced on p. 347, Fig. 4 takes us back to the seventeenth (and even the late seventeenth).
2 Op. cit., pp. 640ff. — The first edition was in 1906.
3 Hilaire de Barenton, *La Dévotion au Sacré-Cœur* (Paris: Librairie St François, n.d.).

Part VIII: Diverse Representations of the Heart of Jesus

to spoil the thesis of the "anticordicoles," those who oppose the extension of the worship rendered to the heart of Jesus Christ under the pretext that it is a new form of piety in the Church, unknown to her before the Holy Visitandine of Paray.

A first work published in 1925, *Devotional and Ascetic Practices in the Middle Ages*, by Dom Gougaud, a Benedictine monk,[4] contains a chapter entitled: "The antecedents of devotion to the Sacred Heart," in which the author speaks in particular of English depictions in which the heart wounded by the spear appears between the pierced hands and feet of Jesus Christ; and so, he states, "the earliest representations of the Sacred Heart date back to the time when the first engravings to promote devotion to the five wounds began to spread."[5] It is indeed the "Sacred Heart" that is thus figured, but it is not true that these are its "oldest representations": there are some prior to this realistic grouping of wounded limbs, some in which the Sacred Heart appears alone, as for example on the host-mold of the bishopric of Vic, in Spain, where the heart of Jesus is unrelated to the five wounds.

But Dom Gougaud makes no mention of the remarkable items collected in Germany by R. Karl Richstaetter, S. J., nor of those published in various other countries, nor of those that we have reproduced for several years, with all needed references, in the former journal *Regnabit*. He has no doubt felt that his limited framework did not allow for this, only the question he deals with is, by this very fact, singularly truncated.

Much broader and more comprehensive is the framework of another book published by Auguste Hamon, S. J., also in 1925: *History of the Devotion to the Sacred Heart*.[6] The author shows great talent as a writer and tells us openly of written

---

4 Dom Louis Gougaud, *Dévotions et Pratiques ascétiques du Moyen-Âge* (Paris: Lethielleux, 1925; Eng. ed., London: Burns Oates & Washbourne, 1927).
5 For the 1927 English translation of the book this whole chapter was entirely recast by the author and the passage no longer occurs. — *Trans.*
6 Auguste Hamon, S. J., *Histoire de la Dévotion au Sacré Coeur*, 5 vols. (Paris: Beauchesne, 1923–39). The author is referencing vol. 2, "L'aube de la dévotion" (1925).

or figurative documentation unfavorable to the so-called Paray school, with which he has however a great kinship of ideas, but on the other hand he is silent about a large number of other documents probably unknown to him, documents that are of considerable import.

Like Dom Gougaud, Father Hamon speaks at length about the representations of the fifteenth and sixteenth centuries where the wounded heart appears on a coat of arms between Jesus's hands and feet pierced by nails. He, too, does not want the figure of the wounded heart to be strictly anything but the evocation of the spear. Surely this heart is that; but by serving as a setting for the wound, it is more than that. It is first of all what it could not have been in the thoughts of the sculptors and painters of that time: it is the heart of him who was crucified for our salvation; it is the natural source of his blood that was shed through love for us; it is the very seat of his love. It is this by the very fact that it is a heart, and, by that, signifies, whatever one might wish or say about it, much more than a hand or foot.

In his appreciation, which makes of this heart accompanying the pierced hands and feet only the hieroglyph of a wound, Father Hamon rejoins Dom Gougaud, who says: "How does one heraldically represent, in the restricted space of the escutcheon, the wound made to the side of Christ by the soldier's spear? To do this, a heart was drawn — the heart of Jesus — a wounded heart, as if the same spear that pierced the side of Our Lord had likewise wounded the heart."[7] — Certainly not: it was not because they did not know how to heraldically represent the wound on the side that our old artists depicted the heart! They have never been hampered in "heraldically" — and in several other ways — representing the five wounds on crests, the wound to the side included! Not prior to or after the vogue for coats of arms bearing the wounded limbs, but at the same time, artists painted or sculpted orbicular or oblong wounds arranged in quincunx on the field of the shield, *two, one* and

---

7 Op. cit. Gougaud (French ed.), p. 89.

Part VIII: Diverse Representations of the Heart of Jesus

two; wounds from which flowed garlands of droplets or ribbons of blood, wounds sometimes crowned with diadems, and which had a heraldic look artistically different from realistic images of the heart and severed limbs.[8] Only the heart had, I repeat, the privilege of adding, to the simple evocation of the wounds received by our Savior on the cross, the idea of the love that had made them accept this, and that simply because it is the *heart*, the natural organ of love, and the idea, too, of the absolute in this sacrifice, because it is the very reservoir and source of blood and life.

Fig. 1. — *The mystical coats of arms of Jeanne de Valois.*

That is why, still at this same period, it sometimes appears on escutcheons, without the other four holy wounds being represented there other than by orbicular or oblong wounds. And this is what Blessed Jeanne de Valois, daughter of Louis XI, expressed on her mystical crest[9] (Fig. 1).

On the beautiful Labarre Psalter of Marseilles, which is also of the fifteenth century, the lateral wound is figured alone; between its lengthy oblong margins and within its depths the heart appears,

---

8 See the crests of Sidmouth Church and Cambridge for example, Part 3, Chap. 8, p. 115, Fig. 3 and p. 116, Fig. 4.
9 Cf. Part 6, Chap. 20, iii, p. 346, Fig. 3.

injured by the tip of the weapon. Is the heart being represented here to frame the wound? Or, to the contrary, are not the margins of the latter widely opened to show us, in the depths of their purple frame, the seat of the Savior's love, the first principle of our redemption?[10]

Father Hamon describes and perfectly interprets the trademark of the Parisian printer Pierre Levet, from the end of the fifteenth century, on which the heart is represented on the cross, wounded by the spear and surrounded by the crown of thorns.[11] He also speaks, a little less happily in my humble opinion, of two of the trademarks of the printers Nicole and Antoine de la Barre, on which a heart is shown with, for the uninformed, less pronounced features, because the trademarks of this era are full of hidden meanings. It would have been good for Father Hamon to know the other mark of Antoine de la Barre, where three hearts are depicted: at the bottom, that of the printer; at the top, two others, one of which is marked with the symbol IHS, *Jesus*, and the other with the letters MA, *Maria*.[12]

Also, how does Father Hamon fail to recognize the heart of Jesus on the sixteenth-century trademark of Jean Corbon, even though the Savior is represented in person holding this heart in his hand?[13]... and how have the trademarks of the printers Vérard and Le Caron, where the heart of Jesus, marked IHS, is placed in the very text of a prayer, been passed over in silence?[14]

I am so much the more regretful in having to point out these shortcomings since Father Hamon has truly favored me unduly by speaking of the "real treasures of iconography" that I have contributed in its day to the journal *Regnabit* and which I have taken up again in this work. That would be saying too much, even if the distinguished Jesuit had had the opportunity to read every installment of *Regnabit*; for, whether he speaks of the carving of Langeac, the drinking-fountain of Poitiers, and the

10 Cf. Part 2, Chap. 4, iii, p. 81, Fig. 4 and p. 82, Plate ii.
11 Cf. Part 6, Chap. 17, iv, p. 266, Fig. 16.
12 Ibid., p. 271, Fig. 20.
13 Ibid., p. 275, Fig. 23.
14 Ibid., p. 265, Fig. 15.

sculpture of Bois-Rogues while, without equivocation, recognizing in these the heart of the Divine Master, or whether he disputes the heart on the seal of Couret and has reservations about the heart in the keep of Chinon, he would surely have yielded, if he had known them, before this heart, at the center of the cross and under which the word *Xristus* is legible, chiseled on a host-mold from the bishopric of Vic[15] (Spain) to be impressed on a priest's host; before, also, this wonderful marble from the Charterhouse of Saint-Denis-d'Orques,[16] from the end of the fifteenth century or beginning of the sixteenth, where the broadly wounded heart, surrounded by a radiation of glory, is at the center of the celestial circle of the seven planets and that of the constellations of the zodiac. And I could recall as well twenty other artifacts that I have already introduced in this book.

With regard to the heart engraved on the wall of the donjon of Chinon, whose Templar origin and Christic character are more and more accepted by specialists in medieval hermeticism, Father Hamon acknowledges that it is not impossible that it is that of Jesus Christ, since it is juxtaposed with the instruments of the Passion, and he is astonished that there are also, to the side, remarkable signs: the open hand and others...[17] It should not be forgotten, however, that we are here in the presence of a composition in which oriental influences are manifest, where a perfectly orthodox hermeticism mingles with common religious figurations. In the former journal *Regnabit*, René Guénon has spoken, with his incontestable authority, about this Christian hermeticism, whose existence and important role in the Middle Ages it would be childish to dispute.[18]

Father Hamon mentions the silence of Richaud, in his *Histoire de Chinon*, with respect to this representation of the radiant heart in the graffiti of the donjon of this city! I was the first to

---

15 Ibid., p. 248, Fig. 7.
16 Cf. Part 6, Chap. 21, p. 354, Fig. 1.
17 Cf. Part 6, Chap. 16, iv, p. 235, Fig. 16.
18 René Guénon, *Le Sacré-Cœur et la légende du Saint-Graal*, in *Regnabit*, Aug.–Sept., 1925, p. 192.; *Insights into Christian Esoterism*, trans. H. D. Fohr (Hillsdale, NY: Sophia Perennis, 2001), p. 89.

point out this shortcoming, which proves absolutely nothing. I was told — is this the truth? — that Richaud refused to see a heart in the representation that interests us because its summit does not present the bend or double curve usually seen at the top of hearts. I have difficulty believing such an objection on his part; for it would suffice to refer to the heraldry of the heart in France and England, in the fourteenth and fifteenth centuries, to convince oneself that the heart of Chinon is not unique in its form. I have pointed out and reproduced several others in the present work which, exactly similar, appear between the pierced hands and feet of the Savior, therefore...

Father Hamon denies the divine character of the heart on the seal of Estème Couret (Fig. 2) because the rays seen there do not touch the heart but indeed rather the foot of the cross which surmounts this heart. I absolutely maintain that they cannot be related to the cross[19]: the rules of heraldry, which governed sigillography in the fifteenth century, like those from before and after, formally forbade the irradiation of the foot of a cross when its upper part, which carried the divine victim, is not so; the opposite, if it were possible, would be absurdly nonsensical.

Fig. 2. — Small seal of Estème Couret.

The rays of the Couret seal are no more attached to the cross than to the circumference of the heart. Placed where they are, their function is not to enhalo the heart: they can only issue from the breach made in the heart by the cross planted in its summit. Even though the engraver has not indicated it better, impeded either by the smallness of the seal or by its metal, yet the fact remains that they cannot, rationally, come from anywhere else.

The seal of Couret is related exclusively, by its very nature and by its engraved ornamentation, to the fields of sigillography and religious heraldry; it can be appreciated only in accordance

---

19 Cf. Part 6, Chap. 17, iii, p. 255-56.

with the rules and the spirit that governed these arts at the end of the Middle Ages, and it is by these alone that one must inquire about the seal's true meaning. Like almost all the emblems of the day, the heart that I see there seems to have two functions: first, to serve as a canting coat of arms for the name of Couret, which derives from "coeur" [heart], the other, to turn one's thoughts toward the heart *par excellence*, that of the Savior Jesus Christ. Surely, this is a matter of appreciation, but this is also, I believe, the truth.

In all of these so very meaningful questions, and in which it is quite interesting to follow Father Hamon, our authors' or researchers' personalities are nothing; the only important thing is the faithful pursuit of the truth. On this point we all agree.

Indices

INDEX OF NAMES

BIBLICAL, LEGENDARY AND MYTHOLOGICAL NAMES

A
Adam, 187, 215, 269
Adonis, 170
Ammon, 221
Amon, 217, 218, 223
Anubis, 217
Apollo, 127, 411-12
Arthur, 190-92, 199
Athena, 413
Aton/Aten, 215, 220
Attis, 189
Atum, 215, 217

B
Bacchus, 256
Bohors, 191, 198

C
Caiaphas, 57, 271, 335
Calliope, 412
Ceres, 413
Clio, 412
Cybele, 189
Cypris, 513

D
David, 95, 108, 159, 223, 367, 377, 497
Dionysius, 413
Dona, 189-90

E
Enos, 188
Eros, 95
Eurydice, 412
Eve, 187, 269 150

G
Galahad, 190-91, 198
Galeriet, 190
Gawain, 190

Geb, 217
Guenivere, 190

H
Hector, 190
Hera, 413
Hermes, 216, 411, 419
Herod, 57, 206, 271, 335
Horus, 221-22

I
Indra, 418
Isaiah, 100-102, 121-22, 127, 164, 194
Iscariot: *see* Judas
Isis, 217, 219, 410

J
Janus, xvi, 294, 376-77
Jeremiah, 151
Jesus: this work in its entirety is dedicated to Christ and to his wounds
John (saint, evangelist), 70, 76, 85, 95, 105, 122, 125, 173, 230, 252, 261-62, 290, 367, 370, 377, 420
John the Baptist (saint), 159
Joseph (spouse of the Virgin Mary), 473-74
Joseph of Arimathea, 70, 78, 173, 188, 192, 196, 390
Judas, 57, 283
Juno; *see* Hera
Jupiter; *see* Zeus

K
Keu, 190
Kore, 413

L
Lancelot, 190, 193
Linus, 412

529

Longinus, xix, 83, 85, 233, 272
Lucifer, 187, 197, 207
Lug, 189-90
Luke (saint, evangelist), 125

M
Maat, 218-19
Malchus, 482
Mark (saint, evangelist), 70, 125
Mary; *see* Virgin Mary
Mary Magdalene, 138, 173, 194, 245
Matthew (saint, evangelist), 70, 125, 155, 157, 400
Melchizedek, 216
Michael (archangel), 187, 218, 461-62
Midas, 411
Minerva; *see* Athena

N
Nephthys, 217
Nicodemus, 70, 207, 231-32
Nut, 217

O
Ormuzd, 419
Orpheus, 377, 412-19
Osiris, 189, 215, 217-19, 419

P
Pan, 411
Parzival, 191, 197
Paul (saint), 220, 290, 303
Pelles, 191
Perceval, 190-91, 193, 198
Persephone; *see* Kore
Peter (saint), 5, 57, 108, 188, 271, 381, 387, 481-83
Pilate, 57, 70, 83, 87, 155, 157, 164, 173, 271, 335, 483
Ptah, 221

R
Ra, 215

S
Satan, 218, 283, 305, 372, 462, 510
Saturn, 377
Set, 217
Seth, 188
Sheba, Queen, 206
Shu, 217
Solomon, 164, 184, 197, 206, 308

T
Tammuz, 189
Tefnut, 217
Thoth, 221
Titurel, 191, 197
Tristan, 190, 193, 356
Typhon, 411

V
Venus, 170
Veronica (saint), 331
Virgin Mary, 76, 83, 129, 173, 245, 252, 267-68, 270, 272, 275, 292, 298, 319, 331, 336, 356, 371-72, 386, 424, 442, 453-57, 461, 470-71, 473-74, 476, 481, 483-84, 492-94, 499, 507

Y
Yvain, 190

Z
Zagreus, 413, 419
Zeus, 411, 413
Zoroaster, 418

Index of Names

ANCIENT AND POST-BIBLICAL NAMES

A

Adamnanus (monk), 205
Akhenaten (Amenhotep), pharaoh, 220-21
Albert the Great, 104
Alcuin (priest), 317
Alet (Victor, priest), 347, 519
Alexios Comnenos (byzantine emperor), 22
Alfonso I, king of Portugal, 342-43
Alfonso II, king of Aragon, 41, 43
Alfonso VI, king of Portugal, 55
Alpais, 12-13
Ambrose (saint), 9
Amenhotep (also known as Akhenaten, pharaoh), 220-21
Angeliers, 260
Anizan (Félix, priest), xii, 90, 239, 282, 285, 330, 401, 409, 420, 498
Anne of Austria, queen of France, 454
Anne de Montmorency (duke), 330
Anthony of Padua (saint), 304, 308, 311
Arculf (bishop), 74, 205, 209
Argenteau (Reynald), 47
Arion, 417
Armailhac (d', priest), 71
Arman-Demeyer, 495
Arnoldi (dom Henry), 306
Arundel, 393
Augustine (bishop of Hippo, saint), 9, 104, 122, 230-31, 510
Autichamp (d'), 453
Autun (John of), 207
Averti, 435
Aymard VI (count), 21

B

Bacheleau, 25
Baguenier Desormeaux, 435
Bainvel (Jean Vincent, priest), 507, 519
Bajazet (sultan), 74
Ballu (Albert, priest), 127
Banéat (Paul), 251
Bara (Hiérosme de), 54-55
Barbier de Montault (Mgr), 14, 36, 38, 40, 166, 230, 243-44, 251, 319, 350, 371, 417, 472, 474, 481-83, 486, 496, 517
Barenton (Hilaire de, priest), 254, 343, 519
Barère, 447
Bata, 217
Baudouin, 468, 470, 472-73
Baudouin, emperor of Constantinople, 74
Baudry d'Asson (Gabriel), 434, 452
Baye (Joseph de, baron), 26
Bazin, 434
Beauvollier, 452
Beche (Thomas, abbot), 383
Bede, Venerable, 74, 205
Bégouën (count), 511
Béjarry, 452
Beka, 219-20
Bellay (Pallu du), 509
Belot (Jean, priest), 137, 356-58, 362
Belsunce (Mgr. de, bishop), 420, 485
Benard (Jean, chaplain), 445
Benedict XIV (pope), 74-75
Bérault (Marie), 321
Bérenger (counts), 41
Bergère (nicknamed Silver-Leg), 441
Berjat (canon), 177
Bernard of Clairvaux (saint), 101-3, 114, 117, 166, 229, 231, 237, 304, 343, 389
Berry (house of), 78, 88, 209, 449, 475
Berthier (Miss Madeleine), 301, 349-50
Bierley(family), 49
Binet (Estienne), 180
Blainville (house of), 49
Blanchet (priest), 17, 19-20, 23, 29, 247
Blehen (Jehan de), 47

531

Bocard, 266
Bonaventure (saint), 109, 166, 305
Bonchamp, 452, 501
Bondone (Giotto di, painter); *see* Giotto
Bonnard (Dom Fourrier), 58
Bonvarlet (family), 48
Bord (docteur), 511
Borel (counts), 41
Boron (Robert de); *see* Robert de Boron
Bouillé (counts of), 503
Boulanger (Jacques), 81, 198
Bourbon (house of), 316, 349, 448, 455
Bourgade-La-Dorie (de), 71
Bourgogne (house of), 55, 257
Boutrais (Frédéric), 118
Brancaccio (cardinal), 234
Breasted, 221
Bridaine, 423
Broussolle (Jules-César, priest), 155
Bruges (Master of, painter), 204
Bruno of Asti (saint), 164
Bullant (Jean), 331
Buron (Lucien, priest), 282, 344, 405, 420, 485

C

Caillaut, 80, 113, 195
Canute le Grand, king of England, 23
Capel (Mother de), 420
Capuano (Antonio, priest), 248, 398-99
Carlos I, king of Portugal, 55
Cathelineau (counts of), 448, 503
Cathelineau (Jacques, Vendean general), 436, 446-49, 452, 502
Catherine of Siena (saint), 307
Catteau (J., priest), 168
Caussade (priest), 423
Caesar (Julius), emperor, 256
Cesbron (lord of the manor), 369
Chabas, 219
Chabot (Guesdin), 193
Chabot (house of), 193
Chalon (Jean de); *see* Jean de Chalon

Champagne (Thibaut de), 182
Chantal (saint Jeanne de); *see* Jeanne de Chantal
Charbonneau (Pierre, canon), 461
Charette (house of), 442, 444, 503
Charette de la Contrie (Athanasius, knight), 442-44, 452, 502
Charlemagne, 190, 256, 317
Charles de Lorraine (archbishop), 126, 168
Charles II (the Bald), king of France, 40
Charles V, king of France, 385-86
Charles VIII, king of France, 329, 345
Charles X, king of France, 449, 468, 475
Charrier (Cl., Mrs.), 353
Chauveau (count), 28
Chégut (A., Mrs.), 372
Cheops, pharaoh, 214
Chephrem, pharaoh, 214, 222-23
Chevalier (priest), 502
Chrétien de Troyes, 191-92, 390
Cicoteau (family), 47
Cintré (Marquise de), 128
Claire (saint), 415
Claire of Assisi (saint), 51
Clement V, pope, 234
Clement XI, pope, 481
Cleves (dukes of), 183
Clifford (lord), 383
Clisson, 317
Cloquet (L.), 517
Colloigne, 193
Colson (commandant), 71
Compagnon (Pierre), 276, 278-79
Confex-Lachambre (family), 316
Constable (R., sir), 394
Constantine, Roman emperor, 5, 17, 22, 37, 131, 198, 290, 365, 367
Copernicus, 357
Copin, 257
Corbon (Jean), 274-75, 523
Cornaro (famille), 52
Cornelius (saint), 38

Coste (Jehan), 78, 80, 113, 194
Coudun (dom Aimery de), 327-30
Courbe (François), 470
Couret (Estème), 255-56, 258, 524-26
Courteaud (abbé), 133, 456
Crudel, king of Norgales, 188-89
Cumont-Damas (Charles de), 27

D
Darcel (Alfred), 384
David (A., priest), 480
Davin (canon), 78, 194, 482
Deblet (René, prior), 292
Delaage (Yves), 71
Delattre (Louis, priest), 142, 226-29
Deloche (Max), 34, 36, 40, 455-56, 466, 474
Delouche (Joseph), 434
Demmin (Auguste), 28, 75
Denys the Carthusian, 281, 353
Dominic of Trier, 281, 353
Dougny (priest), 425
Dreux (Parcival de), 82
Drotiault (Roger), 319
Du Bartras, 105
Du Tremblay (Joseph, capuchin), 316
Dünwegge (Victor and Heinrich, painters), 69
Dupuy-Vaillant (A.), 441
Durand (Paul, doctor), 60
Durandus of Mende (William, bishop), 6-7, 16, 156-57
Dürer, 391
Dutuit (collection), 103, 128

E
Eck (collection), 36
Edward VI, king of England, 393, 397
Eginhard, 256
Elbée (d'), 452
Ennodius (bishop), 9
Erasmus, 358
Erman, 221
Eschenbach (Wolfram von); *see* Wolfram von Eschenbach
Essarts, 452
Eudes (Jean, priest), 518
Eygun (François), 59, 256, 425-26

F
Faber (priest), 363
Faulcon (Jean), 296
Faure (E.), 71
Fedegius, 19
Ferdinand, king of Aragon, 43
Ferdinand the Catholic, king of Aragon, 43
Ferdinand, king of Portugal, 344-45
Fiévé (G., doctor), 426, 438
Fillon (Benjamin), 19, 335, 338, 445
Fillon (collection), 384-85
Fisher (bishop), 396
Flann, king of Ireland, 31
Fleury (Rohault de), 156, 207
Fontaines (Gabriel de), 25, 29, 136
Fortunatus of Poitiers (saint), 56, 59, 131, 143-44, 360, 366, 382
Fox (bishop), 392-93
Francesco Miguel y Badia (collection), 398
Franciosi, 306-7, 309
Francis of Assisi (saint), 297, 299, 385
Francis de Sales (saint), 254, 278-79, 309
Francis I, king of France, 100, 321
Frédol (cardinal), 234
Freppel (Mgr), 446
Fulgent (brother), 454
Fuligno (Niccolo da, painter), 201

G
Gabard (priest), 423
Gaddi (Taddeo, painter), 203
Gaignières (Roger de), 80
Galileo, 357
Galloys (Jean), 327
Gaudeau (canon), 506-8
Gaudin (Jean, priest), 296-97
Gauzelin (saint), 38
Gellé (Claude), 346

Indices

Gentius, king of Illyria, 171
Geoffroy-Martel (count), 326
Germijs (Hubert, abbot), 242
Gertrude (saint), 228-29, 418
Gilles de Rais, 502
Ginot (Émile), 470, 494
Ginther (Anton, priest), 341-44, 389
Giotto (painter), 146-48, 202, 390
Giovanni (don Lorenzo di), 117
Girard (painter), 80
Giraudon, 63, 68-69, 86, 147-49, 160, 186, 200-4
Givry (Claude de Longwy de, cardinal), 250
Gobillaud, 457
Godefroy de Bouillon, 51-52
Gonzaga, 119
Gonzalez y Gea (priest), 400
Gouffier (dukes), 103
Gougaud (dom Louis), 520-21
Gould (Carruthers, sir), 339
Goudon de la Lande (counts), 371
Goyet (Georges, priest), 311
Grandmaison (Millim de), 208
Gregory of Tours (saint), 74
Gresham (John), 309
Grèzes (Henri de), 305
Grignion de la Bachellerie (Louis-Marie, Father de Montfort, saint), ix, 423, 446, 450, 456, 479-81, 484-86, 493
Grimaldi (G.), 74
Grimouard de Saint-Laurent (Henri-Julien, count), x, 4, 146, 261, 278, 298-99, 343, 517
Gros (priest), 423
Grünewald (Matthias, painter), 157, 160
Gudiol (don), 248-49
Guénon (René), xiv-xvii, xix-xx, xxii-xxiii, xxv, 132, 145, 524
Guéranger (dom), 142
Guesclin, 317
Guignard (abbé), 438
Guyot de Provins, 191

H

Hacumblen (Robert), 90-91, 116, 153
Hamon (Augustin, priest), 296, 298-301, 503, 520-21, 523-26
Hangest (Hélène de), duchess of Roannais, 103
Hardouin (Gilles), 268, 342
Hardouin (Jean), 267-68
Hatshepsout, queen of Egypt, 222
Hébert (P., superior general), 447
Heitz (collection), 429
Hennesy (Jean), 508
Henriquez (Alfonso I), king of Portugal, 44, 45, 55-56, 262
Henry of Burgundy (duke), 55, 343
Henry of France; see Henry V, count of Chambord
Henry II, king of France, 103, 253
Henry III, king of France, 372
Henry IV, king of France, 316, 455
Henry V, count of Chambord, 461, 475-76
Henry VIII, king of England, 309, 383, 393, 396
Héraudière (counts of), 371
Hérouard (doctor), 71
Herrarde (abbess), 122
Heussner (A.), 414
Hippolytus (saint), 186
Honorius of Autun, 164
Houdaille, 470
Hucher, 189
Hugo (Victor), 179
Hugh of Saint-Victor, 104
Huré (S.), 276
Huysmans (Joris-Karl), 172, 381

I

Ignatius of Loyola (saint), 296, 301, 510
Igny (Guerric of), 229
Innocent VIII, pope, 74

J

Jacobi (Pierre), 273-75
Jacobus de Voragine, 207

Index of Names

Jacques de Molay, 58, 233-34
James I, king of Aragon, 43
James II, king of Aragon, 43
James the Conqueror, king of Majorca, 43
Jean de Chalon (the Elder), 388
Jean de France; *see* Berry (house of)
Jeanne de Chantal (saint), 218
Jeanne de France, 264; *see* Jeanne de Valois *and* Berry (house of)
Jeanne de Valois (blessed), duchess of Orléans, 345-46, 522
Jerome of Stridon (saint), 164
Joan of Arc (saint), 25
John I, king of Aragon, 43
John II, king of Aragon, 43
John Chrysostom (saint), 304, 310
John the Good, king of France, 80
Joinville (Jean de), 388, 422
Joly (Edmond), 171
Jouanneaux (Guy), 346
Jouin (bishop), 506-8
Jourdin (doctor), 257-58
Jousseaume (collection), 29
Joussemet (Catherine), 445-46
Justinian II, byzantine emperor, 379

K

Kempf (dom Nicolas), 307
Kerver (Tielman), 357
Klauber, 364-65, 498

L

La Barre (Antoine de), 271-72, 523
La Barre (Nicole de), 268-70, 523
La Billiais (family of), 445
La Colombière (Vulson de), 48
La Lande (family of), 371
La Rivière (family), 275
La Rochebrochard-Tinguy (madame de), 457
La Rochejaquelein (family of), 436-37, 453-53, 468
La Rochejaquelein (Henri de), 452, 468, 502

La Sayette (marquis de), 371
La Tour d'Auvergne (Robert de), 8
La Tourette (Gilles de, doctor), 314
La Ville-Beaugé, 452
Labarre (Pierre), 81-82, 162-63, 522
Labbé (Arthur), 33
Labitte (Alphonse), 162
Lacordaire (doctor), 372
Lacouloumère, 468, 470, 472
Lactantius, 216
Lagrillère (abbé), 383
Lambin (Émile), 145
Lancelot, 168
Landel (Hubert), 372
Landulf, 83
Langeac (Jean de, bishop), 321-22
Lanspergius (the Carthusian), 281, 284-87, 308, 353, 408
Lartigue (madame), 469
Laufer (Hans), 455
Launoberger, 34
Laurain, 441
Le Blant (Edmond), 143, 416
Le Caron (Pierre), 264-66, 523
Le Cour (Paul), 71, 145, 182
Le Moine (cardinal), 48
Le Rouge (Pierre), 266
Leclercq (dom Henri), x, 3, 5, 7, 14, 19, 31, 33, 37, 135, 142, 225-29, 366, 414
Leo XIII, pope, 246, 264
Leon de Lyon (priest), 61, 92, 167, 172
Lerosey, A. (canon), 4, 96
Lescure (marquis de), 437-38, 452, 502
Levet (Pierre), 266-67, 298, 325-26, 523
Lévis-Mirepoix (Marguerite de), 162
Levrier (Gérard), 449
Lhuillier de la Chapelle, 439, 458
Liesborn (Master of, painter), 63, 68
Littlechild (W.P.), 90, 116
Llado (don Juan, canon), 248, 253, 398
Lombez (Ambroise de, priest), 423
Longis (Jehan), 272-73
Loth, 198
Lothaire, king of France, 20

Loudun (Geoffroy de, bishop), 353
Louis I (the Pious or the Fair), emperor of the West, 20
Louis II, king of Bavaria, 28
Louis IX (saint), 58, 74, 198, 230-31, 250, 420, 453
Louis XI, king of France, 253, 345, 462, 522
Louis XII, king of France, 122, 207, 252, 492
Louis XIII, king of France, 316, 454-55, 476, 499
Louis XIV, king of France, 294, 349, 372, 420, 451, 455, 466, 506
Louis XV, king of France, 462, 467
Louis XVI, king of France, 320, 435, 447, 462, 469, 476
Louis XVII, royal prince of France, 349
Louis XVIII, king of France, 448-49, 468, 474
Louis d'Anjou (saint), 231-33
Louis-Philippe (d'Orléans), king of France, 475
Lubin (Barthélmy), 153
Luchesini (Ignatio), 85
Lucian (saint), 415
Ludolph of Saxony, 281, 284, 307, 353
Luini (Bernardino, painter), 111
Lulle (Raymond, blessed), 358
Lusignan (family), 52
Lutgarde (saint), 229

M

Mabillon (dom), 15
Machault (Guillaume de), 180
Macrobius, 225
Madiot (priest), 341
Maillard (Olivier, priest), 83-84, 155, 270, 309, 408
Maindron, 75
Mâle (Émile), x, 84, 105, 121-22, 125, 155, 193, 195, 339, 356, 362
Mantegna (painter), 241
Map (Walter), 191-92, 208

Marbode (bishop), 184
Marchand (Guyot), 274, 356, 368
Margaret Mary (Alacoque, saint), xiii, 318, 461, 506, 518
Maria of Aragon, queen, 43
Maria of Castille, queen, 43
Marienlebens (Master of, painter), 186
Marigny, 452
Marigny (lord of), 369
Marigny (vicar general), 257
Martin (Arthur), 225
Martin (Jean, collection), 109
Martin, king of Aragon, 43
Martineau, 80, 113, 194-95
Mary Tudor, queen of England, 397
Maspero, 215, 221-22
Matthew the Great (constable of France); see Montmorency (Matthew II)
Matthiolus, 151, 161, 169, 171
Maunoir (priest), 423
Mauroy (marquis of), 434
Maximian, Roman emperor, 415
Maximin (saint), 366
Mechtilde (saint), 228-29
Meliton (saint), 9
Merovech, king of the Franks, 17
Mesia de La Serda (house of the), 56
Michael, byzantine emperor, 22
Micheneau, 434
Molay (Jacques de); see Jacques de Molay
Mondion (Pierre de), 467
Monmouth (Geoffrey of), 206
Montfort (Father de); see Grignion de la Bachellerie (Louis-Marie, saint)
Monti de Rezé (Claude of, count), 168, 179
Montmorency (house of), 330
Montmorency (Matthew II of, Matthew the Great), 330
Montpensier (dukes of), 250
Mordrain, king of Scotland, 189
Moreau (priest), 36
Moreau de la Ronde (André), 415, 515

Index of Names

Moreau de la Ronde (collection), 137, 515
Moreau de la Ronde (Joseph), ix, 100, 414
Moreno, 510
Moret (Alexandre), 215-16, 220-22
Moreux (Théophile, priest), 214-15, 356, 358, 362
Morus (chancellor), 396
Mougon (of Poitou or of Touraine), 19
Moulier (Marie); *see* Bérault (Marie)
Mourry (Claude, "dit Le Prince"), 348
Mowart, 251
Musekin (Jacques), 256-59, 306
Mycerinus, pharaoh, 214

N

Napoleon, emperor, 208, 452, 474
Nassau (Flandrine of, abbess), 350
Naundorf; *see* Louis XVII
Navarre (Agnès de), princess, 180
Nefer-Neferu-Aten (Nefertiti), queen of Egypt, 220
Newland (John of, abbot), 300
Nicolo (Andrea di, painter), 149
Nigronus, 301
Nikeforos Botaneites, byzantine emperor, 22
Nitze, 198
Noaillat (Georges de), 401
Noguier de Malijay (priest), 71
Nouhes, 452

O

Oeagrus, king of Thrace, 412
Ollier (canon), 324
Orléans (Girard d', painter), 80

P

Papebrock, 9
Papini, 283
Parenteau (Fortuné, collection), 24, 109, 247, 439, 441, 445, 454, 457, 461-62, 502
Pascal II, pope, 52
Patrick (saint), 190
Paul I, tzar of Russia, 172
Paulinus of Nola (saint), 228
Paulownia (Anna), 172
Pauphilet, 198
Payns (Hugues de), 235
Pepi II, pharaoh, 217
Perrault (Charles), 502
Peter II, king of Aragon, 43
Peter IV, king of Aragon, 43
Peter of Alcantara (saint), 183, 308
Petit (Jehan), 83, 155, 309
Petit (Max), 40
Philip (bishop), 16
Philip I, king of France, 20
Philip II; *see* Philip Augustus
Philip IV; *see* Philip the Fair
Philip Augustus, king of France, 137, 237, 330, 515
Philip the Bold, king of France, 193
Philip the Fair, 234
Pia (signor), 71
Picard (Bernard), 12
Picard (colonel), 496
Pidoux de la Maduère, 387-88
Pie (Mgr), 453
Pieto Gérini (Nicolas di), 146, 157
Pigouchet (Philippe), 266, 356
Pius VI, pope, 435
Pius XII, pope, 481
Place (cardinal), 451
Plantagenets (family), 182
Plat (priest), 330
Plumant (Madame), 484
Poncet de la Rivière (Michel, bishop), 295
Prost, 80, 257
Prou (Maurice), 31, 37
Pythagoras, 417, 419

Q

Quantin (John), 155
Quentel (Peter), 286

R

Raadt (Johann Theodor de), 47, 242
Rabelais, 135, 358
Radegonde (saint), queen of the Franks, 366, 379
Rais (Gilles de), 502
Ramessids, pharaohs, 221
Ramses II, pharaoh, 217
Ramses VI, pharaoh, 219
Razilly (marquis de), 477
Receveur (Antoine), 423
Regnart (Pierre), 298-99, 301, 332, 409
Rémuzat (Anne de), 420
Renaud, count of Sens, 21
Renvoisé (canon), 330
Rich, 75
Richard (priest), 243
Richaud, 524-25
Richelieu, 137
Richstaetter (Karl, priest), 161-62, 166-67, 210, 388, 391, 520
Rigaud (Pierre), 254, 276, 278-79
Rilly (François de, count), 379, 381, 499
Robert, king of France, 343
Robert de Boron, 191-92, 196, 390
Rochebrune (Raoul de, count), 28, 34, 108-9, 225, 247, 255-56, 310, 375, 466, 468, 473-74, 476
Rodolph, 243
Romanus Argyrus, byzantine emperor, 22
Ronsard, 105
Rose Tromp (J.), 393
Ross (Alexander), 165
Rossi (Jean-Baptiste de), 38
Rossollin (E.), 82, 419, 422
Rothschild (collection), 103
Rouhault, 193
Roux (priest), 254
Royrand (de), 452

S

Saint-André (family of), 462
Saint-Laurent de la Cassaigne (chevalier, de), 436-37
Saint-Luc (Victoire de), 445
Saint-Périer (René de), 511
Saint Thierry (William of), 229
Sancho, king of Majorca, 43
Sapinaud (de), 452
Sarachaga (Alexis de, baron), 230-31
Sauvageo (collection), 103
Schomberg, 183
Schultze, 414
Séjourné (dom Paul), 102, 109, 330-32
Sévigné (Madame de), 30
Sforza (Maximilian), 100
Sicotteau (familles), 47
Sigefroi, Anglo-Danish king, 50
Smith (Th. S.), 396
Soest (Konrad von, painter), 68, 86
Solutive (Barthélémy), 293
Stephan (dom J.), 383
Stofflet (general), 442, 452
Suzannet, 453
Suzy (Étienne de, cardinal), 234

T

Taillandier (Robert), 276, 278-79
Taliessin, 410
Talmont (prince of), 452
Targé (Alain), 441
Tauler (John), 155, 305-6
Theodelinda, queen of the Lombards, 38
Theodora, byzantine empress, 22
Thévenin (priest), 388
Thom (J.), 90
Thomas Aquinas (saint), 90, 104, 392
Thomas of Villanova (saint), 308
Tonnelat, 198
Tunc (Gérard), 235
Tut-Ankh-Amon, pharaoh, 217, 223
Typotius, 344

U

Ulrick, landgrave of Alsace, 27
Urban VIII, pope, 85
Uzureau (François, canon), 437, 447

Index of Names

V

Vallette (René), 483
Valois (house of), 21, 27, 78, 256, 345
Van den Berghe (Oswald), 197-98
Van Eyck (Jan, painter), 110, 511, 514
Vandervelde (Doctor), 71
Varro, 225
Vasari, 146
Vérard (Antoine), 261-66, 356, 368, 523
Vériville (Miraud de), 162
Verthamon, 503
Vignon (Paul), 71-72, 75
Viguiers, 43
Villehardouin (William of), prince of Achaia, 21
Villeneuve (Geslin de, count), 445
Villoutreys (Jean de, count), 459, 462
Vincent of Beauvais, 104
Vincent IV of Gonzaga (duke), 185
Viollet-le-Duc, 16
Virey (Philippe), 45, 215, 217-18
Vivian (Matthieu), 275-76
Voragine (Jacobus de, archbishop of Genoa); *see* Jacobus de Voragine

W

Westerburg (family), 49
Weston (Miss), 198
Wilde (Mrs. Edith E.), 32, 91, 116-17, 310, 339, 392
William of Normandy, 104
William of Tyr, 206
William VI (count), 20
William X (saint, count), 20
Wolfram von Eschenbach, 191-92, 197
Woolcombe (C.K., vicar), 91, 116

Indices

SUBJECT INDEX

A
Abalone, 146
Acacia, 150, 509
Adonide, 170
Advent, 422
Albigensians, 36
Alchemy, 356, 358, 360, 502
Almighty, 135, 187, 223, 348, 456, 504
Aloes, 70–71, 232
Alpha, 61, 272, 377
Amaranth, 168–70
Amulet, 450, 503, 515
Anchor, 3, 30, 61, 249, 476–77
Angel, 57, 80, 156, 161, 180, 188, 218, 263, 267–68, 295, 322–24, 348, 390, 393, 400, 402; bearing a cup, 196, 199; collecting blood, 194, 201–4, 390; holding a heart, 285; holding a host, 12–14; holding a rose, 166–67; of the Rose of the Winds, 370–71; of Saint Matthew, 125; shield-bearing, 59, 88, 161, 325
Annunciation, 457
Anointings, 6
Apocalypse, 105, 164, 230, 290, 367, 370, 387
Apostle, 125, 205, 207, 286, 343, 371, 407, 423, 446, 485, 497
Aquamarine, 183
Arma Christi, 159, 167, 271, 282
Arrow, 70, 268, 271–72, 285, 420–21, 468, 511; flaming, 364; of love, 129
Art, Christian, ix, 4, 121, 143, 173, 304, 335, 339
Ascension, 9, 308
Astrology, 356, 358, 360
Astronomy, 214, 356, 358, 360, 405
Augustinian, 58, 99, 230
Axe, ix, 25
Azure, 47, 49, 54, 56, 183, 342, 346, 371, 420, 440, 448

B
Balance, 5, 218
Balm, 151, 156
Baptism, 4, 84, 193; sacrilegious, 512
Barrel 125, 316
Basin, 57, 91, 95, 105, 108, 118, 127, 206, 320, 334, 354; of Dona, 190; magic, 189; river, 187; sacred, 189
Belt, sword, 24, 26–27; white, 436
Benedictine(s), 15–16, 228, 313, 317, 326–27, 350, 383, 404, 417, 518, 520; of Calvary, 314, 316, 417; Craon, 499–500; Fontevrault, 297, 316, 333, 382; Saint-Jean d'Angely, 474
Bestiary of Christ, xii, xvi–xviii, xxiii, xv, 159, 174
Bewitchment, 511–12, 515
Bezel, 19, 41, 179, 466, 473
Bible, 136, 188, 215
Bible, of La Roche-Clermault, 349–50
Bible, of Saint Paul Outside-the-Walls, 40
Bird, 84, 89, 95, 103–4, 305, 307, 311, 411–12, 415, 492; divine, 222–23
Blasphemy, 504–6
Blazon, 46, 56, 182, 323, 325, 337, 342, 349, 371; of Jesus Christ, 57, 324; of the Passion, 59
Blazonry, 46–47, 243, 325, 343, 346
Blood, xix, 3–4, 7, 45, 53, 56, 59, 72, 77–78, 81, 84, 87–91, 103–5, 109, 113–14, 121–22, 125–29, 141, 152, 155, 157, 163–65, 168, 170, 177, 181, 184, 187–88, 190, 192–93, 195–96, 199, 208, 213, 216, 242, 246, 249, 275, 280, 303, 307, 320, 334–35, 338, 347, 377, 387–90, 393–95, 398, 403, 410, 419, 442, 444, 446–47, 449, 453, 463, 472, 484, 487, 503, 521–22; Adonis', 170; Body and, 10; Christ's/Jesus's/the Savior's, xiv, 9, 53, 56, 87, 165,

540

Subject Index

168, 184, 201–2, 223, 334, 348, 392; clotted/coagulated/congealed, xiv, 169, 177, 180, 336; collected in a cup, 188, 200–204, 207, 390; divine, 80, 95, 104, 121, 131, 152–53, 166, 170, 177, 181, 197, 199, 209, 245, 282, 305, 334; eucharistic, 183; and light, 182; martyrs', 290; precious, 88, 105, 185, 327, 360, 387, 420; redemptive, 7, 43, 51, 56, 74, 78, 81, 88, 114, 121, 152, 165, 167, 194, 282, 291, 305, 389; sweat of, 141, 335; and water, xix, 67, 83–84, 88, 131, 188, 197, 231, 245, 283, 307–8, 360, 390, 395
Bloodstone, 197
Book of Hours, 60, 82, 161–62, 194–95
Books, sacred, 99, 151
Bowl, 106, 320; of a chalice, 275; of a ciborium, 187; of a cup, 194, 208, 213; sacred, 206
Boxwood, 146, 310
Bramble, 157, 160
Branch, 4, 49–50, 105, 142–44, 146, 150, 153, 156, 162, 209, 225, 227, 237, 239, 243, 246, 274, 316, 331–32, 336, 373, 379, 382–83, 388, 403, 444, 455, 482, 504, 507, 509
Bread, 6, 47, 188, 208, 389, 395, 415
Bronze, 17, 24, 37, 51, 88–89, 116, 119, 179, 184, 189, 228, 255, 484, 512, 515
Brotherhood, 253, 268–69, 498; Christ the Black, 385, 399–400, 421, 498; Christ of Succour, 399; hermetic-mystical, 136; Penitents of Trinité-Vieille, 419, 422
Butterfly, 108

C

Calvary, 6, 19, 24, 56–57, 78, 131, 133, 166, 173, 190, 192, 204, 232, 235, 239, 245, 248–49, 252, 259, 284, 290, 316, 345, 398, 498; *see also* Golgotha
Calvaries (wayside crosses), 33, 423, 426, 480

Candle, 150, 292; Paschal, 8–10, 21, 61–62, 87, 141, 367
Capetians, 21, 27, 190; kings, 191, 330
Capuchins; *see* Order of Saint Francis of Assisi
Carmelite(s), 297, 313, 319, 442; *see also* Order of Carmel
Carnelian, 164, 177, 179, 183–84, 197
Carthusian, 281, 283–87, 297, 306–8, 353, 355, 358, 360–61, 363–64, 367, 374, 408, 518
Cartouche, 43, 103, 294, 296, 301, 323, 373, 375–77, 382, 422, 444, 509
Cask, 125
Casket, 109, 206, 218
Cat, black, 512
Cauldron, sacred, 189
Celts, 189
Cemetery, 32, 36, 169, 366, 473, 517
Centaur, 128
Chalice, 10–11, 31, 109, 113, 117, 165, 194, 200–205, 208–10, 213, 275, 398, 403
Chalice, surmounted by a host, 346, 390, 392, 394–96
Chapter of Saint Gal, 322, 325
Charity, 261, 273, 299, 349, 476
Chastity, 197, 299, 301
Cherry tree, 150
Chevalerie du Graal, 198
Chivalry, xi, 45
Chrism, 4
Chrismon, 61, 143; with spear, 284; *see also* Monogram of Christ
Christ of Pity, 241
Christianity, xiii, xix, 26, 30, 107, 132, 136, 187, 216, 224, 308, 359, 414, 512
Christmas, 377
Circle, 12, 19–21, 76, 135, 138, 173, 208, 248, 336, 394, 407, 445, 467, 480, 505–6; of cherubim, 254; cross-bearing, 31, 38, 55, 133, 235, 360; planetary, 355–61, 363, 524; of the zodiac, 362
Circumcision, 166, 376, 501

Cistercians, 50, 518
Clay, 29, 102, 260, 366, 511; human, 109
Cloak, 199; of flesh, 427; large (*saga*), 37; white, 53
Coat of arms, canting, 113, 256, 526; of Christ, 271, 282, 328-29; mystical, 345; of the Passion, 57, 59, 324; true and rational role, 292; with Sacred Heart, 448; of our salvation, 271; *Signaculum Domini*, 47, 49, 52, 55-56; with five wounds, 114-16, 153, 342; *see also* Crest, Escutcheon
Column, 88, 143, 271, 329, 400
Confraternity, 301; Estoile Internelle, xiv, xvi; mold for, 250-51, 401; penitent, 50, 301
Conifer, 150
Conscience, 137, 433
Convolvulus, 11, 224
Coping, 100
Coral, 164, 177, 183-84, 197
Cord, 57, 295, 322, 385, 462
Cordelier, 298-99, 301, 313, 384-85
Cordiform, 228, 410
Corpus Christi, 6
Council, 317, 459; Fine Arts, 321; Nicea, 9; Troyes, 237
Counter-Church, 510
Crescent, 4, 20-21, 46, 62, 78, 88, 113, 194, 244, 252, 371, 421
Crest, 43, 242, 263, 267, 325, 334, 342-43, 348-49, 392-93, 455, 508, 521; divine, 167; of God, 282; of a helmet, 49, 290; mystical, 522; of our salvation, 272; of the Five Wounds; *see also* Coat of Arms, Escutcheon
Cromlech, 190
Cross, *passim*; altar stone, 6-7, 21, 26, 50, 87; of Anjou, 23; Breton, 493-94; byzantine, 14, 37; of Calvary, 96, 259, 284, 345, 398; ecoté, 243; equal-armed, 4; fleuroned, 29; folly of, 121; forked, 31, 142; "gammated," 19; Greek, 12, 15, 19-20; humetty, 43; of Jerusalem, 49, 54; Latin, 17, 49-50, 252, 468; of Lorraine, 23; Lychnis-, 165; Maltese, x; La Maurienne, 494; mission, 422; of Father Montfort, 479, 484-86; office of, 162; pattee, 26, 47, 50, 252; pectoral, 382-83, 485, 499-500; potent, 41, 50, 52-53; radiant, 330; redemptive, 101, 360, 387; Rose, 508; Savoyard, 494; made of spearheads, 37; starry, 3; *Symbolism of the*, xvi, 145; true, 13, 23, 327, 379, 381-82, 386-87; wayside, 422; in an X, 3, 21, 38, 243
Crosslet, 4-5, 12, 17, 19-21, 25-26, 29, 36, 38, 43, 46-47, 49-53, 76, 87, 111, 171, 244, 386
Crow, 512
Crown, 20, 22, 177, 179, 222, 263, 319, 330, 347-48, 377, 442, 454, 466-69, 472, 476; Arthur and knights, 199; bramble bush, 157, 160; of cherubim, 254; English, 393; of flames, 476; fleur-de-lysed, 347; flowered, 344, 346; glorious, 109; golden, 114, 348; hawthorn, 157; of hearts, 364; holy, 387-88; imperial, 54; magpie's nest, 157, 160; of rope, 504; royal, 55, 268, 445, 454-55; of thorns, 57-59, 89-90, 156, 158, 163, 172, 194, 239, 242, 267-68, 271, 279, 283, 287, 298, 311, 319-20, 325, 328, 332-33, 335, 347, 374, 382-83, 385, 394, 399-400, 403, 424, 426, 441, 447, 450, 452, 482-83, 499, 523
Crucible, 126, 213, 390, 430
Crusader, 45, 51-52, 151, 206
Crusades, 45, 52-53, 171, 205
Cruciata, 171
Crucifix, 76-77, 80, 157, 177, 249, 422, 430, 480-81, 484, 486
Crucifixion, xix, 19, 34, 36, 79, 88, 150, 160, 239, 273, 298, 335, 360, 501
Crucifying, 171, 298; of Our Lady, 385
Crystal, 14, 180, 379-81; rock, 177, 183
Curse, 511, 513

D

Danse macabre, 356
Deer, 108; fallow, 256; roe, 256
Diamond, 177, 179, 183, 469
Divinity, xix, 9, 183, 189, 214, 220, 222, 418, 508
Doe, 95, 109; black, at Ardales, 512
Dog, 367
Dogma, 132, 223, 334, 402
Dolphin, 61
Donkey, 411
Dove, 61, 83–84, 89, 95, 108–9, 142, 144, 197, 295, 305, 307–9, 311, 402, 415, 494
Downpour, 91
Dragon, 412, 462; palm, 150
Dragon's blood, 151
Drop of blood, 170

E

Eagle, 125, 245
East, 136, 151, 189, 329, 370; Christian, 52, 205, 244
Easter, 9
Eden, 187–88
Eglantine, 157, 166
Egyptians, 45, 214, 223, 355, 410
Elephant, 224, 511
Ellipse, 88, 90, 187
Emblem of the Five Wounds, 20, 41, 46, 56, 61, 77
Emerald, 14, 177, 183, 187, 197, 206–8, 386
Enamel, 11, 14, 26, 182, 505
Engraver, 118, 155, 236, 252, 254, 277, 291, 299, 319, 346, 348, 355, 455, 525
Escarbuncle, 88, 141, 179–80, 185–86, 197; *see also* Rays of the, 182–83, 186
Eschuteon 167, 236; *see also* coat of arms, crest
Estoile Internelle, xiv, xvi–xx, 180, 185, 195–97
Eternity, 306, 360, 367, 377, 392

Etimacia, 60, 159
Eucharist, 10, 84, 104–5, 109, 205, 209, 216, 227, 334, 389–91, 501, 512
Evangelary, 33, 38–40
Evil, 143, 219, 225, 307, 372, 411, 450, 510, 513
Ewer, 96, 105, 271, 483
Executioners, 164, 335
Exercise of the Crucified Heart, 300, 408
Ex-libris, x, 49, 295, 497
Exudation, 150–51

F

Faith, 76, 137, 173, 190, 213, 234, 246, 253, 261, 274, 315, 333–34, 338, 366–67, 395, 397, 402, 414, 416, 426, 446, 450, 456, 465, 477, 487, 510, 518; Catholic, 117; Christian, ix, 24, 53, 334
Fibula, 37, 378
Fir, 150
Fireplace, x
Firmament, 135, 356, 459
Fish, 3, 61, 107
Fisher King, 191
Five beads (rosary), 268
Five grains of incense, 8–9, 21
Five points, 38, 48, 54; emblematic, 12, 268; symbolic, 22
Five Wounds, ix, xx, 6, 17, 20, 41, 46, 56–57, 61, 76–77, 90, 105, 114–17, 229, 239, 243–45, 259, 267–68, 286–87, 327, 342, 520–21; Mass of, 163; redemptive, 111; shield, 324
Flame, 8, 99, 230, 254, 278–79, 281, 330, 381, 398, 403, 409, 430, 442, 469, 501; of love, 254, 277
Flank, 87, 442; right, 70
Fleur de Lys, 21–22, 249, 252, 268, 280, 382, 434, 444, 456, 469, 484
Flood, 131, 188, 360
Florary/Flower lore, xix, xxiii, 165, 170
Flower, red, 170–71; mauve, 173; purple, 163

Indices

Foliage, 108, 144–46, 148, 252, 329, 355, 506
Font, baptismal, 47, 135, 315, 327
Fountain, 80, 91, 95, 99–102, 105, 107–8, 114, 118, 326, 523; of comfort, 91, 117, 392; of consolation, 102; of grace, 91, 112, 117–18, 392; heart-, 103, 105; of holiness, 102, 398; of (everlasting) life, 91, 102, 105, 113, 117, 194, 282, 334, 356, 392, 398; of mercy, 91, 117, 392; of piety, 117; of pity, 392; of purification, 194; of regeneration, 194; of salvation, 100, 193; of the Savior, 101, 194; of wisdom, 91
Franciscan, 74, 85, 92, 167, 229, 239, 254, 297, 332, 384, 409, 518–19
Freemason, 508
Freemasonry, 505
Fresco, 55, 143, 146–47, 166, 323, 356

G

Gall, 131
Gallows, 96, 142, 157
Gamma, 38, 40, 244–45
Garden, x, 32, 70, 100, 118; of Olives, 141, 335; of the Virtues, 150
Garment, 57, 121, 335, 466; blood-stained, 122; red, 122, 164–65, 184
Garnet, 177, 183
Gem, 4, 54, 128, 177, 179, 182–83, 219, 379, 466, 470; vegetal, 152
Genesis, 164, 216, 372
Gentian, 171
Gift, eucharistic, 109, 117
Gloss, 109, 113
Goat, 257, 512
God-Man, 61, 177
Gnomonics, 368
Gnostic, 4
Goldsmith, 15, 387, 469, 495
Golgotha, 87, 205–6, 208–9, 249, 336; *see also* Calvary
Good Friday, 56, 131, 197, 360
Gospel, 22, 37–38, 70, 89, 95–96, 108, 163, 188, 190, 197, 216, 239, 322, 354, 376, 390, 400
Gothic, x, 26, 78, 83, 114, 116, 218, 229, 256, 265, 284, 314, 316, 321–22, 345, 357, 362, 390, 403, 468, 519
Grail, 78, 80, 113, 180, 187–93, 197–99, 205, 207–9, 390
Grace, 3, 91, 102, 107–9, 112–14, 117–18, 131, 141, 227, 264, 295, 343, 392, 420, 454, 459, 510; divine, 117, 131; pilgrimage of, 393–96
Graffiti, 132, 135–37, 258, 306, 524
Grape, 95, 121–22, 125–26, 164, 226–28, 230, 332, 334
Gravestone, 31, 327
Great Refuge, 136, 449
Green, 56, 99, 169, 206, 208, 349, 438–39, 445, 505
Grenadille, 171
Griffin, 95
Gum, 150–53; *see also* Resin

H

Habitation, 135, 304, 311; mystical, 289, 309; spiritual, 227, 289, 302, 312
Hammer, 57, 172, 271, 282, 314, 330, 335, 337, 384, 454, 482–83
Happiness, 3, 107, 189–90, 217, 411, 413
Harness, 457
Hawthorn, 146, 157
Healing, 119, 151, 153, 191, 308
Heart (predominantly that of Christ), *passim*; ablaze, 421, 500; adored, 325, 487; *all*, 298, 338; of the apostles, 497; bewitchment of, 511–12, 515; blasphemous, 504; surrounded by bones, 268; Breton, 493; burning, 442; of the Calvaries, 423; center of the universe, xii, 358; bound with a chain, 505; above a chalice, 210; Christ-, 367; Christian, 227, 291, 403, 450, 486; of the cross, 48; surmounted by a cross, 99, 252, 255, 269, 447, 476; by a double cross, 310; marked with the cross, 247;

surmounted by a crown, 348; by a crown of flames, 476; surrounded by the crown of thorns, 311, 383, 441; crucified, 300–306, 338, 390, 406–9, 494, 496; divine, 101, 126, 167, 213, 223, 231, 252–53, 256, 258–59, 266, 286–87, 291, 306, 319, 325, 344–45, 376, 385, 389, 403, 418, 427, 447, 453, 456, 472, 486, 495, 506, 519; emblematic, 300, 329, 386, 473; enigmatic, 330, 406; eucharistic, 389, 395; faithful, 254, 259, 278, 291–93, 297, 300, 302, 310, 312, 318–19, 381, 402, 425; faulty, 297; feminine, 507; flaming, 364, 403, 426, 439, 509; belted with flowers, 505; as fountain, 91, 102, 105; four, 40, 239, 242, 244–45; gilded, 424; of God, 217, 221–23, 309, 368, 398, 410; glorified, 255, 495; glorious, 353; golden, 81, 385, 451; as grape, 126–27; heraldic, 515; hieroglyphic of, 216; human, 70, 129, 216–17, 220, 223, 229, 311, 364, 373, 410, 424, 426–28, 430, 494, 497, 499–500; of humanity, 506; iconography of, 129, 300, 397, 496; inflamed, 292, 439, 483; source of intellect, 410; irradiation of, 356; jewel-case of, 78; of Joseph, 474; leaden, 447, 454; lyre-, 417–18; magical, 515; masculine, 507; Merovingian, 378; metaphorical, 217, 223; monogram inscribed on or above, 291, 294, 298, 319, 367; with nails, 296, 298, 301; natural, 512; one, 407; opened, 67, 106, 245, 259, 305, 390; paternal, 507; all-perfect, 297; physical, 77, 223, 306; pierced, 152, 167, 245, 267, 286; Poitevin, 466–73, 487, 491, 493, 495; profane, 254, 454; radiant/radiating, 258, 279, 306, 363, 367, 498–99, 524; red, 224, 243, 420, 438–40, 442, 505, 511; redeeming, 213; bound with rope, 503–4, 510; royal, 345, 454; Sacred, xii–xiii, xxii, 99–100, 102, 114, 117, 194, 213, 223, 228, 230–31, 249, 254, 276, 294, 296, 306–7, 310–11, 318–19, 327, 329–31, 333, 343, 346–47, 349–50, 358, 372, 374, 381, 393, 395–96, 398, 400–401, 403, 420–22, 426–27, 433, 435–39, 441–52, 454, 461–62, 466, 471, 473, 480, 482, 484, 498, 501–3, 506–7, 509–10, 517–20; Savoyard, 494; sorrowful, 330; as summary, 218; -sun, 369; symbolism of, xv, xxv, 7; thirty-three, 399; transpierced, 60, 81, 327, 331, 420; transverberated, 81, 285; triangle of, 126; in a triangle, 502; in an inverted triangle, 508; united, 372; Universal, 363; as vase, 218, 222; Vendean, 445, 466, 468; of the Virgin Mary, 129, 272, 319, 371–72, 386, 424, 442, 453, 455–56, 470, 473–74, 476, 492, 507; votive, 424, 427–28, 430; vow to the Sacred, 476; of wax, 512; white, 56; of the Word, 409; of the World, 359; worship of, 480, 494; wounded, xix, 12, 59, 62, 77, 80–81, 84–85, 96, 115, 117, 161, 245, 267, 281–82, 285–86, 315–16, 318, 321, 324–25, 364, 367, 375, 389, 391, 394, 398, 408, 453, 483–84, 521, 524; wounded after death, 242; wounded with nails, 293; of Zagreus, 413, 419

Heart-shaped, 4, 11, 224–26, 243, 319, 369, 425, 457, 509

Hebrews, 122, 216, 223

Hell, 3, 144, 183, 290, 367

Helmet, 27–28, 49, 290

Hematite, 164, 177, 179, 183–84, 197

Hen, black, 512

Heraldry, x, 21, 45–47, 49–50, 52, 56, 61, 87, 118–19, 132, 185, 243, 253, 271, 291, 343, 467, 484, 509, 525

Hermetic, Hermetism, ix, xvi, 46, 132–33, 136–37, 197, 216, 356, 359, 508, 524

Holy Crown, 295; see also Crown of thorns
Holy Face, 331, 400
Holy Family, 473-74
Holy Grail; see Grail
Holy of Holies, 74, 304-5, 310
Holy Land, 54, 205, 208
Holy Places, 52, 205-6
Holy Shroud of Turin, xx, 36, 71, 73-75, 155
Holy Spear, 69, 74-75, 78, 168, 190
Holy Spirit, ix, xiv, 402, 418, 494
Holy Wound, 118, 194, 334, 408, 522
Hope, 3, 17, 34, 56, 113, 163, 234, 246, 303, 366, 408, 414, 465, 476-77, 486, 505
Horseman, 164
Hospitalers of Mercy, 314
Host, 12, 166, 192, 197, 247-49, 253-55, 259, 277, 298, 306, 345-46, 390, 392, 394-96, 398, 403, 429, 441, 512, 520, 524; Lord God of, 442
Host-mold, 247-49, 253, 255, 259, 298, 306, 345, 520
Hyacinth, 177
Hyssop, 157-59

I

IHS, 22, 264, 272, 291-92, 294-96, 301, 310, 314, 371-73, 375, 381, 384, 395, 398, 402-3, 417, 422, 471, 484, 497, 501, 523; see also Monogram of the name of Jesus
Illuminator, 81, 155, 161, 256, 260-61, 291, 377
Image-maker, 83, 114, 119, 337-38
Immortality, 170, 413-14, 416
Infinity, xviii-xix, 220, 325, 358, 363
Infusion, 156
Initiation, 132, 231
Instruments of the Passion, 59-60, 81, 167, 172, 194, 251, 253, 258, 272, 381, 403, 484, 524
Intelligence, 137, 217, 221, 280, 363
Ivy, 224-25

J

January, xxiii, 85, 294, 361-62, 375-77, 435, 506
Jacinth, 183
Jasper, 184
Jesuits, 213, 296, 301, 314, 318, 423, 519, 523; see also Society of Jesus
Jewel-case, 78, 81, 302, 410, 466, 487
Jewel of love, 74
Jews, 70, 83, 155, 482
Joy, 100-102, 105, 194, 299-300, 410, 497
Juice, 121, 125
Jupiter, 357, 359-60, 413
Justice, 67, 91, 101, 115, 122, 164, 214, 218, 334, 365, 510

K

Kabbalah, 356
Key, 24, 74, 206, 377, 388, 413
Key, of Saint Meliton, 9
Keystone, 57, 159, 283-84, 353
Kingdom of Blessing, 136
Knighthood, 132
Knights of the Golden Fleece, 400; of Malta, x-xi, 235, 314; of the Precious Blood, 185; of the Round Table, 81, 191, 198; of the Royal Order of Saint Michael, 459, 461-62; of Saint Catherine of Mount Sinai, 53; of Saint John of Jerusalem; see Knights of Malta; of the Holy Sepulcher, 53-54, 62; Templar, 233-34
Knoll, 95, 108
Knowledge, ix, xxiii-xxiv, 71, 91, 137, 214, 221, 358, 363, 377, 517

L

Labarum, 5, 499
Ladder, 271
Lamb, 108-10, 117, 145, 159, 193, 230, 246, 347; paschal, 192, 208
Lantern, 57, 271, 331
Lapsit exillis, xvi, 197
Larch, 150

Subject Index

Last Supper, xiv, 190, 192, 199, 206–8, 210, 262, 390, 393
Laurel, 4, 274, 331, 373, 455, 506–7
Law, Christian, 52
Law, Mosaic, 52, 158
Law, Salic, 379
Leaf, 11, 88, 126, 169, 173, 226–27, 230, 355, 410; convolvulus, 11, 224; four, 5; grape vine, 226, 228, 332; heart-shaped, 4, 11; ivy, 225; oak, 145; St. John's wort, 156; strawberry, 161–63
League of Nations, 508–9
Legionnaire, 76, 88, 91, 152, 239, 245, 416, 482
Lens, 72, 88
Lent, 422
Lenticular, 87–92
Lentisk, 150
Life, eternal, 108, 114, 117–18, 188, 308, 392
Linden, 224
Lion, xvi, 22, 125, 245, 307, 440, 442
Liquor, divine, 125
Liturgy, 7–9, 12, 61, 136, 144, 159, 223, 367, 376–77, 389, 450, 512–13
Logos, 419
Longanimity, 299
Love-lies-bleeding, 169
Lychnis, 165
Lyre, 246, 317, 409, 411–19
Lyre, mystical, 317, 417

M

Macrocosm, 137–38
Magi, 216
Magic, 224, 413, 502, 511–12
Magician, 180
Man of Sorrows, 77, 334
Mango tree, 410
Map, 364
Maple, 146
Mappemonde, 133
Marble, x, 6–7, 224–25, 230, 353, 411, 524

Marble, astronomical, 354–63, 365, 367–69, 405
Mars, 359–60
Martyr, 3, 6, 13, 107, 161, 163, 290, 379, 414, 420, 444, 446, 453
Martyrdom, 435
Martyrium, 205–6
Mass, 6–7, 11, 136, 142, 163, 207, 262, 316, 376, 396, 420, 518
Massenie du Saint Graal, 198
Mast, 3
Mauve, 173, 469
Megaliths, 132–33
Menhir, 32, 132, 190
Mercury, 357, 359–60
Mercy, xii, 91, 102, 114–17, 136, 264, 305, 314, 368, 392, 437, 445, 499
Merovingian, 7, 13, 17, 29, 38, 40, 76, 133, 135–36, 259, 367, 378, 499
Microcosm, 137–38
Millepertuis, 156
Monasticism, 132
Monogram, 52–53, 101, 143, 153, 227, 228, 260, 263, 265, 310, 314, 330, 374, 384, 403, 442; of Christ, 108, 143, 182, 226, 367; see also Chrismon; Constantinian; of the name of Jesus, 100, 226, 264, 271–72, 275, 283–84, 289–98, 300–302, 315, 319, 372–73, 375–76, 381, 383, 402–3, 415, 417, 422, 471, 473, 484, 501; see also IHS; of the name of Mary, 271–72, 275, 298, 319, 471, 473
Moon, 230, 252, 357, 359–60, 471
Moors, 56, 342; see also Muslims
Mount of the Skull, 336
Murex, 164
Muslims, 51; see also Moors
Myrrh, 70, 151, 231
Mysteries, 189, 198, 363, 377, 413
Mystery, xx, xxii, 209, 216, 221, 247, 300, 334, 358, 405, 410, 413, 419, 494
Mysticism, 138, 253, 264, 286, 343, 428; Christian, 302; Jewish, 136

547

N

Nail(s), xix, 4, 6, 10, 13, 34, 36, 46, 57–59, 77, 88, 90, 131, 157, 163, 168, 172, 179, 236, 239, 243, 267, 271, 282–83, 286, 293, 306, 319, 325, 332, 334–35, 337–38, 360, 368, 373, 384, 394–96, 428, 482, 521; four, 5, 15, 19, 31, 36, 48, 58, 92, 250; Holy, 14, 16, 26, 56; three, 36, 48, 59, 89, 273, 279, 289, 296–302, 328, 331, 420
Negative, xviii, 27, 71
Nest, 84, 109, 146–49, 307–8; magpie's 157, 160
New Testament, 52
Nimbus, 22, 89, 237, 254, 268, 402, 497–98
North, 191, 222, 329, 498; angel of, 370

O

Oak, 144–46, 274, 284, 331, 371, 444, 455, 507
Obedience, 90, 299, 301
Oil(s), 21, 141, 156; Holy, 6
Old Testament, 52
Olive tree, 141, 274, 374, 506–7
Olivine, 183
Omega, 61, 272, 377
Opening of the Heart, 324; see also Wound to the Heart
Order of Carmel, 442; see also Carmelites
Order of Cîteaux, 191, 237
Order of the Holy Sepulcher, 56
Order of Mathurins, 314
Order of Saint Augustine; see Augustinians
Order of Saint Benedict; see Benedictines
Order of Saint Bruno, 282–83; see also Carthusians
Order of Saint Francis of Assisi; see Franciscans
Order of Saint Michael of the Chouans, 459, 461–62
Order of the Temple, 58, 197, 233–34, 236–37; see also Knights Templar
Oriflamme, 448
Orthodoxy, 4, 85, 132, 272, 501, 524
Owl, wood-, 459
Ox, 125, 142, 245

P

Palm (tree), 107, 150–51, 161, 349, 367
Palmette, 355–56, 368
Paradise, earthly, 269, 308
Passion, of Our Lady, 386
Passionflower, 171
Paten, 10–11, 293, 366, 394
Patience, 299
Paulownia, 172–73
Peace, 3, 107, 131, 136, 142, 189, 198, 299, 305, 397, 433, 486, 507
Peach, 150
Peacock, 95, 108, 144
Pearl, 37, 179, 183, 209, 302, 333, 386, 467–68
Pelican, 103–6, 109, 128, 146–49, 501
Penitents, White, 301, 419, 422
Petal, 21, 88, 171
Phoenix, 108
Pickaxe, 246, 315
Pilgrimage, 47, 205, 250, 401, 403–4, 450; of Grace, 393–96
Pillar, 262; scourging, 57, 80, 155 267, 287, 322, 324, 331, 384, 481, 510
Pincers, 271, 282, 482–83
Pine, 150–51
Pitch, 150
Planisphere, 133
Plant, eucharistic, 332
Plants, 88, 141, 156, 158, 161, 189
Points, diacritical, 38; see also Signaculum Domini
Poppy, 164–65
Poverty, 299, 301, 303, 327, 507
Precinct, triple, xvi, 131–38
Priesthood, 132, 214, 216, 220
Promised Land, 122
Prudence, 91, 115, 261

Purple, 16, 103, 114, 144, 163, 165, 170, 334, 381, 388, 420, 451–52, 523
Pursuit, mystical, 367

R

Rays of the Escarbuncle, 182–83, 186
Rebus, 273–74, 405, 407, 409, 491, 495
Red, xvi, 81, 88, 151–52, 159, 163–66, 168–71, 177, 179–80, 183–84, 197, 224, 243, 346, 385–86, 395, 420, 422, 438–39, 441–42, 445, 447, 449–51, 463, 502, 505, 508, 511; blood-, 11, 164, 169; brick-, 422
Redeemer, xii, 3, 9–10, 12, 19, 24, 57, 61, 77, 85, 91, 96–97, 122, 126, 170, 177, 183, 213, 252, 264, 269, 283, 292, 296, 303, 331, 335, 338, 342, 368, 384, 390, 423, 510, 518
Redemption, 4, 22, 34, 60, 74, 77, 101, 104, 132–33, 137, 141, 325, 334, 338, 359, 421, 430, 523
Reed, 57, 97, 156–57, 249–50, 411
Refuge, 84, 275, 301, 306–9, 363, 434; Great, 136, 449; in Holy of Holies, 310; mystical, 408; sacred, 303, 304
Regnabit, xii, xv, xx, 63, 68–69, 86, 110, 147–49, 160, 178, 186, 195, 200–204, 243, 285, 388, 390, 401, 409, 420, 429, 447, 480, 485, 498, 520, 523–24
Reliquary, 13–16, 26, 51, 56, 109, 185, 379–82, 384–87, 400
Remedy, 90, 116, 153
Repentance, 163, 234, 236
Resin, 150–53, 512; *see also* Gum
Ring, 19, 34, 36, 74, 182, 244, 250, 402, 454, 491–92, 495; engagement, 274; Gallo-Frankish, 31, 36; Holy Family, 473; Love-, 491; Poitevin, 466, 469; with Sacred Heart, 473–74, 487; signet, 15, 34, 40–41, 48
Robe, seamless, 57, 88, 283
Rods, 59, 80, 155, 158, 239, 242, 283, 323–24, 335, 483
Rooster, 57, 271, 384, 481, 483
Root, 161, 171, 367, 517

Rope 125, 271, 331, 335–36, 384, 503–4, 510
Rosary, 268, 321, 436
Rosary of the Five Wounds, 167
Rose, 4, 164, 166–68, 220, 244, 268, 308, 320, 344, 410; bush, 157, 167; of the Passion, 165–66; red, 165, 168; of Saint John, 174; of the Winds, 370
Rose Cross, 508
Rosewood, 380
Round Table, 81, 190–92, 199
Ruby, 77, 164, 177–80, 182–83, 308, 386, 469
Ruby, balas; *see* Ruby
Ruby, escarbuncle, 180, 182, 197
Rushes, 156–57

S

Sacrifice, 6, 34, 56, 89, 128, 133, 158–59, 163, 248–49, 335–36
Sages, 221, 418
Sagro Catino, 127, 206–10
Saint Gal (chapter of), 322, 325
Salvation, 8, 34, 77, 89, 101, 234, 245, 303–4, 387, 486, 505, 521; coat of arms of, 271–72; fountains of, 100, 193; instrument of, 3, 142; tree of, 142; of the world, 56, 177, 472
Sandalwood, red, 151
Sap, 150–52, 517
Sapphire, 183
Sarcophagus, 416
Saturday, Holy, 367
Saturn, 359–60, 377
Scale (weights), 218–19; (musical), 418
Scales, silver (sign), 266
Scapular of the Sacred Heart, 437–38, 446–47, 450
Scepter, 51, 57, 157, 347, 377
Science, xix, 48, 71, 132, 214–15, 272, 334, 356–57, 505–6
Scourging, 57, 155, 157, 163, 267, 283, 287, 324, 331, 481

Seal, x, 14, 16, 41–43, 46–47, 78, 80, 87, 113, 119, 144, 182, 194, 227, 242, 245, 250, 253, 255–59, 292, 295–96, 302, 305, 320–21, 357, 455–56, 461, 474, 500, 502, 508–9, 524–26; of Christ, 10, 34, 55; *see also Signaculum Domini* and *Signaculum Christi*; of God, 4, 220, 497; *see also Signaculum Dei*; Heart, of Jesus, 461–62; Heart, crucified, 496; of the Lord, 12, 25, 38; mystical, 41, 59, 153; of redemption, 22; seven, 347

Serpent, 143, 372

Shedding of blood, 3–4, 43, 51, 53, 56, 77, 87, 104, 121, 129, 131, 141, 164–65, 177, 209, 213, 249, 338, 395, 410, 444, 472, 487, 521

Sheep, 90, 275, 416

Shekhina, 136

Shell, 461–62, 513, 515

Shepherd, 3, 90, 107, 253, 272, 275, 356

Shipping, 132

Shroud, xx, 70–71, 246; *see also* Holy Shroud

Sickness, 303

Sigillography, 61, 144, 255–56

Sign of God, xx, 4

Signaculum, 12, 14, 27, 31–32, 220; *Christi*, 4–6, 9–10, 20, *see also* Seal of Christ; *cordis*, 497; *Dei*, 4, 76; *see also* Seal of God; *Domini*, xx, 3–4, 10–11, 13–17, 21–24, 26, 28–31, 34, 37–38, 40–41, 43, 45–50, 52–57, 61–63, 87–88, 99, 167, 177, 185, 229, 244, 387; *see also* Seal of the Lord; mystical, 50; *see also* Seal, mystical; of the five wounds, 53

Signs, astronomical, 355–56, 361

Signum, 41, 246

Signum Dei, 4

Skull, 336, 483, 515

Société des Antiquaires de France, 109, 251

Société des Antiquaires de l'Ouest, 7, 29, 99, 102, 293, 295, 310–11, 369–70, 455, 466, 470, 484, 494, 496

Society of Jesus, 296, 302

Society of Mary, 479

Sorcery, 512

Sorrow, 333, 337, 410, 483

Source, 4, 87, 101–3, 112–14, 116–17, 131, 181, 197, 221, 245, 287, 305, 338, 358, 362–63, 369, 390, 472, 486, 500, 503, 521; of [the] blood, 7, 74, 77–78, 167, 196, 291, 389, 419–20, 522; bodily/fleshly, 81, 223, 282; of beauty, 223; of comfort, 392; of devotion, 510; eucharistic, 109, 113; of glory, 237; of [everything] good, 197, 274, 510; of grace, 102, 109, 114, 392, 510; of healing, 153; of [its] heart, 105; of heat, 107; infinite, 274; inner, 390; of intellect, 410; of justice, 115, 510; of [eternal] Life, 106, 114–15, 118, 398, 522; of light, 107, 153, 237, 366; of love, 512; of mercy, 102, 114–15, 392; mystical, 118; of pity, 392; of prudence, 115; of redemption, 101, 325; of regeneration, 113; of remedies, 116; of salvation, 101; of strength, 115; of the Savior, 102, 117; of wisdom, 102, 114–15; of zeal, 102, 114, 239

South, 171, 191, 222, 370, 374, 495, 497–98

Space, 357–58, 361, 371, 376, 405, 418

Spear, xix, 6–7, 57–59, 67, 69, 76, 78, 80–81, 83, 85, 88, 92, 117, 128, 131, 152, 167, 172, 180, 188, 190, 231, 233, 235, 240, 242–43, 245, 249–50, 258–59, 267, 273, 282, 286, 292, 299, 302, 306, 309, 315, 324–26, 328, 331–32, 344, 351, 354, 360, 363, 390, 398, 427, 439, 445, 454, 482–83, 518, 520, 521, 523; bleeding, 191; and chrismon, 284–85; and cup, 189–90; holy, 69, 74–75, 78, 168, 190; of Lug, 190; magic, 189; and

Subject Index

nails, 10, 163, 334; spearhead, 10, 37, 46, 75–76, 81, 88, 233, 235, 319, 343; spear-thrust, 67–68, 72, 77–78, 84, 86, 166, 181, 241, 375, 390; and sponge, 90, 239, 242, 271, 310, 319, 321, 392, 424, 481; talismanic, 189; traversing the Heart, 81, 92, 342; *see also* Spear wound
Spell, evil, 225
Sphinx, xvi, 359, 419
Spirit of Evil, 450
Sponge, 57–59, 80, 90, 97, 157–59, 194, 239, 242, 267, 271, 283, 287, 310, 319, 321, 392, 424, 481
Spring [season], 234, 237, 362
Spring [water], 95, 107–8, 410; mystical, 109, 114, 118; of the Sacred Heart, 114; of the Savior, 102, 107, 115, 119, 348, 392
Square, 12, 25, 43, 109, 133, 136–38, 236, 318, 369, 373, 396, 425, 436, 438–39, 446–47, 509
Stag, 95, 109, 367
Star(s), xviii, 19, 41, 46–47, 131, 133, 197, 246, 257, 326, 356, 358–60, 362–63, 365, 371, 459, 469, 499, 505–7; dead, 358; invisible, 358; morning, 367; symbolic, 492
Stone, altar, 6–8, 11, 21, 26, 50, 87, 174, 194
Stone, precious, 14, 39, 152, 177, 179, 180, 183, 185, 196, 209
Stone, red, xvi, 14, 177, 179–80, 183, 197
Store of spiritual consolation, 91
Stoup, holy water, 106, 320
Strawberry, 161–63, 327
Strength, 17, 91, 115–16, 121, 137, 173, 191, 250, 303, 308, 335, 456, 484, 508
Sun, 99, 107, 126, 152, 215, 230, 252, 355–60, 362, 365, 367–70, 418, 471, 499, 508; Christ-, 367, 371; heart-, 369; -God, 499
Sundial, 355, 368–75, 378, 405
Sweat of blood, 141, 335
Swastika, 19

Sword(s), ix, 25–26, 57, 180, 189, 344, 440, 442, 444–45, 462, 508; -belt, 24, 26–27; flaming, 188; of Peter, 271, 482; seven, 129
Symbol, x, xiv–xv, xx, 5, 9–10, 16–17, 20, 23, 29, 37–38, 45, 52, 57, 61–62, 84, 109, 111, 126, 129, 132–33, 135, 141–42, 222, 225–26, 253, 344, 405, 427, 471, 484, 498–99, 507–8, 510; circuit, astral, 357; cross, 360; eucharist, 105, 227–28; glory, 254; heart of Jesus, 345; IHS, 523; lambs, 108; love, 254; Mary, 252; pelican, 104; reversal of, 515; sacrificial bull, 142; springs, mystical, 108; sun, winged, 355; wound, radiant, 186; wounds, five, 17, 229, 287
Symbolism, ix, xvi, xviii, xxiv–xxv, 4, 8–9, 22–23, 30, 99, 104, 106, 132–33, 136, 141–42, 145, 150, 161, 165, 169–70, 183–84, 223, 258, 277, 291, 338, 372, 515; of the blood, 152, 165, 184; byzantine, 14; Catholic, 61; Christian, xv, xvii, xx, xxii–xxiv, 12, 95, 97, 133, 141, 166, 177, 190, 227, 252, 259; christic, 182, 196; of colors, 505; of desire, 95; of the evangelists, 244; of flowers, xxiii; of the heart, xv, xxv; hidden, 87; medieval, 118, 126; of the rose, 168; of the Sacred Heart, xii, 213, 507; of spiritual light, 153; of stones, xxiii; of the tree-cross, 146; of the divine torture, 31, 141; of the hieroglyphic vase, 223
Symbology, xii, xiv, xviii

T

Talisman, 236, 290, 465, 503
Tau, 30, 142, 218
Temperance, 299
Terebinth, 150
Terror, 336, 433, 452
Thirst, 95–97, 108, 157, 363
Thorax, 72, 75
Thought, divine, 221

Throne, 22, 37, 40, 52, 187, 190, 218, 223, 254, 277, 348, 448, 453, 459
Time(s), 125, 281, 350, 361, 371, 375, 377–78, 480
Topaz, 177, 183
Torment/torture, 3, 10, 24, 31, 70, 95, 141, 143, 155, 163, 171–72, 290, 331, 334–35, 338, 409, 466, 487; redeeming, 240, 236, 253, 279, 310
Transubstantiation, 199
Treasure, 91, 125, 157, 177, 179–80, 188–89, 191, 209, 217, 248, 385, 388, 400, 420, 442, 523; of the Poor, 348
Tree, Christ, 143
Tree-Cross, 142–43, 145–46
Tree, forked, 142; incense, 150–51; resinous, 88, 153; symbolic, 143; wine, 152
Tree of Knowledge, 358
Tree of Life, 105, 145, 147, 222
Tree in the Midst, 145, 150
Triangle of the heart, 126
Triangle, inverted, 126, 502, 508
Triangle, trinitarian, 364, 474, 501
Trident, 3
Trinity, 221, 326, 328, 402, 418, 474, 509
Troubadour, 191
Trouvere, 191
Truth, 215–16, 218–19, 338, 343, 378, 387, 404, 413, 435, 486, 506, 517, 525–26
Turtledove, 307–8
Turquoise, 183

U

Universality, 363–64
Upper Room, 188, 207
Ursulines, 314, 388

V

Vase, 97, 99, 103, 106, 109, 113, 189–90, 205–6, 216, 232; Azewladour, 190; of the Holy Blood, 193; earthen, 109, 113; eucharistic, 11–12; hieroglyphic, 218, 223; of life, 220, 392; liturgical, 40; magic, 189; sacred, 187–88, 190
Vat, 121–22, 125, 200, 334
Veil of Veronica, 331
Venus [planet], 359–60
Vessel, 11–12, 40, 77, 157, 172; blood, 72, 403; emerald, 206; holy, 188–92, 197–98; of life, 398; precious, 192, 196; sacred, 213
Victim, xix, 77, 81, 157, 173, 177, 231, 415, 446; divine, 4, 67, 142, 162, 525; expiatory, 453; sacrificial, 194, 233
Vine, 122, 125, 226–27, 332, 507; mystical, 166
Vinegar, 97, 158
Vintager, 122
Virgins of Pity, 334
Visitandines, 254, 297, 314; of Loudun, 318–19
Volunteers of the West, 448, 503
Vulnerary, ix, xii, xvi, xix–xxv

W

Wars, counter-revolutionary, of the Vendée, 434, 450, 458, 465, 502; religious, 473
Water, holy, 106, 320, 512
Wax, 8–10, 43, 78, 247, 250, 257, 292, 305, 470–72, 511–12
Well, 91, 100–101, 103, 106, 114, 392
Wellspring, 10, 105
West, 10, 12, 26, 29, 90, 107, 136, 150, 168–69, 171, 205, 244, 287, 366–67, 370, 433, 435, 438, 444, 446–47, 451, 459, 461, 469, 473, 475–76, 479, 485–86, 502, 512
Western Rebellion, 371, 393, 396
Whip, 57, 59, 80, 156, 239, 242, 271, 283, 322–25, 331, 335
Will, xxiii, 28, 89, 137, 216, 220, 270, 418, 510; good, 188, 507
Window, stained glass, 28, 90, 92, 114, 122–24, 250, 310, 319–20, 327–30, 348

Subject Index

Wine, 6, 21, 122, 125, 151, 156, 183, 188, 208, 243, 316, 389, 392
Winepress, divine/mystical, 113, 121–29, 164, 334
Wisdom, 91, 102, 114–15, 413, 418, 481
Word, 216–17, 221, 359, 377, 409–10, 412, 414, 418–19
World's Fair, 384
Wound(s), *passim*; to the chest, 72; divine, 11, 13, 19, 31, 78, 88, 113, 116, 122, 166, 194, 243, 396; to the feet, xx, 6, 12, 19, 36, 62, 67, 92, 115, 117–18, 157, 239, 242, 259, 286, 306, 325, 334, 384, 395, 504, 520–21, 525; to the flank, 70, 87; to the right foot/left foot/right hand/left hand, 114–15; to the hands, 6, 12, 19, 62, 67, 92, 117–18, 157, 239, 242, 259, 286, 306, 325, 334, 383, 395, 504, 520–21, 525; of/to the Heart, 12, 56, 59, 62, 77, 91, 102, 115, 117, 229, 242, 315, 343, 345, 348, 520; *see also* Opening of the Heart; to the Heart by an arrow, 272, 285, 420–21; from which a host issues, 390, 429; lateral, 70, 75, 88, 91, 109, 113, 117, 213, 236, 239, 258–59, 284, 289, 304, 438, 522; lenticular, 88–89, 91–92; to the four limbs, 34, 87, 102, 113–14, 157, 337, 398; to the four members, 37; redemptive, 10, 21–22, 77, 223, 334; sacred, 33, 51, 76, 83, 113, 115, 117, 177, 195–96, 231, 306, 342; from scourging, 155; in/to the side, 62, 67–68, 77–78, 80–81, 84–85, 88–89, 168, 177–81, 183, 186–87, 229, 232, 283, 303–4, 307, 343, 521; of the spear, 10, 128, 240, 242–43, 258–59, 284, 292, 302, 306, 332, 351, 398, 427, 439, 454; *see also* Spear-thrust; to the wrists, xx

Y
Yew, 146

Z
Zodiac, 355–58, 361–63, 524
Zouaves, papal, 448, 503

SCRIPTURE INDEX

Genesis
   22:18 • 216
   49:11 • 164

Leviticus
   14:2–8 • 159
   14:49–53 • 159

Numbers
   13:23 • 122
   19:6 • 159
   19:18 • 159

Psalms
   41:2 • 108
   42 (Vulg. 41):2–3 • 95
   51 (Vulg. 50) • 159
   56 • 122

Song of Songs
   2:13–14 • 305
   2:14 • 309
   4:3 • 184
   5:2 • 277
   5:10 • 184
   8:6 • 220

Jeremiah
   8:22 • 151
   46:11 • 151

Ezekiel
   47:1–12 • 105

Isaiah
   12:3 • 194
   12:3–4 • 100
   63ff. • 164
   63:1–2 • 184
   63:1–3 • 122

Enoch
   77:2 • 136

Matthew
   6:22 • 400
   12:34 • 410
   26–27 • 155
   26:39 • 89
   27:27–31 • 157
   27:54 • 231
   27:59–60 • 70

Mark
   14:36 • 89
   15:39 • 231
   15:45–46 • 70
   16:17, 18 • 164

Luke
   2:21 • 376
   22:42 • 89
   22:44 • 141
   23:47 • 231

John
   1:9 • 181
   1:29 • 159
   3:10 • 232
   7:37 • 95
   19:28 • 97
   19:28–30 • 158
   19:33–34 • 85
   19:34 • xix, 67, 197
   19:38–42 • 70
   19:39 • 232

Acts of the Apostles
   4:32 • 407

Galatians
   2:20 • 220

Philippians
   2 • 290

2 Peter
   1:19–21 • xiv

Apocalypse
   12:1 • 252
   19:13 • 122, 164, 184
   22:1–2 • 105

www.ingramcontent.com/pod-product-compliance
Lightning Source LLC
Chambersburg PA
CBHW030742250426
43672CB00028B/332